Developing Cultural Literacy
Through the Writing Process

Related Titles of Interest

Oral Communication Problems in Children and Adolescents, Second Edition
Sol Adler and Deborah A. King (Editors)
ISBN: 0–205–15089–6

Getting It Together: A Process Workbook for K–12 Curriculum Development, Implementation, and Assessment
Judy F. Carr and Douglas E. Harris
ISBN: 0–205–14173–0

Language and Literacy Learning in Multicultural Classrooms
Leslie W. Crawford
ISBN: 0–205–13922–1

Integrating Reading and Writing Through Children's Literature
Kathy Everts Danielson and Jan LaBonty
ISBN: 0–205–15314–3

The Child's View of Reading: Understandings for Teachers and Parents
Pamela A. Michel
ISBN: 0–205–13784–9

Literacy Development in the Early Years: Helping Children Read and Write, Second Edition
Lesley Mandel Morrow
ISBN: 0–205–14043–2

A Handbook for the K–12 Reading Resource Specialist
Marguerite C. Radencich, Penny G. Beers, and Jeanne Shay Schumm
ISBN: 0–205–14081–5

The Beginnings of Writing, Third Edition
Charles Temple, Ruth Nathan, Frances Temple, and Nancy A. Burris
ISBN: 0–205–14518–3

Developing Cultural Literacy Through the Writing Process

Empowering All Learners

BARBARA C. PALMER
The Florida State University, Tallahassee, Florida

MARY L. HAFNER
Educational Consultant, Tallahassee, Florida

MARILYN F. SHARP
Leon County Schools, Tallahassee, Florida

Allyn and Bacon
Boston London Toronto Sydney Tokyo Singapore

Copyright © 1994 by Allyn and Bacon

A Division of Paramount Publishing
160 Gould Street
Needham Heights, Massachusetts 02194

Library of Congress Cataloging-in-Publication Data
Palmer, Barbara C.
    Developing cultural literacy through the writing process :
empowering all learners / Barbara C. Palmer, Mary L. Hafner, Marilyn
F. Sharp.
        p.   cm.
    Includes bibliographical references and index.
    ISBN 0–205–13989–2
    1. English language—Composition and exercises—Study and
teaching. 2. English language—Rhetoric—Study and teaching.
3. Civilization—Study and teaching.   I. Hafner, Mary L.
II. Sharp, Marilyn F.   III. Title.
PE1404.P35   1994
808′.042′07—dc20   93–23669
                                                                CIP

Printed in the United States of America
10 9 8 7 6 5 4 3 2 1   98 97 96 95 94

Contents

PART II FOCUSING ON PROCESS

CHAPTER 3
Prewriting: Generating and Planning   47

CHAPTER 6
Revising and Editing   153

PART III   MOVING FROM PROCESS TO PRODUCT

CHAPTER 7
Technology and Composing   185

CHAPTER 8
Modes of Publishing   207

PART IV EMPOWERING WRITERS

CHAPTER 9
Journal Writing: A Heuristic Activity   225

CHAPTER 10
Metacognitive Awareness and Self-Monitoring   255

CHAPTER 11
A Portfolio Approach to Assessment and Other Types of Evaluation   281

Preface

Approaching the turn of the century, educators are acutely aware of the ever-increasing knowlege base that exists to be passed on to our students; and we are fully cognizant of the fact that it is impossible to teach them everything. Therefore, we must teach students how to be lifelong learners. We also concur with the wisdom of the Native American who once said that "the value of knowledge increases as it is shared." As leaders in education, science, medicine, and the humanities throughout the world work together to solve common problems and to plan for a better tomorrow, we realize just how small our global society has become during this age of technology and jet travel. Today's classrooms reflect this reality; our schools are composed of students from many different backgrounds. As a result, sociocultural and linguistic differences are to be expected and become an asset when the richness of these varied cultures is shared. As students learn more about one another and discuss the myriad events that have shaped their lives, they are expanding their knowlege base naturally in contexts that have real meaning for them. An atmosphere that encourages sharing and exploration within meaningful contexts contributes much toward empowering students who are learning how to take more responsibility for their own education. Concomitantly, these students are developing the kinds of responsible behaviors needed for good citizenship in their communities. To further meet the demands of good citizenship, our students need to learn how to think critically and to communicate clearly using the language processes of listening, speaking, reading, and writing. As the Chinese philosopher Confucius (c. 551–479 B.C.) noted, "In language, clarity is everything."

Developing Cultural Literacy Through the Writing Process: Empowering All Learners contributes uniquely to education by combining the expansion of cultural literacy with the development of process-based writing. The book, written for teacher educators, teachers, and students in teacher education programs, thoroughly addresses each stage of the writing process, with emphasis on the recursive and overlapping nature of these stages. Additionally, many related model activities at the end of each chapter show how to develop the writing process, while expanding the writer's knowledge base and providing opportunities for the writer to think critically. These model activities, which translate theory into practice, demonstrate how knowledge can be used to build on knowledge. This knowledge-building concept, advocated by E. D. Hirsch, Jr., author of *Cultural Literacy* and founder of the Core Knowledge Foundation, is the basis of his drive to strengthen academic content by teaching a sequence of core knowledge. Unlike Dr. Hirsch, who has offered a definition of what a core knowledge should include, the authors of this book have created model activities around a sampling of knowledge from many areas. Content from across subject areas is included in the model activities with an intent to strike a balance between knowledge and thinking. Of course, integrating the curriculum whenever possible is recommended. The model activities are intended for educators' consideration and modification to meet the specific learning needs of their students; such activities should be used as part of a total learning environment. Students should be encouraged to explore and develop their own interests; as they do, extensive exposure to the different genres of related literature should become a major ingredient in the learning environment. As learners expand their knowledge base through reading and thinking, they are in a better position to construct meaning actively as writers, to think critically about how the experiences of others (both real and fictional) have influenced them, and to make responsible decisions about their own lives.

Developing Cultural Literacy Through the Writing Process: Empowering All Learners has many features that make it particularly appealing to today's educator who already has a full schedule. The style of the book is both readable and interesting. Model activities and checklists are provided for efficacy of teacher time management. Visuals have been used appropriately to clarify content and to enhance the reader's knowledge about persons or topics addressed in activities. The book encourages the concept of teacher and students working together as co-learners, exploring interests and subjects in depth in a creative manner. Peer teaching and learning are also encouraged as educators prepare students for the cooperative atmosphere that is an intrinsic part of today's workplace. Part I of the book sets the stage for writing instruction by providing an overview of the writing process and by discussing how teacher expectations and mental rehearsal contribute to successful writing. Part II focuses on process, with chapters on prewriting, drafting and translating, sharing and responding, and revising and editing. Part III moves from process to product with a chapter on technology and composing, followed by modes of publishing. The empowerment of writers is emphasized in Part IV, with chapters on journal writing, metacognitive awareness and self-monitoring, and a portfolio approach to assessment. Each chapter opens with an appropriate quote; throughout the book the reader also finds vignettes, interviews with leaders in the field, and comments from reflective teachers currently working with students. Taken as a whole, this book and the accompanying activities will assist teachers immensely as they create an environment where there is great enthusiasm for learning.

Acknowledgments

We would like to acknowledge the scholars across the ages whose thinking influenced the foundation for this book. We extend thanks to our colleagues as well as to the many students, teachers, administrators, and other educators who have shared ideas and experiences with us over the years; they were instrumental in creating our vision of educational excellence for all learners. The encouragement and support given by Allyn and Bacon, especially Mylan L. Jaixen, associate publisher, and Susan Hutchinson, editorial assistant, deserve special mention. We owe a debt of gratitude to the three reviewers of our manuscript, Rebecca Guthrie, Rock Springs Elementary School, Apopka, Florida; Sharon Kane, State University of New York, Oswego, New York; and Shirley Karasik, Uniondale Public Schools, Uniondale, New York. Their careful review and thoughtful suggestions contributed much to the quality of this book. Finally, we thank our families for their encouragement, help, and patience throughout the process of writing this book.

Developing Cultural Literacy Through the Writing Process

CHAPTER 1

The Stages of the Writing Process and Their Recursive Nature

Which is greater—the spoken word or the written word?

—Arthur W. Dake, Portland, Oregon

The question above is an interesting one to ponder, particularly for those of us who are educators. When Marilyn vos Savant, columnist for *Parade Magazine* (1990, p. 14) and listed in the *Guinness Book of World Records Hall of Fame* for "Highest IQ," was asked this question, she responded that the written word was superior to the spoken word because authors can utilize a process that includes planning, organizing, and revising. Also, the written word has the advantage of reaching not only today's readers but future generations as well.

In today's learning environment, our goal is to integrate instruction among the language processes of listening, speaking, reading, and writing, so that students are involved actively in making and conveying meaning in natural ways. Goodman (1986) emphasized that "integration is a key principle for language development and learning through language" (p. 30) and that "expression (writing) and comprehension (reading) are built during functional, meaningful, relevant language use" (p. 39). Hennings (1990) recommended that "students should spend considerable time talking about life, language, and literature before, during, and after reading and writing." Furthermore, Hennings stated that oral language is "the connecting thread" to the other language processes and suggested that, as shown in Figure 1.1, there is a "natural flow among the language arts in an integrated approach" (p. 13).

So, while the authors of this text concur with vos Savant up to a point, our response to the question raised by Dake would emphasize the importance of both the spoken word and the written word. Given that both are forms of thinking, both can be used to construct meaning. We might go a step further and tell Mr. Dake that good writing is not always easy and may be a challenge even for our best students. This is more often than not the case when students haven't been taught that writing is a learned process that takes time and concentrated practice. We should also tell him that writing is a top priority in many U.S. classrooms today, perhaps in response to the ever-growing concern about the increasing dropout rate and the fact that too many graduates are not prepared adequately to meet minimum communication requirements of the job market.

The value of writing as a way of learning and the need to provide instruction on the writing process have been stressed by educators (Applebee, Langer, Mullis, & Jenkins, 1990; Applebee, 1984; Emig, 1977; Mayer & Lester, 1983). We know that writing requires complex thinking; the process of writing involves problem solving and decision making. According to Lundsteen (1989), " . . . writing is a tool for getting along in the world" (p. 261). Obviously, written communication is a requirement for succeeding in our world of high technology. But what may not be so obvious is how best to teach

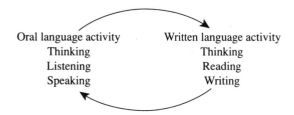

Oral language activity   Written language activity
Thinking   Thinking
Listening   Reading
Speaking   Writing

FIGURE 1.1 The Natural Flow among the Language Arts

Source: Dorothy Grant Hennings, *Communication in Action: Teaching the Language Arts,* Fourth Edition, Figure 1.2, p. 13. Copyright © 1990 by Houghton Mifflin Company. Used with permission.

developing writers so that they evolve into the kind of writers capable of capturing their experiences and communicating them through the written word.

Let's start with attitude. A positive attitude on the part of both the student and the teacher is extremely important in any learning environment. In Chapter 2 you will read about the self-fulfilling prophecy and its impact on learning. Teachers who provide writing instruction know just how valuable it is for students to believe that they can become better writers. Also, in our society we stress the importance of doing one's best with any given task. In preparation for introducing and/or reinforcing the process of writing, consider letting students ponder the meaning of the following statement attributed to the American novelist and short-story writer, Ernest Hemingway (1899–1961): "I have tried simply to write the best I can; sometimes I have good luck and write better than I can."

When one creative middle school teacher in an urban setting gave her students the opportunity to think about the foregoing statement, she realized two things: (1) students need *time* to massage and share their ideas, using their present knowledge base; and (2) when their knowledge base is limited, it can be expanded through instruction, thus enabling students to become better comprehenders of text as well as better writers. She also observed that students grow more quickly when they feel confident about expressing their ideas with one another. The following comments, questions, thoughts, reactions, and asides were noted as the middle school students responded to the Hemingway statement:

"What does it mean to do the best you can? Aren't some people just more gifted at certain things than others?"

"Is learning to write anything like learning to ride a bicycle?" (This question caused much laughter, which was not discouraged by the teacher.)

"Didn't Hemingway become one of the most famous writers of his time? I wonder what it was about his style that made his writing so popular?"

"Do you think Hemingway thought of himself as being an excellent writer? What was he like as a person?"

"Well, I think his luck ran out when his health started failing. How did he spend his last years?"

Many good discussions evolved from the timely introduction of the Hemingway statement; during the remaining months of that semester, several students became Hemingway experts as they enjoyed his short stories about war, hunting, fishing, and bullfighting. Others, with the teacher's encouragement, began considering the possibility of writing as a career option after they read two of Hemingway's brilliant novels, *The Sun Also Rises* and *The Old Man and the Sea.* Too, several students observed that Hemingway's writing reflected his experiences in different parts of the world; for example, *The Sun Also Rises* reflected his life in Paris, and *The Old Man and the Sea* reflected his life in Cuba. Naturally, as they read more about Hemingway and shared with one another, they began to experience, as Hemingway had, the real need to address writing as a process. Richards (1968) aptly made reference to Ernest Hemingway's apprenticeship as a writer and his growth in the writing process in the following statement:

He was a writer who did not imitate the traditional styles of great literature. With clean, powerful strokes he forged his own style of writing—a natural, realistic style that was refreshingly different from any that had been seen before. He labored to perfect this style with a devotion seldom seen, even among great novelists, and he never compromised his standards for the opportunity to make money. His long, hard, self-imposed apprenticeship made him a master when other writers had stopped trying to improve. (p. 89)

The author study that had evolved naturally in this classroom afforded both students and teacher the opportunity to experience vicariously the reality that good writing more often than not involves rewriting and fine-tuning, both of which take time and hard work. Hemingway often said that easy writing makes hard reading. The teacher reported that the word *apprenticeship* conveyed to her a message of great importance in regard to her students' writing: Students benefit immensely when a process, such as writing, is modeled. Not only do students grow through their exposure to the works of great writers, but they develop as writers themselves when they understand how to translate their own thoughts into print and revise as needed to get the quality they are capable of producing at that point in time. Like Hemingway, developing writers must internalize the desire to improve; they need and deserve effective teachers who are good writers themselves to model process-based writing.

Donald H. Graves, well known for the landmark publication, *Writing: Teachers and Children at Work* (1983), stressed the importance of process and how to implement the writing process in today's classroom. Having been a teacher, school principal, language supervisor, university professor, and director of a writing process laboratory, Graves believes that teachers should also be writers; otherwise, teachers won't know how the process of writing feels. In an interview by DiAnn Waskul Ellis (1988) on Graves's thoughts on writing, reported in *The Whole Language Catalog* (Goodman, Bird, & Goodman, 1991), Graves made several observations about how the best teachers of good writing operate:

DiAnn: How do the best teachers of writing operate? You have had a chance to observe quite a few good teachers.

Don: Number one, they write themselves. Number two, they share their writing. Number three, their students have different voices. They don't all sound like the teacher. And that requires, on the part of the professional, a fair amount of knowledge about the teaching of writing. Usually they are people who, on the one hand are quite outspoken, and who have real tension with the world and the issues of the world. On the other hand, they respect you for your unique perspective of the world—but they're going to challenge you, too. (p. 130)

In a report on the National Writing Project (NWP), Goldberg (1984) stressed the importance of teachers having opportunities to write "on the job," thus modeling process-based writing for students. The highly publicized Bay Area Writing Project, which began in 1974 in Berkeley, California, and was the beginning of the National Writing Project, succeeded in developing better teachers of writing by implementing this principle. As teachers

are willing to share their work-in-progress, which naturally continues from one day to the next, students have visible models that allow them to realize that even the experts are challenged by the endeavor of translating thoughts to print. In the words of Nancie Atwell (1987), "We need to write, share our writing with our students, and demonstrate what experienced writers do in the process of composing, letting our students see our own drafts in all their messiness and tentativeness" (p. 18). As teachers share their revisions, whether several or many, students observe the reality of what it means to expand ideas, clarify meaning, and perhaps completely reorganize information. This observation holds true, also, for topic selection, which is often the greatest challenge for developing writers who find themselves enmeshed in a seemingly complicated environment. Both students and teachers acknowledge that process-based writing requires a great deal of time to implement. Yet, the benefits of treating students as real writers are significant. Jan Loveless (1991), an instructional designer for the Learning Center of Dow Chemical Company, Pittsburg, California, has said that "when students are treated as real writers, they begin to function as writers" (p. 263). Directing what she called her "learning club," Loveless tried very hard not to be an authority figure—just more experienced—as she worked with her students. Sometimes, the wonderful ideas of a learning club such as the one Loveless directed seem almost impossible to implement because of time limitations and class size; for example, it is quite a challenge to write along with students when teachers have the number of students that many do today. Thus, it is understandable that the issue of time continues to surface as a problem for educators who see the need for and the benefits of teachers becoming writers themselves.

As youngsters move into adolescence, they will experience many changes within themselves and in their view of what is important in the world. Some of these changes may cause students to feel upset, and some are, in reality, traumatic. Not only will the ability to write serve them intellectually, but it can benefit them emotionally as they get in touch with their inner thoughts and feelings or, as Vygotsky (1962) said, their "inner voices." Researchers, reporting in various journals of the American Psychological Association, suggest that writing about the trauma experienced can actually serve as a vehicle for improving the writer's health.

In a 1991 *Tallahassee Democrat* newspaper article, "Writing About Your Trauma Can Ease Pain," findings from several research studies were reported indicating that "people who are able to write about their inner thoughts and feelings may enjoy better mental and physical health" (p. 2B). For example, James W. Pennebaker, a professor of psychology at Southern Methodist University in Dallas, had participants in several studies write about their traumatic experiences for twenty minutes per day over four consecutive days; the participants in comparison groups wrote about superficial topics such as describing a room. According to the article, "Pennebaker found that people who wrote about traumatic experiences visited doctors much less often than they did before and significantly less than people who wrote about trivial topics" (p. 2B). Probably even more interesting were the findings of Janice Kiecolt-Glaser and Ronald Glaser at Ohio State University, who used blood tests to determine the effects of writing on the health of the participants in their study. These researchers "found significantly higher levels of T-cells, which help fight infection and virus, among people who wrote about traumatic experiences" (p. 2B). It appears that both physical and mental stress are reduced through the process of writing. According to Pennebaker, "Writing is a powerful tool to organize overwhelming events and make them manageable" (p. 2B). It appears that once these thoughts are organized, unresolved issues are more easily resolved. Think of the impact on society if all students had this information and were encouraged to write about their problems. Principals and guidance counselors could certainly benefit through use of this technique with troubled youngsters.

Several seasoned teachers, discussing the foregoing findings, concluded that there are numerous advantages to the use of silent sustained writing in today's learning environment, including the enhancement of everyone's health. With students and teachers quietly writing together and, at appropriate times, sharing their work-in-progress, a sense of community is possible in any classroom. As developing writers experience acceptance of their contributions, they are motivated internally and externally to continue the process. Particularly for students who do not have acceptance elsewhere, this is an opportunity to enhance self-esteem, an important component of one's overall sense of well-being. With the permission of the teachers who participated in this discussion, the following sample comments and suggestions were recorded randomly by the professor who conducted the class they were attending as part of their inservice:

"If students today know it's okay with us, I think they will write about topics that may be upsetting their lives."

"Perhaps, sometimes, we're a little uneasy when students address topics such as drugs or abuse in their writings. I think a big part of helping them is listening to their thoughts and feelings."

"When students share personal problems in their journal writings, they often ask for confidentiality. Sometimes I feel torn between respecting that request or getting help for them."

"When I started using sustained silent writing, I found it helpful to begin my writing a few minutes after the students did and to finish shortly before they did."

"Well, sometimes I write uninterruptedly for a while and then I circulate around the room; I think there are probably lots of different ways to implement the concept of sustained silent writing."

"I don't think I'll ever feel guilty again about writing alongside my students; when I share my journal entries with them, they seem more open about sharing theirs."

A HISTORICAL PERSPECTIVE ON WRITING AS A PROCESS

The desire to improve the teaching of writing is probably about as old as writing itself. Some believe these concerns always will be present. In a 1988 article published in *Phi Delta Kappan,* Jenkinson stated that "the search for ways to improve the writing of students began centuries ago and will never end, for the young will always be criticized for their inability to write" (p. 713). Jenkinson reported that it was the Sumerians who were credited with giving the world writing. Jenkinson also shared the findings of one researcher—Daniels (1983)—who reported the Sumerians' concern about students' writing ability thousands of years ago (p. 714):

On a clay tablet of the early Sumerians was recorded the agonized complaints of a Sumerian teacher about the sudden drop-off in students' writing ability. Now this teacher

Cuneiform tablets of the ancient Sumerians

was probably more an instructor of scribesmanship than composition, but it is at least interesting to discover that the reports from "Bonehead Sumerian" were about the same 4,500 years ago as they are from "Bonehead English" today. (p. 33)

Learning more about the Sumerians is an interesting topic to pursue and can be used to expand the cultural literacy of students through writing. Model Activity 1.1 integrates acquiring knowledge about Sumerians with process-based writing.

   Just how new are our ideas about the stages of the writing process and their recursive nature? Using stages in process-based writing is not new at all but is a method practiced by classical writers and journalists through the ages. Able teachers, also, long have taught writers using a variety of methods that included common elements. Likewise, according to Jenkinson (1988), Porter Perrin made reference to the concept of the recursive nature of writing in his 1942 publication *Writer's Guide and Index to English,* which was already in its fourth edition by 1965. In "Stages in Writing a Paper" in Porter Perrin's popular *Writer's Guide,* the author delineated the following eight stages in the writing process (p. 39):

1. Focusing on a subject—Definition of topic, sensing of problems involved and of possible sources of information.
2. Gathering material—Notes (in mind or on paper) from memory, observation, interviews, reading, speculation.
3. Deciding on methods of development—The ways of approaching and exploring the subject.
4. Organizing the paper—A synopsis or outline of the paper.
5. Writing the first draft—Tentative copy of the paper.
6. Revising—Necessary changes in material, corrections and improvements in words, sentences, paragraphs.
7. Preparing the manuscript—The completed paper, ready for reading or for printing.
8. Seeing the manuscript into print—The printed copy.

As one carefully reviews Perrin's stages, it is readily apparent that good writing requires thinking; writing is really a form of thinking using the written word. Keep in mind Perrin's emphasis that a writer does not necessarily move through these stages as delineated; on the contrary, Perrin suggested, what the writer learns in one stage may cause him or her to return to an earlier stage, and so forth. More than forty years after Perrin's book first appeared, this insight was reaffirmed by Humes (1983), who stated that the process does not move in a straight line. Tierney and Pearson (1983) pointed out that the writing process has overlapping and recursive stages. Lundsteen (1989, p. 266) offered the following explanation of the concept of the recursive nature of writing:

That is, we do not plan everything we have to say, then put it down on paper, and finally go over it to edit, recopy, and turn it in to the teacher. Instead, writing is recursive; it goes back and forth. We plan a little, put words on paper, stop to plan what we want to say next, go back and change a sentence, or change our minds altogether.

Tremmel (1992) also emphasized the need for educators to be vigilant about keeping the concept of process fluid when teaching writing. In this regard, he addressed reification as a potential problem and suggested that educators give special consideration to "those points where theory gets translated into practice" (p. 21). The stages of the writing process are fluid; they become both recursive and overlapping as writers weave back and forth to construct meaning. In all likelihood, no two compositions will have gone through exactly the same process, for writers will modify their own developing process as necessary to translate their ideas clearly into a written form of communication.

During the last couple of decades, more and more has been written about the importance of process with regard to good writing as opposed to simply reacting to a finished product. Many consider the work of Emig (1971) with twelfth graders to be related directly to this change in attitude. She concluded that it is important to watch writers at work and assist them throughout the process of writing, rather than simply evaluating the finished product. Along with the important work of Emig (1971), many other researchers and writers have contributed to the movement toward process writing. For example, the work of Moffett (1968) is considered seminal in its influence on recent thinking about writing theory, which advocates making a closer connection between speech and writing. Elbow (1985) supported this speech–writing connection by recommending that the students' oral language skills be applied to writing. A few years earlier, Elbow (1981) had encouraged the use of freewriting, a technique that allows writers to let their thoughts flow on paper without having to focus on mechanics or organization. He suggested the use of two types of freewriting, unfocused and focused, along with other techniques for helping writers master the writing process. In a 1988 article, Leopold and Jenkinson offered the following brief bibliography in response to a request for significant books about process writing published during the last twenty years:

Learning to Write and Writing to Learn: A Brief Bibliography. * A teacher attending a conference on writing across the curriculum made this request: "List 20 books—not articles—written during the last 20 years that I can study to discover what is significant about process writing, writing across the curriculum, and writing to learn. Include only one book per writer. After I read one

**Source:* E. B. Jenkinson, "Learning to Write/Writing to Learn," *Phi Delta Kappan, 69* (10), June 1988, p. 745. Reprinted with permission.

book, I might want to read more by the same author. Some of the books should be collections of significant articles on the topics." In response to this interesting challenge, I offer just such a brief bibliography.

Applebee, Arthur N. *Writing in the Secondary School: English and the Content Areas.* Urbana, Ill.: National Council of Teachers of English, 1981.

Britton, James. *Language and Learning.* New York: Penguin Books, 1972.

Calkins, Lucy McCormick. *The Art of Teaching Writing.* Portsmouth, N.H.: Heinemann, 1986.

Cooper, Charles R. and Lee Odell, eds. *Research on Composing: Points of Departure.* Urbana, Ill.: National Council of Teachers of English, 1978.

Elbow, Peter. *Writing with Power: Techniques for Mastering the Writing Process.* New York: Oxford University Press, 1981.

Emig, Janet. *The Composing Processes of Twelfth Graders.* Urbana, Ill.: National Council of Teachers of English, 1971.

Fulwiler, Toby and Art Young, eds. *Language Connections: Writing and Reading Across the Curriculum.* Urbana, Ill.: National Council of Teachers of English, 1982.

Gere, Anne Ruggles, ed. *Roots in the Sawdust: Writing to Learn Across the Disciplines.* Urbana, Ill.: National Council of Teachers of English, 1985.

Graves, Donald H. *Writing: Teachers and Children at Work.* Exeter, N.H.: Heinemann, 1983.

Hays, Janice et al., eds. *The Writer's Mind: Writing as a Mode of Thinking.* Urbana, Ill.: National Council of Teachers of English, 1983.

Harste, Jerome C., Virginia A. Woodward, and Carolyn L. Burke. *Language Stories & Literacy Lessons.* Portsmouth, N.H.: Heinemann, 1984.

Hillocks, George, Jr. *Research on Written Composition: New Directions for Teaching.* Urbana, Ill.: National Conference on Research in English, 1986.

Kirby, Dan and Tom Liner. *Inside Out: Developmental Strategies for Teaching Writing.* Montclair, N.J.: Boynton/Cook, 1981.

Macrorie, Ken. *Writing to Be Read.* New York: Hayden, 1968.

Maimon, Elaine P. et al. *Writing in the Arts and Sciences.* Cambridge, Mass.: Winthrop, 1981.

Moffett, James. *Teaching the Universe of Discourse.* Boston: Houghton Mifflin, 1968.

Murray, Donald M. *A Writer Teaches Writing: A Practical Method of Teaching Composition.* Boston: Houghton Mifflin, 1968.

Newkirk, Thomas and Nancie Atwell, eds. *Understanding Writing: Ways of Observing, Learning & Teach-*

ing K-8, 2nd ed. Portsmouth, N.H.: Heinemann, 1986.

Shaughnessy, Mina. *Errors and Expectations: A Guide for the Teacher of Basic Writing.* New York: Oxford University Press, 1977.

Tchudi, Stephen. *Writing in the Content Areas: The NEA Inservice Training Program.* West Haven, Conn.: National Education Association, 1984.—EBJ

In the 1980s, researchers such as Flower and Hayes (1981) formulated cognitive-process theories of writing in an attempt to describe the complex activity of writing. Flower and Hayes (1981) developed a model of writing based on their research with college students; they described writing as a process of problem solving and emphasized the recursive nature of this process as writers monitor themselves. According to Lundsteen (1989), "The view of writing as problem solving is at the heart of the cognitive-process theories of composing" (p. 268). "The process theories describe several components or subprocesses of the writing activity in order to clarify what is actually going on in our minds as we write" (Lundsteen, 1989, p. 266). Like the process of reading, it is difficult to clarify what is actually occurring in the mind as one thinks and writes. What we do know, according to Brozo and Simpson (1991), is that "students construct meaning" (p. 149). Students are actively building their own meanings as they interact with print material or write their own thoughts (Kucer, 1985). Tierney and Pearson (1983) reported that, rather than being mirror images of one another, reading and writing are parallel processes in that they are both constructive. For example, students are constructing meaning as they understand and attempt to explain and/or write about the relationship between the atoms of hydrogen and oxygen that make up a water molecule. Students begin to create their own texts in their minds before explaining verbally and/or in their own written words. Too, students may examine diagrams to visualize the explanation of H_2O, the scientific symbol for the water molecule meaning that two atoms of hydrogen (H) and one atom of oxygen (O) come together to form a molecule of water. The foregoing is also a good example of how to integrate the subject of science with the development of the language processes, particularly writing.

THE STAGES OF THE WRITING PROCESS

In considering the relationship between problem solving and the writing process, educators agree with Lundsteen (1989) when she stated that this process "is a complicated intellectual undertaking . . . Writers need to be creative enough to generate ideas and goal directed enough to organize those ideas into meaningful text" (p. 268). As developing writers move through this process to produce, eventually, a piece of writing that accurately represents their thoughts, they are problem solving. If the goal of writing is to communicate meaning to ourselves and others, thinking will occur as the writer (1) generates ideas, thoughts, and images; (2) creates an order to those thoughts; and (3) communicates this meaning to others through interesting text that, ideally, is well written. Furthermore, Reutzel and Cooter (1992) emphasized that a process approach to writing helps "students learn and use phases of authorship" (p. 417).

As discussed earlier in this chapter, the idea of overlapping and recursive stages of the writing process is not new. On the contrary, the 1942 work of Porter Perrin makes us most aware that we are revisiting ideas that outdate most of us. Brozo and Simpson (1991) emphasized that the various stages presented by different educators throughout history do have much in common: "While there is considerable diversity in the labeling of these stages, the common motif across them all appears to be a concern for prewriting, writing, and postwriting" (p. 149). Jenkinson (1988, p. 714) stated that

teachers who focus on the writing process in a variety of disciplines take students through some variation of these steps: (1) prewriting activities (jotting down ideas, listing thoughts, brainstorming, gathering information, and so on); (2) writing a draft; (3) peer review of the draft; (4) revising; (5) editing; (6) writing the final draft; and (7) publishing.

Furthermore, Jenkinson suggested that a comparison of the foregoing and Porter Perrin's eight stages is interesting because of their similarities. Others, such as Humes (1983), have suggested that this process be examined under the following four headings: planning, translating, reviewing, and revising. Lundsteen (1989) emphasized the importance of "treating revision separately because it is during this important subprocess that the teacher has a particular opportunity to be especially helpful or, conversely, especially detrimental to the child writer" (p. 266). For purposes of this text, the following stages of the writing process, presented in Maimon's 1988 article "Cultivating the Prose Garden," are recommended with minor modification and with the reminder that these stages are overlapping and recursive:

The Stages of the Writing Process.*   The stages of the writing process presented here are derived from *The Art of Teaching Writing,* by Lucy McCormick Calkins (Heinemann, 1986), and from *Writing: Teachers and Children at Work,* by Donald Graves (Heinemann, 1983).

Prewriting.   Sometimes called "rehearsal," prewriting is the time to gather information, to experiment with ideas, and to plot a course. It is time for students to get ready to write, and it is time to think about where they are going. But they should also remain open to new directions that they may discover.

Teachers should encourage all types of processes of discovery—daydreaming, role-playing, drawing, reading, any activity that prepares students for writing. Students should also experiment with such heuristic exercises as listing, clustering, cubing, and journal writing.

Drafting.   This is the stage of the writing process that most people think of as "writing." During this stage, students translate their thoughts and ideas into sentences and paragraphs. Drafting should always be done with a particular purpose and audience in mind.

Sharing.   This is the first opportunity for the writer to achieve mental distance from a piece of writing. The writer reads the piece aloud—either to peers or to the teacher. The listeners then respond with questions and comments. The purpose of the conference is to help the writer clarify the piece for its intended audience.

Revising.   During the process of revision, the writer expands ideas, clarifies meanings, and reorganizes information. Heuristic devices may be used to generate additional text.

Editing.   During the editing phase of the writing process, the writer focuses on the conventions of language. Spelling, punctuation, syntax, and structure are analyzed and corrected. Students should have access to dictionaries, thesauruses, style sheets, and other reference materials at this stage. They should be encouraged to do as much of their own editing as possible. Teachers should remember, however, that even professional writers have the benefit of an editor.

Publishing.   The publishing of student work can take a variety of forms: individual books, class books, newsletters, literary magazines, bulletin board displays. Of course, not all pieces of writing need to be presented in a polished form, but student writers should have opportunities to celebrate their authorship. —*Joyce Gulley,* research associate, Cummins Engine Foundation Writing Project at Indiana University, Bloomington.

Model Activity 1.2 is designed for the teacher's use in modeling the stages of process writing for students. Of course, teachers may choose to substitute content that reflects other topics.

GOVERNING PRINCIPLES

After considering theory and research findings, Klein (1985) developed seven governing principles for writing development through the elementary and middle school years and discussed related implications for the classroom teacher, including his belief that "learners should see composition as consisting of three important phases—prewriting, writing, and revision" (p. 81). In particular, Klein stressed the importance of revision as a natural part of the writing process, stating that revision "remains a problem for writers of all age categories" (p. 81). Reflecting on this concept of revision, for example, one has to wonder if the American author Carl Sandburg (1878–1967) revised any of the lines before completing his well-known poem "Fog."

Fog*

The fog comes
on little cat feet.

**Source:* Elaine Maimon, "Cultivating the Prose Garden," *Phi Delta Kappan, 69*(10), June 1988, p. 736. Reprinted with permission.

**Source:* C. Sandburg, *Chicago Poems* (New York: Henry Holt and Company, 1916).

It sits looking
over harbor and city
on silent haunches
and then moves on.

Any reader quickly realizes that the simple statement, "The fog moved in and out of the city," is lifeless compared to Sandburg's words. In this brilliant piece of free verse, Sandburg metaphorically characterized the fog as a cat. Probably the various analogies associated with a cat and its actions did not come to Sandburg without serious contemplation and revision.

From an account offered by the writer and director Norman Corwin (1993; Berman & Goldman, 1992), who had Carl Sandburg as his house guest for about a month when Sandburg was eighty years old, we know that the poet gave much thought to the lines of his poetry; it appears from the reported exchange that he was in the habit of revising. The pair were sitting at breakfast one day. Corwin noticed that Sandburg kept fishing little scraps of paper with writing on them in and out of his pocket. After noting that the scraps were quite old, Corwin asked what they were. The following conversation took place:

"Oh, they're scraps of poems that I've been carrying around."
I read some of them. They were each three, four, five lines or so, and they were beautiful things, little gems.
"Carl, have these been published?"
"No, no."
"But they're wonderful. Why haven't they been published?"
"Because I'm not through with them."

Other principles presented by Klein as being relevant for pre-K through grade 8 included the following; of course, many of these principles apply to all age categories.

[Most writers] . . . in the primary grades produce more and higher-quality writing when operating in an informal learning environment that permits them considerable freedom in choosing topics and defining their own strategies for completing the writing assignment.

[Most writers] . . . in the primary grades turn inward for the content of their writing. Personal experiences and immediate family and friends are the critical root sources of their writing.

Writing serves different purposes—to inform, to describe, to explain, to persuade or argue, to entertain—none of which are age-specific. Beginning writers, older children, and adult writers alike employ writing for these purposes. It is only the degree of sophistication that differs and not the range or general character of the purposes.

The writer writes for different audiences: the self, the known or personal you, and the unknown you. During the intermediate school years, students need to develop necessary skills in adapting written structure and content to context and audience.

Students should write often.

Writing occurs in many forms—stories, poems, essays, journals, notes, letters, reports, scripts for plays. These forms incorporate a more limited number of discourse modes—exposition, narration, argumentation, and fiction. [Note: In Klein's discussion of this principle, he suggested that while "all modes of writing should receive attention in all grades, emphasis shifts somewhat toward the logical and analytical writing demands as the learner matures" (p. 82).] (pp. 78–83)

In many of today's schools, students do write often as the curriculum and language processes are integrated. Following the reading of Sandburg's poem "Fog," for instance, might be a good time to introduce Model Activity 1.3, which can be used to integrate study about the weather into a poetry-writing assignment. As one teacher who was well into the process of moving to an integrated approach said, "It's really quite a relief not to have to split up the hours of the school day into a lesson for writing, a lesson for reading, a lesson for social studies, and so forth." She did report, however, the real need for students to have chunks of time for writing. This is consistent with the first of Atwell's (1987) seven principles related to teaching and learning in a classroom established as a reading and writing workshop:

Writers need regular chunks of time—time to think, write, confer, read, change their minds, and write some more. Writers need time they can count on, so even when they aren't writing, they're anticipating the time they will be. Writers need time to write well. (p. 17)

Atwell's other principles follow:

- Writers need their own topics.
- Writers need response.
- Writers learn mechanics in context.

- Children need to know adults who write.
- Writers need to read.
- Writing teachers need to take responsibility for their knowledge and teaching. (pp. 17–18)

During a recent visit to classrooms of a beginning kindergarten teacher and several of her colleagues from other grades, it was observed firsthand that there is a growing propensity to integrate reading and writing from the first day that a child comes to school as well as throughout the continuing grades. Like Atwell (1987), these wise teachers reported that they saw writing as a way for students " . . . to think about and give shape to their own ideas and concerns" (p. 17). Furthermore, one experienced teacher added, "With this philosophy, tasks such as topic selection are simplified immensely."

Brozo and Simpson (1991), concerned primarily with secondary school students, stressed the importance of writing as a process. Like other educators, they recommended sufficient class time for students to prewrite, write, and revise, and emphasized that time is not ever to be considered wasted when students are getting ready to write. Also, process writing experts consistently recommended that writing assignments have real audiences. When working in a content area, Brozo and Simpson supported Tchudi and Huerta (1983) in their assertion that content should be kept at the center of the process of writing. In this regard, they made the following practical suggestion: "Before designing a writing activity, ask yourself what you want your students to learn about your content area. Then select the activity that will best accomplish this objective; it may or may not involve writing" (p. 152). Other recommendations of Brozo and Simpson (1991) included the following: "Design writing assignments that encourage active learning; vary the assignments and the discourse modes, moving from simple to complex; and include publication of your students' writing in the final phase of the writing process" (pp. 152–153).

Students, of course, should be encouraged early on to share their writing. For example, students often share their pieces orally with their peers in the hope of eliciting comments that will help them revise their work to improve it before publication. One only has to watch youngsters during the preteen and teenage years writing notes to one another or to one of their parents begging permission for something believed to be impermissible, to realize that youngsters do understand the value of revision. Surely you've overheard young people having conversations of this nature:

"Let me see; let me see it! Wait! Tell him that Susie likes him, and that if he likes her to write his phone number."

"No, no! Listen! Write, 'Do you like Susie? Yes or No?'"

"There."

"Okay. Now, put a box after Yes and No for him to check!"

And another:

"Ask your mother if you can spend the night with me Friday night and we'll go to Midnight Madness."

"She'll never let me go."

"Sure she will if you ask her nicely. Tell her you'll clean up the house and be home by 10:00 A.M. Saturday to help her get ready for her party."

"Okay. Let's write down how to ask her."

"Okay."

Mom,
Can I spend the night with Joanie Friday night?
Her mom says it's okay.
"Don't forget to tell her you'll be home early Saturday morning."

Oh, yeah. If I can, I promise to be home early Saturday morning to help you . . .

Publication, broadly defined, means to place before the public. This public may be one person only, as in the notes above, or as vast as the school newspaper or a national contest. Sometimes even publication becomes recursive as copy after copy of a selected piece is drafted, lengthened, or shortened for submission to various places for various audiences.

CONCLUSION

Each stage of the writing process will be discussed in the subsequent chapters, with emphasis on the recursive and overlapping nature of these stages. Additionally, you will find numerous related instructional model activities that may be used as you teach these vital steps to students. These model activities, designed to translate theory into practice, demonstrate how students' knowledge of cultural literacy can be expanded while enhancing their critical thinking. Subject matter from across the content areas was selected for inclusion in the model activities with an intent to strike a balance between knowledge and thinking. No attempt has been made to present a core of knowledge such as that suggested by E. D. Hirsch, Jr., author of *Cultural Literacy* (1987), and founder of the Core Knowledge Foundation. The authors do support and recommend that educators apply the words of Hirsch (1989), "Knowledge builds on knowledge" (p. xiv).

It is suggested that when educators use the model activities of this text, they also introduce students to related literature, music, and art, in an attempt to help students develop an appreciation for scholarship and the beauty of the arts. Thus, the instructional activities are part of a total learning environment. Teachers and students are encouraged to consider each model activity as an invitation to learn more about the given topic. Although choices of writing topics are suggested, they are not meant to be limiting, for the authors encourage students throughout the model activities to explore and write about subjects that interest them. It is hoped that students, as they share, process, and write about information, will begin to think more critically and become better problem solvers.

Approaching the turn of the century, we realize just how small our global society has become in this age of technology and jet travel. Today's classrooms reflect this reality; our schools are composed of students from many different cultures. Therefore, educators are encouraged to build on the strengths of the diversity of their students, sharing multicultural traditions and authentically representing pluralistic institutions. The students of today will shape the future; by preparing them to be lifelong learners and capable problem solvers, they will succeed in creating a better tomorrow.

REFERENCES

Applebee, A. N. (1984). Writing and reasoning. *Review of Educational Research, 54,* 577–596.

Applebee, A. N., Langer, J. A., Mullis, I. V. S., & Jenkins, L. B. (1990). *The writing report card, 1984–1988: Findings from the nation's report card.* Princeton, NJ: National Assessment of Education Progress, Educational Testing Service.

Atwell, N. (1987). *In the middle: Writing, reading, and learning with adolescents.* Portsmouth, NH: Boynton/Cook.

Berman, P. L., & Goldman, C. (1992). *The ageless spirit.* New York: Ballantine Books.

Brozo, W. G., & Simpson, M. L. (1991). The active learner and writing in the secondary classroom. In *Readers, teachers, learners: Expanding literacy in the secondary schools* (pp. 147–175). New York: Macmillan.

Calkins, L. M. (1986). *The art of teaching writing.* Portsmouth, NH: Heinemann.

Corwin. N. (1993, July). Norman Corwin: Writer, director. *Guideposts,* p. 32.

Daniels, H. A. (1983). *Famous last words.* Carbondale: Southern Illinois University Press.

Elbow, P. (1981). *Writing with power: Techniques for mastering the writing process.* New York: Oxford University Press.

Elbow, P. (1985). The shifting relationships between speech and writing. *College Composition and Communication, 36,* 283–303.

Ellis, D. W. (Ed.). (1988, March–April). An interview with Donald Graves. *The California Reader, 21*(3), 3–8.

Emig, J. (1971). *The composing process of twelfth graders.* Research Report No. 13. Urbana, IL: National Council of Teachers of English.

Emig, J. (1977). Writing as a mode of learning. *College Composition and Communication, 28,* 122–128.

Flower, L., & Hayes, J. R. (1981). A cognitive process theory of writing. *College Composition and Communication, 32,* 365–387.

Gardner, J. L. (Ed.). (1981). *Reader's Digest atlas of the Bible.* Pleasantville, NY: Reader's Digest Association.

Goldberg, M. F. (1984, January). An update on the National Writing Project. *Phi Delta Kappan, 65*(5), 356–357.

Goodman, K. S. (1986). *What's whole in whole language?* Portsmouth, NH: Heinemann.

Goodman, K. S., Bird, L. B., & Goodman, Y. M. (Eds.). (1991). *The whole language catalog* (pp. 130–131). Santa Rosa, CA: American School Publishers.

Graves, D. H. (1983). *Writing: Teachers and children at work.* Exeter, NH: Heinemann.

Hennings, D. G. (1990). *Communication in action: Teaching the language arts,* 4th ed. Boston: Houghton Mifflin.

Hirsch, E. D., Jr. (1987). *Cultural literacy: What every American needs to know.* Boston: Houghton Mifflin.

Hirsch, E. D., Jr. (1989). *A first dictionary of cultural literacy.* Boston: Houghton Mifflin.

Humes, A. (1983). Research on the composing process. *Review of Educational Research, 53*(2), 201–216.

Jenkinson, E. B. (1988, June). Learning to write/Writing to learn. *Phi Delta Kappan, 69*(10), 712–717.

Klein, M. L. (1985). *The development of writing in children.* Englewood Cliffs, NJ: Prentice-Hall.

Kucer, S. L. (1985). The making of meaning: Reading and writing as parallel processes. *Written Communication, 2,* 319–336.

Leopold, A. H., & Jenkinson, E. B. (1988, June). The Cummins Engine Foundation writing project: A cooperative venture with public schools. *Phi Delta Kappan, 69*(10), 740–745.

Loveless, J. B. (1991). As teachers see it. In K. S. Goodman, L. B. Bird, & Y. M. Goodman (Eds.). *The whole language catalog* (p. 263). Santa Rosa, CA: American School.

Lundsteen, S. W. (1989). Learning to compose. In *Language arts: A problem-solving approach* (pp. 260–303). New York: Harper & Row.

Maimon, E. P. (1988). Cultivating the prose garden. *Phi Delta Kappan, 69*(10), 734–739.

Mayer, J. S., & Lester, N. B. (1983). Putting learning first in writing to learn. *Language Arts, 60*(6), 717–722.

Moffett, J. (1968). *Teaching the universe of discourse.* Boston: Houghton Mifflin.

Perrin, P. G. (1965). *Writer's guide and index to English,* 4th ed. Chicago: Scott, Foresman.

Reutzel, D. R., & Cooter, R. B., Jr. (1992). *Teaching children to read: From basals to books.* New York: Macmillan.

Richards, N. (1968). *People of destiny: Ernest Hemingway.* Chicago: Children's Press.

Sandburg, C. (1916). *Chicago Poems.* New York: Henry Holt and Company.

Tchudi, S. N., & Huerta, M. C. (1983). *Teaching writing in the content areas.* Washington, DC: National Education Association.

Tierney, R. J., & Pearson, P. D. (1983). Toward a composing model of reading. *Language Arts, 60,* 568–580.

Tremmel, R. (1992). A habit of mind. *English Education, 24*(1), 20–33.

vos Savant, M. (1990). Ask Marilyn. *Parade Magazine,* November 18, p. 14.

Vygotsky, L. S. (1962). *Thought and language.* (E. Hanfmann & G. Vakar, Trans.). Cambridge, MA: MIT Press.

Writing about your trauma can ease pain. (1991). *Tallahassee Democrat,* March 11, p. 2B.

MODEL ACTIVITIES

The activities that follow are meant to serve as models; such activities should be used as part of a total learning environment. These model activities were designed to demonstrate how the writing process can be developed while expanding the writer's knowledge base and providing opportunities for the writer to think critically.

The Sumerians of Ancient Times

Have you ever wondered what it would have been like to live over five thousand years ago? Fortunately for us, some ancient people, the Sumerians, developed a system of writing called *cuneiform* that tells us how they lived around 3500 B.C. Listen as this Sumerian statue comes to life through his writings to tell you about his people (based on Gardner, 1981):

Hello. I am a Sumerian. My people—a nation of traders—settled in a place in Southern Mesopotamia where the Tigris and Euphrates Rivers join together before flowing into the Persian Gulf. We called our land Sumer. You can see how we dressed; we liked fringes at the bottom of our garments. Our special hairstyles and the way the men styled their beards made us look very distinctive.

When my people came to Sumer, they dug irrigation canals and dikes so we could grow wheat, barley, and other crops. We built cities out of what we had plenty of—mud. We shaped bricks, let them dry in the sun, and built walls around our cities for protection from enemy warriors. Our people were very creative; we used the arch in building and the wheel for transportation. We fashioned sculptures of our gods and rulers from stone, designed pottery, and made bronze for which we found many uses.

We Sumerians used a number system based on 10's and 6's. I understand that you still use our system in the way you tell time. We also developed the earliest known law code. Our biggest achievement, though, was our development of a system of writing. Our clay tablets carried the beginning of written history. In addition to the oral tradition, mankind could now pass on wisdom of the past to future generations in a new way, writing. We were happy to be able to do that, and I hope you will carry on this fine tradition of telling others about yourself in writing.

Goodbye for now. It's time for me to step back into the pages of ancient history books.—A Sumerian

Directions: Would you like to record something in writing for future generations to read? First, spend some time thinking about the life and culture of our day. Expand the cluster below to include some areas of interest to you. If you're feeling especially creative, expand the concept map with different categories or structure it in a different way.

Write quickly as thoughts come to you.

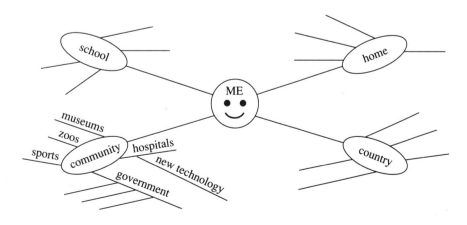

13

Now, choose one topic from your cluster. In the space below write a paragraph to inform future generations about some part of the time in history in which you live. You may also draw an illustration if you like.

_____

_____

_____

_____

_____

_____

_____

_____

_____

_____

_____

_____

_____

_____

After drafting your paragraph, share your writing with one or two classmates or your teacher. They may have suggestions that will help you to improve it. Make any revisions that you feel will improve your paragraph better as you rewrite it below.

_____

_____

_____

_____

_____

_____

_____

_____

_____

_____

_____

_____

_____

_____

Did the students in your class choose many different topics to write about? _____ You may want to keep these paragraphs in your writing folder for a cooperative class project to be worked on at another time.

ACTIVITY 1.2

Let's Practice Writing

This activity is designed to introduce you to the stages of the writing process.

Prewriting

Work through the following activity for practice with the generating stage of writing, using the suggested steps.

1. Pick a subject area:

   safety   nutrition   drug abuse
   recycling   weather   (your example): _____

2. Write down all the ideas about the subject you chose that come into your mind. An example is given on the subject "Nutrition."

Nutrition

eggs	grocery shopping
phosphorus	orange juice
planning menus	iodine
potatoes	good smell of bread baking
checking dates on cans	meat
cheese	magnesium
fresh fruits	eating with friends
picnics	fish
green vegetables	cereals
iron	making a grocery list
gardening	milk
sugar	beans
dining out	bread
calcium	

3. Review your ideas and then organize them under related headings. For example, if you chose the topic of nutrition, the following subject areas might emerge:

   tasks associated with providing meals
   pleasures of eating
   minerals needed by the body
   sources of vitamins
   proteins
   carbohydrates

4. Using the generating and planning ideas given thus far, plan a framework for a writing draft on your chosen topic. You may find the form that follows useful.

Title: _____

Paragraph 1

  A. Subject: _____

       Ideas: _____

            _____

            _____

Paragraph 2

  B. Subject: _____

       Ideas: _____

            _____

            _____

Paragraph 3

  C. Subject: _____

       Ideas: _____

            _____

            _____

Consider the following questions:

What are the main ideas in my writing?
What would make a good title?
What order should be used to express ideas?
What should be at the beginning?
What should be at the end?

Drafting

5. Using the preceding plan as a guide, write on the chosen topic. As you write, consider the following:

Who is my audience?
Is the message clear to me?
Will the audience, the readers, understand?
Is the appropriate written form for the audience being used?

_____

_____

_____

_____

_____

_____

_____

_____

_____

_____

Sharing

6. Read your draft aloud to your classmates. Encourage them to respond with questions and comments about your writing. Ask if they understand everything that you have written, and make sure you understand their suggestions regarding your work-in-progress.

Revising

7. After considering all the feedback received when sharing the draft, you may decide that changes are necessary for clarity; you may even decide to reorganize your material. Incorporate changes into your work-in-progress, keeping in mind the intended audience. You may also feel a need to expand some ideas, to create a different tone, or to add interest.

_____

_____

_____

_____

_____

_____

_____

_____

_____

_____

Editing

8. Now reread what you have written. Check for any omissions and/or remaining errors in mechanics such as punctuation, capitalization, and spelling. Work with a partner, serving as copy editors for each other. After making all your corrections, proofread one last time prior to publishing.

Publishing

9. Not all pieces of writing need to be taken through the stage of publishing. However, publication is a means to celebrate written work. You and your classmates may want to publish your writing by posting it on a bulletin board or compiling it in the form of class booklets, newsletters, class histories, and the like.

ACTIVITY 1.3

Poetry about Weather

Directions: Read the following passage about fog and what causes it. Then read the poem "Fog" by Carl Sandburg.

Fog is a cloud close to the ground or surface of a body of water. Fog, like clouds, is made up of tiny drops of water.

Fog forms much as the cloud of steam does that appears over a boiling teakettle. The moisture in the warm air coming out of the kettle hits the cooler air outside and condenses, or turns to small drops of water. In the same way, fog is formed when the wind blows warm, moist air over a cold surface of land or water. The more of these tiny particles of water there are, the thicker the fog is. Fog disappears when the ground warms up or when a brisk wind blows it away.

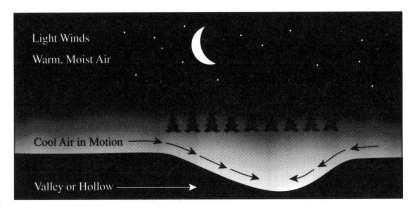

There are many accidents in fog because people cannot see their way. Air traffic is sometimes delayed because of the danger during takeoffs and landings when fog is heavy.

San Francisco and London are cities that are famous for their fog. Carl Sandburg (1878–1967) wrote about fog in Chicago in the following poem:

Fog

> The fog comes
> on little cat feet.
>
> It sits looking
> over harbor and city
> on silent haunches
> and then moves on.

Writing a Poem about the Weather

The weather has long been a topic of choice for many poets. Besides "Fog" by Carl Sandburg, the following are a few examples. You may wish to locate one or two of these poems to read before completing this activity.

"The Rainy Day" by Henry Wadsworth Longfellow
"A Day of Sunshine" by Henry Wadsworth Longfellow
"Snow-Bound" by John Greenleaf Whittier
"The Sky is Low" by Emily Dickinson
"When the Frost Is on the Punkin" by James Whitcomb Riley
"Song of the Rain-Chant" from Indian folklore

Source: C. Sandburg, Chicago Poems (New York: Henry Holt and Company, 1916).

Look over the following list of weather words. You may add others if you wish.

fog	hail	lightning	sunshine
rain	sleet	tornado	clouds
snow	thunder	hurricane	frost
wind	_____	_____	_____

Choose one weather word as the topic of your poem:

_____

In the space below, jot down ideas that come to mind when you think of the kind of weather described by that word.

_____

_____

_____

_____

_____

_____

_____

_____

_____

Now you are ready to draft your poem. Use ideas that came to you while brainstorming. Your poem may be written in free verse or in a rhyming pattern.

_____

_____

_____

_____

_____

_____

_____

_____

_____

_____

_____

Share your poem draft with a classmate. Work together on any revisions that may improve meaning, meter, or rhyme (if it is used). Then recopy your revised poem; if you plan to display the poem, consider using colored paper for backing. Your class may wish to make a weather collage for the bulletin board. Use all the poems written about the weather during this writing activity.

CHAPTER 2

Teacher Expectations and Mental Rehearsal for Successful Writing

Curiosity is one of the permanent and certain characteristics of a vigorous intellect.

—Samuel Johnson (1709–1784), English lexicographer and author

WHAT YOU EXPECT IS OFTEN WHAT YOU GET

When teachers expect their students' writing performance to develop optimally, they communicate this positive attitude throughout the instructional process. Likewise, students who are taught how to visualize their own success become better writers. "Success breeds success."

In many cases, people short-circuit the potential of others merely by expecting less of them than they are capable of producing. Conversely, by expecting the best from individuals, it is possible to influence their motivation toward improvement and success. Participants in any group enterprise tend to be more productive when they are respected, feel valued, and believe that their contribution will make a difference. It might be well, then, to look at what one successful teacher is doing to accomplish this.

Judith Thies (Lindley, 1990), a poet and a teacher of creative writing as a survival skill in one of the Kansas City, Missouri, school district's magnet schools, fought the reality of gangs as well as their associated psychological problems. With a positive attitude despite these circumstances, she boldly stated, "None of my creative writing students will ever be gang members." After teaching at an exclusive private school, Thies jumped at the chance to head the creative writing program at one of the city's magnet schools that pulls in a mix of students with specialties such as science, the arts, history, or high-technology skills, tapping the talents of low-achieving students while offering others a chance to focus and do better. Thies said of her students:

The passion and the melodies are there in their writing. If I had to put music to the sounds of their writing, I'd put a guitar to the voice of my Hispanic students and, of course, the blues to my black students. My Orientals are the imagists, so I'd pick flutes, the clear, piercing sounds of the high instruments.

The inner city gets trapped inside their heads. It becomes a beast. By allowing them to write every day about it, if nothing else it's a survival tool. (p. 1B)

This caring teacher has been a real force in that school, encouraging her students with statements such as these: "You are unique. You are special. There's no one else out there with *your* voice." She also has reminded them that the emotional quality in their writing is powerful and has told them to "get their voices out there for the world to hear."

In today's classrooms, which are composed of students from diverse cultural and language backgrounds, teachers must give even more consideration to the impact that their expectations will have on actual student performance. Students frequently tend to live up or down to the expectations of their teachers, expectations that often turn into self-fulfilling prophecies.

SELF-FULFILLING PROPHECIES

According to Merton (1957), a self-fulfilling prophecy occurs when a false definition of a situation causes behavior that makes the false definition come true. In a worst-case scenario, a teacher in the early 1960s made it a practice to note each of her student's IQ scores in the margin of her grade book at the beginning of each term. According to this misguided teacher, these IQ scores helped her determine the potential of each student early in the term. Predictably, she reported that the students performed in accordance with her predetermined expectations. It would seem that the point of this teacher's pen held tremendous power over her students. One can only speculate about how she actually treated the students in the classroom.

Around this same time, Rosenthal and Fode (1963) and Rosenthal and Lawson (1964) were conducting studies of the effects of experimenter bias with ordinary rats. In both studies, ordinary rats were randomly divided and labeled "bright" or "dull"; experimenters were led to believe that the so-called bright rats had been bred to be superior performers with maze tasks. In the first study, the rats labeled "bright" actually improved daily, whereas the "dull" rats only improved through the third day before regressing. Working with "bright" rats led the experimenters to assess their rats more positively in terms of brightness, pleasantness, and likableness. Also, the experimenters with the "bright" rats interpreted their own behavior more positively. For example, the "bright" rat experimenters reported that they not only handled their rats more often but did so more gently and observed their animals more carefully as well. These studies led psychologists to speculate that students who were thought to be "brighter" or more intelligent by their teachers would also live up to that expectation by high achievement in the classroom.

PYGMALION IN THE CLASSROOM

In this classic study, Rosenthal and Jacobson (1968) conducted an experiment that demonstrated that teachers' expectations for student performance influenced student achievement. Their study, *Pygmalion in the Classroom,* was carried out in a public school setting, and all participating students were pretested with a standard intelligence test. The teachers were led to believe that several of the students in their classes showed great academic potential. In fact, these students had been selected at random. After one semester, all students were retested with the same IQ test; they were tested again a full academic year later. When IQ scores were compared, the students in early primary grades who were expected to bloom intellectually showed greater gains in IQ than students for whom such an expectation did not exist. Naturally, these significant findings captured the attention of educators throughout the nation.

Since the publication of *Pygmalion in the Classroom,* there have been numerous research studies demonstrating that teacher expectation influences student achievement. According to Cooper and Tom (1984), research since the classic *Pygmalion* study indicates that "although the factors that influence student performance are multiple and complex, teacher expectations do play a role in how well and how much students learn" (p. 77). One must also keep in mind that the teacher–student relationship in the classroom, unlike the laboratory, is bidirectional; student ability, motivation, and even appearance influence what teachers think about students (West & Anderson, 1976).

Teachers' attitudes about their own experiences and themselves are also related to how well they enable students in the learning environment of the classroom. For example, teachers who truly enjoy poetry are far more likely to introduce various kinds

Attitude Is Everything

Reprinted with special permission of King Features Syndicate.

of poetry and to encourage students to write their own poems. Likewise, teachers who appreciate poetry themselves frequently study the lives of favorite poets and model for students the process of understanding the poet's perspective. This often necessitates a close look at the historical period during which the poet created. In the following example, a teacher chose to begin a class discussion by sharing specific information about one of the United States' best-known poets; this teacher also encouraged her students, who represented a variety of cultural backgrounds, to share information about their favorite poets.

Teacher: One of my favorite poets is Robert Frost (1874–1963), a man who was considered a New Englander even though he was born in San Francisco. He lived during part of my lifetime and wrote about his feelings and things that were dear to his heart. I probably admire him most, though, because he didn't give up even when life became very challenging.

Student A: What do you mean by that?

Teacher: During certain periods of his life, he actually considered himself a failure. Just think about this: He was forty years old before he had any public recognition. After that, Frost received more honors than any other contemporary poet in the U.S.; he won the Pulitzer Prize for poetry four times.

Student B: I think I'd like to learn more about Frost. Do you know much more about him?

Teacher: What kind of things would you like to know?

Student B: Well, what did he do when he wasn't writing poetry?

Everyone laughed at that question! Then they lightly joked among themselves, speculating about what else Frost did besides writing poetry.

Teacher: For openers, he worked in a textile mill, became a chicken farmer, married his high school classmate and had a large family, studied, taught, read and reread Emerson, and enjoyed searching for rare flowers. Unfortunately, he also experienced a lot of personal grief and loss during his lifetime.

Throughout this dialoguing, the teacher was actively involving the students in the learning process, building their background experience and piquing their curiosity. In this example, she purposely name-dropped Emerson, thus introducing Ralph Waldo Emerson (1803–1882), an American poet and essayist much admired and read by Frost. She wanted to use this "teachable moment" to point out that Emerson stressed the importance of the individual and wrote an essay called "Self-Reliance."

At this point, a teacher could seize the opportunity to guide students through the process of reading some of Frost's poetry, finding print material that would unveil his fascinating life, and helping them relate his poetry to their own lives. Just hearing Frost's "Stopping by Woods on a Snowy Evening" will give students a feel for one of his poems of endurance. Through the teacher's reading, students will hear how good poetry sounds; also, the students will see that there is value in writing, even though it often is hard work.

Model Activities 2.1, 2.2, and 2.3 relate to the

poetry of Frost and Emerson; they are versatile in that they can be used during one or more of the stages of the writing process. For example, if they are used for prewriting (generating ideas and gathering information before writing to enhance the composing process), one likely result might be a trip to the school or public library. Students may want to build their background experience through reading as they become curious and interested in the content. Many students who previously balked at the idea of studying poetry may do an about-face when it is presented in a way that causes them to relate personally; at some point, they may want to try their hand at writing poems.

ENTHUSIASM IS CONTAGIOUS AND ENABLES LEARNING

Research findings indicate that there is a positive relationship between teacher self-concept and teacher effectiveness (Okech, 1987; Manning & Payne, 1987). Thus, it is important that teachers be concerned about their own feelings and attitudes. Apparently, when teachers genuinely feel good about themselves and the way they have chosen to spend their professional lives, they are likely to exhibit more enthusiasm in classroom interactions with students. There is much common sense in the adage that enthusiasm is contagious, given the influence of teacher modeling. Teachers who are capable enablers themselves will be more effective at enabling their students. With regard to this topic, Hanson (1990) stressed the importance of teachers enabling students "to learn and discover themselves" (p. 265).

The role of the teacher is dynamic, particularly when teachers also perceive themselves as learners. For example, in his writing process laboratory, Donald H. Graves implements the idea of letting students show him (the teacher) how to help them write (Walshe, 1981). By implementing this approach in the classroom, teachers facilitate their own continued growth alongside their students. According to Lester and Onore (1986), the educational process is demonstrated as teachers move through a cycle of seeking answers, finding more questions, and so on. Reflective practitioners such as Wellington (1991) also have emphasized the importance of inquiry-oriented teaching, which "engages the teacher in a cycle of thought and action based on professional experience" (p. 4). In such a process, learning occurs as a result of active participation; learning is also more enjoyable for both student and teacher. Furthermore, through natural interaction with students, Yetta Goodman (1989) suggested that teachers "are not just discovering what students know about any particular learning but are also using the moments of interaction to question the student, to encourage, to stimulate, and to challenge" (p. 11). Students need to be encouraged to think reflectively about their writings. According to Canning (1991), questions such as the following should be useful for prompting student reflection about their writings (p. 19):

Can you talk more about that?
Why do you think that happens?
What evidence do you have about that?
What does this remind you of?
What if it happened this way?
Do you see a connection between this and _____?
How else could you approach that?
What do you want to happen?
How could you do that?

Canning uses detailed questions such as these in her effort to push "the writers to be specific" (p. 19). As they address her questions, they are also being encouraged to assume responsibility for their decisions about their work-in-progress. Her intention is to have the students "speak in their own voices" (p. 19) and to know that she trusts each of them. Canning also uses affirmations when appropriate within the context of learning to communicate her trust; she offered the following as examples (p. 21):

You can find a way that works for you when you are ready.
You can change if you want to.
You can grow at your own pace.
You can know what you need and ask for help.
You can experiment and explore. I will help you.
You can learn from what doesn't work for you.
You can feel your feelings.
Your needs and reflections are important.
I like talking to you like this.

SOCIOCULTURAL AND LINGUISTIC DIFFERENCES

E PLURIBUS UNUM—Latin slogan engraved on U.S. coins, meaning "one formed from many"

Today's classrooms are composed of students from many different backgrounds. The resulting sociocultural and linguistic differences can be an asset when the richness of these cultures is shared. In the United States, these differences will increase in the future. According to Hodgkinson (1985, p. 10), the following changes in the public school system can be expected:

• More students from poverty-stricken households
• More students from single-parent households
• More students from minority backgrounds
• A larger number of premature babies, leading to more learning difficulties in school (partially the result of an increase in teenage pregnancies)
• An increase in the number of black middle-class students
• An increase in the numbers of Asian-American students

Valdivieso (1986) also pointed out that Hispanics constitute the fastest growing population in the United States because of their high birth rate. According to a report from the U.S. Bureau of the Census (1987), by the end of the 1990s Hispanics will surpass blacks as the largest minority group in the United States. According to William A. Henry III (1990), by the year 2020 "the number of U.S. residents who are Hispanic or nonwhite will have more than doubled, to nearly 115 million, while the white population will not be increasing at all" (p. 28). Further projections to 2056 indicate that "whites may be a minority group" (p. 30). These changes will alter much in our society, including education. As we consider today's classrooms and look to the future, various issues related to differences in our student population must be of primary concern as instruction is designed.

Given that students' "culture may affect who they are as communicators" (Lundsteen, 1989, p. 491), it is essential that each culture represented in the classroom be understood and respected; this often requires a new level of awareness on everyone's part, for each culture or subculture has its own rules for learning. For example, students who are expected to succeed usually receive more eye contact. Consider this question, then: What happens when a teacher is working with students who are from a culture where eye contact with the teacher is considered disrespectful? Although an answer to this complex question would require a thorough understanding of that particular culture, the situation creates a good discussion topic and also provides an opportunity for students to write about their differences and accompanying feelings. When considering academic interactions and acknowledging that successful students create more, keep in mind that some cultures actually discourage working together and may even equate such cooperation with cheating. The antithesis is true as well: In some cultures, individual competition is highly discouraged, with team playing being the only game in town. Lundsteen (1989) suggested that "while we need to avoid stereotyping, . . . some generalizations help explain differences" (p. 491).

THE CLASSROOM AS A LITERATE COMMUNITY

As teachers become more aware of themselves and their students, they are in an ideal position to encourage developing writers. For students to be empowered as writers, it is important that they feel accepted and valued for who they really are, so that intrinsic motivation is more likely to occur. As students in the classroom feel respected and valued, they will select writing topics that are relevant to them. According to Vygotsky (1978), "Writing should be meaningful for children . . . an intrinsic need should be aroused in them, and that writing should be incorporated into a task that is necessary and relevant for life." Writing, a part of our culture, should emerge as a natural part of life. As creators of the literacy environment in the classroom, Cairney and Langbien (1989) suggested that "the major challenge . . . is to create classroom environments in which all children come to value reading and writing as natural extensions of their lives." Doing so, they suggest, will give students a place for sharing and growing "as members of a literate community" (p. 567).

Kenneth Goodman (1986) recommended that students themselves should author some of the print materials contributing to the "literature environment" of the classroom. Having students contribute to the printed materials available to be read allows them both to write something to be read by others, and to read what others have written. Both acts involve students in their own literacy development. By not overlooking the fact that students entering the classroom possess considerable literacy knowledge, and by building on that base, teachers can play a crucial role in the empowerment of students through literacy. Ideally, such a classroom would also include a wide range of literacy materials—for example, good literature, newspapers, magazines, and the content texts. As Robert Frost is said to have remarked, "The best way to get kids to read [and write] is to surround them with so many books that they stumble over them" (Zakariya, 1985, p. 21). Other reading materials, such as baseball cards, travel brochures, posters, pictures, and even drivers' license handbooks, should also be included as a part of the classroom environment. According to Fagan (1989), "The presence of 'environmental literacy materials' helps the low achievers think of themselves as readers and writers since they are often aware of such materials in their lives, and

often do not think of these literacy tasks as reading and writing" (p. 577).

Because it is known that some homes from which students come do not have literacy materials, it is imperative that they be provided in the classroom. For example, the daily newspaper provides high-interest, real-life content that students want to read and write about; it reports history as it happens. As students develop the habit of reading newspapers, they naturally increase their knowledge of both their community and the greater world. Also, newspapers provide excellent models for writing and numerous opportunities for students to think critically. Likewise, history related to newspapers can be used to enhance cultural literacy. Students will benefit from discussions about the concept of a free press and associated implications, as well as what various leaders across time had to say about this topic. Leaders such as Thomas Jefferson (1743–1826), who served as the third president of the United States from 1801 to 1809, will seem more real to students when they consider remarks attributed to him such as the following: "The press is the best instrument for enlightening the mind of man, and improving him as a rational, moral, and social being." Furthermore, the findings of the research conducted by Palmer (1989) to investigate the effects of newspaper-based instruction on reading vocabulary, reading comprehension, and writing performance of at-risk middle and secondary students, indicated that newspaper-based instruction should be used consistently over time in the classroom, and that newspaper use is most beneficial when combined with a whole language approach to instruction. In this study, the whole language involvement included the integration of critical observing, reading, writing, speaking, listening, and even role-playing. This whole language philosophy of teaching integrated all the language arts in a context that had personal meaning for the students. As students made choices about what they would read in the newspapers, they were naturally assuming more responsibility for their own learning. At the middle school level, for example, Palmer found that as more time was allocated to the newspaper with instruction treatment, gains in writing performance increased. Another particularly interesting finding was that secondary school males' reading vocabulary benefited most when they used newspapers.

In the newspaper-based Model Activities 2.4, 2.5, and 2.6, the emphasis is on integrating the reading and writing processes. Without content of their own, these processes are applied to all content areas. Through such activities, students should understand better that writing is a process that involves thinking.

Finally, it is important to keep in mind that the concept of the classroom as a literature community is not limited to students of any particular age. Reporting the findings of a "teachers as research-

ers" project, Rousculp and Maring (1992) said that "among the key elements of our literate environment and community of learners were the course text, library collections, activities for encouraging bonding and collaboration, and the writing portfolio" (p. 379). As students collaborated with one another, sharing their ideas and work-in-progress, bonding occurred naturally; this was particularly important given the diversity of their backgrounds.

MENTAL REHEARSAL AND THE ENHANCEMENT OF EDUCATION

Ralph Waldo Emerson wrote that the secret of success lies within the power of oneself: "Self trust is the first secret of success." In addressing the ingredients of success, Maxwell Maltz, author of *Psycho-Cybernetics* (1960) and of *The Magic Power of Self-Image Psychology* (1964), contended in the latter that one basic maxim was as follows: "Believe in yourself and you'll succeed!" (p. 55).

Students should be encouraged to practice visualizing themselves as successful writers. Visualizing success, however, does not imply that their first drafts won't need further development. As even the most successful inventors have learned, hard work must accompany a positive and persevering attitude. Thomas Alva Edison (1847–1931), one of North America's most famous inventors, with 1,093 patents to his credit (more than anyone before or since), is a good example. Called Al by his friends, he attended school for only three months when he was eight years old. By the time he was twenty-one, he had completed his first invention, a vote recorder, but no one wanted it (Doyle, 1980). Edison claimed he had only about a 10 percent success rate. Yet, that success rate gave us the follow-

ing: the phonograph, which he created with the black inventor Charles Batchelor; waxed paper; the electric light bulb in 1879; the camera; and the world's first movie studio, which he called the "Black Maria" after the 1847 police patrol wagons because the whole building was painted black. Edison also is credited with improving both the telephone and the stock ticker. He said that he never considered his experiments that didn't work as failures; each time, he had learned something else that would not work. His creative genius he attributed only to hard work: " 'one percent inspiration,' Edison would say, 'ninety-nine percent perspiration'" (Doyle, 1980, p. 24).

Through the process of self-correction and practice, success is likely to follow. The old proverb, "If at first you don't succeed, try, try again," implies that we will have failures and opportunities to change those failures into success experiences. Nowhere is that maxim more true than in learning to be a writer, for successful writers rarely offer a composition's first draft as a finished product for others to read.

MENTAL IMAGERY OR MENTAL REHEARSAL

The idea of imagery goes back hundreds of years. It is said that the Greek philosopher and mathematician Pythagoras (about 497 B.C.) taught his students to solve problems by using imagery. Aristotle (384–322 B.C.), another Greek philosopher, believed that thought was housed in images. Aristotle also was convinced that "man by nature seeks to

know" (Eisner, 1991, p. 14). In recent years, according to Wheatley, Maddox, Anthony, and Coe (1987, p. 150), "Mental imagery, the formation of pictures of external objects or events in one's mind," ... has been the focus of many research studies. Findings of these mental imagery or mental rehearsal studies are consistent with current learning theories of Piaget and Inhelder (1971) and Paivio (1971). In 1986, Paivio (p. 227) hypothesized that cognition involves both a verbal linguistic system and a nonverbal imaging system for information processing. Recent studies have shown the efficacy of using mental imagery to enhance the educational process (Greeson & Zigarwi, 1986; McDaniel & Einstein, 1986). Of particular interest is the work of Gaylean (1980, 1983), who used guided imagery with low-achieving students. Lowery (1982) also reported the effectiveness of mental imagery in educating gifted students. According to Weaver and Cotrell (1986), the utilization of mental imagery as a tool for enhancing the learning process extends throughout the educational curriculum, including areas of athletics, such as football, soccer, basketball, baseball, and tennis, as well as literacy development. With Olympic games receiving international attention, and with more and more pressure on players and coaches to win, mental rehearsal has become a popular technique for enhancing an athlete's performance.

Kraig (1990) reported that researchers at the University of Chicago, who wondered if reports of athletes improving through mental rehearsal were true, conducted an experimental study. Three basketball teams were assembled. Each person's ability to shoot free throws, unhindered shots from behind a set line, was measured. One team was told to practice free throws an hour a day for 30 days, another team was told not to think about basketball for 30 days, and the third team was told to visualize themselves successfully throwing free throws for 30 days. At the end of that time, those who had mentally pictured success were almost as successful as those who actually practiced, showing 23 percent and 24 percent improvement in accuracy, respectively. Those who did not practice in any way showed no change. By mentally experiencing the success associated with sinking the basket, these team members had engaged in practice of a sort; mental rehearsal was taking place. Similar results have been reported with other sports—snow skiing, golf, and even throwing darts. Today, the most successful athletes spend time in both mental rehearsal sports practice and actual physical practice. Educators need to learn from this and to incorporate mental rehearsal into their lessons.

OUR MARVELOUS MINDS

Along with better utilization of techniques such as mental rehearsal, educators are considering the instructional implications of research findings related to the brain. Although its workings still are not understood fully, the current body of research indicates that the brain's neocortex is divided into two halves, which are joined by nerve fibers, the corpus callosum. These two hemispheres develop varying, but complementary, ways of processing information. The American astronomer, author, and educator, Carl Sagan (1934–   ) reported that solutions to complex problems require the utilization of both sides of the brain; Sagan believes that the path to the future lies through the corpus callosum. The left hemisphere of the brain is orderly, verbal, sequential, and analytical. On the right side, the brain is creative and artistic and sees things totally, rather than in parts (Wheatley et al., 1987, p. 150). It is the more creative right hemisphere that looks for divergent views and thinks in visual images; art, drama, and music draw on this hemisphere's abilities. The nervous system is connected to the brain in a crossed-over fashion; at the base of the brain the signals are twisted so that the right side of the brain controls the left side of our body and vice versa. The left side of the brain is slightly more dominant, which accounts for why about 90 percent of people are right-handed (Bogoch, 1988, p. 565).

In contrast to current researchers, nineteenth-century scientists defined the left hemisphere as dominant or major, with the right brain subordinate or minor. Based on that nineteenth-century thinking, most of our educational system was designed to cultivate the verbal, rational, objective, logical left hemisphere.

Rudyard Kipling (1865–1936), English author and Nobel Prize winner, is well known for classics such as *The Jungle Book, Just So Stories,* and the poem "Gunga Din." But this creative writer must have been aware of the two sides of the brain when, at the beginning of the twentieth century, he wrote a poem, "The Two-Sided Man," expressing gratitude for the two separate sides of his head (Kipling, 1927).

Twentieth-century discoveries about how the brain works are important for educators: We now know that instruction must be designed to cultivate efficient use of *both* hemispheres of the brain, relying on many interconnections between the two halves. Given that the brain has an unlimited capacity to learn (Johnson, 1985), we must make every effort to stimulate both hemispheres mentally while challenging our students; this can be accomplished by actively involving students in learning experiences that combine the forces of both hemispheres. For example, to involve students actively in problem solving, teachers should encourage them to conceptualize possible solutions; an insight to the problem may materialize in the right hemisphere as a visual image; then, the left hemisphere will transform this into a more abstract representation so that the student can describe it verbally and then put that description down on paper. We must remember that when students are actively involved in constructing meaning, they are most likely to learn and remember. Also, keeping in mind that students have different learning styles, it is advantageous to present material in a variety of forms while integrating in-

struction and to encourage students to expand their schemata (organized prior knowledge) independently and cooperatively. To be good writers, students must be willing to become good thinkers, for writing is a form of thinking. When instruction is designed to challenge our students, both sides of the brain will be activated, and these interconnections will result in optimal functioning of the brain, which Teyler (1978) described as probably the most complexly organized matter in the universe.

[Because of] . . . an explosion of recent findings in brain science—aided by new computer programs that can simulate brain cells in action . . . [we now know] . . . that the brain is far more intricate than any mechanical device imaginable. [It has been likened to] . . . a beehive or a busy market place, a seething swarm of densely interconnected nerve cells—called neurons—that are continually sending electrochemical signals back and forth to each other and altering their lines of communication with every experience (How the Brain Really Works Its Wonders," 1988, p. 48).

CREATIVE THINKING

In our society, very young children are encouraged to share their stories of imaginary friends and fantasy trips. Most parents of preschoolers would agree with Lauren Bacall (1924–   ), an American-born actress who has enjoyed success on stage and screen, that "imagination is the highest kite one can fly." As these same youngsters start school and move through the early grades, we strive to make sure that these students learn the difference between what's real and what's imagined; furthermore, daydreaming is too often regarded with suspicion and discouraged. Then, by the time they reach fourth grade, we start wondering why students are not very creative. Is it possible that their creativity has been suppressed by our educational system, which focuses the most instructional time and attention on the left hemisphere of the brain?

Albert Einstein (1879–1955), a brilliant American (German-born) physicist, firmly believed that "Imagination is more important than knowledge." Einstein is said to have once remarked that when trying to solve a problem, "The answer will come while you're eating an apple." One creative classroom teacher, who chanced upon these words while

doing other research, began to apply this concept to her daily life. If she wanted to recall an answer, she simply implanted the question in her brain and went on her merry way. If she consciously tried to remember something that would not immediately come to mind, she could not produce the answer; but if she stored the question, the answer would come, usually within the next few minutes. What was this magic?

The understanding came as she began to study mental imagery. We've all heard of people who seem to solve problems while they are asleep. Some authors have been said to have awakened with whole chapters of books written in their heads, waiting only to be written hurriedly on their typewriters or computers. Ghiselin (1952) reported that Einstein solved his theory of relativity while imagining himself riding a beam of light; and that the great Austrian-born musician Wolfgang Amadeus Mozart (1756–1791), who began composing at the age of five, often reflected upon imaginary experiences before creating a piece of music. It appears that the dominant left brain suppresses imagery during our normal activities. Only during periods of relaxation—"while eating an apple"—does our visual imagery surface. Today, the positive use of mental imagery/rehearsal training has moved from theory to practice. Thousands of people each year seek the help of physicians and hypnotists to reduce stress, lose weight, or quit smoking. Thousands more buy self-help tapes on how to take tests or make better speeches; these tapes all begin in a similar way: "Relax. Feel your mind beginning to relax. Now, begin to imagine (visualize) yourself succeeding in any way you choose."

IMPLEMENTATION IN THE CLASSROOM

Combining mental rehearsal with verbal and written language in the classroom is not as easy as one would at first *imagine*. Students, who all too often have become more accustomed to answering specific literal questions and parroting answers, will need to learn or relearn how to think more critically and creatively, to imagine things on their own. Furthermore, as developing writers, these students will use a private inner language to think (Vygotsky, 1962); with this inner voice, students talk to themselves, in a sense, before they translate their thoughts to written language. The use of imagery should be particularly beneficial for these students, although it may take some practice. "The basic underpinning of all mental techniques is to manifest creative images during periods of relaxation" (Wheatley et al., 1987, p. 156). Therefore, the teacher may use calming music, deep breathing exercises, or some other relaxation techniques, perhaps including the suggestion that the mind is beginning to relax.

One high school teacher has her students relax by sitting back, closing their eyes, and imagining they are climbing inside a giant soap bubble resting on the grass in a field. She then leads them floating over trees, houses, and lakes and asks them to think about what they see. Finally, she brings them mentally back to earth and has them write about their imagined experiences. She confides that at first her students become dependent on the bubble and don't want to think creatively on their own, preferring to have her lead and direct their thoughts. But this is just her introduction to fantasy thinking; after only a few bubble trips, she encourages students to let their minds wander without her help.

The stimulus does not have to be a bubble. It can be a play, an assignment—anything. Model Activity 2.7 was designed to allow learners to practice imaging, one of the marvelous functions of the brain's right hemisphere. By using the mind's eye to "see" an imaginary picture, students will be better prepared to describe its detail in writing.

Mental rehearsal is advantageous because it dispels distractions and quiets students' mental chatter. Gaylean (1983) found that students who used mental imagery scored significantly higher on oral and written communication measures than those who did not. The value of mental imagery and rehearsal is in enhancing students' self-concept and helping writers improve by expecting positive results. As Wheatley et al. (1987) stated, "The value of mental imagery techniques to enhance the education process has been demonstrated in virtually every area of academic endeavor." These authors call mental imagery "valuable pedagogical technology" (Wheatley et al., 1987, p. 156) that can definitely be used to enrich your classroom.

A MUSICAL NOTE

If you choose to utilize calming music to enhance relaxation, perhaps even to reinforce some positive daydreaming, consider starting with music by Chopin. Later, this experience will serve as the perfect springboard for studying the life of Frédéric François Chopin (1810–1849), Polish pianist and composer. Students who have heard and appreciated the music of a particular composer are far more likely to express an interest in learning more about the composer and the period of history in which the composer lived. In addition to enhancing relaxation, the music also stimulates the brain. Remember, "It is the right hemisphere of the brain that arranges visual and musical sensations into patterns" (Wheatley et al., 1987, p. 153). Also recommended for relaxation is the music of the German organist, composer, and choirmaster Johann Sebastian Bach (1685–1750). After learning the calming effect of Bach's music firsthand, students may appreciate the humor in the following article, "Bach Reduces the Barking," from *Parade Magazine* (Shearer, 1990):

In 1697, the British playwright William Congreve penned the following line: "Music has charms to soothe a savage breast." Fortunately, says Peter Gott—the manager of SSI Kennels, near Nottingham, England—he recalled that line from his school days when neighbors began complaining to him about the loud barking of his dogs.

Substituting "beast" for "breast" in Congreve's quotation, Gott decided to try music to lower the volume of the barking being generated by his canine guests. "The result, when we began playing music for them," Gott reports, "was amazing. They seem much happier and more relaxed. We play the music through speakers. Some dogs even have their own headsets."

More than 100 dogs of every type stay at SSI Kennels, and, according to Gott, the majority find the music of Bach most relaxing and tranquilizing.*

The scores of Wolfgang Amadeus Mozart (1756–1791) seem to achieve the most perfect balance between the relaxing and energizing effects of sound. Students will be fascinated as they learn about Mozart's unusually early start as a composer. At the age of three, Mozart delighted his Austrian composer father, Leopold, by picking out a piano melody with ease. By the age of six, he had composed a minuet and was traveling with his father or his mother from court to court in Europe to perform for royalty. Mozart's sister Nannerl, also an excellent musician, often performed with him on the harpsichord. Mozart was well known as an improviser; given a tune of only a few notes, he would add to those with his own variations and play

creatively and spontaneously for ten or fifteen minutes.

Mozart taught music and wrote music on commission. In addition to composing operas, symphonies, and twenty-seven piano concerti, the busy Mozart even composed a tune for Benjamin Franklin's set of musical glasses. Nonetheless, when he died of typhoid fever in November of 1791, at the age of thirty-six, he was buried in a pauper's grave. Activities 2.8, 2.9, and 2.10, which focus on Mozart, were designed to model the integration of reading and writing instruction with music, history, geography, and other areas; students are asked to think critically as they respond in writing.

One of the greatest composers of all time created his mightiest works after becoming practically deaf. This was Ludwig van Beethoven (1770–1827), a German composer whose family was of Flemish origin; his huge Ninth Symphony, called the "Chorale," was the composition. Although he was sent to an elementary school, Beethoven had no regular schooling after the age of eleven except in music. At this time, he was already a notable improviser and had published his first composition. On his first visit to Vienna in 1787, Beethoven met Mozart, who was at the height of his fame. It has been said that Mozart gave Beethoven a few lessons at this time. Mozart, recognizing Beethoven's potential, said that he would "give the world something worth listening to." Beethoven loved the country, particularly wandering through the woods, and always carried a piece of paper in his pocket for jotting down ideas or themes. It was there in the woods that he worked out the great music of some of his masterpieces. He's well known for his romantic "Moonlight Sonata," which he dedicated to a countess with whom he had fallen in love for a brief time. Other well-known pieces include Beethoven's Fifth Symphony, recognized by the opening four notes, *da-da-da DUM*; and his "Ode to Joy," known to many as the tune of a beautiful hymn, "Joyful, Joyful, We Adore Thee."

Developing writers will respond positively to your introduction of classical music, even though it may seen a bit complex at first. It will achieve your purpose of relaxation and, at the same time, pique students' interest in the orchestra; many students may become interested in learning more about the string, woodwind, brass, and percussion instruments played by the large group of musicians. Other notable composers of classical music include Brahms (1833–1897), Haydn (1732–1809), and

Source: Lloyd Shearer, "Bach Reduces the Barking," *Parade Magazine,* November 4, 1990, p. 9. Reprinted with permission of Lloyd Shearer.

Tchaikovsky (1840–1893). What better way to develop students' cultural literacy and provide a springboard for writing than by listening to music that has stood the test of time through the centuries.

REFERENCES

Bogoch, S. (1988). Brain. *World Book Encyclopedia* (Vol. 2, pp, 561–570). Chicago: World Book.

Browne, D. (1989). Hagar the horrible (cartoon). New York: King Features.

Cairney, T., & Langbien, S. (1989). Building communities of readers and writers. *The Reading Teacher, 42*(8), 560–567.

Canning, C. (1991). What teachers say about reflection. *Educational Leadership, 48*(6), 18–21.

Cooper, H., & Tom, D. (1984). Teacher expectation research: A review with implications for classroom instruction. *Elementary School Journal, 85*(1), 77–90.

Doyle, J. E., Jr. (1980). *Thomas Edison: The story of a dream builder.* Belleville, NJ: Techni-Com, p. 5.

Eisner, E. W. (1991, February). What really counts in schools. *Educational Leadership, 48*(5), 10–11, 14–17.

Fagan, W. T. (1989). Empowered students; empowered teachers. *The Reading Teacher, 42*(8), 572–578.

Frost, R. (1916). *Mountain interval.* New York: Holt.

Gaylean, B. (1980). The effects of guided imagery activity on various behaviors of low achieving students. *Journal of Suggestive-Accelerative Learning and Teaching,* 87–97.

Gaylean, B. (1983, March). Guided imagery in the curriculum. *Educational Leadership,* 54–58.

Ghiselin, B. (Ed.). (1952). *The creative process.* Berkeley: University of California Press.

Goodman, K. (1986). *What's whole in whole language?* Portsmouth, NH: Heinemann Educational Books.

Goodman, Y. M. (1989). *Evaluation of students: Evaluation by teachers of.* In K. S. Goodman, Y. M. Goodman, & W. J. Hood (Eds.), *The whole language evaluation book* (pp. 3–14). Portsmouth, NH: Heinemann Educational Books.

Greeson, L. E., & Zigarwi, D. P. (1986). Modeling and mental imagery use by multiply handicapped and learning disabled preschool children. *Psychology in the Schools, 23,* 82–87.

Hanson, G. R. (1990). Whole language, whole teaching, whole being: The need for reflection in the teaching process. In K. S. Goodman, Y. M. Goodman, & W. J. Hood (Eds.), *The whole language evaluation book* (pp. 263–272). Portsmouth, NH: Heinemann Educational Books.

Henry, W. A. III (1990). Beyond the melting pot. *Time, 135*(15), April 9, pp. 28–31.

Hodgkinson, H. L. (1985). *All one system: Demographics of education—Kindergarten through graduate school.* Washington, DC: Institute of Educational Leadership.

How the brain really works its wonders (1988). *U.S. News & World Report, 104*(25), June 27, pp. 48–51, 53–54.

Johnson, V. R. (1985, March). Concentrating on the brain. *Science Teacher, 52,* 32–36.

Kipling, R. (1927). *Rudyard Kipling's Verse.* London: Hodder & Stoughton.

Kraig, D. M. (1990, October). I see by the papers. *Fate, 43*(9), 5–18.

Lester, N. B., & Onore, C. S. (1986). From teacher-teacher to teacher-learner: Making the grade. *Language Arts, 63,* 724–728.

Lindley, M. A. (1990). A magnet school's pull is partly in its teachers. *Tallahassee Democrat,* October 23, p. 1B.

Lowery, J. (1982). Developing creativity in gifted children. *Gifted Children Quarterly, 26,* 133–139.

Lundsteen, S. W. (1989). Children with special needs in the language arts. In *Language arts: A problem-solving approach* (pp. 481–496). New York: Harper & Row.

Maltz, M. (1960). *Psycho-cybernetics.* Englewood Cliffs, NJ: Prentice-Hall.

Maltz, M. (1964). *The magic power of self-image psychology.* New York: Simon & Schuster.

Manning, B. H., & Payne, B. D. (1987). Student–teacher classroom interactions and self-perception of personality. *Journal of Instructional Psychology, 14,* 140–147.

McDaniel, M. A., & Einstein, G. O. (1986). Bizarre imagery as an effective memory aid: The importance of distinctiveness. *Journal of Experimental Psychology: Learning, Memory, and Cognition, 12,* 54–65.

Merton, R. K. (1957). *Social theory and social structure.* New York: Free Press of Glencoe.

Neville, J. (1993). Telephone interview.

Okech, J. G. (1987). Self-concepts and attitudes towards teaching as predictors of effective teaching. *Journal of Instructional Psychology, 14,* 27–35.

Paivio, A. (1971). *Imagery and verbal process.* New York: Holt, Rinehart and Winston.

Paivio, A. (1986). *Mental representations: A dual coding approach.* New York: Oxford University Press.

Palmer, B. C. (1989). *An investigation of the effects of newspaper-based instruction on reading vocabulary, reading comprehension, and writing performance of at-risk middle and secondary school students* (Report No. CS 009–935). Akron, OH: Knight Foundation. (ERIC Document Reproduction Service No. ED 315 732).

Piaget, J. & Inhelder, B. (1971). *Mental imagery in the child.* New York: Basic Books.

Rosenthal, R., & Fode, K. L. (1963). The effects of experimenter bias on the performance of the albino rat. *Behavioral Science, 8,* 183–189.

Rosenthal, R., & Jacobson, L. (1968). *Pygmalion in the classroom: Teacher expectation and pupils' intellectual development.* New York: Holt, Rinehart and Winston.

Rosenthal, R., & Lawson, R. (1964). A longitudinal study of the effects of experimenter bias on the operant learning of laboratory rats. *Journal of Psychiatric Research, 2,* 61–72.

Rousculp, E. E., & Maring, G. E. (1992, February). Portfolios for a community of learners. *Journal of Reading, 35*(5), 378–385.

Shearer, L. (1990). Bach reduces the barking. *Parade Magazine,* November 4, p. 9.

Teyler, T. J. (1978). The brain sciences: An introduction. *Education and the Brain* (pp. 1–32). Chicago: University of Chicago Press.

U.S. Bureau of the Census (1987). *The Hispanic population in the United States.* Current Population Statistics, Series P-20, No. 416. Washington, DC: U.S. Government Printing Office.

Valdivieso, R. (1986). *Must they wait another generation? Hispanics and secondary school reform.* New York: ERIC Clearinghouse on Urban Education.

Vygotsky, L. S. (1962). Thought and language. (E. Hanfmann & G. Vakar, Trans.). Cambridge, MA: MIT Press.

Vygotsky, L. S. (1978). *Mind in society: The development of higher psychological processes.* In M. Cole, V. John-Steiner, S. Schribner, & E. Souberman (Eds.), Cambridge, MA: Harvard University Press.

Walshe, R. D. (Ed.). (1981). *Donald Graves in Australia—Children want to write.* Rozelle, NSW, Australia: Primary English Teaching Association.

Weaver, R. L., & Cotrell, H. W. (1986). Imaging: Classroom instruction technique. *The Clearing House, 59,* 268–271.

Wellington, B. (1991, March). The promise of reflective practice. *Educational Leadership, 48*(6), 4–5.

West, C., & Anderson, T. (1976). The question of preponderant causation in teacher expectancy research. *Review of Educational Research, 46,* 185–213.

Wheatley, W. J., Maddox, E. N., Anthony, W. P., & Coe, F. S. (1987, Fall). Enhancing education through the use of mental imagery. *Reading Improvement, 24*(3), 150–159.

Zakariya, S. B. (1985, August). Spotlight on reading. *American School Board Journal, 172*(8), 17–23.

MODEL ACTIVITIES

The activities that follow are meant to serve as models; such activities should be used as part of a total learning environment. These model activities were designed to demonstrate how the writing process can be developed while expanding the writer's knowledge base and providing opportunities for the writer to think critically.

ACTIVITY 2.1

The Figure a Poem Makes

Directions: Read the following and then write a few sentences about your thoughts or reaction.

In 1939 Robert Frost compared the writing of a poem to love in the following words:

The figure a poem makes. It begins in delight and ends in wisdom. The figure is the same as for love.

Frost is describing his impressions of poetic construction. Love, according to Frost, also begins in delight and ends in wisdom. Do you think love is like the writing of a poem? In what ways do you think they are the same? How do you think they are different?

_____

_____

_____

_____

_____

_____

_____

_____

_____

_____

_____

_____

_____

_____

_____

_____

_____

_____

_____

_____

_____

_____

_____

35

Choosing Paths in Life

Directions: The following, written by Robert Frost (1874–1963), is considered one of his best known poems.

The Road Not Taken

Two roads diverged in a yellow wood,
And sorry I could not travel both
And be one traveler, long I stood
And looked down one as far as I could
To where it bent in the undergrowth;

Then took the other, as just as fair,
And having perhaps the better claim,
Because it was grassy and wanted wear;
Though as for that the passing there
Had worn them really about the same,

And both that morning equally lay
In leaves no step had trodden black.
Oh, I kept the first for another day!
Yet knowing how way leads on to way,
I doubted if I should ever come back.

I shall be telling this with a sigh
Somewhere ages and ages hence:
Two roads diverged in a wood, and I—
I took the one less traveled by,
And that has made all the difference.

Have you ever felt that you were in a situation similar to the one described in this poem? Have you ever been in a position where you had to make an important choice? After making that choice, did you ever have regrets? Did you spend energy thinking about the rejected alternative? Describe what happened to you and how you felt about it:

_____

_____

_____

_____

_____

_____

_____

_____

Source: Robert Frost, *Mountain Interval* (New York: Holt, 1916).

Which lines from this poem spoke to you in some special way?

_____

_____

_____

_____

_____

_____

_____

_____

_____

_____

_____

_____

_____

_____

Describe your specific feelings:

_____

_____

_____

_____

_____

_____

_____

_____

_____

_____

_____

_____

Concord Hymn

Directions: Read "Concord Hymn," written by Ralph Waldo Emerson (1803–1882) about the first battle of the Revolutionary War, which took place in the late 1700s. Then respond to the related questions that follow.

Historical Situation: The American colonists opposed Great Britain's control of American trade and didn't think they should have to pay taxes to the British. The Americans went to war for their independence.

Your Opinion, Please:
1. Did the Americans make the right decision?

_____

2. How do you think life today would be different had the American colonists not started the Revolutionary War?

_____

_____

_____

_____

Phrase Search: Find the phrase "the shot heard round the world" near the beginning of Emerson's "Concord Hymn." This famous phrase refers to the first shot fired in the Revolutionary War; it took place at Lexington and Concord, Massachusetts.

Your Opinion, Please: Do you think a gun shot was heard literally around the world? If you answered "no," then what do you think Emerson *might* have meant?

_____

_____

_____

_____

_____

For Your Information: Historian Joe Neville (1993), when asked his opinion of what "the shot heard round the world" meant, replied that this was the first time a colony had challenged its mother country. Shortly after the American Revolution, there was a French Revolution; a short, unsuccessful Irish Revolution; the mutiny on the ship *Bounty*; and several other ships' mutinies where the crews sat down and refused to work in order to obtain better food and working conditions. After Americans revolted against their mother country, others did likewise.

Note: You may want to do some additional reading about Great Britain and its vast holdings at the time of the Revolutionary War. Some have said that the British Empire was so extensive that the sun never set on it.

Fun with the News

Directions: Take some time to read a current edition of a newspaper, mentally noting articles that appeal to you in some way. Then, using the newspaper as a springboard, make a list of things that you think you might enjoy doing before you are thirty years old.

Things I'd Like to Do List: **Priority**

_____   _____

_____   _____

_____   _____

_____   _____

_____   _____

_____   _____

_____   _____

_____   _____

_____   _____

_____   _____

_____   _____

_____   _____

Now, prioritize your list, noting which thing you'd like to do first, second, and so on. Write a paragraph describing your first choice and tell what in particular interested you.

_____

_____

_____

_____

_____

_____

_____

_____

_____

_____

_____

_____

_____

_____

ACTIVITY 2.5

Newspaper-Picture Group Storytelling

Directions: First, individually read the newspaper. Then, in your small group of three students, select several pictures from the newspaper that you found interesting; brainstorm how they might fit together. Next, create a group story connecting all the pictures. Write down the story and revise and edit it in your small group. Finally, choose a group member to read the story aloud to the entire class.

Newspaper Reporter Interview

Directions: Pick a person whose name appears somewhere in your daily newspaper. Now, imagine that you are the reporter sent to interview this person. Write the interview questions you would most like to ask. Role-play the interview with another student, and record his or her answers. Finally, trade places with your partner and repeat the interview process.

Name of person selected for interview:

_____

List of interview questions:

_____

_____

_____

_____

_____

_____

_____

_____

_____

_____

_____

Your reaction to your experience as a newspaper reporter:

_____

_____

_____

_____

_____

_____

_____

_____

_____

ACTIVITY 2.7

Exploring Mental Images

Directions: Close your eyes and think about *a spring day* or *a thunderstorm.* Think of sounds, sights, and feelings. Then write about these thoughts.

Images   **Descriptions**

   Example:

_____Trees_____   _____Light green new leaves_____

Your Turn:

_____

_____

_____

_____

_____

Now, put numbers after each of the above images and descriptions to show how you would sequence them to write a paragraph or short essay.

Write an idea for a title. If you wish, create a drawing like the image in your mind. Then write a draft about it, describing your thoughts and feelings. Share your work-in-progress with classmates, and consider moving your draft toward publication. Whether you publish this piece or not, exploring mental images should prove to be a useful technique as you write again in the future.

_____

_____

_____

_____

_____

_____

Mozart, Musical Prodigy

Directions: Read the paragraph below and then write your response to the questions that follow:

Mozart (1756–1791), a musical prodigy, was treated as a genius at the royal courts of Europe. Exploited by his father for the money he could earn as a performer, Mozart spent over a decade (from age six to seventeen) traveling from court to court where he would play the harpsichord and the violin and would improvise for royalty. At that time, no railroads existed; stagecoaches were used to travel the dirty, often muddy, bumpy roads from city to city.

How comfortable do you think traveling was during the days of Mozart?

_____

_____

_____

Does this part of Mozart's life appeal to you in any way?

_____

If yes, in what way or ways?

_____

_____

Describe how travel today differs from travel during Mozart's time.

_____

_____

_____

_____

Use the answers you have written and your feelings about what you know about Mozart's life to write a paragraph, pretending you are Mozart during his teen years.

_____

_____

_____

_____

_____

_____

_____

_____

43

Music for All Time

Directions: Read the following statement made about Mozart during his lifetime, and then offer your opinion.

"The boy's music will be remembered after all of us are forgotten."

—Hasse, a composer famous during the life of Mozart

Do you think the statement about Mozart's music being remembered after all of us are forgotten was accurate? Why or why not?

_____

_____

_____

Describe your favorite music and tell why it appeals to you.

_____

_____

_____

_____

_____

_____

What would you like to be remembered for?

_____

_____

_____

_____

_____

_____

Why?

_____

_____

_____

_____

_____

_____

ACTIVITY 2.10

Mozart Featured the Violin

Directions: Read the following facts about the violin and then offer your written opinion.

In the early 1500s the violin was invented in the country of Italy. Mozart, who was born in another country, Austria, more than two hundred years later, loved to play the violin. He featured it in his symphonies (long pieces of music with parts called movements played by an orchestra), writing the first of his forty-one symphonies at the age of eleven. Now, entering the twenty-first century, it is interesting to note that more music has been written for this four-stringed instrument than for any other instrument in known history.

Your Opinion, Please: Why do you think the violin has been so well received over time?

_____

_____

_____

_____

Other stringed instruments of an orchestra include the harp and the cello. Tell which of the two you would prefer to play and why.

_____

_____

_____

_____

_____

_____

_____

_____

_____

_____

_____

_____

_____

_____

_____

Even if you were a musical prodigy (a highly talented child) like Mozart, you would probably have to practice for hours each day. Describe what you think an ordinary weekday would be like in your life if you played the instrument you chose in the preceding question.

_____

_____

_____

_____

_____

_____

_____

_____

_____

_____

_____

_____

_____

_____

_____

_____

_____

CHAPTER 3

Prewriting: Generating and Planning

Writing, like life itself, is a voyage of discovery.

—Henry Miller (1891–1980), American writer

Prewriting involves generating ideas and gathering information before writing to enhance the composing process. The first thing any writer does is generate ideas in response to a stimulus or purpose. Robert Louis Stevenson (1850–1894), a Scottish author who contributed several classics to the world of children's literature, including *Treasure Island, Kidnapped,* and *A Child's Garden of Verses,* said that his prose tales often came to him as dreams. "In the small hours one morning," wrote his wife in the 1800s, "I was awakened by cries of horror from Louis. Thinking he had a nightmare, I awakened him. He said angrily: 'Why did you awaken me? I was dreaming a fine bogey tale.'" This was *The Strange Case of Doctor Jekyll and Mr. Hyde* (1886), a novel in which the extremes of good and evil are played out in one character when the kindly physician Dr. Jekyll discovers a drug that changes him, first at will and later involuntarily, into the evil monster Mr. Hyde.

Stevenson was not the only person who thought things out in his repose. As you will recall from Chapter 2, Einstein's remark, "The answer will come while you're eating an apple," implies that if you just enter a problem into the subconscious area of your mind, the brain will often think of a solution. Your mind will massage an idea and begin to organize it for you. All this can happen before writers actually begin to write; this subconscious organizing is a form of prewriting.

In this chapter, you will find ideas about effective instruction for prewriting, as well as numerous rehearsal strategies that can be used to empower students as writers. You will discover how the advancement of cultural literacy can be combined with the development of process-based writing. Chapter topics include essentials in a responsive learning environment, the teacher as a writing model, strategies for teaching prewriting, providing time for prewriting, and targeting the audience in prewriting. The prewriting stage of the writing process cannot be overemphasized, for it represents the foundation on which a good writer builds.

PREWRITING DEFINED

The process of writing begins long before a single word is actually written down—at the time a writer decides to write about something. This time to generate ideas, thoughts, and images and to formulate plans for writing is called the prewriting stage; it may also be called *rehearsing* (Calkins, 1986; Hennings, 1990) or *collecting* (Murray, 1987). You will recall from the discussion in Chapter 1 of Porter Perrin's writing, dating back as far as 1942, that the first two of his eight writing stages— focusing on a subject and gathering material—are both prewriting processes (Perrin, 1965).

Today's teachers are focusing more on prewriting strategies to help students become deeply and personally involved in the process of writing. Teaching writing begins with the recognition that each individual comes to the classroom learning environment with concerns, ideas, memories, and feelings. As students get in touch with themselves and these feelings, they will select writing topics that are of real concern to them. Farnan, Lapp, and Flood (1992) recommended that educators "encourage a wide spectrum of writing behaviors, which can include brainstorming; freewriting; reading about a subject; talking to others for purposes of gleaning ideas, clarifying thoughts, and getting feedback; or perhaps simply sitting quietly, thinking" (p. 555). Educators need to listen actively, thereby facilitating students' discovery of the things about which they know and care. As students are encouraged to order their thoughts, thus creating meaning for themselves, a natural desire to

communicate this meaning to others usually follows. As Calkins (1986, p. 17) stated, "Rehearsal is, above all, a way of living." Students who write regularly develop a sense of *being writers*. Just as artists see potential paintings everywhere they turn, those who write regularly begin to find ideas for stories in all aspects of their lives.

Prewriting is not necessarily a silent activity; talking is often an important tool. Students talk to themselves silently or out loud, informally to classmates and teachers, and to one another in teacher-guided groups. Students must also learn strategies for thinking through relationships before writing (Hennings, 1990). Each person uses a private inner language (Vygotsky, 1962) to think, to reinforce personal concrete experiences, and to link experiences to those of others. That private inner language is used again to recall, order, and monitor oral speech or written expression. In getting ready to write, students remain open to new directions that may come along as they experiment. Creativity, spontaneity, self-expression, freedom of opinion, initiative, and excitement are to be encouraged during prewriting.

ESSENTIALS IN A RESPONSIVE LEARNING ENVIRONMENT

In 1849, the American writer Nathaniel Hawthorne had just lost his government position as surveyor of the Salem, Massachusetts, customshouse. He went home, dejected and almost desperate. When his wife learned the reason for his gloom, instead of giving way to reproaches, she set pen and ink on the table and, lighting a fire in the grate, put her arms about his shoulders and said, "Now you will be able to write your book." Hawthorne took her advice and, in 1850, enriched the world with *The Scarlet Letter,* regarded as his masterpiece and a classic of American literature.

So, too, are teachers responsible for creating a learning environment that encourages writing. Students learn to write by writing; trial-and-error experimentation is a great teacher of the writing process. Successful teachers set the stage for the positive development of their evolving writers' first attempts to compose. A classroom atmosphere that encourages students to become involved actively in successful prewriting activities contributes much to the success of the students' writing endeavors. The

recommendations that follow are particularly essential to the success of prewriting activities.

A Place That Is Supportive, Comfortable, and Relaxed

"Our students are changing their ideas about writing because we are changing our classrooms—beyond a work setting to a learning environment" (Lindquist & Ligett, 1992, p. 2). A literary-rich environment that is friendly, relaxed, comfortable, positive, and exciting, with an awareness of each student's worth, is conducive to the generation of ideas for writing. A responsive classroom is characterized by students' knowing how to support and challenge one another. As Hansen (1992) advised,

Learners know they need support for their efforts. If they do not get enough encouragement, they may be afraid to try something new. If they don't venture into the unknown, they won't grow, change, learn, all of which takes courage—courage to move onward. (p. 101)

Writing is particularly important as a means to help young people understand their lives. If students are carefully guided in a writing program to a point where they can trust the teacher and their peers, they often begin to use writing as a way of finding meaning in their lives. As Chenfield (1987) wrote,

Your students will write in your room if they feel safe. If they know that they will not be humiliated, put down, harshly criticized, or ignored, they will write. If they know that you, their teacher, care about and appreciate their creative efforts and feel that their ideas are of value, they will write. If your students trust you, know that you will not betray them, know that you will protect their dignity and spirit as fiercely as conservationists protect endangered species, they will write. (p. 327)

Because developing writers will have individual needs, there should be flexibility in the range of activities offered to encourage students during prewriting time. A feeling of success on the part of students during this stage tends to continue during further writing stages and, indeed, through all of learning. In studying the effects of the social environment on learning, Walberg (1990, p. 475) found the following:

Many correlational studies suggest that *classroom morale* is associated with achievement gains, with greater interest in subject matter, and with the worthy outcome of voluntary participation in nonrequired subject-related activities. Morale is assessed by asking students to agree or disagree with such statements as "Most of the students know one another well" and "The class members know the purpose of the lessons." Students who perceive the atmosphere as friendly, satisfying, focused on goals, and challenging and who feel that the classroom has the required materials tend to learn more. (emphasis in original)

A Classroom Where Creative Ideas and Activities Abound

Creative thinking and expression are needs and rights of all people. Young people, especially, have the urge to create. As Klein (1985, p. 81) stated,

Instilling a sense of writing as a nonending accumulative process whose open-ended character is to be accepted and even enjoyed must be a major goal in the writing program. And, perhaps, of all the aspects of this writing process, none is more important or demanding of the teacher's creative planning skills than the prewriting phase.

Teachers can turn their rooms into writing places to encourage this creativity with a variety of environmental literacy materials as described in Chapter 2. Pets, plants, and collections, for example, also may be useful catalytic agents for prewriting activities. A good supply of writing material is ideal. This is a good opportunity to recycle paper that has been used previously, such as unused sides of computer paper or clean backs of old photocopied sheets. Wallpaper and wrapping paper provide interesting texture and design for prewriting experimentation and may whet creative appetites. One of the best ways to meet students' needs is to set up writing areas with specific resources in the classroom. Another way is for teachers to have resources relating to relevant topics packaged in folders or envelopes and readily available to students. Some teachers also suggest that students, particularly at the elementary level, keep their own writing supplies—paper, pens, pencils, and the like—in envelopes or zip-lock bags. Regardless of how teachers choose to organize their classrooms for writing, student exploration is encouraged when learning environments contain a variety of resources that are rich in cultural literacy and related to topics of interest to the students. Teachers who stimulate these developing writers to use freely the resource books and other materials found in the classroom, as well as in school and community libraries, empower their students to become creative thinkers and writers.

Creativity is not a quality possessed only by a chosen few; people of all ages and from every culture are potentially creative to some degree. "We recognize that all writing that is not simple copying is creative, and we want our students to recognize that, too" (Cooper & Brown, 1992, p. 42). Creativity can be developed by a nurturing process that encourages students to discover who they are and what they have to say. The complex nature of creativity, however, is often difficult to identify and measure, and generalizations can be unfair. Prewriting offers a perfect time to set the stage for creative learning and practice through individualized, nongraded activities that allow all students to express their creative potential. If creative writing is to be fostered, students must be given time to think and daydream. According to Newbery Award–winning children's author Lois Lenski (1949), creative expression should never be confused with teaching the techniques of writing. Creation, as described by

Lenski, is a flowing of ideas; when stimulation is given, ideas may pour from the mind as water flows from a fountain. And a teacher's positive, encouraging comments about the student's work, as well as one-to-one interaction, are helpful during rehearsal for writing.

Semantic mapping, also called *webbing* or *clustering,* can be used to create a visual representation to help writers generate, expand, clarify, and organize ideas. Consider making the first experience with mapping a group activity in which you model how easily ideas developed during brainstorming can be charted, expanded, and organized. For example, all students can participate as a web of the Fourth of July is developed and mapped on the chalkboard (see Figure 3.1).

To provide an opportunity for students to use clustering individually as a means of generating ideas, Model Activity 3.1 draws from students' past experiences. In Model Activity 3.2, the cluster is developed after reading a short passage about a famous historical figure.

One creative classroom teacher skillfully guided students into exploring an area of great importance to them—finding the answer to the question, "What is a seventh grader?" (Of course, any grade could be used.) This involved planning how students would go about the task, how they would gather information, and how they would choose relevant informa-

tion. Then plans were formulated for how the class would compile and analyze the gathered information, make sense of it, and share it with the rest of the school. As you reflect on the preceding example, consider prewriting possibilities that might appeal to your students: Gathered information such as height and weight, favorite books, favorite television programs, and most liked and disliked foods can be compiled into lists. Interviewing one another to answer such questions as "What do you like most about our school?" or "What would you like to see changed in our school?" yields information to be shared and compiled. Interesting personal details about individuals can also be obtained in a nonthreatening way through Model Activity 3.3, which uses art to describe students' interests and hobbies. Students may think of this activity as a game because it is fun, but the results are often surprising and rewarding. The question "What is a seventh grader?" has generated numerous ideas for prewriting activities. It is easy to see how an enthusiastic group of students could carry this project through many exciting writing activities, culminating with publishing the results of the study to be shared with others.

In summary, an environment that encourages the creative urge in developing writers allows for risk taking without threats to self-worth. It encourages students to be in touch with their own feelings and

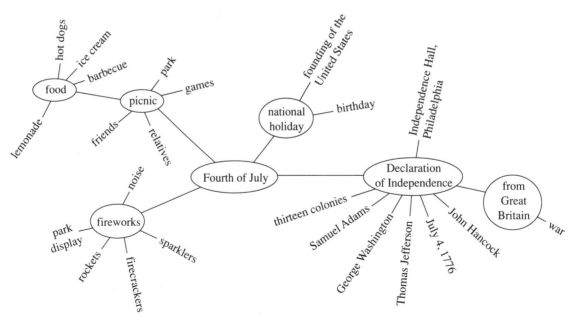

FIGURE 3.1 A Web of the Fourth of July

protects their right to be different from others. At the same time, respect for the rights of others occurs in a healthy, responsive classroom. The prewriting stage of the composing process offers endless opportunities for nurturing the creative potential inherent in all students, and a trusting atmosphere is essential.

A Place to Move and Explore

Exploration and movement in the classroom are important for prewriting success. Handling things, touching objects, and taking class trips supply ideas and subject matter for student prewriting activities. Klein (1985) suggested that students be allowed to change the direction of their writing while participating in the writing process. He also recommended that they be allowed to take physical breaks from their writing—and that means walking around. "We must remember that during the writing process, it is normal for people to write in spurts—brief periods of sustained production interrupted by contemplation and physical movement" (p. 76). Outside the classroom, writers often choose not to write at desks. Robert Frost, for example, avoided writing at a desk. He liked to compose in a rocking chair with a writing board resting on the chair's arms.

One creative teacher used some freshly picked eucalyptus leaves from Palo Alto, California, to give her students the experience of touching while teaching about marsupials, with a writing experience incorporated into the activity. Both local leaves and leaves from other parts of the country or the world can serve as a catalyst for integrating science, reading, geography, history, and other subjects with writing and critical thinking. Model Activity 3.4 is an example of how to incorporate the examination of artifacts and other real objects into prewriting activities.

A Setting for Peer and Student–Teacher Interactions

The renowned Polish pianist Ignace Paderewski (1860–1941) is said to have suffered a discouraging first experience in a piano class at the Warsaw Conservatory. "Not hands for playing," the teacher declared. "That thumb, that third finger, too short." He gave Ignace a trial, then told him to leave, to take up some other instrument (Kellogg, 1956).

Think of what the world might have missed if this young Polish lad had been too discouraged to continue because of this unfortunate student–teacher interaction. Paderewski went on to become a popular concert pianist, and his "Minuet in G" is a beloved classic. Also a statesman, Paderewski was devoted to the cause of Polish independence and made concert tours to raise funds for Polish relief.

Students usually will give of themselves more comfortably if they know and trust their teacher. That trust will come more quickly if the teacher emerges as a personality with real feelings—joy, sadness, anger, serenity—and also as someone who sometimes makes mistakes. Teachers who show that they care about their students as individuals and strive to make sure that those in their classroom are receiving the best instruction available are most likely to have the respect of their students. As a result, students are more receptive, and teaching is more successful. Being available for student–teacher discussions is especially important during prewriting, when ideas can be clarified and expanded and questions addressed in an informal manner.

It has been pointed out that the connection between teachers and students is more pronounced during the middle school years than at any other time (Calkins, 1986). In this period of identity formation, students often try to mask their own feelings and ideas in order to conform to what they feel their teachers and peers expect, thereby stifling creativity and individuality. These years are a time of physical and emotional as well as intellectual changes. Moods swing from one extreme to the other. Feelings of shyness, fear, and inadequacy suddenly emerge; if these students' past experiences have led them to associate writing assignments with a lot of red ink in the margins, they may use all kinds of tactics to avoid writing. The concerned teacher uses prewriting to help these young people see writing as a safe activity, with a supportive group of peers who are all learning to be noncritical of each others' writing endeavors.

Allowing for peer interactions, as well as student–teacher discussions, is desirable. It is important for students to have feedback from peers, and constructive criticism from peers is healthy. To accomplish this goal, tables, desks, and chairs can be arranged to facilitate small-group or one-on-one discussions. Activities that are nonthreatening in their demands and allow for interaction among classmates can be helpful in drawing out shy or withdrawn students. Model Activity 3.5, for example, is fun and an effective method for practicing the concept of plot, especially for students who are unsure of themselves. The given prompts make students eager to get started, and the forced combinations contribute to stories that are absurd and humorous.

A Place Where Use Is Made of Current Technology

Students can be taught to use computers as tools for writing instruction; computers provide an easy way for students to collect prewriting ideas and thoughts and to rearrange them as often as desired. Using a word-processing program at the prewriting stage can reduce the anxiety that some students feel about writing. If students feel they know nothing about a topic or are unsure about where to begin, they can freely and quickly brainstorm ideas once they know the keyboard. Computers facilitate deleting, adding, and rearranging material; categories can be formed, labeled, and ordered—so useful at the prewriting stage. The use of computers in the writing process is examined at length in Chapter 7 of this book.

THE TEACHER AS A WRITING MODEL

The role of the classroom teacher has been evolving from a model whereby teachers transmit knowledge to students, to one where teachers facilitate students' more active construction of meaning. This latter model assumes that learning is student-centered and process-oriented, as described by Pahl and Monson (1992), as follows:

In this model, the teacher plays a central role in facilitating student learning by acting as a catalyst for problem solving and by creating the environmental conditions that support active learning. Since the purpose of learning is to construct meaning, the teacher must provide demonstrations of the learning process and must model the use of meaning-making strategies. (p. 519)

The teacher who is a writer becomes a model for students. Modeling or demonstrating the process of writing by writing along with students is a primary part of the instruction provided by an effective teacher. By writing and sharing that writing with students, the teacher sends a message to students that writing is important. "What a teacher does at the prewriting stage is likely to be even more important in fostering quality than what is done by 'marking' at the end" (Walshe, 1979, p. 54).

Cox (1988) reported that students, in some cases, do not connect the type of writing they are encouraged to do with the writing they see the teacher doing. For example, when teachers use the time while students are writing in their journals to complete reports, plan lessons, or work on report cards, they are modeling a different kind of writing than what students are being asked to do. Think of how you might feel if you enrolled in a technical school's cabinet-making class and the teacher gave you tools, the name of a project to construct, and a set of directions to follow—but neglected to model the how-to aspect of your task. One likely scenario is that you might become discouraged and not develop much real skill in cabinet making. Yet, writing often has been taught in this manner.

Developing writers, who often lack understanding and insights about their own composing processes, can be helped through teacher modeling and by exposure to the practices of experienced writers. Farnan and colleagues (1992) described how student writers can learn from experienced writers as follows:

. . . Novices tend to concentrate on finished products, to worry about displaying correctness instead of spending time planning, drafting, rethinking, and redrafting. In contrast, experienced writers report focusing on processes of thinking, planning, and generating ideas, which, sooner or later, happen to result in a finished product which has been worked on and reworked myriad times. These insights can inform novices' ways of thinking about writing processes, providing alternative ways of approaching tasks as they develop their own writing behaviors. (p. 554)

One teacher uses short generating activities, at times when a break is needed, to relax students after working on a difficult study problem or to calm students settling down after the lunch break. Model Activity 3.6, "Attention with Awesome Alliteration," is one such activity. After students were given copies of the activity and directions were read, this teacher modeled her sentence on the chalkboard.

Affectionate, astray aliens arrived at Abbeyville aboard an aerodyne and arranged ample appetizers for all applauding adolescents.

A brief discussion followed to be sure all students understood the meanings of all words used. *Aerodyne* (a heavier-than-air aircraft that derives its lift from motion), for example, would not be a word familiar to all students. This might be a good time to teach the word *alliteration,* the occurrence of the same letter or sound at the beginning of several words in succession. Alliteration is to the beginning of words what rhyming is to their endings. The tongue twister "She sells sea shells by the seashore" is a familiar example of alliteration. Given the diversity of backgrounds represented in our classrooms today, tongue twisters may be unfamiliar to some students. Therefore, modeling simple tongue twisters, emphasizing the alliteration, is a good idea; modeling how to construct a tongue twister is also important. After students have had time to write a few of their own sentences using alliteration, as suggested in Model Activity 3.6, they may choose to share some of their favorites with classmates. This model prewriting activity demonstrates how alliteration, besides being used for playful tongue twisters, is often used by newspapers for eye-catching headlines. Students might find a knowledge of alliteration helpful in writing poetry or if they decide to create a class or school newspaper.

Teacher modeling continues as encouragement is given to each student in a positive, enthusiastic manner. Journals and their use in the writing program are discussed at length in Chapter 9. Mention is made of journal writing here, however, because of the many excellent opportunities provided for the teacher to demonstrate writing by actually writing along with the students and by sharing what has been written. A teacher who keeps a journal for daily writing, for example, may share with the class:

Here's what I have written in my journal: "Yesterday while studying gravity and how its pull keeps the moon orbiting the earth and the earth in place around the sun, our class had some unanswered questions, particularly about weightlessness in space. Today we'll see if we can work together to discover what we need to know to better understand gravity and its forces."

Students see firsthand that the teacher has put the writing journal to good use—to help remember from one day to the next. The usefulness of journal writing has been modeled.

Murray (1982) stated: "Instead of teaching finished writing, we should teach unfinished writing, and glory in its unfinishedness. . . . We share with our students the continual excitement of choosing one word instead of another, of searching for the one true word" (p. 15). For teachers, then, prewriting is the time to begin modeling the writing process by prewriting with their students. All the prewriting strategies discussed in the next section—from warm-ups and brainstorming to topic selection—will be more readily understood by students when teachers first model effectively as part of the instructional process.

STRATEGIES FOR TEACHING PREWRITING

Students view the prewriting stage differently and, therefore, need different strategies or combinations of strategies for getting started. In the classroom, prewriting activities take many forms and often involve no actual writing with paper and pencil or at the computer. Successful prewriting activities lead students into an awareness that writing is thought and speech written down. The students' interest in personal writing evolves as they acquire an appreciation of themselves as writers. Students may come to school with limited writing experiences or feeling discouraged from lack of success in previous writing experiences. Interesting prewriting sessions can do much to guide these disenchanted learners back to a renewed eagerness to learn.

Warm-up Activities

Writing is a physical as well as a mental activity. Just as basketball and football players warm up by exercising and practicing, writers may need to warm up, too. When using warm-ups to generate words and ideas, students should be encouraged to forget about mechanics and just write. Some days, teachers find that students have difficulty getting started writing. On those days, warm-up exercises such as those modeled in Activity 3.7 may be helpful.

Word Association Techniques

A good method to generate ideas is the association of one word with other words. These word association techniques may be presented in various forms and offer excellent ideas for prewriting activities. Students enjoy browsing through books of lists or facts and are intrigued to discover that movie stars John Wayne, Robert Redford, and Bob Urich all attended college on athletic scholarships or that Ann Landers, Bette Davis, Dinah Shore, and Joanne Woodward were all Girl Scouts. Young achievers in your class will delight in learning that in 1776, the year of the Declaration of Independence,

James Monroe (fought in Revolutionary War; became fifth president of the United States) was eighteen.

Alexander Hamilton (American statesman) was twenty-one.

James Madison (known as "Father of the Constitution"; became fourth president of the United States) was twenty-six.

Thomas Jefferson (principal author of the Declaration of Independence; third president of the United States) was thirty- three.

Half of the population of the United States were under sixteen.

Three-quarters were under twenty-five (Elmo, 1981).

A classroom that makes available some books of lists and facts as well as special dictionaries and trivia games provides students with examples to generate ideas of their own. Model Activity 3.7 deals with list making as a prewriting activity.

Clustering, webbing, and mapping are other word association techniques useful for prewriting. Bromley (1991) stated that webbing can do for older students what drawing a picture does for young children: It allows them to plan and organize graphically ideas and relationships. Then they can write or talk about what they have drawn. Webbing supports students' rehearsal and planning for writing; it provides a concrete way to organize ideas and to identify what to include in writing. Webbing is a versatile, flexible teaching tool that can be adapted to fit specific needs of students. Model Activities 3.1 and 3.2, presented earlier in this chapter, make use of webbing or clustering techniques.

Another word association technique is the use of acrostics. They are fun, are easily understood after doing a few, and allow for variety and creativity. A good way to start is described in Model Activity 3.8, in which students choose words from the newspaper, supplying descriptive words.

Brainstorming

Brainstorming is a technique used to generate and collect ideas for writing; it's a way to produce many ideas from a group for the purpose of simple enjoyment or problem solving. Brainstorming encourages a free flow of ideas, imagination, creativity, and flexibility in rehearsing ideas. Thinking, talking, and listening are involved in brainstorming sessions that can be carried out with the class as a whole, in small groups, or individually. Sometimes brainstorming is an oral activity only—to relax, to stimulate thinking, or to air opinions and feelings. At other times, ideas may be recorded on the chalkboard, or students may record their own ideas; students can use the resulting ideas and words in their writing. The webbing, clustering, and list-making activities presented earlier in this chapter all use brainstorming to generate ideas.

Cox (1988, p. 86) offered the following specific guidelines for a planned brainstorming session:

1. Invite ideas—to expand a subject, solve a problem, or plan future activities.
2. Encourage all kinds of ideas—humorous, whimsical, or even nonsensical—and a great number of ideas.
3. In the initial stages, suspend comments or judgments.
4. Record all ideas.
5. Encourage the students to respond to each other's ideas, and to bounce new ones off old ones. Hitchhiking of one student's ideas on another's is valued.

Model Activity 3.9 was designed to use brainstorming to set the stage for a writing activity after a topic has been chosen but before actual writing of the draft begins. It will help the student to discover what is already known about the topic, to list unanswered questions that will need researching, and to make notes about places to go to find answers for those questions.

Freewriting

"Freewriting, or writing continuously without stopping for several minutes, . . . results in a rambling stream-of-consciousness as the mind moves from one thought to another" (Temple & Gillet, 1989, p. 259). Freewriting helps students begin to write easily and with pleasure; it is a technique to help them feel comfortable in their writing. It's a discovery process with no definite purpose, allowing students to write without fear of criticism or grades. "The goal of freewriting is in the process, not the product" (Elbow, 1981, p. 13). It is a useful tool for fairly fluent writers who can write quickly (Temple & Gillet, 1989).

In freewriting, the writer generates words, sentences, and paragraphs to express thoughts, images, and ideas about things they know—themselves, their common knowledge, and the concerns of their age group. Students write random thoughts down on the paper or keep them in the their minds as they find words to express their thoughts. The exercises should be short, within the students' abilities, and able to be completed with students experiencing a sense of accomplishment and satisfaction; they may be developed into first drafts. Freewriting is often part of journal writing, discussed at length in Chapter 9. Freewriting in the classroom fits in at many places—after a field trip or a class movie, following storytelling, after studying a famous painting or other work of art, or in connection with study in some content area. The purpose may be to write about an event just experienced, or it may be a response to a class activity. When asked to freewrite on a favorite color, fifth-grader Janet wrote the following:

Yellow is my favorite color because it makes me happy. I like the sunshine coming in the window of my room. Centers of flowers are yellow, cheese is yellow, and my favorite dress is yellow. I think houses that are painted yellow are pretty, too.

Janet's paragraph is an example of the kind of ideas that freewriting can produce. As this writer reflects on these thoughts, she may decide to simply use some of them as a springboard; thus, freewriting will have served as a vehicle for constructing a more meaningful draft. In referring to the advantages of freewriting, Elbow (1981) said, "It doesn't always produce powerful writing itself, but it leads to powerful writing" (p. 15). Elbow explained how this is accomplished, as follows:

[It is] the peculiar increase in power and insight that comes from focusing your energy while at the same time putting aside your conscious controlling self. Freewriting gives practice in this special mode of focusing-but-not trying; it helps you stand out of the way and let words be chosen by the sequence of the words themselves or the thought, not by the conscious self. In this way freewriting gradually puts a deeper resonance or voice into your writing. (p. 16)

Prewriting in the form of freewriting helps students get started when they have a block or don't feel like writing. It teaches them to write without worrying about the mechanics of writing. Freewriting can be an outlet for feelings that often get in the way when trying to write about something else. And freewriting often leads the way to writing that is alive and forceful. Topics and ideas that are generated in a freewriting session may lead to a draft in the form of a poem, an essay, or some other form of writing.

Using Oral Language

Students who are able to express their thoughts well orally are in a better position to succeed as writers. Therefore, enlightened teachers accommodate this natural development of the writing process by providing instruction that emphasizes oral language growth.

Reading aloud to students exposes them to the variety, beauty, and power of the English language. Exposure to the classics will contribute to their writing styles later, as they listen to kinds of literature they might not choose to read on their own. Teachers also should include different forms of writing, such as poetry, essays, and short stories, when reading aloud to students. Students of all ages enjoy having someone read aloud to them; concomitantly, they become more aware of the many forms that writing takes.

Storytelling is another good vehicle for generating ideas during prewriting; as a story unfolds, stu-

**" 'Writing?' But you'll put all the storytellers
out of work!"**

Source: "Laugh Parade," *Parade Magazine,* September 9, 1990, p. 18. Copyright © 1992;
Reprinted Courtesy of Bunny Hoest and Parade Magazine.

dents should be encouraged to relate their own experiences, reactions, and emotions to the story. Peck (1989) noted that "the art of storytelling is currently enjoying a renaissance, as evidenced by the growing number of professional tellers, associations, and sourcebooks available" (p. 138). Peck reported that storytelling is not the presentation of a memorized script or reading of a written text; it is a personal experience story told in a natural manner. Allowing students to tell their own stories is also a good learning activity and provides opportunity for development of oral expression and a sense of story. Students may pattern their stories after ones they have heard or may borrow themes from a literary work heard in a storytelling session.

Educators recognize storytelling as an excellent vehicle for developing language and cultural literacy. For example, it can be used to introduce students to the traditions, beliefs, and history of folktales. Students of all ages love to hear of the antics of legendary heroes of folklore, such as Paul Bunyan, the rugged logger whose size and strength have come to be associated with the "tall tale." As the Paul Bunyan tales were heard and retold by loggers of America's timberlands, local and personal embellishments were added. Every family also has its own stories to tell, often passed along by grandparents or other family members. Students should

be encouraged to share stories of their choice with classmates.

Drawing/Imaging

Writing is most effective when learners are led to tap the creative aspects of their beings. The visual and the verbal strengthen one another; if a teacher can get a student creating in art, a response in words is likely to follow eventually. Drawing can be a useful prewriting activity to develop creativity; but activities must be carefully designed to fit the needs of the students who, in some cases, may associate traditional verbal and computational skills with "growing up" and consider any kind of artwork as "childish." The concerned teacher can dispel this thinking by the use of carefully selected drawing activities, not only to generate writing activities, but also to achieve the goal of a balanced, integrated future for all learners.

Chapter 2 described how both hemispheres of the brain are involved in higher cognitive functioning, with each hemisphere specializing in a different mode of thinking. Edwards (1979), who has applied recent discoveries in brain research to the teaching of drawing skills, described the left-hemisphere, right-handed mode as "foursquare, upright, sensible, direct, true, hard-edged, unfanciful, and forceful" (p. 38). She defined the right-hemisphere, left-handed mode as "curvy, flexible, more playful in its unexpected twists and turns, more complex, diagonal, and fanciful" (p. 38). In all kinds of activities, the brain uses both hemispheres—at times with one of the halves leading and at other times with the two halves sharing equally.

Today's educators are becoming increasingly more concerned with the importance of creativity and intuition in the learning process. Teachers of the writing process would do well to study ways to help students gain access to their right-brain functions—imagination, visualization, creativity, and inventiveness. Prewriting activities offer excellent means to unleash the right-brain potential. George Orwell (1903–1950), a British writer whose political conscience was expressed in the allegorical fable *Animal Farm* (1945), and the satirical novel of life under the surveillance of Big Brother, *Nineteen Eighty-four* (1949), described the prewriting process as follows:

In prose, the worst thing one can do with words is to surrender to them. When you think of a concrete object, you think wordlessly, and then, if you want to describe the thing you have been visualizing, you probably hunt about till you find the exact words that seem to fit it. When you think of something abstract you are more inclined to use words from the start, and unless you make a conscious effort to prevent it, the existing dialect will come rushing in and do the job for you, at the expense of blurring or even changing your meaning. Probably it is better to put off using words as long as possible and get one's meaning clear as one can through pictures or sensations. (Orwell, 1968, p. 138)

Visualizing and imaging are important to both drawing and writing; therefore, the use of drawing as a prewriting activity not only assists learners in formulating plans for their writing, but also cultivates the functioning of the right hemisphere of the brain.

Studying about Native Americans, for instance, would be a good opportunity to enhance cultural literacy and to incorporate drawing into a prewriting activity that could provide ideas for future writing. The teacher could introduce the activity with a brief discussion that might begin as follows:

Teacher: Early Native Americans kept written records by means of picture writing called *pictographs.* A picture of a footprint meant "travel" or "movement"; a picture of a bird meant "carefree" or "lighthearted." Here is a

sampling of some common Indian symbols (use chalkboard or overhead projector):

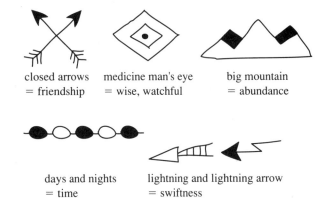

closed arrows = friendship

medicine man's eye = wise, watchful

big mountain = abundance

days and nights = time

lightning and lightning arrow = swiftness

Teacher: North American tribes, the Kiowa and the Sioux, kept a history by drawing with charcoal on stretched animal hides. The American poet Henry Wadsworth Longfellow (1807–1882) wrote about this in his well-known poem recounting an Indian legend, *The Song of Hiawatha* (1855), one of the first long poems in American literature to be published:

> *Such as these the shapes they painted*
> *On the birch-bark and the deerskin*

The Aztec and Maya of Latin America progressed beyond the picture stage to use symbols to indicate sounds, not just situations. By combining the picture of one object with another, the reader could derive a third meaning in terms of sounds. This is called *rebus* writing. Following are some examples of modern-day rebus writing (use chalkboard or overhead projector):

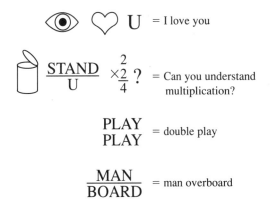

= I love you

= Can you understand multiplication?

= double play

= man overboard

After discussion of the Indians' use of picture writing, with ample opportunity for students to share and ask questions, they can be led to create their own picture language. Encourage them to be inventive. If a student appears to be having trouble getting started, team this student with a classmate who seems to be getting off to a good start. They can work together, and the reluctant student will often be able to contribute after seeing a sample or two provided by the classmate. Remember, as an inscription on a Native American sacred feather says, "The value of knowledge increases as it is shared." Also, what fun when papers are exchanged to be *read!* Some students will be sure to enjoy rebus writing and will surprise classmates and teachers with their creativity. Model Activity 3.10 demonstrates another way to use drawing as prewriting.

Continuing the study of Native Americans, we learn how their writing progressed from the pictorial stage to much more sophisticated forms. The Latin American Mayans developed a kind of writing somewhat like Egyptian hieroglyphics, where each sign or picture stood for a complete word or a syllable in a word. Other Indians were very gifted with language usage, but a Cherokee named Sequoyah, the only person in American history to invent an alphabet, is considered one of the greatest literary geniuses of all time. Model Activity 3.11 provides more information about this great American, Sequoyah.

Many opportunities exist for drawing to be used in the classroom as prewriting. Hennings (1990) described rehearsing for writing as consisting of three elements—pictorializing, talking about, and thinking out. Some developing writers may find a picture series useful in sequencing the content of a report or story; thus, pictorializing becomes a tool for learning to organize their thoughts. The newspaper offers many opportunities for practice. Encourage students to read comic strips and collect their favorites over a period of time. As they become familiar with the comic strip characters, some students may like to draw, with dialogue, an original cartoon situation of their own. Other students may write and perform a skit starring their favorite character. Model Activity 3.12 demonstrates how to organize ideas and thoughts based on a picture series.

Here are some other student activities making use of pictorial material found in newspapers:

1. Choose pictures from the newspaper and clip them out without the captions. Ask students to discuss events depicted in the photographs and develop a dialogue that the characters might use in speaking with one another.
2. Along with the teacher, students look at a weather map, discussing directions and markings. Locate various states and cities on the map and discuss the weather symbols and forecast for the next day. Using the weather map as a guide, take a "tour" of the United States. After deciding on the route for the tour, record in writing the directions to follow, and note the weather to be expected in major cities along the way.
3. Students select an advertisement from the newspaper and make a shopping list from that ad. Then give the shopping list, the ad, and a fictitious purchase amount to a partner, who must calculate the cost of the items on the list and determine the amount of change to be received (Buford, Doyle, & Shapley, 1985).

Drama

The use of dialogue in writing was introduced in the previous discussion of using newspapers and student-created cartoons and comic strips as prewriting activities. Role-playing and acting out stories also support the writing process by encouraging students to think about dialogue and sequencing of events in a story. Educators should take advantage of the opportunities of this method of learning; in particular, middle school teachers find students in this physically active age group most receptive to activities that give them a means of role-playing and acting out some situations of great concern to them, all in a nonthreatening format. Taking the viewpoint of an animal, insect, or some inanimate object, for instance, allows students to be imaginative and removes fear of being judged.

Drama used as a prewriting activity is usually informal, spontaneous, and unrehearsed. Activities include movement warm-ups such as "statue," where a given pose is assumed. Pantomine, the art of conveying ideas without words, is enjoyed by students and allows for interpretation of feelings and moods as well. After a storytelling or reading session, students may act out stories themselves or use puppets to dramatize stories.

Creative drama activities are springboards for student script writing, an excellent means of developing a wide range of composing skills. Garrison (1981, p. 2), a classroom teacher, in "How to Write a One-Act Play," offered the following prewriting (on paper) activities:

1. Write a scenario—a framework (like an outline)—which includes a brief description of the set, entrances, exits, furniture placement, etc. Make a list of characters with a brief description of each. Outline the action of what happens in the play.
2. Decide if the play is character-centered or event-centered.
3. Try to build suspense toward the climax. Each scene should present a small piece of the basic conflict. Show a negotiation between the characters.
4. The climax or crisis scene must satisfy the audience's interest. Avoid "trick" or sensational endings. The audience's reaction should be "of course," not "how surprising." Try for a truthful close.[*]

Students Choose Own Writing Topics

Students have no trouble finding much to talk about but often have great difficulty coming up with something to write about. Students scurrying into the classroom after lunch display no lack of words in discussing clothes, hairdos, skateboards, or television shows. But when the teacher announces free writing time on a topic of their own choosing, students often have a blank look, perhaps because they have become accustomed to being told what to write about and are dependent on the teacher's ideas of what constitutes a good topic. It is up to teachers to direct students toward finding their own

topics, style, and language through modeling topic selection and through skillful use of prewriting activities.

Teachers who are striving to empower their students to take charge of their own writing will find prewriting a good time to encourage students to choose their own writing topics. Pulitzer Prize winner Donald M. Murray (1982) stated:

Grant your students their writing rights—the right to be an authority. The writer has to write with information. Students must write on subjects on which they have abundant information or be given adequate time to collect an abundance of information before they write. (p. 175)

The teacher must refrain from providing a content and must be careful not to inhibit students from finding their own subjects, forms, and language (Murray, 1980). The prewriting stage is a time for working with students so that they will be able to choose their own writing topics and really care about them. Ownership makes all the difference! Giving students the responsibility for choosing their own writing topics requires a great deal of support from the teacher as students are taught how to take ownership of their writing. The teacher helps the students discover subjects and topics they know about, so they can begin to organize their thoughts about them.

PROVIDING TIME FOR PREWRITING

It has been said that the prewriting stage may constitute 85 percent of the composing/writing process. Ample time must be scheduled for prewriting to establish a good foundation on which to build the other stages of writing. As Murray has stated, "I wonder if extensive rewriting is not mostly a failure of prewriting, or allowing adequate time for rehearsal, a matter of plucking the fruit before it is ripe" (Murray & Graves, 1981, p. 113).

Given the demands of their busy daily schedules, how can teachers find adequate time to devote to prewriting? If prewriting activities help students make connections between what they already know or want to know and what they are about to study,

more elaborate concepts are formed and learning will become more focused. Have you observed how eager students are to learn more about a topic related to a field trip they have just taken? Teachers can provide this same advantage for their students through interesting prewriting activities in any content area. Offer relevant generating activities such as discussing, brainstorming, organizing, and writing responses prior to reading text assignments (Brozo & Simpson, 1991).

Model Activity 3.13, designed for use when studying the Revolutionary War period in history or social studies, emphasizes critical thinking and cooperative learning. Although students probably know about preparing time capsules for future generations, this prewriting activity will be to collect items for a time capsule going *back* in time over two hundred years. First, students brainstorm a list

[*]*Source:* Reprinted from "How to Write a One-Act Play," p. 2, with permission of Ruth Sasser Garrison, Writing Teacher, Tallahassee Community College.

of items or pictures of items to be included in a time capsule going back in time to the Revolutionary War period. Then they discuss how eighteenth-century people would have a problem understanding things such as computers, microwaves, digital watches, TVs and VCRs, immunization shots, escalators, and frozen foods. This prewriting activity can be followed by having students each pick an item to be included in the time capsule and write a descriptive paragraph to inform eighteenth-century people about the item.

The prewriting process must be long enough to allow student writers to identify their purposes for writing in addition to choosing their subjects and their targeted audiences. Often this cannot be accomplished in a one-day prewriting session. Although some students will move quickly through the prewriting process, others will need much time; often, students will return to prewriting after some initial drafting. Teachers who recognize and accept the fact that students proceed at different rates at different times avoid the temptation to rush students to start the composition of writing drafts before they are ready. It is sometimes better to carry over prewriting activities from one day to the next.

TARGETING THE AUDIENCE IN PREWRITING

With each new purpose for writing, there will be a different audience with different expectations. The writer must ask: "For whom am I writing? What do I need or want to tell them? How much do they know? What do I hope they will know after reading what I have written?" More advanced writers automatically ask themselves these questions. New writers tend to write for themselves and need practice using visual imagery as an absent audience monitor. Through teacher modeling and appropriate activities, the student can be led to imagine the reader's response to the written work and can adjust the writing accordingly. At times, the audience will be identified at the prewriting stage; at other times, prewriting will be for oneself only, with a future audience being targeted during drafting.

It is helpful for students to read others' writing, to analyze the writing from a writer's viewpoint, and to discuss the purpose and form chosen by the writer. This gives the writer a chance to experience the role of the reader and can increase the writer's awareness of the audience. Student writers need experience writing for audiences other than their teachers. Therefore, the audiences addressed by writing assignments should be varied so that student writers will experience making decisions about how appropriate their writing is for their intended readers.

Teacher modeling can be influential in helping students target their audiences in prewriting. Teachers who share their own writing to show different tones and style, depending on the writing purpose and audience, demonstrate to students how to identify and write for a variety of audiences. Their students can be led to participate in writing for real audiences—peers, younger children in the school, parents, community leaders, newspapers, and literary magazines. A more complete discussion of audience identification, along with a sampling of model activities, will be found in Chapter 4 in the section entitled "A Sense of Audience and Writing Formats."

REFERENCES

Bromley, K. D. (1991). *Webbing with literature.* Boston: Allyn and Bacon.

Brozo, W. G., & Simpson, M. L. (1991). *Readers, teachers, learners: Expanding literacy in the secondary schools.* New York: Macmillan.

Buford, J. W., Doyle, L., & Shapley, B. (1985). *Classroom vavoom! Newspaper activities.* West Palm Beach, FL: Palm Beach Newspapers.

Calkins, C. C. (Ed.). (1975). *The story of America.* Pleasantville, NY: Readers' Digest Association.

Calkins, L. M. (1986). *The art of teaching writing.* Portsmouth, NH: Heinemann.

Chenfeld, M. B. (1987). *Teaching language arts creatively,* 2nd ed. New York: Harcourt Brace Jovanovich.

Cooper, W., & Brown, B. J. (1992). Using portfolios to empower student writers. *English Journal, 81*(2), 40–45.

Cox, C. (1988). *Teaching language arts.* Boston: Allyn and Bacon.

Edwards, B. (1979). *Drawing on the right side of the brain: A course in enhancing creativity and artistic confidence.* Boston: Houghton Mifflin.

Elbow, P. (1981). *Writing with power.* New York: Oxford University Press.

Elmo, D. (1981). *The giant list book.* New York: Modern Promotions/Unisystems.

Farnan, N., Lapp, D., & Flood, J. (1992). Changing perspectives in writing instruction. *Journal of Reading, 35*(7), 550–556.

Garrison, R. (1981). *How to write a one-act play.* Unpublished manuscript.

Hansen, J. (1992). The language of challenge: Readers and writers speak their minds. *Language Arts, 69*(2), 100–105.

Hennings, D. G. (1990). *Communication in action: Teaching the language arts,* 4th ed. Boston: Houghton Mifflin.

Kellogg, C. (1956). *Paderewski.* New York: Viking Press.

Klein, M. L. (1985). *The development of writing in children: Pre-K through grade 8.* Englewood Cliffs, NJ: Prentice-Hall.

Lenski, L. (1949, November). Helping children to create. *Childhood Education, 26,* 101–105.

Lindquist, B., & Ligett, C. (1992, Winter). Teachers write about research: Taking time to wonder. *IRT Communication Quarterly, 14*(2), 2.

Manning, K. R. (1987). Florence Nightingale. *The World Book Encyclopedia* (Vol. 14, pp. 423–425). Chicago: World Book.

Murray, D. M. (1980). Writing as process: How writing finds its own meaning. In T. R. Donovan & B. W. McClelland (Eds.), *Eight approaches to composition* (pp. 3–20). Urbana, IL: National Council of Teachers of English.

Murray, D. M. (1982). *Learning by teaching: Selected articles on writing and teaching.* Montclair, NJ: Boynton-Cook.

Murray, D. M. (1987). *Write to learn,* 2nd ed. New York: Holt, Rinehart and Winston.

Murray, D. M., & Graves, D. H. (1981). Revision in the writer's workshop and in the classroom. In R. D. Walshe (Ed.), *Donald Graves in Australia—Children want to write.* Rozelle, NSW, Australia: Primary English Teaching Association.

Orwell, G. (1968). Politics and the English language. In S. Orwell & I. Angus (Eds.), *In front of your nose, Vol. 4: The collected essays of George Orwell.* New York: Harcourt, Brace and World.

Pahl, M. M., & Monson, R. J. (1992). In search of whole language: Transforming curriculum and instruction. *Journal of Reading, 35*(7), 518–524.

Peck, J. (1989). Using storytelling to promote language and literacy development. *The Reading Teacher, 43*(2), 138–141.

Perrin, P. G. (1965). *Writer's guide and index to English,* 4th ed. Chicago: Scott Foresman.

Staff. (1990). Man's best marsupial. *Time,* September 17, p. 61.

Temple, C., & Gillet, J. W. (1989). *Language arts: Learning processes and teaching practices,* 2nd ed. Glenview, IL: Scott Foresman.

Vygotsky, L. S. (1962). *Thought and language* (E. Hanfmann & G. Vakar, Translators). Cambridge, MA: MIT Press.

Walberg, H. J. (1990). Productive teaching and instruction: Assessing the knowledge base. *Phi Delta Kappan, 71*(6), 470–478.

Walshe, R. D. (1979). What's basic to teaching writing? *English Journal, 68*(9), 51–56.

MODEL ACTIVITIES

The activities that follow are meant to serve as models; such activities should be used as part of a total learning environment. These model activities were designed to demonstrate how the writing process can be developed while expanding the writer's knowledge base and providing opportunities for the writer to think critically.

ACTIVITY 3.1

Childhood Games

Directions: What were some of the games you liked to play when you were younger? Did you enjoy playing Capture the Flag or Hide-and-Seek? What is your favorite game now that you're older? And what is your favorite indoor game for a rainy day? Put your thinking cap on and start writing down all the childhood games that you can remember. Write them down in the box below as fast as you can, going out from the circle, or whatever seems right for you. Stop to relax now and then.

Are you surprised that you remembered so many childhood games? Keep this page in your writing folder. It may be useful for a writing draft at another time.

ACTIVITY 3.2

The Lady with the Lamp

Directions: Read the following paragraph about a famous historical figure.

Florence Nightingale (1820–1910) was an English lady who founded the nursing profession as we know it today. She grew up in a wealthy family prominent in British society and enjoyed traveling in Europe. But, even as a child, Florence liked to help others. When she grew up, Florence went to study in a hospital in Paris and later entered nurses' training in Germany. After becoming a nurse, she directed nursing operations and tended wounded soldiers in the Crimean War. She was known as "the lady with the lamp" as she walked through the hospital at night, taking care of the injured. Florence Nightingale was a hospital reformer and introduced sanitary practices to reduce the spread of infectious diseases. She founded the Nightingale Home for Nurses in London and was an adviser for many countries concerning military hospitals. She received many honors and was the first woman to be given the British Order of Merit. To all the word, the light that Florence Nightingale carried has come to mean care for the sick, concern for the welfare of every human being, and freedom for women to choose their own work. (Manning, 1987)

Now, in the space below, use the information you learned while reading the preceding paragraph to make a cluster of information about Florence Nightingale. If you know other things about her, use those also. You may want to add to your cluster something telling how you feel about Florence Nightingale and her work. Remember that you are brainstorming, and your thoughts and spelling will not be graded. Jot down quickly all ideas that come to mind.

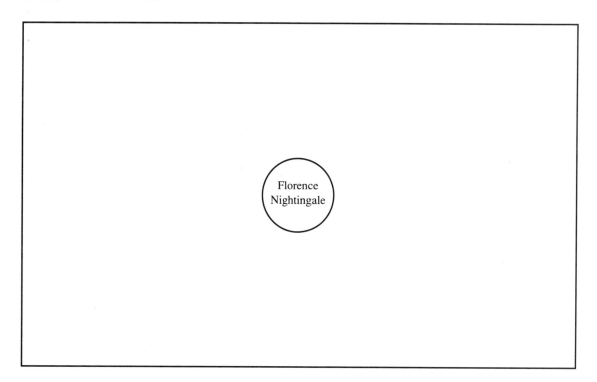

File this activity in your writing folder. It may be expanded into a writing draft in the future.

Me, Myself, and I

Directions: Draw your first name or nickname in large, fat letters in the space below. An example of a name is given to show you how to draw the letters.

Next, make a drawing or cartoon character out of each letter of your name so that it will tell something about you. Here is our example, Katie, done for you. You can see that Katie likes to roller skate; has a hard time waking up; and enjoys music, hot dogs, and reading a favorite book.

Have fun . . . and if you need help, ask your teacher or a classmate.

ACTIVITY 3.4

No Leaves for Lunch

Directions: After touching the eucalyptus leaf, like the one shown below from Palo Alto, California, read the following passage about koalas.

A koala bear, which is not a bear at all, is a marsupial (a mammal that has a pouch for carrying its young). After the birth of a koala baby, which is approximately one inch long, it crawls into the mother's pouch and lives there for about six months. Other examples of marsupials are the kangaroo and the wallaby. These Australian marsupials aren't found in the United States except in zoos. The only marsupial in North America is the Virginia gray opossum, which some people say is the oldest wild animal on this continent.

Zoo-goers find koalas—even with their mournful eyes—fun to watch, particularly because of their keen sense of balance. Even when asleep, koalas have no difficulty perching on a branch. Usually they choose a resting spot where branches come together; there they brace themselves with their sharp claws for napping. Because they need a fresh supply of eucalyptus leaves every day, and these don't grow in many places, koalas are rarely found outside of Australia where, up until recent times, there were no problems associated with food supply.

The koala, Australia's informal mascot, is in jeopardy. Their numbers in Australia once reached millions; today that number has been reduced to about 400,000. What has caused their numbers to dwindle? Fur hunters have taken their toll. Also, koalas have been threatened by disease and have suffered from traffic accidents on the roads of developing areas. As the animal's habitat has become threatened, with the eucalyptus forest continuing to shrink, the home and food supply of the koala have been put at risk. Without preservation measures, the koalas won't have a future. Research into koala ecology is currently receiving worldwide attention. (Staff, *Time,* 1990)

66

Now, read and discuss the following questions. Be sure you understand the importance of the eucalyptus leaf for the koala. Finally, share your opinion about the best way(s) to save the koalas in today's changing world.

1. How are marsupials different from other mammals?
2. Which country has the koala as its informal mascot? Is that country also a continent? Where is it located in relation to where you live? Can you find it on a globe?
3. Why is the koala population dwindling?
4. If it is true that koalas are the world's favorite marsupial, why do you think we rarely see them in U.S. zoos?

Your Opinion, Please: I think the best way(s) to help koalas survive in today's changing world is/are

_____

_____

_____

_____

_____

_____

_____

_____

_____

_____

_____

_____

_____

_____

_____

_____

_____

_____

_____

_____

ACTIVITY 3.5

An Unbelievable Plot

Directions: Start with three pieces of paper. On one, write a place (setting). It may be a real or an imaginary place. On each of the other two pieces of paper, write the name of a person (character) who is real, imaginary, or in fiction; it could be an animal. You now have a setting and two characters for a story.

Next, a student or the teacher collects all the pieces of paper in three separate containers. After mixing up the slips in each container, each student draws one piece of paper from each container.

Now, you have two characters and a setting. Use them to write a story plot in the space given. Plan to share your plot with the class when everyone has finished.

Examples of story ideas other students have written when doing this activity show you how much fun this can be.

"George Washington enjoys a picnic at a TV studio with Kentucky Colonel Sanders, who brings the fried chicken."

"Michael Jordan lets Garfield borrow his sneakers as they go sightseeing in Paris."

Your Story Plot:

_____

_____

_____

_____

_____

_____

_____

_____

_____

_____

_____

_____

_____

_____

_____

_____

File this activity in your writing folder. You may wish to expand your plot into a story in a future writing assignment.

Attention with Awesome Alliteration

Directions: When several words in succession all begin with the same letter or sound, this is called *alliteration*. Pflugerville High School in Texas once won 55 football games in a row for a state record. When a game was lost, the local newspaper had the following headline: "Pflugerville Pfinally Pfalters." A tongue twister, such as *Peter Piper picked a peck of pickled peppers,* is another example.

Write as long a sentence as you can for each of the initial letters below. You may use little words such as *the, a, an, and,* and *or;* but the rest should begin with the given letter.

Example: *s*   <u>Salesman Smith sold shiny snow shovels.</u>

t _____

n _____

sh _____

Your letter choice:

— _____

— _____

— _____

— _____

Put an asterisk (*) by your two favorites to share with your classmates.

You might find a knowledge of alliteration helpful if you decide to write for a class or school newspaper. Alliteration may also be useful when writing poetry.

ACTIVITY 3.7

Warm Up with Lists of Things

Directions: Make lists of things asked for in the items below. Work fast, and don't worry about spelling or neatness.

1. Things that could fit in a coat pocket:

   _____   _____
   _____   _____
   _____   _____

2. Things you'd see on a city street at night:

   _____
   _____
   _____

3. Things that are

   shiny: _____
   round: _____
   soft: _____
   jagged: _____
   ridged: _____
   huge: _____
   smooth: _____
   sour: _____
   scary: _____
   pretty: _____
   useful: _____

Extra! Extra! Read All about It!

Directions: Clip a short story or paragraph from the newspaper and paste in the space below. Choose one word from the news item, and print it on the line to the right of your clipping. Now use each letter in the word to make other words and print those words vertically. Use your imagination.

An Example:

Atlanta Hosts Olympics The 1996 Summer Olympic Games in Atlanta, Georgia, marks the seventh time that a U.S. city has been chosen to host this international event. These games are held every four years at a different site, and amateur athletes of all nations are eligible to participate.

	A		g		s		
g	t	g	a		w		
O	L	Y	M	P	I	C	S
l	a	m	e	r	m	r	u
d	n	n	s	i	m	o	m
	t	a		z	i	w	m
	a	s		e	n	d	e
	t			s	g	s	r
	i						
	c						
	s						

Paste your
newspaper
clipping
here

Your word: _____

Brainstorming

This activity uses brainstorming to show you how to develop a topic of your choice before starting a draft.

An Example: Sheila chose the topic of *hot air balloons* and brainstormed the following:

What I already know about hot air balloons:

1. They are pretty.

2. They can be used in races.

3. Usually only one or two people ride at a time.

4. They fly above the trees and houses but not high like airplanes.

What I need to find out about hot air balloons:	Where will I find this informaiton?
1. What fuel is used?	Library
2. How safe are they?	Ask Bobby's father
3. How does one learn to	
fly a hot air balloon?	Ask Bobby's father
4. Are they ever used for	
anything other than	
recreation?	Library

Directions: Choose a topic you wish to write about. Then brainstorm ideas about the subject that come to mind and write under the headings given. Don't worry about spelling and punctuation now.

My Topic: _____

What I already know about _____ :
                                          (write in your topic)

_____

_____

_____

_____

_____

_____

_____

_____

What I need to find out about _____ : (your topic)	Where will I find this information?
_____	_____
_____	_____
_____	_____
_____	_____
_____	_____
_____	_____
_____	_____
_____	_____

You may wish to keep this activity in your folder for a future writing project.

Can You Read This?

Directions: Choose one or more of the following short passages and tell the story through drawing. You can use your own style of drawing. This could be in pictograph or rebus writing, or you may want to do a series of drawings as in a comic strip. When you are finished, see if a classmate can "read" your drawing.

1. On May 20, 1927, Charles Lindbergh took off from New York in his plane, the *Spirit of St. Louis.* About nine and a half hours later, he landed in Paris. He was the first person to fly alone across the Atlantic Ocean.

2. A tornado is a violent storm in which the wind moves upward in a narrow, circular funnel. The winds in a tornado move fast enough to destroy buildings and trees in its path.

3. The pyramids are huge stone monuments in Egypt. Each has a square base, with four triangular sides that come to a point at the top. In ancient times, they were built as tombs for the Egyptian rulers, called pharaohs.

Save this activity in your writing folder. You may want to find out more about Lindbergh, tornados, or pyramids to expand into a future writing draft.

Sequoyah, the Cherokee Genius

Directions: First, read the following selection about Sequoyah. After a brainstorm session about the topic, draw a web or cluster to organize your thoughts.

Sequoyah (1773–1843), inventor of the Cherokee alphabet, was the son of a Cherokee Indian woman and a white trader. He wanted his people to have the white man's secret of the "talking leaves" and began by making a pictograph for each word in the Cherokee vocabulary. When Sequoyah's wife became angry at his neglect of the house and garden and burned his thousands of notations, he started again. But this time he made symbols for Cherokee sounds and, in 12 years, refined his system to 86 characters, which he presented to the Council of Chiefs in 1821. During the 12 years of working on his system of writing, Sequoyah was treated as an outcast by most of his tribe for meddling with the white man's secrets. However, hundreds of Cherokees were learning to read and write their own language within months following his winning approval of the tribal council. Books and a newspaper were printed in the new alphabet, and Sequoyah was looked up to as a genius by his people. To honor Sequoyah, the giant redwood trees of the Pacific coast of the United States were named for him. (Calkins, 1975)

Now, brainstorm—as a class or in small groups—what you have just read about Sequoyah. Consider the following questions along with those you may have.

1. What do you think motivated Sequoyah to work on his project for so many years when it seemed that everyone else was so against it?

   _____

   _____

   _____

   _____

   _____

   _____

   _____

   _____

2. Have you ever worked on something that did not seem to be going well but later turned out to be successful? If so, please share this.

   _____

   _____

   _____

   _____

   _____

   _____

   _____

3. From what you have read in the preceding paragraph, brainstorm a list of words that you might use to describe Sequoyah.

_____   _____

_____   _____

_____   _____

_____   _____

_____   _____

_____   _____

_____   _____

_____   _____

Now, draw a web about Sequoyah. Use information from this activity and include other things you may know about Sequoyah or the Cherokee Indians. You may wish to research this topic further in your school or public library.

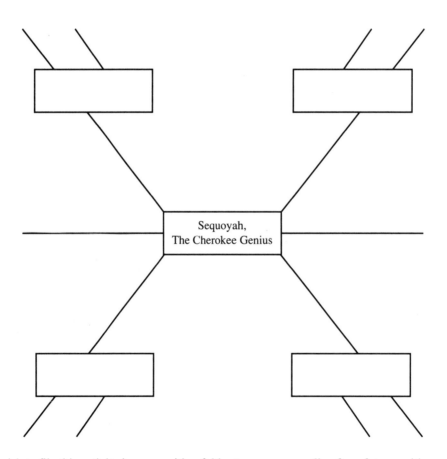

You may wish to file this activity in your writing folder to use as an outline for a future writing project.

ACTIVITY 3.12

New Kid in Town

Directions: Choose a favorite comic strip from the newspaper or from your collection. Now, invent your own new cartoon character (person, animal, robot, or extraterrestrial) to add to the strip. Using your imagination, give this character a name and an individual style and personality. Decide what traits make the character come alive and have the dialogue reveal those particular characteristics. Below, draw a picture of your created cartoon character and tell a few things that describe the character.

Next, add your new character, with dialogue, to a comic strip you have clipped from the newspaper and pasted in the spaces below. Or, you may choose to create and draw a series of frames of your own. Use the spaces below.

77

ACTIVITY 3.13

Turning Back the Clock

Directions: Pretend that you are collecting items for a time capsule to be sent back to the people of the Revolutionary War period. What would you like for these people to know about us? Remember, they have not seen computers, televisions, escalators, frozen foods, and many other things. List below items or ideas that you think should be included in a time capsule to be sent *back in time* to the Revolutionary War period.

_____   _____

_____   _____

_____   _____

_____   _____

_____   _____

_____   _____

Now, choose one of the items above and write a descriptive paragraph to inform eighteenth-century people about that item.

_____

_____

_____

_____

_____

_____

_____

_____

_____

_____

_____

_____

_____

_____

_____

_____

_____

_____

CHAPTER 4

Drafting and Translating

Composing requires an orchestration of experience. There are different ways to say things, and all are worthy of investigation.

—NCTE Committee on Curriculum Bulletins

The thinking, observing, collecting, reading, listening, talking, and reflecting of prewriting advance to a time when writers begin to feel ready to transcribe their ideas into words on a page. This urge to get something down in writing will not be reached in the same amount of time for individuals tackling different kinds of writing. This readiness to write does not mean, nor should it mean, that the composition is shaped completely in the writer's mind or in prewriting notes. On the contrary, students actively construct meaning as they write. When this urge to get one's thoughts written into words and sentences is acknowledged and acted on, the result typically takes the form of a first draft. This first draft is usually just one of an evolving series as students develop their topics. Murray (1982) stressed the need for students to feel free to write as many drafts as needed.

Grant your students their writing rights: . . . The right to produce drafts. The student should have the right to write the way the writer does, through a series of evolving drafts. The student attempts a draft, reads it to see what worked and didn't work, and then writes another draft. These drafts are not failures, but represent natural stages in a journey toward meaning. (p. 175)

Producing a first draft may be the fastest part of the writing process. On the other hand, a writer may realize that more needs to be learned about the chosen topic before continuing; when this happens, prewriting is revisited. Since composing does not occur in a linear fashion, the writer may look ahead to the next draft to see what must be reworked or added (revision) or reach back to collect more information or plan a different strategy for the composition (rehearsal). Once writing has begun, the overlapping and recursive nature of the various stages of the writing process is readily evidenced.

At the drafting stage, a writer may struggle to craft words into sentences, paragraphs, and sections. The writer's concern at this time is the content—selecting and organizing ideas. Thinking and writing shape one another to construct meaning; Edward Albee (1928–), American Pulitzer Prize–winning playwright, stated, "I write to find out what I'm thinking about." Murray (1982) also noted that students gain insight into their thoughts by putting them on paper.

The writer is constantly learning from the writing what it intends to say. The writer listens for evolving meaning. . . . To learn what to do next, the writer looks within the piece of writing. . . . Writing can be a lens; if the writer looks through it, he or she will see what will make the writing more effective. (p. 21)

Thus, the first draft takes its form with an emphasis on the construction of meaningful thoughts; it is important that this stage of writing not be disturbed lest a thought of the moment be lost forever. For some writers, attending to spelling and grammar at this point would be interruptive; these mechanics can be dealt with at a later time.

When students actually begin drafting, teachers can guide them toward using techniques that will facilitate their work-in-progress. For example, drafts can be written on lined paper, using every other line and leaving large margins. This format makes revision easier; but, more important, it announces at the onset the writer's intent to make changes. Another tool that is practical and fun for students to use is the DRAFT stamp. If teachers keep a rubber DRAFT stamp handy and encourage its use after modeling for students how best to use it, students are more likely to believe that it is all right to share drafts with others. This technique has been particularly successful with students who are oriented toward perfectionism. The DRAFT stamp becomes the student's license to get thoughts down on paper without concern for creating a perfect product. Of course, developing writers seem to feel less pressure when a draft becomes bona fide with the press of the stamp. A portion of one teacher's first draft, which served as a model for her students, appears in Figure 4.1.

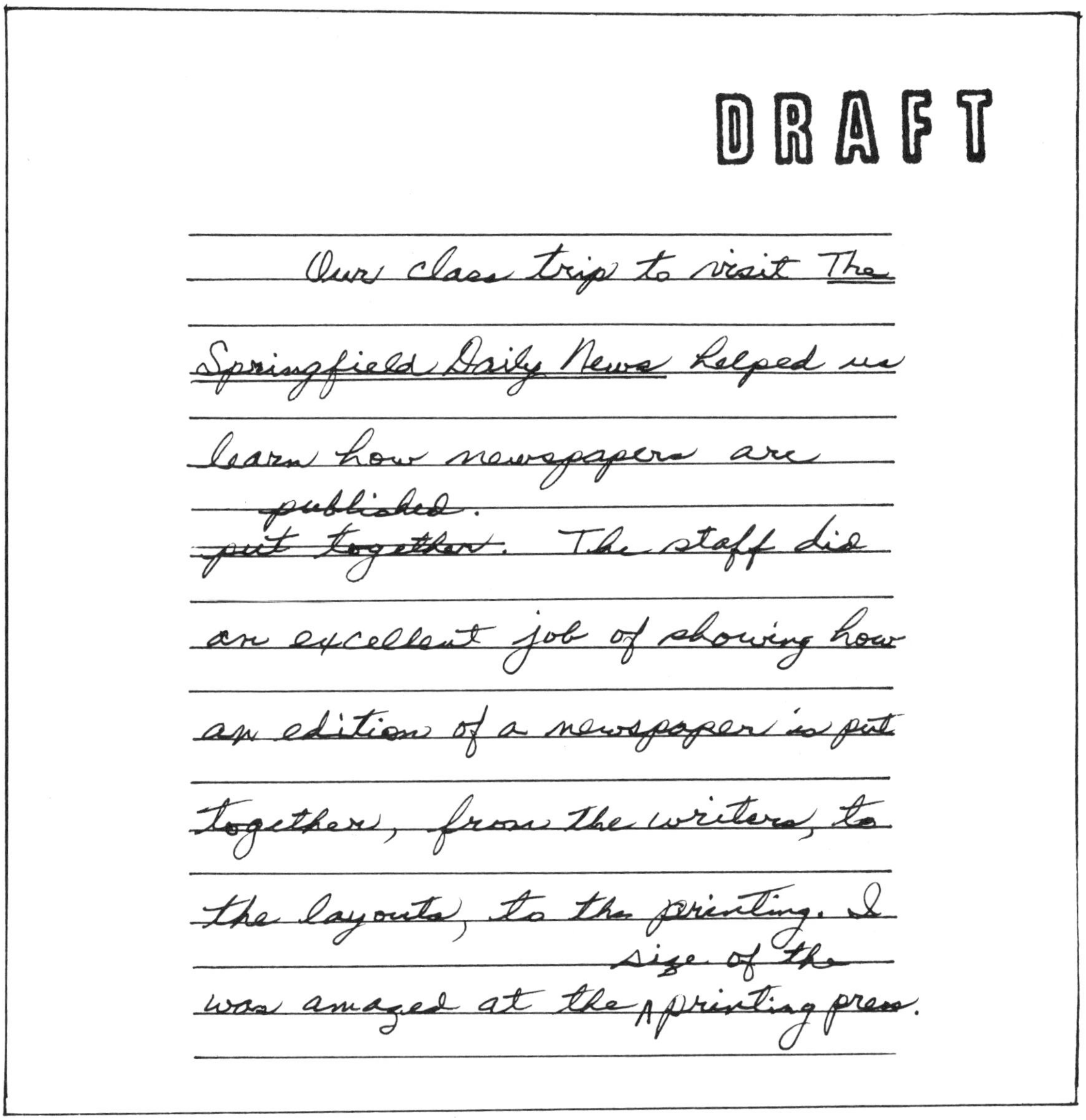

FIGURE 4.1 Portion of a Teacher's First Draft

Model Activity 4.1 was designed to help students get started on a first draft and examine their reasons for learning to write well. Model Activity 4.2 offers an opportunity for free writing practice, allowing for individual and personal thoughts to be expressed in a first draft.

Many opportunities exist for writing instruction to be a daily experience in the classroom. Students in Linda Jemison Smith's classroom at Troy Elementary School in Troy, Alabama, enjoy sharing their poems and stories from the Author's Chair. Smith (1990) modeled writing for her students by composing the following literacy vignette, "The Author's Chair":

> Do you like the Author's Chair?
> It sits and waits for me.
> I think, I write, then write again,
> The chair—it waits for me.
>
> I work hard as an author,
> I write and do my best.
> When I'm in the Author's Chair,
> I become the guest.
>
> I take my seat, I'm very proud,
> I'll read my works for you.
> When I'm in the Author's Chair,
> My dreams—they all come true.[*]

Smith helped her students see how she felt as an author and teacher by modeling poetry writing. Professional writers of literature read by students also serve as models for student writers and offer insights to teachers regarding instruction. In a collection of interviews with selected authors of adolescent literature edited by Weiss (1979), interviewer Paul Janeczko asked author Milton Meltzer the following question: "In your opinion, what is the essence of good writing?" Meltzer's reply was as follows:

I think, to speak in your own true voice, and that's the hardest thing to find. I never think mechanically of something that people label "style." Whatever that may be comes out of your own experience, and the influences you have been subject to, as a reader first of all, from your early years on. On paper you really find out what you think and what you feel; you often don't know that until you try to put it down on paper. Sometimes you are very much surprised about what emerges. (p. 69)

Pechan (1991) described how one elementary school generated interest and growth in writing by inviting a professional author to inspire developing writers to tell their personal stories through process-based writing. After a successful one-day visit by author Elaine Moore, sharing the magic of writing with students, teachers, and parents, this school made plans to have the author return to work directly with students for a full week the following year. This writer-in-residency program gave students and teachers time to participate with the professional in all stages of writing and to see these stages through an author's eyes. The enthusiasm of the week translated into improved teaching and writing after the week ended; Pechan reported the following response from one group of teachers:

We can now look at literature through an author's eyes and writing through a reader's eyes. Because they had been shown and not told how strongly writing and reading affect each other, they were now able to make that connection *with* their students and not *for* them. (p. 34; emphasis in the original)

Any school or class can look to its own community for professional writers who may be invited to visit and share with students, whether it be for one class period or an extended period of time.

THE STUDENT WRITER

Murray (1982) offered the following definition: "A student writer is an individual who is learning to use language to discover meaning in experience and communicate it" (p. 11). Ideally, the responsibility for learning shifts progressively from the teacher to the student; the writing draft offers one of the best opportunities for students to make this transition in adapting independently to their environment. Middle school students, experiencing a period of accelerated growth, come to the classroom with tremendous variation in interests, aptitudes,

---

[*]*Source:* From "Literacy Vignette: The Author's Chair" by Linda Jemison Smith, *The Reading Teacher, 44*(1), p. 74. Reprinted with permission of Linda Jemison Smith and the International Reading Association.

and abilities; a good program of individualized instruction is essential to meet their needs. As Calkins (1986) said, "Human beings have a deep need to represent their experience through writing. We need to make our truths beautiful. . . . We write because we want to understand our lives" (p. 3). Model Activity 4.3 was designed to provide students with an experience of drawing on their individual interests and expectations as they practice a writing draft.

Middle school students should experience all modes of discourse. Narrative, descriptive, expository, and persuasive writing are among the modes used when students write for a variety of purposes, for a variety of audiences, and in a variety of forms. Paired writing assignments and projects in which students produce joint compositions are especially effective in the middle school grades (Mangieri, Staley, & Wilhide, 1984). Students of this age are often beginning to find their own writing a satisfying means of expression, and they look to others for advice about improvement. When S. E. Hinton, au-

thor of *The Outsiders,* was asked in an interview by William Walsh (Weiss, 1979) if any of the youngsters who wrote to her asked about their own writing, she gave this response.

Yes, they do. A lot of them want to write and don't know where to begin. I always say that, first of all, they've got to read. Just read everything. I never studied writing consciously. But if you read a lot, like I did, subconsciously, structure is going to drop into your head, whether it's sentence structure, paragraph structure, chapter structure, or novel structure. Pretty soon, you're going to know where things go—where the climax is supposed to be, where the ending's supposed to be, how to get there, how to describe people. You can absorb it subconsciously. I, personally, never tried to copy any one person's style because I feel you should write the way you think. But reading lots of different styles will expose you to different ways of thinking. My big recommendation is to read and then practice. Write yourself. I wrote for eight years before I wrote *The Outsiders.* I advise writing for oneself. If you don't want to read it, nobody else is going to read it. (pp. 36–37)

WRITING FOR MEANING

The goal of all writing is to construct meaning for ourselves and to communicate that meaning to others. When we write, we generate ideas, thoughts, and images. We create an order to these thoughts, which we then express in writing. If we have translated well, then the reader is more likely to comprehend fully our intended ideas. Figure 4.2 shows the various language processes.

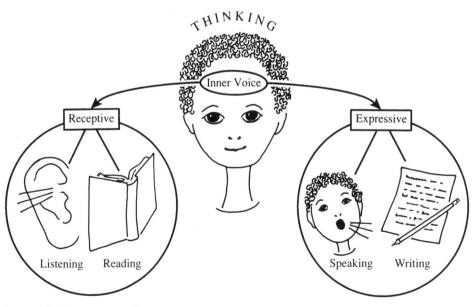

FIGURE 4.2 Language Processes

Each person uses a private inner language to think (Vygotsky, 1962). With our "inner voice," as Vygotsky called it, we talk to ourselves to reinforce our own concrete experiences; to link our experiences to those of another as that person talks or we read another's words; and to recall, order, and monitor as we express ourselves in oral speech or writing. From concrete experience—to oral language—and to written language, the process of making meaning with language becomes more abstract and more subject to standardized language forms.

Of the language processes—listening, reading, speaking, and writing—writing is most closely related to speaking (Mykelbust, 1973). This is because writing and speaking are both expressive, requiring the speaker or writer to generate personal images, thoughts, and ideas to be expressed through words, sentences, and paragraphs. Through the language processes of listening and reading, meaning is constructed from information provided; one's inner voice is used to read what was written, to listen internally to hear what was written, and to check internally to determine if the written words do make sense.

The inexperienced writer may lack practice using an inner voice to check internally and coordinate the language processes of writing, listening, reading, and speaking, as well as the mechanical aspects of writing: spelling, grammar, punctuation, and capitalization. The writing problems of many students stem largely from a lack of experience in coordinating these complex processes. The developing writer may get discouraged with the mechanical processes before adequately thinking through the meaning to be communicated; when this happens, the result often is a text of short, choppy sentences or long, rambling sentences with many mechanical errors. As indicated earlier in this chapter, capitalization, punctuation, spelling, and grammatical forms may be distractions to the creative meaning-making process of drafting. Therefore, at this stage, students should be allowed to risk making mechanical errors while concentrating on the flow of language.

Over time, with much practice, writers mature and learn to integrate the many tasks of writing. In the meantime, an effective teacher can help students concentrate on one aspect at a time and further aid them by placing a priority on their desire to create meaningful, interesting texts. Drafting is the time for writers to get their ideas down on paper; later, they can check to see if the ideas make sense and whether they have made spelling, punctuation, or other mechanical errors. Teachers expect students' writing to have errors; these errors should be utilized as teaching/learning opportunities at the proper time. Maimon (1988) advised that "when we look at a student's first try at a difficult assignment, we should shift our focus away from 'what this is not' to 'what you can make this become'" (p. 734). Model Activity 4.4 provides an opportunity to practice writing for meaning while producing a first draft.

THE TEACHER'S ROLE

Marva N. Collins (1991), a dedicated teacher and founder and director of the inner-city Westside Preparatory School in Chicago, stated the following:

I teach because I believe Plato was right when he said: "Education is cumulative and it affects the breed." To think that I have given a generation the torch of literacy that can be passed to their heirs is truly the denouement of living. (p. 137)

The teacher who wishes to make the experience of drafting enjoyable, exciting, and successful for developing writers will work hard. This may mean reflecting on one's own attitudes about writing, positive or negative, that are often passed on to students. Almost a century ago, Rollo Walter Brown (1915), writing about composition in French schools, addressed this point. Although much progress has been made since that time in the way writing is taught, it is interesting that much of what he said is still relevant.

We are strangely illogical. If we do even the smallest piece of writing ourselves, we think upon it, and only after we have digested it thoroughly do we venture to write. Nevertheless, when we assign a theme, which, to begin with, is looked upon by the pupil as a mere task set by someone else, we frequently do not discuss the material in any thoroughgoing manner, and we do not always show the pupil how he might become interested in his subject by talking to his classmates and friends about it. We do not help him far in getting ideas, save in a very general way, and we hesitate to put a plan on the blackboard, lest he copy it and use it. We give him only the lightest straw to clutch—sometimes only a title of four or five words—yet expect him to come out safely, and to find pleasure in the struggle. He probably does neither. His mind is unaccustomed to catching up stray ideas and putting them in order. He may not even do his best in trying to learn how. He writes what little is in his mind, or fits together some ideas that he has garbled from a book, and calls the result his "composition." Then we spend many precious minutes showing him, or trying to show him, how to tear his ideas all apart and rewrite them into a new theme. Certainly there is little pedagogical or personal defense for our practice. If the teacher helps his pupils to enrich, quicken, and organize their material before they begin to write, he not only stimulates them to their best efforts, but saves himself infinite pains. (pp. 222–223)

Writing drafts should be as individual as the students who compose them and will vary according to students' individual development, their skill, and their involvement with the task. A concerned teacher who observes students as they are drafting can learn much about what each student is doing that is helping or hindering the process of composing. This teacher further observes when and where to intervene in order to help a student develop a more efficient method of writing. Tonjes (1991) suggested that the role of today's writing teacher is, first, to help students recognize their own strengths, and, next, to encourage them to work on particular weaknesses—a few at a time. Although students will not produce perfect products each time with this approach, they will be working toward becoming more confident, purposeful writers as they practice. And creativity, individual development, and expression of new ideas will have a rightful place in their writing drafts. Referring to the importance of a teacher's role, Albert Einstein is attributed with having said that the supreme art of the teacher is to awaken joy in creative expression and knowledge.

Graser (1983) shared suggestions of ways that teachers can help students make the transition from prewriting to drafting.

Beginning writers may need the teacher to sense with them the moment when they can move from thinking of what they want to say into drafting. The teacher may intervene, remind of a deadline, and encourage the writer to see what it looks like on paper. (p. 69)

A writer who is at a standstill in the first draft may need to be directed to further prewriting or an ex-amination of notes in the writing folder or journal. Or, if the student is stuck on the opening sentence, the suggestion to work on the ending or another part of the draft may be all that is needed to get the developing writer started. Murray (1982) emphasized that one can work on a piece of writing only after completing a draft.

All writing is experimental. There is little anyone can say before an experiment begins, because no one knows how it will work out. The teacher can help the student see what works and doesn't work in a draft only after it is completed. (p. 175)

There are other times when teachers must intervene to help writers who are struggling with a first draft. Perhaps a chosen topic isn't working well and needs to be reconsidered; this is a good opportunity to teach students that real situations or subjects that they want to talk about and explore further almost always make the best topic choices. Unless a chosen topic is of genuine interest to the student, it probably will never evolve fully. Providing relevant pictures, charts, graphs, or maps can often give students nonverbal information that is useful to them as an impetus for their developing drafts. Many teachers suggest joint writing projects, which allow flexibility among individual students and encourage working with a partner or in small groups during drafting. The reluctant or timid writer often feels more secure writing on a common class topic, while at the same time drawing from his or her own experiences and interests to create a draft. Of course, when using joint writing projects, it is important to make sure that each writer believes that he or she has a contribution to make—that is, has something to say that is worth sharing. The teacher may also help a student choose an appropriate form for the developing draft. Sometimes a poem is a good choice, whereas other drafts may be more successful if written as a first-person account or a fictional story. All intervention by the teacher to motivate writers to produce drafts is best accomplished if the goal is to empower students to make good choices rather than depending on the teacher to make assignments.

Teachers who write with their students *know* that writing is challenging but rewarding, and they pass this valuable insight along to their students through modeling. Students quickly learn that when people write, they work hard. They may become frustrated

"It's worse than it looks...That's just the *first* draft."

Source: "Laugh Parade," June 23, 1991, *Parade Magazine,* p. 17. © 1992; Reprinted courtesy of Bunny Hoest and Parade Magazine.

and discard parts of their drafts, they talk with other people about their ideas, and they rewrite; eventually, however, a draft evolves that they are proud of and wish to share with others.

As students develop their drafts, keep in mind that all will not finish at the same time; and time schedules must be met. Unfinished drafts should be kept in student writing folders so that students are free to write when they have extra time and when they have the urge to continue composing.

The evolution of writing drafts takes time, and the demands of any busy classroom are tremendous. To devote adequate time daily to writing, Maimon (1988) suggested that classroom practices reflect the concept of work-in-progress and that "we then read early drafts with an eye to responding to the seeds of thought that might be ready for cultivation" (p. 735).

To build able writers, we must remember that internal motivation is the ideal, while we provide encouragement where needed at the various stages of writing. Of course, students of any age appreciate praise; and, as the old saying goes, "Nothing succeeds like success." As teachers form the habit of modeling good writing and providing feedback on students' work-in-progress, such as brief comments, praise, and questions, there will be less need for extensive grading and correcting of mechanical errors on writing papers because students will be involved actively in developing their own drafts through a process that is oriented toward success. Ideally, students are developing as writers while learning the subject matter. Thus, the integration of writing with learning can take place across the curriculum—in social studies, science, math, art, or any other area of study.

WRITING DRAFTS IN THE CONTENT AREAS

Tonjes (1991) noted that study-writing has been shown to improve thinking, learning, and reading. There is no better way to master a body of knowledge than to write about it. Teachers have the opportunity to take advantage of this role of writing by using writing across the curriculum to assist students' overall learning. Composing not only helps students comprehend better and see relation-

ships among ideas, but also brings about the organization of their ideas. Furthermore, incorporating writing with content area study gives variety, motivation, and personal interest to assignments. History or social studies teachers might select, for example, biographical sketches of famous people to learn more about a particular era or topic. Model Activity 4.5 incorporates a writing assignment with learning about George Washington Carver and his work.

Writing is often used to think. Fulwiler (1982) pointed out that people from all walks of life think by writing, from penciled notes to material stored in computers. The ability to ask appropriate questions leads to comprehension; thus, writing to learn occurs when students jot down questions they would like to have answered. Writing predictions based on given clues and then checking to discover if they were right can contribute to learning in many subject areas. Notetaking to remember, writing to organize material, and first drafts about topics of interest to students are other examples of writing to learn. Some teachers find that having students use learning logs for each of their subject areas is valuable. The form of the logs—notebooks, cards, or files—does not matter, but it is important that the logs are used for learning in the subject areas rather than as a means of checking on what students already know. The value of this thinking and learning is enhanced when students discover a topic to develop further in the form of a written composition such as a poem, essay, or report. Furthermore, writing can serve as a vehicle for thinking as students explore the various content areas and develop their cultural literacy.

Writing and Reading

Research and theory support the practice of integrating writing and reading instruction. Much of this emphasis on the writing–reading connection comes from studies of "early readers"—those who learn to read and write before they enter school. Durkin (1966) studied early readers and found that their scribbling and writing before starting school contributed to their success in learning to read at an earlier age than most children. From this finding she inferred that writing and reading should be taught together.

As students progress through the grades, the advantages of the reading–writing connection become even more evident. Dionisio (1983) found that writing not only caused gains in reading achievement, but also had a powerful motivational effect. She found that teaching reading through writing was the best approach for her "turned off to reading" sixth-grade remedial students. When she modeled writing with the students and gave them ample opportunities to read their own works as well as the writing of their classmates and their teacher, the students'

reading abilities improved—even without formal reading instruction. Advocates of the whole language approach to learning certainly recommend teaching writing and reading together, using material that has relevant meaning for students (Goodman, 1986).

May (1990) found that students' motivation to learn improved by moving from a traditional reading emphasis to a writing emphasis. Writing, with its many opportunities for decision making while choosing a title or a topic, deciding on a plot, creating characters, or developing good arguments, gives students the right to make decisions and to take control. This setting provides autonomy, especially helpful for remedial students, and presents a school setting where, with proper teaching conditions and strategies, students can learn to really enjoy writing! Strong (1991) suggested that content area reading and writing help students connect what they already know to whatever it is they are trying to learn. Writing serves to focus thinking and rehearse concepts, linking main ideas with details and organizing knowledge. This linkage contributes to long-term learning and comprehension. The act of writing is a highly demanding one and involves the author in two roles—composer and reader. As the writer is forced to slow down in order to transcribe thoughts (sentences) in a connected way, he or she often discovers unexpected insights and connections. And "good writers know how to take the role of reader to evaluate their own writing" (Askov & Otto, 1985, p. 267).

May (1990) advised using a different approach from the one used by many teachers when thinking about teaching reading and writing; that is, he proposed having the writing experiences precede the reading experiences. May also stressed the importance of a teacher realizing that a student's "concept of writing influences greatly his concept of reading. In fact, as he learns to write, he gradually learns what reading is all about" (p. 257). This positive motivational effect of writing before reading was reinforced by Hamann, Schultz, Smith, and White (1991), who discussed the power of autobiographical writing before reading:

When students write about relevant autobiographical experiences prior to reading, they are more on-task, offer more sophisticated responses to characters, and like the texts more. And, perhaps more important, they seem to invest more, to care more deeply about the stories and about their own reactions to literature. (p. 28)

In today's classroom, writing has become a valuable tool for thinking and a means of learning content. "Writing before starting the reading assignment can help students retrieve background knowledge that is needed to comprehend ideas in the written material. Activation of such knowledge can be beneficial to reading achievement" (Roe, Stoodt, & Burns, 1991, p. 258).

Model Activity 4.6 was designed to teach both reading and writing, using sentence combining. This technique gives practice in focusing attention on relationships between spoken and written language, helps to develop short-term memory, and gives practice in problem solving and interaction (Strong, 1991). Sentence combining is a good prereading motivator to create interest and an eagerness to learn more about a story or book to be read. Model Activity 4.6 is based on two books by Newbery Medal–winning authors. The Newbery Medal, presented in honor of an eighteenth-century British bookseller and publisher who first thought of publishing books just for children, has been given yearly since 1922 to the author of the most distinguished contribution to American literature for children. Runners-up are called Newbery Honor Books.

Writing and Mathematics

Writing, literature, and mathematics were integrated as upper elementary students built activities around a study of *Gulliver's Travels,* a novel by Jonathan Swift (1667–1745), an English writer and Anglican clergyman who lived much of his life in Ireland. In this satire on political institutions, Swift expressed his convictions through Lemuel Gulliver, a ship's physician who kept a journal of his voyages to unusual places: Lilliput, where people were only six inches tall; Brobdingnag, where people were giants and Gulliver was a Lilliputian; Laputa, where "wise" men lived; and Houyhnhnmland, where horses ran the government. These experiences convinced Gulliver that reason had been corrupted by humanity.

On the basis of Swift's classic novel, a curriculum model entitled *My Travels with Gulliver* (Education Development Center, 1991) was developed to enhance thinking and learning in mathematics while students also broadened their cultural literacy, using writing as a powerful vehicle. This curriculum model was discussed by Kliman and Klei-

man (1992). Students became notetakers and researchers traveling with Gulliver to Brobdingnag, conducting mathematical investigations and reporting this information through journal entries and stories. "Instead of learning by memorizing and practicing, students working on these activities learn by reading, discussing, imagining, creating and describing concrete models, and writing" (Kliman & Kleiman, 1992, p. 128). As students wrote drafts, describing the experiences they would encounter in a Brobdingnag environment, they actively used mathematics. Kliman and Kleiman related integrating the famous classic with mathematics as follows:

The story of Gulliver served as a springboard for students' mathematics learning. In order to understand and describe giant lands better, students learned mathematical skills and techniques such as using scale factors to calculate giant sizes, estimating large sizes, making size comparisons, and creating scale drawings. Teachers felt that their students developed new understandings about mathematics through writing, reading, and discussing stories incorporating mathematical information and relationships. Students learned to appreciate that mathematics can be used to make descriptions of people, objects, and events more meaningful. They also came to see that a mathematical perspective can enhance enjoyment of books and stories. (pp. 133–134)

Other stories can be selected to make writing an integral part of the math class. Kliman and Kleiman (1992) suggested guidelines for teachers who encourage mathematical writing:

If students are to come to view mathematics as meaningful and relevant and are to understand the role mathematics can play in stories, they must work in a communication-rich classroom environment that values the creating and sharing of mathematical writing and the expression and discussion of mathematical ideas, strategies, and imaginings. (p. 135)

Stories that contain mathematical ideas and information can be chosen, mathematical writing can be discussed and modeled, and mathematics appropriate to the story can be introduced. Student drafts often seem more realistic if students can assume the role of a character in the story. Two examples of stories containing math concepts are *The Phantom Tollbooth* by Norton Juster and *Sideways Arithmetic from Wayside School* by Louis Sachar.

Students become better equipped to understand the role that mathematics plays in their world when their writing activities lead them to listen and observe teacher modeling, read to gather information, share with others, and respond to written material. "One of the most exciting possibilities and new realities in current math teaching is the idea of students using writing to reflect on their reasoning processes" (Routman, 1991). Writing about math concepts offers students the opportunity to think about what they have been doing and make needed changes. The part that writing plays in promoting better understanding of concepts in math also occurs when writing is used for learning in any content area.

Writing and Other Content Areas

An example of how students integrated writing and science, as well as technology and art, is described by Bruce Robert Dean (1992), a Massachusetts art teacher and a 1992–1993 Christa McAuliffe Scholar. Over a six-week period, students created a computerized field guide to all the nature around their school. The outdoors became a classroom as they collected information from the plant, animal, and insect kingdoms, using field sketchbooks for making written notes and sketching drawings of plants, insects, birds, and animals. They researched their findings, then added information in their sketchbooks. They opened a database and designed the forms for recording scientific information about living things observed. When the time came to assemble the field guide, each student was responsible for writing one entry for a species of animal, bird, insect, or plant. As students finished these drafts, they were formatted with the word-processing program to fit the design of the field test. Student drawings were pasted in the final draft of the field guide. A product of this project was a bound book donated to the school library for student use and enjoyment. The most important outcome of the project, however, was stated by Dean: "Through this project my students will gain a sensitivity to the common elements of nature and learn to be keener observers of their environments. When they see an ant, they may look at it in a new way" (1992, p. 68).

Science is studied to help students understand the world in which they live through investigation and explanation of natural phenomena. Science includes health education, which helps students understand themselves. Writing can be a powerful tool for learning about the concepts, generaliza-

tions, and theories associated with scientific material. When students use writing to connect science content that they read to their own experiences, learning becomes more meaningful. Likewise, students learn from one another as they share their written drafts; for example, insights gained while problem solving and/or performing experiments can be discussed, written about, and shared again. When laboratory reports are to be written, teacher modeling by conducting an experiment and writing a cooperative laboratory report on the chalkboard or by using an overhead projector is helpful as students learn to become independent report writers. Opportunities abound while studying science for the integration of writing and cultural literacy. Whether learning about constellations, radioactivity, clouds, or earthquakes, or about the work of Einstein, Galileo, or Newton, writing is a tool to enable students to think, express their own ideas, and focus on the material being studied.

The content area of social studies includes history, geography, political science, philosophy, and sociology. In social studies, students learn about their own culture and the many other cultures that make up our world. Integrating writing, cultural literacy, and social studies is a natural avenue to help students think critically and creatively and better understand the viewpoints of others. Writing drafts, along with the ongoing sharing and responding that occurs in process writing, encourages students to develop new attitudes and better decision-making techniques. Students may come to realize they have the power to make positive changes in their own lives; for example, students may lead their families to begin a home recycling program after a study of environmental problems. Or a family preparedness plan, as described in Model Activity 4.10, could save lives. Many of the model activities presented in this book integrate social studies with writing and cultural literacy. Teachers will certainly find many opportunities for their students to integrate writing and cultural literacy as they move through the social studies curriculum.

The content areas where writing can be valuable to assist learning are not limited to those described in the preceding paragraphs. Writing is a valid means of learning any content material, including art and music, foreign language, physical education, and technology. Writing in the content areas becomes a means for gaining new knowledge and promoting retention of material studied. Along with these benefits related to learning content, fluency in writing is being acquired. With a focus on cultural literacy, the model activities in this book were designed to give teachers ideas for integrating writing instruction across the curriculum.

A SENSE OF AUDIENCE AND WRITING FORMATS

If, when reading a draft of one of your developing writers, you note that "this sounds just like Charlie," Charlie can be applauded because he has demonstrated voice. This student has gained a sense of authority and control over his topic and the writing process, shown by revealing his own voice; he is writing for himself. In like manner, the process of reading is most successful when the student can say, "That's just how I feel!" as he or she reads. This personal connection in reading and writing becomes meaningful when the reader or writer can say, "I could do that!" or "I'd like to try that."

Writing for oneself is a valuable first step in learning to write for many purposes and adjusting what one writes for an absent audience. Audience has already been addressed at the prewriting stage, but it needs to be kept in mind at each stage of the writing process. Because writing serves many functions, the writer must choose an appropriate form and constantly be aware of the absent audience involved. The writer is, therefore, both creator and reader, always rereading what has been written to be sure the absent audience will understand. The writer must first ask, "To whom am I writing?" Other questions that follow may include: "What do I need or want to say?" "How much is already known?" "What do I hope the audience will know after reading what I have written?"

Writers use many means to communicate with their audience. Some of these are listed here:

- Introductory sentences that tell the reader why the writer is writing:

I want to thank you for the great book you sent for my birthday.
I am applying for admission to your summer sports camp.

- Closing sentences that summarize what the writer has written:

I hope, then, that you and your mother will be able to pick me up from the airport next Tuesday.

- Expected formats to help the reader anticipate meaning:

Thank you for responding to my request.
To Whom It May Concern:

- Statements in personal notes that help readers know that you are adapting your writing to them.

Please call me at any time if you need a ride to school.

- Events placed in order of their occurrence.

First . . . then . . . later . . .

- Transitions created from one thought to another that help the reader's thoughts to flow with the writer's.

Therefore . . . because . . . however . . . before . . . in conclusion . . .

- Images or concrete examples evoked to describe a complex idea.

I've been holding my breath waiting for the end of the story.
This news puts me on top of the world.

Model Activity 4.7 was designed to help student writers think like readers when writing. Model Activity 4.8 was constructed to demonstrate voice and develop audience awareness. This activity is intended to be used over time.

Audience awareness requires the writer to consider the audience's experiences and level of understanding before creating a meaningful context in which words can be understood. Some words have multiple meanings, and it is only through the writer's good use of context that the intended meaning is revealed. For instance, when one writes, "It was hot," the reader must have other information to know which of the following is meant:

It was hot.

OR

It was hot.

It is also the writer's task to choose the appropriate written form for the identified audience. For example, which would better suit my purpose for this communication—a memo or a letter?

Although the functions of writing have been classified in various ways, the six functions or purposes for writing identified by Takala (1982) will be delineated in this chapter as follows: reflective, documentative, expressive, artistic, informative, and persuasive. Many types of writing overlap in function; for example, a personal letter may be both informative and persuasive. Students should be given instruction that enables them to define each writing purpose and apply its expected conventions.

Reflective Writing

We often write for ourselves as a means of organizing our thoughts and/or providing ourselves with reminders. Reflective writing frequently requires grouping a number of items for practical purposes. Students use reflective writing when they jot reminders about homework assignments in their notebooks or keep a list of telephone numbers of friends. Prewriting activities, such as those presented as models in Chapter 3, often require reflective writing—for example, brainstorming lists or clusters to identify a topic about which to write. Also, given that much of journal writing is reflective, Chapter 9 includes a section describing use of the reflective journal. That section of Chapter 9 describes how students are led to find their own voices by using a three-step model of thinking to reflect their own beliefs and opinions. Reflective writing encourages thinking and is another means of putting students in touch with themselves and their feelings. Activity 4.9 asks students to reflect on their personal belongings in order to place them in a more orderly arrangement. Activity 4.10 requires reflective thinking to determine the best plan for a home fire drill; the writing becomes informative, also, as each student's fire drill plan is completed.

Documentative Writing

Although documentative writing usually does not require complex composing skills, certain types of writing skills are required. When reporting what was witnessed at an accident, for instance, it becomes important to separate facts from opinions

and generalizations. And a knowledge of how to fill out forms properly will be a valuable asset later when your students use checking accounts, apply for needed services, complete job application forms, and the like. Some important concepts to teach students about most forms are as follows:

- The purpose for most forms is documentative, requiring a person to give personal information in a standardized format. Forms often become legal papers when signed.
- Accuracy and neatness are important because errors could have legal or other important consequences. A miswritten telephone number or address could prevent a person from receiving services. Misspelled words on a job application may put the job seeker at the bottom of the list of considered applicants.
- Forms are standardized; once a person practices filling out a particular type, writing one the next time will be easier.
- Before filling out an important new form, students should write their answers on a separate sheet of scratch paper or on a blank photocopy of the form, correct any errors, and then copy their answers neatly in the appropriate places on the form.
- Each type of form has its own special vocabulary that students need to learn.
- Date, address, telephone number, date of birth, Social Security number, and signature are predictable requests that each person should be prepared to write.

Model Activity 4.11 offers students practice in filling out two forms: an application for a library card and a job application.

Expressive Writing

Expressive writing is the way people communicate with one another most often; it is much like written speech. Britton (1972) described writing in the expressive voice as being much like conversation and as the form used most often by young children and beginning writers. Students using the expressive voice often write as if they know their readers; they assume their readers know the same things they know; and they feel that their readers are personally interested in them. Britton (1972) described writing in the expressive voice as focusing on the writer's personal ideas, feelings, and experiences.

Expressive writing conveys attitudes, emotions, mood, and so forth. Personal letters, notes, and cards are usually expressive; of course, they may be informative or persuasive as well. Good expressive writing takes advantage of the skillful use of description. Model Activity 4.12 allows students to express their viewpoints about their rights as citizens as found in the Bill of Rights.

Artistic Writing

Creating a poem, a short story, a tall tale, or an essay falls into the category of artistic writing, although any piece of writing might have other functions also—for instance, being persuasive or informative. Poetry is a medium for experimentation in writing that generally allows students to experience success. Poetry is similar to oral language in that it relies on rhythm, intonation, concrete images, and personal description. Students have used oral communication to describe personal events, persuade others, and share information. When students write poetry in the classroom, they should be encouraged to practice prewriting before starting their drafts just as they do in other kinds of writing. Also keep in mind that students who experience success in prose forms will most likely enjoy the adventure of creating verse.

Burk (1992, p. 27) made the following four observations about what poets do.

1. Poets make decisions about rhyme.
2. Poets arrange their words on the page to suit their own purposes.
3. Poets say things in ways they have never been said before.
4. Poets revise.

These observations were made after ten years of teaching writing, including six years at the seventh-grade level. Recognizing the importance of poetry as a means of expression, Burk has made it an integral part of his writing classes; "and I want the poet's habits of arranging words purposefully and choosing them boldly to influence all my students' writing—poetry or not" (p. 31).

If students are to appreciate poetry and become writers of poetry, it might be wise to follow the advice of Mary Yanaga George (1970), who recommended that "the teacher does some of the work, but Robert Frost and Carl Sandburg do more and better" (p. 94). Exposure to a variety of good poetry is the best preparation for students to develop a feeling for poetry as a writing form. The reading of poetry aloud by teacher and students encourages an appreciation for it. As favorite poems are being read aloud, some listeners may want to follow along with a copy in hand; in any case, it's a good idea for everyone to have a copy to store in the writing folder for rereading. Most poems bring more pleasure and understanding to the reader when read more than once; as one middle school student shared, "My feelings and emotions surfaced after I reread a poem about justice that I first heard in class."

Students discover that poetry is very personal, and the same poem may have different meanings for different individuals, depending on their past experiences. DeHaven (1983) defined poetry as "more a feeling than a form. It is not written just to be read; it is written to be experienced. . . . It is [a poet's] *response to something* rather than *a report of something*" (p. 219; emphasis in the original). Blake (1992) wrote of his conviction that virtually all humans can learn, through poetry, how to express feelings; live, work, and love others; and listen to others in order to share their thoughts.

Through writing poetry we may witness the miraculous reality around us, use words to reveal the human condition, and tell people some things they didn't know or hadn't themselves put into words before. But we write poems in order to know. At the core of myself as a person is the capacity for access to my feeling life. (p. 20)

Students come to learn that writing good poetry usually requires honesty and simplicity, and that poems can be funny or very serious. DeHaven (1983) suggested that students write group poems to involve them in writing poetry in a supportive setting. Through this vehicle, they are encouraged to share their opinions, feelings, and emotions. One way to begin this is through a teacher-guided discussion of a topic with phrases or sentences voluntaered by students; they will be able to observe the poem taking shape as offered material is recorded on the chalkboard. Another type of group poem suggested by DeHaven consists of short, individually written responses (one- or two-line rhyming couplets) combined into one poem.

Spiegel (1991), writing about materials to introduce children to poetry, said the following:

If children are encouraged to become poets, they must be allowed to experiment freely with different forms, rhythms, and images. Insistence on strict adherence to a particular pattern (rhyming, diamante, etc.) may frustrate budding poets and surely will place form as more important than content in the minds of young authors. (p. 42)

When students are allowed to respond to poetry in their own ways, their responses will differ. For any poem heard, one student may notice the sound of the words or the imagery, another will focus on the rhythm, while yet another may react to the overall message of the poem. Since poetry offers such an excellent opportunity for students to create meaning for themselves, it is best that teachers resist the temptation to impose their own meaning; when teachers offer their interpretations, they should speak as fellow learners, not as authorities. As Tom Hansen (1992) advised,

. . . We need to extricate ourselves from the role of Keepers of the Meaning and to turn poems over to our students. Any activity we devise, as long as it motivates them to explore their own way into a poem until they begin to experience it imaginatively, will serve this purpose. (p. 24)

Three ways of exploring poems by involving students actively in the process were suggested by Tom Hansen (1992): "Draw me a picture of the poem, . . . make a video of the poem [that might include a script], . . . [and] perform the poem as if it were a play" (pp. 24–25).

Model Activity 4.13 takes students through the process of creating a first draft of a poem; this activity can be used more than once. Poetry can be taught in different ways; for example, many students would like to become song writers. They enjoy writing new lyrics to existing tunes or pop hits. They may even go on to form a musical group to perform the numbers they write. Model Activity 4.14 focuses on a folktale told in ballad form.

An eighth-grade teacher in a Texas middle school related how she discovered a technique that motivated her students to read and write poetry (Kiaune, 1992). Noticing that her students enjoyed circulating personal photos among classmates, Kiaune decided to turn this interest of middle schoolers into an opportunity to teach poetry, using their collections of photos as textbooks for the week. Cooperative learning groups of three shared photos and asked questions that often required the owner of the photo to relive the scene. "My students rediscovered the feelings and emotions of a familiar

experience through a concrete association, and I gained invaluable insight into their lives" (p. 70). Students then selected one photo and began prewriting by mapping descriptive words and phrases appropriate to their photo. These words and phrases became poetic descriptions that evolved into short poems. Students framed their photos with their poetry alongside. Kiaune observed, "Because their project was based on emotional ownership, my eighth graders recreated the experience freely through concrete imagery. The simple result was 'phoetry'" (p. 71).

Most writing in the classroom will draw on students' own experiences and should be seen as a means for personal growth and the communication of ideas with others. Developing writers can be encouraged to experience the various kinds of artistic composition—the short story, poem, essay, and tall tale—in their class activities. And some may want to give fiction writing a try. Calkins (1986) warned that it is not easy to give students successful experiences with the writing of fiction, particularly in the upper elementary and middle school grades. Their rough drafts often go on and on, with endless detail or no detail at all, and their chosen topics are often sensational, "far-out" subjects about which they know very little. It seems students often think that writing fiction means writing the opposite of the truth. Calkins (1986) offered the following insights about teaching fiction writing to students:

. . . My first priority would be to help them write from feelings and insights that matter to them; my second priority would be to help them create and attend closely to their own fictional dreams. I would teach the components of fiction—plot, character development, mood, setting, etc.—only as parts of this dream. Rather than discussing character development one day and plot another, I would try to show children that each of these elements is woven into the fabric of fiction. I would want children to understand that fiction means creating a motion picture of one's own, and that we create this motion picture by standing in our characters' shoes, and by feeling with their hearts. (p. 325)

"Students need to examine and appreciate models of quality fiction before they can be expected to write fiction themselves" (Routman, 1991, p. 167). Teachers can guide students to notice the way an author has created a mood in a fictional work. Observing the settings and main characters, the descriptive words and phrases used, and the beginnings of good stories by published authors provides students with insights into what authors do when writing fiction. Studying fiction gives teachers wonderful opportunities to introduce relevant cultural literacy writing activities, such as creating story maps of selected authors' works, comparing various versions of traditional folktales and fairytales, and comparing and analyzing characters. Although great literature provides the best models of language, examples of high-quality writing by students and teachers are also useful as models for others.

Students will find that fiction writing usually will be more successful if they write from experience, dealing with interests and concerns of their own age group. Before drafting fictional stories, prewriting is an important and useful stage for the writer; for example, drawing a picture of the main character, along with descriptive notes, helps the writer visualize the character when writing drafts. "Because students knew one another's characters through the pictures and brief accompanying notes, subsequent suggestions to peers for revisions were specific and helpful" (Routman, 1991, p. 182). Another useful prewriting activity to use before drafting fiction is to create a story map that leads students to think about the main events of the story and to plan an ending. Student–teacher conferencing before writing drafts may help students produce stories that are more focused and better organized. Of course, it is important that teacher comments be selected carefully to ensure that the student retains ownership of all drafts. If peer sharing of fictional drafts follows, feedback from others may help writers identify strengths and weaknesses in their drafts.

Beautiful picture books have a universal appeal to people of all ages. One interesting technique for using picture books to encourage fictional writing was described by Miletta (1992):

Classroom teachers in the intermediate grades can use picture books to illustrate writing techniques and to expose students to models of literary forms. Children can discover elements of plot, setting, character, style, theme, and humor by comparing and contrasting folk and fairy tales, myths and legends, and fantasy and realistic fiction. Wordless picture books can provide vivid imagery for students to write original stories suitable for younger children. (p. 555)

Selection of picture books with appropriate topics is vital to success in motivating upper grade students to write. Miletta suggested stories of war and peace, the environment, relationships between generations, and self-development—topics to inspire "students to extend their own learning, lead to their own discussions, and write their own stories" (p. 556).

The value of humor in the learning environment is often underestimated. Because early literary memories are often funny ones, teachers can encourage students to make use of humor, when appropriate, in their writing. Burke (1986) said that a sense of humor is developmental but also highly individual; students in the same age group will probably laugh at the same things, but within any group, individuals will also laugh at different things. We are all familiar with the delightful ways that authors and illustrators bring smiles to the faces of the readers of their works. Burke also suggested the following list of major comic elements that can be used by student writers who wish to add humor to their writing: "visual exaggeration, plot or character exaggeration, verbal exaggeration, nonsense, surprise, incongruity and illogic, ludicrous situations, slapstick, and word play" (pp. 122–123).

Informative Writing

Informative writing is used to convey information such as in a report, a business letter, a memo, or a note. The writer must learn to be clear and concise so that the reader will know what is to be done with the information. To help students conceptualize the goals of informative writing, one useful prewriting technique is to provide a role-playing experience, requiring one student to give directions or information to another who is unaware of the speaker's intentions. Model Activity 4.15 provides an opportunity for students to draft an informative note, giving directions.

Many real situations that occur from day to day in the classroom can provide settings for worthwhile informative writing sessions. For example, there might be the need to draft a memo to the principal giving information about the student-authored poetry from your class on display at City Hall. Another example might be writing a letter to the editor of the local newspaper to inform others about a special recycling project. Real needs always provide the best writing opportunities for students—that is, when they can convey a real message to a real audience.

Persuasive Writing

Consumer complaints, letters to the editor, advertisements, and job application letters are all examples of persuasive writing, targeted to influence others. Audience awareness is very important in persuasive writing.

Letter Writing

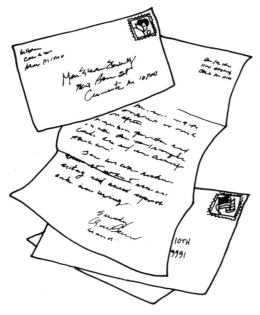

One of the most important reasons for learning to write well is to be able to communicate through letters. Students should be encouraged to write different kinds of letters, business and personal, and to develop the proper attitudes, habits, and skills necessary for letter writing. Many opportunities exist

for students to practice writing various kinds of letters: letters inviting speakers to the class, thank-you letters following school trips or to speakers, friendly letters to ill classmates, or invitations to parents and friends to attend some class project or play. Kay W. Bindrim (1991), a teacher of grades 6 and 7, offered a suggestion that will contribute much toward student writing becoming a real experience when she advised keeping a file of important and often-used addresses in the writing center of the classroom. The file might include addresses of the president, governor, mayor, and other government officials; the school principal, teachers, and staff; museums and zoos; area businesses; local authors and artists. Add others to represent your area. Students will eagerly go to the address file as they choose to write to real people or organizations.

Two excellent ideas targeting real audiences for student letter writing were provided by Marna Bunce-Crim (1992). The first suggestion is for teachers gathering materials for a planned teaching unit:

Let your students do the work! The next time you're planning a unit on the environment, for instance, explain your plans to the class and have them compose letters requesting free materials from local environmental agencies. It's a great way to involve students in a unit of study before it even begins. (p. 18)

The second idea, if your school is near a college or university, is to "try teaming up with instructors in the education department. Your students will enjoy writing letters to college students, and the undergraduates will get a firsthand view of developing writers that no lecture course could provide" (Bunce-Crim, 1992, p. 18). Formats for personal and business letters, along with the opportunity for students to practice drafting letters and envelopes, are presented in Model Activities 4.16 and 4.17.

CONCLUSION

Drafting and translating become a part of the writing process when developing writers begin to take ownership of their writing. Consider the timely advice of Jane Hansen (1992), who stated:

To understand that a written piece of information could

usually contain more—that it contains whatever the author decided to put in and that the author's decisions about what to put in may not necessarily match the decisions that all readers would have made if they had written it—is a basic understanding about the nature of print that carries writers beyond the rough drafts of their community into the final drafts of professional writers. (p. 102)

Calkins (1986) advised that for first drafts, "the goal is fluency, voice, and an organizing image" (p. 289). Students at all grade levels should be presented with writing techniques to help them in the process of developing a style of their own.

This chapter has presented a variety of writing formats to accommodate some of the many purposes served in writing. An effective classroom writing program shows the various forms of expository writing that exist in the real world and gives the students practice emulating them. To ensure student success in writing drafts, the successful classroom teacher will provide support and encouragement while allowing students to tackle real problems in written communication.

REFERENCES

Askov, E. N., & Otto, W. (1985). *Meeting the challenge.* Columbus, OH: Merrill.

Bindrim, K. W. (1991). Write about it. *The Mailbox, 13*(2), Intermediate, p. 11. Greensboro, NC: The Education Center.

Blake, R. W. (1992). Poets on poetry: The morality of poetry. *English Journal, 81*(1), 16–20.

Britton, J. (1972). *Language and learning.* New York: Penguin Books.

Brown, R. W. (1915). *How the French boy learns to write: A study in the teaching of the mother tongue.* Cambridge, MA: Harvard University Press.

Bunce-Crim, M. (1992). Real writing for real audiences. *Instructor, 101*(8), 18.

Burk, D. (1992). Teaching the terrain of poetry. *English Journal, 81*(3), 26–31.

Burke, E. M. (1986). *Early childhood literature: For love of child and book.* Boston: Allyn and Bacon.

Calkins, L. M. (1986). *The art of teaching writing.* Portsmouth, NH: Heinemann.

Collins, M. N. (1991). Why I teach. *The Educational Forum, 55*(2), 135–138.

Dean, B. R. (1992). Take technology outdoors. *Instructor, 101*(9), 66–68.

DeHaven, E. P. (1983). *Teaching and learning the language arts,* 2nd ed. Boston: Little, Brown.

Dionisio, M. (1983). Write? Isn't this reading class? *The Reading Teacher, 36,* 746–750.

Durkin, D. (1966). *Children who read early: Two longitudinal studies.* New York: Teachers College Press.

Education Development Center. (1991). *My travels with Gulliver.* Scotts Valley, CA: Wings for Learning.

Fulwiler, T. (1982). Writing: An act of cognition. In K. Erle & J. Noonan (Eds.), *Teaching writing in all disciplines.* San Francisco: Jossey-Bass.

George, M. Y. (1970). *Language art.* Scranton, PA: Chandler.

Goodman, K. (1986). *What's whole in whole language?* Portsmouth, NH: Heinemann.

Graser, E. R. (1983). *Teaching writing: A process approach.* Dubuque, IA: Kendall/Hunt.

Hamann, L. S., Schultz, L., Smith, M. W., & White, B. (1991).

Making connections: The power of autobiographical writing before reading. *Journal of Reading, 35*(1), 24–28.

Hansen, J. (1992). The language of challenge: Readers and writers speak their minds. *Language Arts, 69*(2), 100–105.

Hansen, T. (1992). Reclaiming the body: Teaching modern poetry. *English Journal, 81*(1), 21–26.

Kiaune, J. A. (1992). "Phoetry" in the middle school. *English Journal, 81*(3), 70–71.

Kliman, M., & Kleiman, G. M. (1992). Life among the giants: Writing, mathematics, and exploring Gulliver's world. *Language Arts, 69*(2), 128–136.

Laugh Parade. (1991). *Parade Magazine.* New York: Parade Publications, June 23, p. 17.

Maimon, E. P. (1988, June). Cultivating the prose garden. *Phi Delta Kappan, 69*(10), 734–739.

Mangieri, J. N., Staley, N. K., & Wilhide, J. A. (1984). *Teaching language arts.* New York: McGraw-Hill.

May, F. B. (1990). *Reading as communication: An interactive approach* (3rd ed.). Columbus, OH: Merrill.

Miletta, M. M. (1992). Picture books for older children: Reading and writing connections. *The Reading Teacher, 45*(7), 555–556.

Murray, D. M. (1982). *Learning by teaching.* Portsmouth, NH: Heinemann.

Mykelbust, H. R. (1973). *Development and disorders of written language* (Vol. 2). New York: Grune & Stratton.

National Park Service, U.S. Department of the Interior. (1990). Brochure, George Washington Carver National Monument, Missouri.

Pechan, S. (1991). The real thing: Bringing children's authors into the classroom. *Reading Today,* June–July, p. 34.

Roe, B. D., Stoodt, B. D., & Burns, P. C. (1991). *Secondary school reading instruction: The content areas,* 4th ed. Boston: Houghton Mifflin.

Routman, R. (1991). *Invitations: Changing as teachers and learners K–12.* Portsmouth, NH: Heinemann.

Smith, L. J. (1990). Literacy vignette: The author's chair. *The Reading Teacher, 44*(1), 74.

Spiegel, D. L. (1991). Materials to introduce children to poetry. *The Reading Teacher, 44*(6), 428–430.

Strong, W. J. (1991). Writing strategies that enhance reading. In

B. L. Hayes (Ed.), *Effective strategies for teaching reading.* Boston: Allyn and Bacon.

Takala, S. (1982). On the origins, communicative parameters, and processes of writing. In A. C. Purvis & S. Takala (Eds.), *An international perspective on the evaluation of written composition* (pp. 209–230). Oxford: Pergamon Press.

Tonjes, M. J. (1991). *Secondary reading, writing, and learning.* Boston: Allyn and Bacon.

Treviño, E. B. de. (1965). *I, Juan de Pareja.* Toronto: Collins.

Voigt, C. (1989). *Seventeen against the dealer.* New York: Fawcett Juniper.

Vygotsky, L. S. (1962). *Thought and language* (E. Hanfmann & G. Vakar, Translators). Cambridge, MA: MIT Press.

Weiss, M. J. (Ed.). (1979). *From writers to students: The pleasures and pains of writing.* Newark, DE: International Reading Association.

MODEL ACTIVITIES

The activities that follow are meant to serve as models; such activities should be used as part of a total learning environment. These model activities were designed to demonstrate how the writing process can be developed while expanding the writer's knowledge base and providing opportunities for the writer to think critically.

ACTIVITY 4.1

Why I Want to Learn to Write Well

Writing serves many purposes. This activity will help you discover the purposes *you* have for learning to write well. Think of the various uses you now have for writing, then imagine some writing skills needs for the future.

Prewriting: To help with your planning for writing, read over the following list of purposes for writing. Place a check mark by those you feel are important to you. Add to the list any other matters that are important to you.

_____	work I can be proud of	_____	interviews
_____	my feelings being expressed	_____	advice column
_____	my journal	_____	gossip column
_____	notes to friends	_____	advertisements
_____	letters	_____	commercials
_____	poetry	_____	comic strips
_____	stories	_____	jokes
_____	class newspaper	_____	letters to the editor
_____	books	_____	_____
_____	book reports	_____	_____
_____	skits and plays	_____	_____
_____	class reports	_____	_____

Directions: Write a paragraph on the topic "Why I Want to Learn to Write Well." Remember, *your* ideas are important. Just as professional authors write about topics and ideas that are important to them, you will find more satisfaction in writing about things of interest to you.

This is a first draft. It will *not* be graded. Write quickly so your ideas can flow freely.

_____

_____

_____

_____

_____

_____

_____

_____

_____

_____

Good Neighbors

The preamble to the Charter of the United Nations says one of the reasons that the nations of the world have united is "to practice tolerance and live together in peace with one another as good neighbors." Robert Frost's poem "Mending Wall" says that good fences make good neighbors. Find this poem and read it to see if you can discover what Frost means by that statement.

Prewriting:

1. *List* several things that make someone a good neighbor to you: _____

   _____

   _____

2. *List* some things you do that make you a good neighbor to others: _____

   _____

   _____

   _____

3. What do you think Frost meant when he said, "Good fences make good neighbors"? Read "Mending Wall" again; then write your answer to this question: _____

   _____

   _____

Writing a Draft: Now, write a paragraph or two on the topic "Good Neighbors." Tell what you think makes a good neighbor. Also discuss how you think the nations of the world can be good neighbors. Write freely; don't worry about spelling, capitalization, punctuation, and grammar. Try your best to communicate *your* ideas and feelings about the topic.

_____

_____

_____

_____

_____

_____

_____

_____

_____

_____

File your draft in your writing folder. You may want to use it for future revision, editing, and publication.

ACTIVITY 4.3

Daydreaming about My Future

We all have thought at times about different careers or types of work that we would like to experience in the future. Sometimes we've shared these ideas with our friends. Perhaps you already have changed your mind several times about plans for your life's work. Very likely, you will change your mind again before the time actually comes to make a career choice. Occasionally a person will choose a career that was selected early in life, but this is not usually the case. Most often, the lasting choice evolves as a person grows and continues in school. Just for fun, this activity involves daydreaming about some of the thoughts you have for your future.

Directions: In the first column of the following chart, list some jobs or careers that you think might be of interest to you. Then complete the second and third columns, jotting down advantages or disadvantages (or both) that might apply to each career chosen. An example is provided.

My Career	Advantages	Disadvantages
Example: doctor	service to humanity good income	many years of education needed long hours

Now, look back over your lists and put stars by those careers that you think most appeal to you. Finally, choose one career and draft a short paragraph or two to describe yourself working in that career sometime in the future. Remember, you are just pretending—but try to imagine what it would really be like to be doing the work you choose.

_____

_____

_____

_____

_____

_____

_____

_____

_____

_____

_____

_____

_____

_____

_____

_____

_____

_____

_____

_____

_____

_____

_____

_____

_____

_____

_____

_____

_____

Wise Answers to Important Questions

Over two thousand years ago, in ancient Greece, the people had the idea that every citizen should have a part in the government. This was the beginning of democracy. The ancient Greeks also were among the first to study science and medicine. Many of the world's first great writers, artists, speakers, and philosophers were Greek.

Philosophy is the study of the nature of the world and about how to live a good life. Philosophy means "love of wisdom." Philosophers are people who study and write to try to provide wise answers to important questions.

One of ancient Greece's philosophers was Socrates (c. 470–399 B.C.) who said, "Know thyself." He knew that leading a good life was not a matter of teaching a few rules; it was a lifetime process. So Socrates taught his students by questioning them about their opinions. He felt this was a better way of teaching than telling them what to think. His students were taught to find and correct their own errors. Socrates wanted his students to search for wisdom and a noble life. One of his pupils was Plato.

Plato (c. 427–347 B.C.) stated, "The direction in which education starts a man will determine his future life." He taught that ideas and forms are more real than the physical world. He wrote *The Republic,* describing an ideal government ruled by philosopher-kings. He believed that the ideal state was a goal toward which people should work. Plato opened an academy in Athens and made it the intellectual center of Greece. An interesting bit of trivia about this philosopher is that "Plato" was a nickname, meaning "broad-shouldered."

Aristotle (384–322 B.C.) was a student of Plato. His philosophy was based on the form of reasoning we call *logic.* He wrote about many topics and conducted research in natural science, studying animals. The study of psychology was started by Aristotle. He analyzed Greek drama and gave his reviews; this was the beginning of literary criticism. Aristotle, known as "the Philosopher," lectured by strolling around, and students had to follow him from place to place.

The next part of this activity will focus on your wise answers to important questions as you become the philosopher.

Note: Did you notice the "c." before the dates of the lives of Socrates and Plato? It is an abbreviation for *circa,* a word meaning "around" or "about." The use of "c." means that exact dates are not known and the dates given are approximate.

Prewriting: What are some important questions that need wise answers in today's world? Make a list of things that come to your mind. A few examples are given.

How should we act to make our world a better place? _____

What should be done to protect and save our environment? _____

How can we solve the drug problem in our world? _____

_____

_____

_____

_____

A Writing Draft: Now choose a topic from the list (you may use one of the examples if you like). As a philosopher, write a draft to tell others how you think the question should be answered. Using your own ideas, see if you can get your writing to say what you mean.

_____

_____

_____

_____

_____

_____

_____

_____

_____

_____

_____

_____

_____

_____

_____

_____

Save your draft. You may want to use it later when asked to write about something important to you. In your spare time, you might like to draft your thoughts about other issues you feel are important to you. You will be forming, in writing, your own philosophy of life.

The Plant Doctor

George Washington Carver (1864–1943) was not only an outstanding North American black educator and researcher in the agricultural sciences, to many young people, he was an encouraging model who set standards to which they could aspire. His motto, "To be of the greatest good to the greatest number of 'my people,'" was evident as he taught botany and agriculture to the children of former slaves while working to improve the lot of poor, one-horse farmers. He developed methods to help these farmers achieve self-sufficiency and conservation by planting crops of soybeans and peanuts as well as cotton.

Carver believed that science, art, and religion, instead of being separate entities, strengthened and supported one another. His work was devoted to showing how the natural bounty of the land could be understood better and used for the good of all people. As George Washington Carver said, "It is not the style of clothes one wears, neither the kind of automobile one drives, nor the amount of money one has in the bank, that count. These mean nothing. It is simply service that measures success" (quoted in the brochure for the George Washington Carver National Monument, in Missouri) (National Park Service, 1990).

During the turmoil of the Civil War, George Washington Carver was born of slave parents on the Moses Carver farm in southwest Missouri. Shortly after his birth, he and his mother were kidnapped by Confederate bushwhackers (so called because they hid out in the woods in ambush). George was found and returned to the Carvers, but his mother was never seen again. George and his brother Jim were reared by the Carvers as their own children; George Washington Carver often recalled the love and guidance they showed him. Growing up on the farm, George had time to wander in the woods and enjoyed collecting flowers and rocks. He transplanted plants from the woods in a little garden he had hidden in brush. The flowers grew so well that George was nicknamed "The Plant Doctor" in his community. Rocks collected from the woods and streams were "treasures" he kept throughout his life.

At the age of twelve, George Washington Carver moved to a nearby town to attend school because there was no school for blacks near the Carvers' farm. After working his way through high school in Kansas, he attended Iowa State College of Agriculture and Mechanic Arts (now Iowa State University) and graduated in 1894. He joined the faculty there and continued his research in the botany laboratory. In 1896, he became director of the Department of Agricultural Research at Tuskegee Institute, where he began his experiments with peanuts. He developed several hundred industrial uses for peanuts; this is why he was often referred to as "the peanut man." His gentle manner charmed those he met. Young people, especially, were influenced by Carver and moved in new directions because of him.

Directions: Spend some time brainstorming about the passage you have just read. Use the cluster that has been started to add thoughts and ideas about George Washington Carver as they come to you.

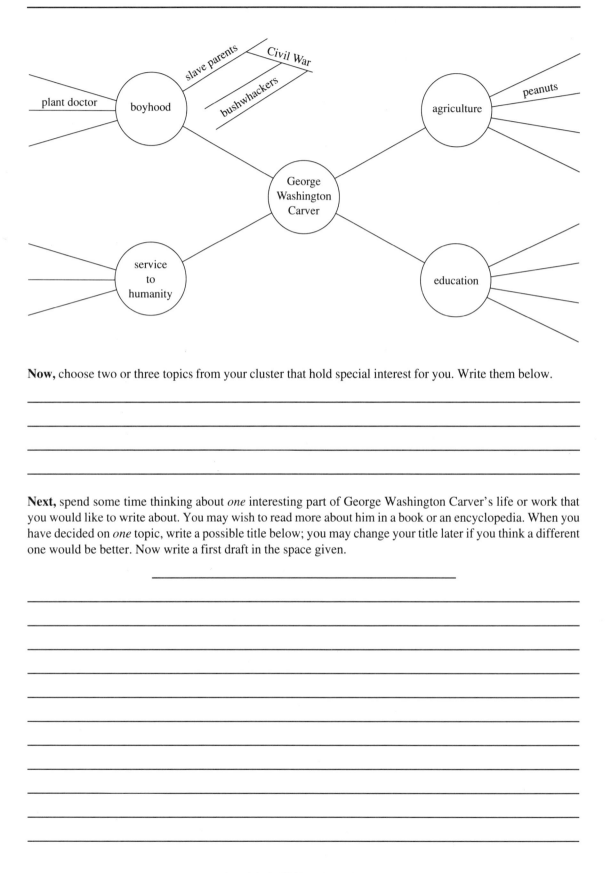

Now, choose two or three topics from your cluster that hold special interest for you. Write them below.

_____

_____

_____

_____

Next, spend some time thinking about *one* interesting part of George Washington Carver's life or work that you would like to write about. You may wish to read more about him in a book or an encyclopedia. When you have decided on *one* topic, write a possible title below; you may change your title later if you think a different one would be better. Now write a first draft in the space given.

_____

_____

_____

_____

_____

_____

_____

_____

_____

_____

_____

_____

_____

_____
_____
_____
_____
_____
_____
_____
_____
_____
_____
_____
_____
_____
_____
_____
_____
_____
_____
_____
_____
_____
_____
_____
_____
_____
_____
_____
_____

After first drafts have been written, discuss Carver's life and work with your classmates and teacher. Your teacher will list, or will choose a student to list all the topics about which students have written. (Of course, some may have chosen the same or similar topics.) With your teacher's help, determine if there are missing links in the class' life history of this famous American. Volunteer groups of three or four students may choose to write about those missing topics to complete this class project.

Keep the draft of your topic in your writing folder; later, you may choose to revise where necessary, edit, and proofread. Select a class committee of students to collect all papers as students finish and organize them into one continuous story of the life of George Washington Carver.

How Can I Say This?

There are many different ways to say the same thing. This activity will give you an opportunity to practice writing along with two Newbery Medal–winning authors. After you have finished this activity, you may want to read their books.

Directions: A paragraph has been chosen from each of two novels, the first a Newbery Award winner. Before you read these books, however, complete the activity that follows. For each passage, the sentences are grouped into related thoughts. Your task is to combine these sentences so that the writing sounds better. You may take out unnecessary words and rearrange the sentences to make the text more readable. The following is an example to demonstrate how one sentence was formed from three:

1.1 Sometimes I drew little designs.
1.2 I drew them on the borders of the letters.
1.3 They were drawn to illustrate some point.

"Sometimes I drew little designs on the borders of the letters, to illustrate some point."

(from *I, Juan de Pareja,* p. 11)

Write individually as you work through this activity the first time. Then form small groups to compare solutions to this exercise. Finally, read the author's original passage, found at the end of this activity.

I. *I, Juan de Pareja,* by Elizabeth Borton de Treviño (1965), p. 133.
   1.1 Another time we were caught on the roads.
   1.2 We were caught by a storm.
   1.3 It was a storm of sleet and rain.

   2.1 Master was chilled.
   2.2 He was chilled to the bone.

   3.1 There were sharp pains in his hand.
   3.2 Once again his hand swelled.
   3.3 It swelled to twice its size.
   3.4 It was feverish.

   4.1 We came to an inn.
   4.2 Master would not leave his room.
   4.3 He was becoming very frightened.
   4.4 I could see this.

   5.1 Why was he frightened?
   5.2 His hand was necessary for him to earn his livelihood.
   5.3 He had earned it this way since he was young.
   5.4 His hand was needed to show his knowledge.
   5.5 His hand was needed to show his skill.
   5.6 His hand was needed to show the art he had learned.
   5.7 It had taken him almost thirty years of steady labor to learn this.

Your Paragraph:

_____

_____

_____

_____

_____

_____

_____

_____

_____

_____

_____

_____

_____

_____

_____

_____

II. *Seventeen Against the Dealer,* by Cynthia Voigt (1989), pp. 190–191.

1.1 Dicey walked out of the shop.
1.2 She walked around to the creek.
1.3 She stood on the short wooden dock.
1.4 She looked down into the water.

2.1 The bottom of the water was muddy and brown.
2.2 Little waves rippled.
2.3 Old tires lay in the water.
2.4 The tires were half-buried, half-covered.

3.1 The water was shallow.
3.2 The water was blown by the wind.
3.3 The water splashed against the flat wooden bulkheading.
3.4 The water splashed rhythmically.

4.1 The pilings were covered with thick ice.
4.2 A few snags were in the water.
4.3 The snags were trees before they were washed away by erosion.
4.4 The branches of the trees looked like bones of hands raised out of the water.

5.1 There were miniature coves where there were no waves.
5.2 Sheets of thin ice floated there.
5.3 It was cold out there.
5.4 Dicey felt very cold.

Your Paragraph:

_____

_____

_____

_____

_____

_____

_____

_____

_____

_____

_____

_____

_____

_____

_____

_____

_____

Now you may read these passages as the authors wrote them.

I. *I, Juan de Pareja,* by E. B. de Treviño, 1965, p. 133:

Another time we were caught on the roads by a storm of sleet and wind, and Master was chilled to the bone. This brought on sharp pains in his hand, and once again it swelled to twice its size and was feverish. When we came to an inn, Master would not stir from his room and I could see that he was becoming very frightened. Any why not? His hand had been his livelihood since he was young; in it was all the knowledge, all the skill, all the art he had learned in almost thirty years of steady labor.

II. *Seventeen Against the Dealer,* by C. Voigt, 1989, pp. 190–191:

Dicey drifted out of the shop and around to the creek. Standing on the short wooden dock, she looked down into the water. The muddy brown bottom was rippled by little waves, and old tires, half-buried, half-covered, lay in it. The shallow water, blown by the wind, splashed rhythmically against the flat wooden bulkheading. Thick ice painted the pilings. A few snags, which used to be trees before erosion brought them down, raised branches like the bones of hands out of the water. Where miniature coves quieted the waves, sheets of thin ice floated. It was cold out there, but no colder than Dicey felt.

ACTIVITY 4.7

Can You Guess?

Directions: Get together with a friend and describe an object you both can see. It might be a tree, an orange, a table, or a chair. Touch it, look closely at it, smell it, and talk about it. Then, working separately, write a description of the object. After you have finished, compare what you wrote with your friend's description.

_____

_____

_____

_____

_____

Now describe something without telling your friend what it is. See if your friend can guess what it is by reading what you wrote. No telling—just describing!

_____

_____

_____

_____

If your friend could not guess, try rewriting your description. Try to make it clear so your friend will understand.

_____

_____

_____

_____

_____

This exercise helps you think as a reader does when you write.

Paul Revere's Ride

Paul Revere (1735–1818) was an American patriot of the Revolutionary War. He worked closely with Samuel Adams and John Hancock and was Lieutenant Colonel of a Massachusetts artillery regiment. He took part in the Boston Tea Party and worked hard for voted approval of the Constitution. He was also a good businessman, a silversmith, and master of his craft. He cast bullets and church bells, created beautiful engravings, designed ornamental false teeth, and made fine silver dishes prized by collectors today.

Paul Revere is best remembered, however, for a famous ride on horseback while serving as a messenger with the Massachusetts patriots. The governor of Massachusetts, General Gage, kept his British troops ready for any rebellion by the patriots who were clamoring for independence. Paul Revere waited and watched in Boston, where he had set up a system of signals using lanterns in the bell tower of Christ Church. The sexton in the church tower would hang one lantern if he saw troops coming by land. Two lanterns meant they were crossing the Charles River in boats. When, late on the night of April 18, 1775, two lanterns appeared in the church tower, Revere started off on his famous midnight ride. He rode swiftly to Lexington and on to Concord, warning colonists that the British had landed and were ready to fight. It was in Lexington that seventy-seven patriot farmers and townspeople known as Minutemen, who had been training with muskets, confronted the British army. A shot rang out from the ranks of the Minutemen, and the Revolution had begun.

This exciting event inspired Henry Wadsworth Longfellow (1807–1882) to write "Paul Revere's Ride," one of the most popular poems in North American literature. Locate and read the poem "Paul Revere's Ride." Then complete the following writing activity.

Directions: After reading Longfellow's poem, write a first draft, choosing your topic from one of the three suggested below; or you may create your own topic. When you're ready, consider sharing your draft with classmates. As you hear various versions of what took place, you and your classmates may want to consider publishing these exciting viewpoints.

1. Pretend you are Paul Revere's horse. Write about this wild night ride from the horse's point of view.

2. Write about Paul Revere's ride from the point of view of someone your age. You may be too young to join the war, but imagine that you have a sixteen-year-old brother and a father who will fight.

_____

_____

_____

_____

_____

_____

_____

_____

_____

_____

_____

_____

_____

_____

_____

3. Write an account of this historic ride by Paul Revere for a history textbook. Explain why the event happened and what took place in the end.

_____

_____

_____

_____

_____

_____

_____

_____

_____

_____

_____

_____

_____

_____

Organizing My Room

Do you keep your room neat and tidy, or is it a disaster area? Either way, this activity will give you an opportunity to think about some things you might do to better organize your personal space. After completing this activity, you may even be motivated to follow up by actually reorganizing your room.

1. Make a list of the things that are kept in your room. If you share a room, you may want to make two lists—one for your own things and one for items shared.

   _____   _____
   _____   _____
   _____   _____
   _____   _____
   _____   _____
   _____   _____
   _____   _____
   _____   _____
   _____   _____
   _____   _____
   _____   _____

2. Classify the items into lists with headings—hobbies, books and school materials, clothing, sports equipment, games, and so on.

   _____ _____ _____ _____
   _____ _____ _____ _____
   _____ _____ _____ _____
   _____ _____ _____ _____
   _____ _____ _____ _____
   _____ _____ _____ _____

   _____ _____ _____ _____
   _____ _____ _____ _____
   _____ _____ _____ _____
   _____ _____ _____ _____
   _____ _____ _____ _____

3. Now, can you think of some improvements that could be made by moving things around? Jot down those changes in another list.

_____

_____

_____

4. Finally, in the space below, draw a plan of your room as you have organized it. Label your furniture and show where you would put your things from each group listed in number 2.

Plan It

Has your family ever had a fire drill at your home? It doesn't take too much effort or time, but it can be a lifesaver. One family's plan is given here, with a layout of the house for illustration. Read this example, then design a plan for your family.

Example Plan: Mom, Dad, and Jason, who is a teenager, discuss what to do if a fire should start in their home. Jeremy, a three-year-old, will participate in his own way, too. Mom and Dad tell us to find shoes and,

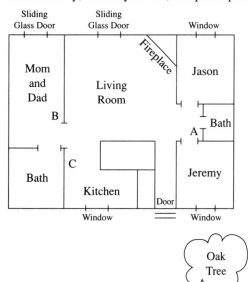

if time permits, something small like a washcloth to cover our noses and mouths to keep us from breathing lung-damaging smoke. They say to leave everything behind and not even to worry about getting dressed. This family's home has two smoke detectors (points A and B). A fire extinguisher is at point C.

The diagram is used to plan routes of escape. If the whole family is home and in bed, Jason will get Jeremy and then escape. Drills are actually done, with the pretend fire being in different locations. (In a real fire, if a door feels hot, one must go a different way.) Jason practices opening the deadbolt lock in a flash. The family designates the big oak tree in the front yard as the meeting point.

Your Plan: Draw a plan of your house in the space below. Then draft your plan for escape in case of a fire. Be sure to include an alternative escape route in case your door is blocked. After you have completed this activity, you may want to share the plan with your family. Perhaps you can conduct a fire drill using your plan.

_____

_____

_____

_____

_____

_____

_____

_____

_____

_____

_____

Filling Out Forms

Forms are used in our society to document information. It is a good idea to get acquainted with forms, because you will be using them as you get older and apply for your driver's license, seek college entrance, or apply for a job. Becoming familiar with filling out forms makes the task easier.

Some Hints About Forms:

Get two forms or make a photocopy. If you have two blank copies to work with, then you can use one for practice and one for the final product.

Accuracy and neatness are important. Write information needed to complete the form on scratch paper first. Be certain that names and addresses of parents, references, and others are spelled correctly. Write on the form only after you have decided what you will say, have written out a draft, and have corrected all errors.

Information requested is similar for all forms. Because similar information is often requested on forms, gather this information and keep it in a safe place so you will have it ready when needed.

- Address and telephone number
- Social Security number
- Date and place of birth
- Names, ages, and addresses of family members
- Name, phone number, and relationship of a person to contact in an emergency
- Names, addresses, and phone numbers of three people who will permit you to list them as references

It is now your turn to practice filling out forms. The first is an application for a library card. Fill out this form as you would if you were applying for a card for yourself.

Glenview Public Library

Please Print:

Name _____   Date _____

Social Security Number _____

Mailing Address _____

City _____   State _____   Zip _____

Telephone Number: Home _____   Work _____

School or University _____

I apply for the privilege to use the library. In exchange for patron privileges, I agree to comply with all rules, regulations, and policies relating to the use of the library.

Applicant's Signature _____

Age _____
(if 17 or under)

Parent's Signature_____
(for applicants 17 or under)

117

The next form given to you for practice is a job application form. Your primary purpose for completing it is to obtain a job that matches your interests and abilities. Keep in mind that the employer's purpose is to hire someone who is competent, reliable, and can get along easily with others.

What important things about you should you tell the employer? Tell the employer about your skills, attitudes, and interests that make you right for this job. Brainstorm your ideas here.

Skills   **Attitudes**   **Interests**

_____   _____   _____

_____   _____   _____

_____   _____   _____

_____   _____   _____

_____   _____   _____

Now practice filling in the sample job application form given. Pretend you are applying for a job in a restaurant, grocery store, or another occupation of your choice. Write your choice here: _____
_____.

Because the application form is often the employer's first impression of you, neatness, lack of errors, and complete answers are important. Make a copy of the form to use for practice, or write on scratch paper. After filling out the form, *proofread* for errors. Ask a friend and your teacher to read it for errors also. *Correct* your errors; then carefully *rewrite* your application on the form provided.

Job Application Form

Name _____   Date _____

Address _____
           Street   City   State   Zip

Telephone Number _____   Social Security Number _____

Age _____   Date of Birth _____
                                     Month   Date   Year

Education:

_____
    School Name   City   Highest Grade Completed

Present or Prior Employment

Employer   From   To   Pay   Reason for Leaving

_____   _____   _____   _____   _____

_____   _____   _____   _____   _____

Type of Work Requested

Part-time ___   Days: M ____ hrs. _____   TH ____ hrs. _____

                    T ____ hrs. _____   F ____ hrs. _____

Full-time ___   W ____ hrs. _____   S ____ hrs. _____

                   SUN ____ hrs. _____

Experience _____ Special Skills _____

Interests/Hobbies _____

Date of Availability for Work _____

References (Not Relatives):

    Name   Position   Address   Phone

1. _____

2. _____

Other Information You Would Like Us to Know _____

_____

I verify that the above is true _____
                                   Signature of Applicant

ACTIVITY 4.12

The Bill of Rights

The first ten amendments to the U.S. Constitution are called the Bill or Rights. They state the most important rights that all U.S. citizens share.

An abbreviated listing of the first ten amendments is given below. You may wish to locate the Bill of Rights in an encyclopedia or history book and read it in its original form before completing this activity. Read together and discuss what these rights mean before you begin to write.

1. Freedom of religion, speech, press, assembly, and petition
2. Right to bear arms
3. Right not to have to house troops
4. Freedom from unreasonable search of person, house, and papers
5. Right to life, liberty, and property, as well as certain rights when on trial
6. Protection in criminal trials—speedy, public trial; impartial jury in state of crime; see witnesses against you; have witnesses in own favor; and legal assistance
7. Right of trial by jury for civil suits of over $20 and right not to be tried twice for the same crime
8. Excessive bail, fines, and punishment are forbidden.
9. People have rights beyond these rights.
10. Powers not delegated to the federal government are reserved to the states and the people.

Directions: Which one of the first ten amendments do you think is the most important? Can you explain why? Generate ideas by thinking, talking with a classmate, and jotting down thoughts in the space below:

_____

_____

_____

_____

_____

Choose one of the ten amendments to write about, and plan what you would like to say by organizing your ideas into a first draft. Be sure to include your own attitudes and express *your* feelings.

_____

_____

_____

_____

_____

_____

_____

_____

_____

_____

_____

_____

_____

_____

_____

_____

_____

Now write a second draft, using the ideas you have organized in your first draft. Think about who will be reading your writing, and decide on a form you would like to use. It could be a letter, a paragraph, a story, or a poem. *You* decide how you would like to write it and use the space below for your second draft.

_____

_____

_____

_____

_____

_____

_____

_____

_____

_____

_____

_____

_____

_____

_____

_____

_____

_____

_____

_____

_____

ACTIVITY 4.13

Writing a Poem

Poetry is language used in a special way. Poems may be descriptions of objects or events and often give messages about feelings or ideas. Poems may use images. You may remember how Carl Sandburg created the image of a cat in his poem "Fog." The example that follows is a short poem by Christina Rossetti (1830–1894), an English poet whose verse shows her love for nature. She wrote some of the best lyric poems in English literature.

Who Has Seen the Wind?[*]

> Who has seen the wind?
>   Neither I nor you;
> But when the leaves hang trembling,
>   The wind is passing through.
>
> Who has seen the wind?
>   Neither you nor I;
> But when the trees bow down their heads,
>   The wind is passing by.

Did the poet paint a picture with words that you could see in your imagination? Could you feel the wind?

Now try writing some poetry of your own. Following the steps given here will help you.

1. Pick a subject—something concrete like a spider web, an orange, a hand, the moon, or rain—or an experience or feeling. Close your eyes and describe it. How does it feel, look, sound, taste?
2. Write down your ideas:

_____

_____

3. Now put your ideas into an order:

_____

_____

_____

4. Write a first draft of your poem:

_____

_____

_____

_____

_____

5. You probably will want to make some changes in your first draft. Most poets write several drafts before they are satisfied with their poems.

[*]*Source:* Christina Rossetti, "Who Has Seen the Wind?" in Kate Douglas Wiggin and Nora Archibald Smith (Eds.), *Pinafore Palace: A Book of Rhymes for the Nursery* (New York: The McClure Company, 1907), p. 129.

ACTIVITY 4.14

The Steel-Driving Man

John Henry was a black man whose story is a legend in North American folklore. We don't know for certain that there was a real John Henry, but the spirit of this hero lives in the hundreds of different versions of the ballad that tells his story.

John Henry was a railroad worker called a steel driver. He worked on the construction of the Big Bend Tunnel in West Virginia, 1870–1873. The tunnel was built to route the Chesapeake and Ohio Railroad through a mountain. In those days, long-handled hammers were used to pound steel rods into rock to make holes for blasting with explosives. John Henry was the best steel-driving man around!

One day a steam drill was brought to the site to do the work of the steel driver. A contest took place when John Henry challenged that he could drive the steel into the rock faster than the machine. This contest is said to have been symbolic of the manual workers' last stand against the machine. John Henry won his race against the steam drill. Then, in the words of the ballad, "He died with his hammer in his hand." It is said that a ghost hammer still rings in the Big Bend Tunnel in West Virginia.

Directions: Read one of the many versions of John Henry's story in a book or songbook. It can be found in ballad form in many folk songbooks. A ballad is a story told in verse and meant to be sung. Many books also contain this famous folktale. *John Henry and His Hammer* by H. W. Felton and *Folk Songs from the West Virginia Hills* by P. W. Gainer are two examples. Your school or community library should be of help to you in locating this story. After you have read John Henry's story, you are ready to continue this activity.

Truth or Fantasy? Because this legend was first passed from one storyteller to another, you will notice that information found in different stories does not always agree, and some things are hard to believe! One book said that John Henry weighed thirty-three pounds and talked when he was born. Another said he used two twenty-pound hammers, one in each hand, for driving the steel rods. Another storyteller said John Henry could lift four tons.

To help separate truth and fantasy in the folk legend of John Henry, complete the following two paragraphs:

1. John Henry was a man who could have _____

_____

_____

_____

_____

_____

_____

2. John Henry probably didn't _____

_____

_____

_____

_____

_____

_____

_____

Writing a Ballad: See if you can write a ballad. To prepare for writing, brainstorm some ideas and jot them down below. Remember, a ballad tells a story in verse form. It could be a story about you, your family, your class, a school sports event, or a news event. It could be true, part true and part fantasy, or all fantasy.

_____   _____

_____   _____

_____   _____

_____   _____

_____   _____

_____   _____

Use these ideas to write the first draft of your ballad. If you want to be able to sing it later, choose a familiar tune that you like. As you hum the tune in your mind, draw a line for each syllable. This will help you know how many syllables each line of your ballad should have if you want to be able to sing it to your tune. Good luck!

_____

_____

_____

_____

_____

_____

_____

_____

_____

_____

_____

_____

_____

_____

_____

_____

The Way to Juanita's House

We sometimes need to provide written information. Use the following information to give directions in writing.

This is a map of Juanita's neighborhood. Her house is marked with an ⊠; she lives at 401 East Circle Lane. Use the lines below to give written directions to help someone get from Liberty Mall to Juanita's house. Make your directions simple, direct, and clear.

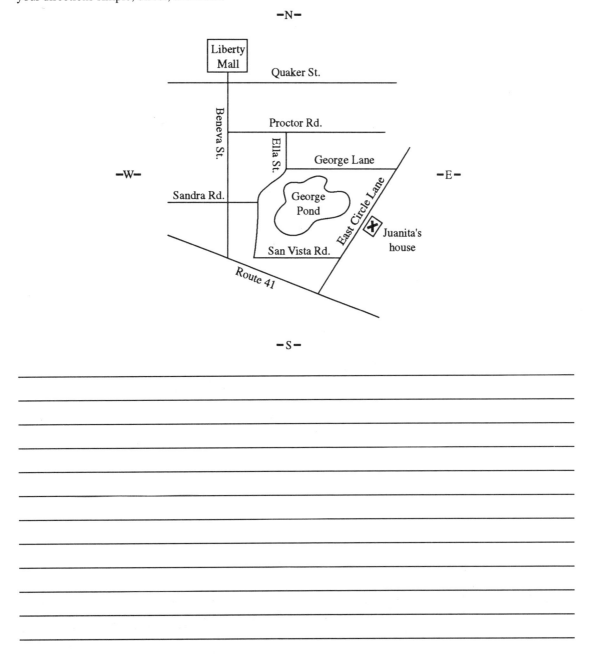

_____

_____

_____

_____

_____

_____

_____

_____

_____

_____

_____

_____

Writing a Personal Letter

Business letters and personal letters are different because our reasons for writing them are different. Personal letters and notes often express a writer's attitudes, emotions, and moods. They may give information, often of a personal nature. Personal letters are written to people we know. Personal letters may be typed or handwritten; but, if typed, the letter should be signed by hand. The form of a personal letter is different from that of a business letter.

Personal Letter Format:

---

                                 123 Oak Street

            (Heading)   Marianna, Florida 32446

                                 April 5, 1998

Dear Joe,   (Opening greeting)

      I have a day off from school this coming Friday, April 10. If convenient for you and your parents, I would like to visit you that weekend. I can get a ride with my aunt, who is going to Atlanta on business.

      Let me know if this plan is all right with you and your family. I really want to see all of you.

                 (Closing)   Your friend,
                               Andy

(Body)

Use the lines below to draft a short personal letter to a friend, a grandparent, or a pen pal. After revising and editing, you can use stationery to copy the final version of your letter for mailing.

_____

_____

_____

_____

_____

_____

_____

_____

_____

_____

_____

_____

_____

_____

_____

_____

Personal Letter Envelope Format

Andy Jones
123 Oak Street   (Return address)
Marianna, FL 32446

(Mailing address) Mr. Joe Jackson
3120 Sunset Street
Atlanta, GA 30349

Now it's your turn to draft the envelope for your letter:

Writing a Business Letter

Business letters often are written to give information. The writer learns to be clear and brief so that the reader knows what is to be done with the information. Business letters often are written to request information or an item. They may be written to influence the reader, as is done with a consumer complaint, a letter to the editor, or an application letter.

There is a standard format for business letters, and you will notice some differences from the format for personal letters. An inside address comes before the opening greeting in a business letter. It includes the name of the person to whom you are writing, followed by his or her title. Then the company name is written, followed by the mailing address. Another difference is that the opening greeting in a business letter is followed by a colon instead of a comma, as is used in a personal letter.

Business Letter Format:

(Heading)   21 Monroe Street
Rocky Ford, Colorado 81067
September 5, 1998

Mr. Carl Smith, Manager
Regency Corporation
2140 Fourth Street   (Inside address)
Chicago, Illinois 60624

Dear Mr. Smith: (Greeting)

Please send me a copy of your free catalog of sound
systems, No. 645, to the above address. I am interesed   (Body)
in placing an order for some equipment.

(Closing)   Sincerely yours,

(Signature)   *Gary Bennett*

Gary Bennett

Now it's your turn to write a short business letter. Use the following lines for a first draft; then revise and edit before writing on stationery.

Heading _____

_____

_____

_____

_____   Inside address

_____

_____

_____   Greeting (Remember to use
a colon in a business letter)

Body

_____

_____

_____

_____

_____

_____

_____

_____

_____

_____

Closing _____

Signature _____

Business Letter Envelope Format:

```
Gary Bennett
21 Monroe Street        (Return address)
Rocky Ford, CO 81067


                          Mr. Carl Smith, Manager
                          Regency Corporation
      (Mailing address)   2140 Fourth Street
                          Chicago, IL 60624
```

Now it's your turn to draft the envelope for your business letter:

CHAPTER 5

Sharing the Draft: Conferring and Responding

Help thy friend's boat across, and lo! thine own has reached the shore.

—Hindu proverb

Writers of all ages tend to feel a sense of accomplishment when they complete their first drafts, but they also tend to yearn for opportunities to continue developing their drafts. When a particular draft is chosen to be published as a classroom activity or sent to someone, ample time must be allocated for reworking the draft to get it in final form for its intended audience. It is at this point that sharing writing efforts and receiving feedback from others—classmates, teachers, parents, or friends—is so effective. Black (1968) emphasized in *The Labyrinth of Language* the need of all human beings to share their writings with others:

Man is the only animal that can use *symbols* (words, pictures, graphs, numbers, etc.). He alone can bridge the gap between one person and another, conveying thoughts, feelings, desires, attitudes, and sharing in the traditions, conventions, the knowledge, and the superstition of his culture: the only animal that can truly *understand* and *misunderstand*. On this essential skill depends everything that we call civilization. Without it, imagination, thought—even self-knowledge—are impossible. (p. 10; emphasis in the original).

Much of the joy of creating is in sharing the product at its various developmental stages. When peers point out a section they especially like or suggest changes they feel would make a better paragraph, the author of the draft senses the need to rewrite in order to incorporate the good suggestions offered and to make additions sparked by discussion of the draft. A need to revisit the draft to refine what the writer intended to say develops; the writer is now learning and practicing the art of composing. A caring and conscientious teacher encourages and carefully guides students through this process. As Murray (1989) stated,

. . . It is the challenge of the writing teacher to become the person with whom the student wants to share work that is still searching for meaning. It is also the responsibility of the writing teacher to create a community within the class that makes such sharing contagious. And as the drafts move toward a completed meaning, the writer needs test readers who can become more critical and still be supportive. (p. 27)

Writing is to be shared at any or all of the overlapping and recursive stages of the writing process, from selecting a topic and prewriting, through drafting, responding, revising, editing, and publication. The act of sharing is a wonderful vehicle for moving writers forward in their search for meaning.

SHARING COOPERATIVELY

Various kinds of learning take place during conferring and responding to written drafts, when students are guided by their teacher to have an attitude of encouraging one another's successes. Learning teams of four to five members can collaborate to ensure mastery of a writing task; at the same time, such thoughtful interactions help develop critical thinking skills. Each student works at his or her own ability level without fear of labeling. Furthermore, sharing the draft provides an excellent opportunity for the teacher to guide students to use their minds to conceptualize, problem solve, integrate and interpret data, reason, analyze, and devise strategies to cope with all kinds of problems. This con-

tively processing the content of each shared draft in their search for clarity of meaning; students are learning from one another.

Crouse and Davey (1989) defined collaboration as follows:

. . . the initiation of a social act for the purpose of learning. . . . It can be as simple as two children sitting beside one another for comfort as they write, or it can be children writing together for a specific goal, initiated and defined by those children. (p. 757).

Even very young children often collaborate without being aware of the term or its meaning as demonstrated in the "Hi & Lois" cartoon that follows:

Source: Browne, C. In *Tallahassee Democrat,* September 23, 1991, p. 4C. Reprinted with special permission of King Features Syndicate.

cept works when classrooms extend beyond a work setting to a learning environment such as that described by Lindquist and Ligett (1992):

What a relief that expertise comes from everyone. Students become teachers and teachers become students. Questions become more important than answers. All learners are engaged in meaningful inquiry. Learning is shared and celebrated with others. It excites the "wonder in the mind"! (p. 2)

As students work in groups cooperatively, they can talk about problems with their writing and consider options for working toward solutions. They can share and celebrate fresh ideas and take risks to write creatively. They can assimilate knowledge of their various cultures along with content area subject matter. Students can become better writers because, when working collaboratively, they are ac-

Elementary teachers Crouse and Davey gathered insights from their students to describe collaborative learning. Their results showed that friendship was valuable in the process; students felt confident and secure working with someone else. Students said they could learn much from one another; together they could plan and organize, help one another make meanings clear, and offer advice about the mechanics of their writing. Ownership was recognized, and writers did not feel compelled to follow every suggestion offered by others. These students came to realize that collaborative learning thrives in a comfortable and pleasant environment with mobility to interact freely with classmates, a variety of accessible materials, liberty to choose their own topics, and freedom to manage their own time (Crouse & Davey, 1989).

One teacher of a fourth–fifth-grade class in an

urban school, Deb Woodman, adopted McMahon and Raphael's (1992) literacy program, The Book Club, to create a literacy environment for reading and writing. A goal of the program, the development of a language to talk about literacy, was obtained as Woodman observed her students participating in discussions and sharing sessions: "They critiqued illustrations, plots, and character descriptions; asked questions about authors' motives for writing and about each other's interpretations of story events; created dramatic interpretations of books they had read; and discussed each other's written text" (p. 4).

Barell (1991) described how students can be empowered to take control of their own learning, which gives them a sense of responsibility for problem solving. This is accomplished not by telling students what they should think but by providing them with opportunities to practice how to think. When students are free to express their ideas, supported by their teacher and peers, and encouraged to take risks, thinking and learning occur naturally. Barell wrote of an incident in the life of Nobel Prize–winning physicist Isidor I. Rabi (1898–1988), an Austrian-born scientist who was one of the leaders of the project that developed the atomic bomb. In describing his childhood, Rabi said that, unlike most parents who ask their children what they learned in school that day, his mother always asked, "Izzy, did you ask a good question today?"

A goal of a classroom setting where conferring and responding occur easily is that students become teachers as well as learners and become proficient in asking those "good questions." In their study of teaching and learning in whole language classrooms, Allen, Michalove, Shockley, and West (1991) observed classes in grades 1, 2, and 5 in an effort to increase successful literacy learning. Through several phases, the researchers identified major issues in the development of students studied, leading to identification of the themes critical to increased success: "engagement with literacy and membership in the literate community" (p. 461).

Allen et al. (1991) found that sharing books and writing with peers was a primary motivational force for reading and writing in the lower grades, but "being a member of the social community seemed more compelling for the fifth graders" (p. 465). They also found that membership in an active com-

munity of learners offered choices for improved behavior for some students having problems in this area.

Children become teachers as well as learners, collaborators as well as friends. They supported each other as risk takers. These were roles some of the children had to learn. When Barbara [teacher] had Jeremiah work in a reading group and a writing group, his usual pouting and squabbling diminished greatly. As one of the more competent readers and writers in these two groups, he began to be viewed as a helpful resource rather than a nuisance by the other kids. After two months of this support, he began functioning more productively as he once again chose his own places and partners for reading and writing.

Over and over, in every classroom, the children encouraged, taught, challenged, and supported each other. . . . As the routines and expectations for interaction in these classrooms became internalized, children developed their roles as teachers, learners, and collaborators in their literate communities. (p. 466)

Hansen (1992) explained how "classrooms characterized by the language of challenge can help upper elementary grade children grow as writers and evaluators of their own literacy development" (p. 100). Sharing groups are successful when teachers teach their students to use the language of challenge; "with everyone committed to it, the language of challenge can become part of the daily life of classrooms. In fact, the children can become so good at it that they surprise their teachers" (p. 101). In time, they will challenge professional writers as well, keeping critical thinking alive. Hansen described a fifth-grade class where students wrote responses to—not summaries of—assigned social studies text material. The discussions and sharing that followed, based on these student responses, provided a fresh look at the text where history was not only a lesson about the past, but a picture of the future. Hansen summarized what can take place in classrooms where students are challenged:

[Students] . . . have learned how to challenge their tests, themselves, their texts, and each other. They use a language of challenge in the midst of a supportive environment where they know how to walk the fine line between challenge and confrontation. This tension is necessary, vital to learning. Without it, forward movement is minimal. With it, everyone takes everyone's learning seriously. (p. 104).

Teachers and students who are not accustomed to sharing cooperatively in groups may need guidance in the beginning; this chapter presents strategies some teacher have used successfully. Teachers can take a few minutes at the end of a sharing session to discuss with students the effectiveness of the session and invite feedback of suggestions for improvement. Model Activity 5.1 can be used for student evaluation of a cooperative sharing session; it

could be used repeatedly as needed for evaluation of any sharing session. It might also be wise at this point to consider the following words of English poet John Milton (1608–1674), as stated in *Areopagitica,* written in 1644: "Where there is much desire to learn, there of necessity will be much arguing, much writing, many opinions; for opinion in good men is but knowledge in the making."

STUDENT–TEACHER SHARING

An individual conference held for a few minutes each week shows students that the teacher is interested in their work and gives them a chance to tell the teacher about their writing plans. Teachers beginning to make use of this model of sharing cooperatively with their students through conferencing may need to make some changes in how they relate to them. As Murray (1989) suggested, "The writer needs response when it can do some good, when the writing can be changed; but in school we too often respond only when the writing is finished, when it's too late" (p. 26). For the student–teacher conference, each student chooses a specific piece of writing from his or her writing folder to share with the teacher; together they analyze its strengths and weaknesses and decide on any suggestions for improvement. As Tiedt and Tiedt (1987) advised, "Don't tell a student too many things; it is usually wiser to make only a few points at any one conference" (p. 238). Duke (1991) stated the following:

Based on what is known about the student's stage of writing development, the teacher selects a focus for discussion that will help the student move ahead and enhance the piece of writing, but not leave the student frustrated because the teacher has asked for too much too soon. (pp. 217–218)

As student–teacher conferences are carried out, teachers will do well to heed the advice of a pioneer in the automobile industry and founder, in 1903, of the Ford Motor Company. Henry Ford (1863–1947) said, "Don't find fault. Find a remedy."

Murray (1985) suggested that a good way to think about responding to student drafts is by asking the following two questions: "What works?" and "What needs work?" As the teacher participant in the student–teacher conference, think of yourself as a writing coach; you want your team member to

play the best game that he or she can and end the game feeling like a winner. But, remember, you are on the sidelines at this point. When coaching the writing game, there are a few simple rules to keep in mind. Although these suggestions were adapted from a presentation by Murray (1989, pp. 123–125) at a seminar of newspaper writing coaches who work with newspaper writers to help them improve their writing, they are timely for the classroom writing teacher as well.

1. The writer is the owner of the text; the teacher is the listener.
2. Working with language should be fun; don't take it too seriously.
3. Since all writing is experimental, we don't know what works until it is tried. Keep in mind that failure is normal if it is a learning tool that points to a way to achieve success.
4. When making suggestions, it is better to point out several alternatives rather than only one. If the student is redirected to his or her game plan with several possibilities, the game can be continued with the player focusing on what is seen as the best way to win the game.
5. Point out how the student's performance in this draft (game) contributes to the student's overall development as a writer (athlete).
6. Avoid generalized praise or generalized criticism; neither makes much of a contribution at this point. Rather, relate to a specific issue. Give examples: "This is a good topic. Remember when you told me you didn't have anything to say?" "This is very well organized; now might be a good time to check the library for some facts to document what you have to say."
7. Provide a model for your student's constructive criticism so she or he will be able to identify problems and work to improve each evolving draft.
8. Don't neglect the better writers. With so much attention and support required by struggling students,

teachers need to be reminded to give the better writers the attention they deserve. These students are eager to do well, they care about their writing, and they need positive reinforcement from you. Their good papers can become better ones.

9. Don't forget to be writing yourself—modeling.
10. Let students speak first, and listen to what they have to say.

Remember that the purpose of the student–teacher conference is not to evaluate or make conclusions. It should be supportive, stimulating, and encouraging. It is important that students leave the student–teacher conference thinking about what has been accomplished and what they will do next as they plan to continue writing.

PEER RESPONSE GROUPS

Student-to-Student

A successful student–teacher conference should lead naturally into student–student conferences. Following teacher modeling during the student–teacher conference, students are more likely to serve as "teachers" within the class, thus developing further a classroom community of writers. As Graves (1984) wrote:

Writing is a public act. It exists to influence others or provide thinking for oneself at another place and time. Too much writing is composed for just one person, the teacher. Young writers don't grow without the expanded horizons of other children's reactions; they possess too limited a concept of the effects of their text. Sharing becomes an orthodoxy when writers are required to share, regardless of where they are in a draft, or at times when they simply do not need help. This is particularly true for older writers beyond the age of eight or nine. (p. 190)

Flexibility within the classroom allows sharing to take place as needed. It may sometimes be desirable for student–teacher or student–student conferences to occur as students are working in larger groups.

Small Groups and Teams

Peer conferencing is an important part of the writing process, and student writing does benefit from it. We also know that peer conferencing needs to be taught, practiced, and reinforced. Students do not always naturally know how to give helpful advice, but they can be guided to learn which kinds of responses are helpful to fellow writers.

Glasser (1986) advocated cooperative learning in teams; and he suggested that students functioning at different levels all benefited when grouped together. He believed that the more advanced students clarified their thinking as they became tutors

for less able students who, in turn, benefited from the shared knowledge and help with writing received form their peers. Glasser saw the teacher as the organizer/manager as described in the following excerpt:

Try to see your class not as individual students who are now in teams, but as learning-teams made up of students selected by you as the manager because you think that they can learn better as this team than as individuals. (p. 124)

Organization into teams or small groups may be carried out by the teacher or the students. Teachers are advised to make group assignments based on what a team can accomplish together that an individual student could not. Whether teams are assigned by the teacher or self-selected by students, the cooperation of each group member should be encouraged.

Teacher modeling continues to be a most important part of the process as writing drafts are shared in groups. Routman (1991) described how she felt that sharing her own writing has helped her to be a better teacher:

My own feelings of vulnerability have helped me be empathetic to students—and teachers—who share their writing and have sensitized me to the need to set up a classroom writing climate that is supportive and encouraging. We all need to feel that our writing and best efforts are valued if we are going to take the risk of sharing writing and accepting responses. (p. 162)

Bunce-Crim (1991) also wrote of the importance of the teacher sharing writing with students.

The first time I tried to include dialogue in a story, for instance, several children pointed out that no ten-year-old would use the words and sentence structure that I had chosen. They anxiously awaited my revisions, just as I looked forward to theirs. We began talking to each other as writers. I had exposed my vulnerability to them, and they had shown me theirs. We had become partners in the writing process. (p. 38)

Successful group conferencing can become a valuable part of process writing programs if teachers model the concept as part of the instructional process. Some teachers have found that making a videotape demonstrating effective conferencing allows students to learn from seeing others working through the process.

Maimon (1988) suggested that when students select writing drafts to be shared, the process will go more smoothly if the writer of the draft attaches a self-analysis form to answer specific questions such as "What further steps are planned for the writing project?" or "How can readers help most?" By doing this, the writer plans for improvement as part of the process; rather than waiting for the teacher and classmates to find problems and point them out, the writer invites assistance from others. Asking for advice also reinforces the idea that the final responsibility for the work-in-progress belongs to the writer. In this regard, students could be encouraged to create their own self-analysis form designed specifically for each piece of writing, and/or the class could design cooperatively a self-analysis form that could be duplicated and made available for all students.

Strong (1991) found that the following guidelines have worked well in peer response groups:

How to Get Feedback on Writing

1. Read your work aloud twice.
2. Don't defend your work.
3. Take notes on what others tell you.
4. Ask questions to clarify what others say.
5. Thank people for their comments.
6. Never apologize for the piece you are going to read.

How to Give Feedback on Writing

1. Listen for the overall effect in the first reading.
2. Make notes and comments during the second reading.
3. Tell what you liked best about the writing.
4. Identify a place in the writing that may need work.
5. Comment on content and organization first, then mechanics.
6. Be specific by pointing to places on the actual page. (p. 167)

As the groups work, the teacher is free to move around the room, participating as a writer with the students, responding favorably to encourage students, and helping to alleviate any problems such as insensitive criticism. A successful group session ends with writers drafting their plans for revision.

Jean M. Daly (1990), a fifth-grade teacher at Setauket Elementary School in Setauket, New York, recognizing that it is sometimes difficult to monitor the conferences and students who stray from the task, offered a strategy to help make peer conferencing a rewarding experience. Daly developed a set of Peer Conference Cards to help students remain on task. Each group of students had a set of six cards, printed on colored paper and laminated. Information given on Daly's cards has been paraphrased as follows:

1. A Reader Card directed a chosen reader to perform certain tasks before reading his or her writing, such as telling the group which part they should listen to with special care or asking for suggestions for a title. Then the author, holding the Reader Card, clearly and slowly read the draft to the listeners. The draft was read twice.
2. A Summarizer Card required the student possessing it to summarize what the reader had said. The card gave some suggested formats, such as "Your main point was . . . "
3. A Questioner Card directed a conference member to ask questions. Again, suggested questions were given, such as "Will you explain more about . . . ?" or "Could you please clarify this part?"
4. A Suggester Card directed the student holding it to make suggestions to the writer after the group had heard the draft and had engaged in group discussion. Again, the card gave possible suggestions if needed: "Have you thought about trying . . . ?" or "Have you talked with . . .?" He/she had the same problem before."
5. A Praiser Card gave clues as to how to praise the writer and his draft, such as "I liked the part where you . . . " or "You made me (laugh, cry, smile) when you . . . "
6. An Observer Card was prepared for use in groups needing rearranging because of absences or additions to the class. The card holder kept a checklist to mark off as each group member completed his or her task.

The cards were rotated around the group until each member had been the reader. Daly observed:

The author often made notes as peers spoke and then decided what to do with the information the peer group offered. The author maintained ownership of the piece, and the decision to act or not act upon the information obtained in the peer conference resided solely with the author. (p. 280)

Daly introduced the use of these cards to her class by modeling the procedure using a group of volunteers. After two to three weeks, she noticed less dependence on the cards as students gained confidence in peer conferencing skills. Soon the cards were no longer needed as students had learned to make efficient use of classroom time during peer conferencing.

In Chapter 4 of this book, Model Activity 4.12 was presented to give students an opportunity to study the Bill of Rights, thus expanding their cultural literacy. The activity continued with writing a first draft about the amendment each student felt was most important. Model Activity 5.2 allows for a continuation of study about the Bill of Rights and offers a writing activity using peer response groups to help students understand the meaning of a free press. Model Activity 5.3 is designed to help students be more aware of the need for protecting our freedom of speech. Model Activity 5.4 may be used as a guide for a writing activity making extensive use of peer response groups working toward the final goal of a class publication.

Cross-Grade Groups

Beverly Keiser (1991), a reading specialist at Casa De Oro Elementary School in Spring Valley, California, found cross-grade peer interaction an excellent way to create a real audience for meaningful student writing. Keiser found that "students will learn the importance of writing for authentic purposes when peers read and respond to student writing" (p. 250). This researcher discussed a strategy implemented after a second-grade class had read and discussed *Cinderella*. Discovering many unanswered questions about the story—"Did Cinderella marry the prince?" "What is Cinderella's stepmother like?" "Is Cinderella happy now?"—they wrote letters to the characters in the book. Each student chose a character and then joined a group of others who had chosen the same character to discuss and share ideas about questions they wanted to ask, as well as information about themselves they wanted to tell the book character. Once the letters

were written, revised, and edited, they were sent to a fifth-grade class for answers.

After the second-grade letters were distributed to the fifth-grade students, the fifth graders formed groups according to book characters to read and discuss the second-grade letters and plan their written responses. Drafts were written, revised, and edited as final copies to be sent back to the second graders. Imagine the excitement of the second graders as they received answers to their letters. As Keiser observed,

Through this experience both groups of students realized that their writing was valued and that such writing was worth the effort required to produce published works. Revisions became much more important because of the desire to communicate with the reader. Students used higher level thinking skills to generate questions in both the initial letters and responses.

An extension activity for this lesson might be to have the older students invite the second graders to a palace luncheon. The older students could organize the luncheon and dress as characters from the book. (p. 250)

Although this activity was conducted in an elementary setting, there is no reason to believe it would be any less successful among middle or high school students writing to another class to inquire about famous people in history, literature, science, or any field. Model Activity 5.5, for example, integrates a social studies topic with writing and cultural literacy as students correspond with some famous historical figures.

The Writing Workshop

Some educators choose to use the writing workshop as the setting for student writing. The writing workshop makes use of group sharing; therefore, many of the strategies already discussed in this chapter will apply to the workshop. When writers are ready to share drafts with more readers, the writing workshop provides the opportunity for developing writers to see potential in their work and solve problems with their drafts. The writing workshop demands that writers make their meaning clear; it is often surprising for writers to find out that something that is so clear to themselves may be difficult for others to understand. Critical thinking is called for in the writing workshop as students and teacher learn to construct and create meaningful text through interaction between writer and reader. Then the student can turn back to his or her draft and decide what needs to be done next.

The workshop sequence, as outlined by Murray (1985), follows:

- The writer comments on the draft.
- The workshop members listen and read the draft.
- The workshop members respond to the writer's comments and the draft.
- The writer responds to the workshop members' responses. (p. 193)

Calkins (1986) encouraged teachers to have a special time each day for the writing workshop. She stressed the importance of a clear, simple structure for the workshop, leaving teachers free to rearrange and adapt to student needs. Calkins continued:

... Teachers with whom I have worked tend to begin their workshops with a four or five minute mini-lesson. After talking to the children or giving them tips about good writing, the teacher sends them off to draft, revise, and confer with each other. The teacher moves around the room, talking with individuals about their writing, quietly managing the flow of the room, and meeting with informal clusters of children. The workshop ends with either a whole-class sharing session or small response groups. (p. 26)

Each teacher will establish the tone of the workshop. It should be relaxed, but students should be kept aware of the task at hand. Both joys and frustrations can be shared in a setting that allows for laughter as well as constructive criticism. The teacher is alert to reactions of students, draws out nonparticipating students, and keeps discussion on track. At the end, as at the beginning, the writer is invited to respond to the workshop and thank the class for their participation and help.

Some teachers also find written responses to drafts helpful, and a number of drafts can be shared at one time in this setting. Several blank pages can be stapled to the drafts; then as these texts are circulated, students may respond in writing to the drafts. The teacher might suggest questions to be answered, such as "Is the meaning clear?" or "I would publish this if . . . " Students also may request the responses they need. The idea is to keep the drafts moving around the classroom. This technique allows student readers to see many drafts at various stages of the writing process, thereby gaining insights that may be helpful in their own writing. Student writers get feedback from a number of peers, which usually points them toward a need to revise. The writing workshop is very useful when a product or composition to be published is the goal.

SHARING WRITING WITH PARENTS

Parents play an important role in the literacy development of their children. Therefore, teachers who involve parents and other adult caregivers as their students use process-based writing are making use of yet another means toward the goal of helping those students become effective writers. Reutzel and Fawson (1990) developed the use of a traveling tales backpack to involve parents with student writing activity, thereby establishing a bridge between the school and the home. Although the backpack idea was developed by Reutzel and Fawson for use with first graders, after they shared their results with teacher colleagues, requests came to use the idea with older students as well.

An assortment of writing materials, along with a laminated guideline sheet, filled the traveling tales backpack. Parents were telephoned beforehand to ensure greater cooperation. Each student had an opportunity to take the traveling tales backpack home

for a couple of days and nights during the next several months of school. When the backpack was to be returned, parents were invited to come to school, if possible, to share the writing completed at home by student and family working cooperatively.

Many interesting incidents were related by parents describing their traveling tales backpack experiences. Often, entire families got involved—brainstorming, planning, and answering questions as the students wrote and revised their drafts. It evolved naturally that the family became a peer conference group to help with the draft revisions and editing. Sometimes, illustrations drawn or selected by family members were added to contribute to the completion of the written work, which was shared with the class as each student returned the traveling tales backpack.

Reutzel and Fawson's traveling backpack idea can be adapted to be used effectively with students of all ages. For example, a class who decided to write about the topic "Grandparents or Other Special Relatives" could collaborate with their families to gather information. Notes from family discussions, interviews, photo albums, and written family records could be kept in large, plastic, zip-lock bags. Imagine the interesting drafts that could evolve from each student sharing something unique about his or her special person. The final drafts could be compiled to make an interesting class book.

SHARING WITH THE LARGER COMMUNITY

One reason for writing is to share ideas with other people. As students discuss differences in style between written work to be read by a particular person or persons and written work to be published in a newspaper, the concept of *audience* is strengthened. Students learn how a letter to their parents might differ from one written to the school principal or city mayor. They see how the informal written messages they share with one another in the classroom differ from a letter mailed to a member of Congress. Writing about one-to-one sharing, then total group sharing, and finally sharing with a specific or larger audience, Amspaugh (1989) stated:

I think that the most important outcome from all of these endeavors is that the children loved to write because they knew something positive would happen to their ideas. The sharing gave purpose and direction to what we were doing. They learned about several very important reasons for writing, and they recognized that they had become competent writers. (p. 188)

It is vital that teachers provide an atmosphere for sharing that encourages acceptance by others as they provide feedback at all stages of the writing process. As students realize that all writers revise, they will learn that the more input and assistance they get by sharing their drafts with others, the better their work will be. Then, in this safe environment, students will look forward to sharing their drafts, thus finding the feedback of others a valuable part of the writing process.

REFERENCES

Allen, J. B., Michalove, B., Shockley, B., & West, M. (1991). "I'm really worried about Joseph": Reducing the risks of literacy learning. *The Reading Teacher, 44*(7), 458–472.

Amspaugh, L. B. (1989). Writing is meant to be shared. *The Reading Teacher, 43*(2), 187–188.

Barell, J. (1991). Teaching for thoughtfulness: Classroom strategies to enhance intellectual development. White Plains, NY: Longman.

Black, M. (1968). *The labyrinth of language.* New York: Frederick A. Praeger.

Browne, C. (1991, September 23). Hi & Lois (cartoon). *The Tallahassee Democrat,* p. 4C.

Bunce-Crim, N. (1991). What is a writing classroom? *Instructor, 101*(2), 36–38.

Calkins, L. M. (1986). *The art of teaching writing.* Portsmouth, NH: Heinemann.

Crouse, P., & Davey, M. (1989). Collaborative learning: Insights from our children. *Language Arts, 66*(7), 756–766.

Daly, J. M. (1990). Successful peer conferencing. *The Reading Teacher, 44*(3), 280.

Duke, C. R. (1991). Evaluating the writing process. In B. L.

Hayes (Ed.). *Effective strategies for teaching reading.* Boston: Allyn and Bacon.

Glasser, W. (1986). *Control theory in the classroom.* New York: Harper & Row.

Graves, D. H. (1984). *A researcher learns to write.* Exeter, NH: Heinemann.

Hansen, J. (1992). The language of challenge: Readers and writers speak their minds. *Language Arts, 69*(2), 100–105.

Keiser, B. (1991). Creating authentic conditions for writing. *The Reading Teacher, 45*(3), 249–250.

Lindquist, B., & Ligett, C. (1992). Teachers write about research: Taking time to wonder. *Communication Quarterly, 14*(2), 2.

Maimon, E. P. (1988). Cultivating the prose garden. *Phi Delta Kappan, 69*(10), 734–739.

McMahon, S., & Raphael, T. (1992). Student book clubs. *Communication Quarterly, 14*(2), 1, 3–4.

Murray, D. M. (1989). *Expecting the unexpected.* Portsmouth, NH: Boynton/Cook.

Murray, D. M. (1985). *A writer teaches writing,* 2nd ed. Boston: Houghton Mifflin.

Reutzel, D. R., & Fawson, P. C. (1990). Traveling tales: Connecting parents and children through writing. *The Reading Teacher, 44*(3), 222–227.

Routman, R. (1991). *Invitations.* Portsmouth, NH: Heinemann.

Sagan, C., & Druyan, A. (1991). Real patriots ask questions. *Parade Magazine,* September 8, pp. 12–16.

Strong, W. J. (1991). Writing strategies that enhance reading. In B. L. Hayes (Ed.), *Effective strategies for teaching reading.* Boston: Allyn and Bacon.

Tiedt, S. W., & Tiedt, I. M. (1987). *Language arts activities for the classroom,* 2nd ed. Boston: Allyn and Bacon.

MODEL ACTIVITIES

The activities that follow are meant to serve as models; such activities should be used as part of a total learning environment. These model activities were designed to demonstrate how the writing process can be developed while expanding the writer's knowledge base and providing opportunities for the writer to think critically.

Becoming Helpful Group Members

Learning to work together and help one another are important. As a result, our classroom can become a place where learning is exciting and fun. Such an environment will also prepare us for being good citizens throughout our lives.

Think about today's group session as you respond by writing in the spaces below.

1. What was the best thing you did to help the group today? _____

_____

_____

2. What was the best thing a classmate did to help you today? _____

_____

_____

3. Do you think you can improve as a group contributor? _____ Give one or two suggestions: _____

_____

_____

_____

4. What bothered you most in today's group session? _____

_____

_____

_____

_____

5. Do you have other questions about today's group session? If so, write them below. _____

_____

_____

_____

_____

_____

6. As you take time to reflect on today's group session, consider how you felt as a group member. If you wish, describe some of those feelings. _____

_____

_____

_____

_____

_____

The Bill of Rights and a Free Press

The federal government of the United States is based on one of history's most remarkable documents, the Constitution of the United States. Drafted in 1787 and ratified the following year, the Constitution is successful because of its ability to adjust to meet needs of changing times and the acceptance of its basic principles by the American people. A source of authority for the Constitution was the Declaration of Independence adopted on July 4, 1776.

Thomas Jefferson (1743–1826), main author of the Declaration of Independence and third president of the United States (1801–1809), was not involved with writing the Constitution because at that time he was abroad, serving as America's ambassador to France. He was very interested in it, however; and when he read the Constitution, he was very pleased— with two exceptions. One was that he feared that, with no limit on the number of terms the president could serve, a president could become like a king. (In 1951, the Twenty-second Amendment limited the presidency to two terms.) Jefferson's second worry was the absence of a bill of rights whereby the average person would be protected from abuses by those in power.

Jefferson's concerns were considered; and, in 1791, the first ten amendments, called the Bill of Rights, were added to the Constitution. Because of the Bill of Rights, we enjoy important freedoms that affect our lives every day, although we often take these freedoms for granted.

Amendment 1 of the Bill of Rights guarantees freedom of speech, freedom of the press, and freedom of religion. It also guarantees people the right to assemble peacefully and to petition the government. In 1816, Thomas Jefferson boldly stated the following about the importance of a free press: "When the press is free and every man able to read, all is safe."

1. In small groups, discuss the Bill of Rights, especially Amendment 1. Study a copy of the original ten amendments, as well as those that have been added since 1791. Check newspapers to find examples of the Bill of Rights in action today. Brainstorm about what the first amendment means to each student in your group.

2. Draft a paragraph or two telling what you think Jefferson meant when he said, "When the press is free and every man able to read, all is safe." Tell also what this statement means to you today.

_____

_____

_____

_____

_____

_____

_____

_____

_____
_____
_____
_____
_____
_____
_____
_____

3. Assemble in small groups to share your first drafts. Help one another with suggestions for changes that will make the pieces of writing better. Also, discuss the possibility of sharing your final products with a larger audience. If the group decides to do so, discuss how you would like to proceed.

4. Rewrite your revised draft in the space below:

_____
_____
_____
_____
_____
_____
_____
_____
_____
_____
_____
_____
_____
_____
_____
_____
_____
_____

Protecting Our Freedom of Speech

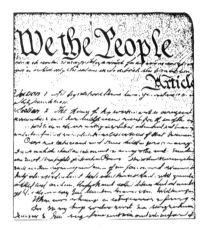

An important part of being an American citizen is knowing how to use and protect our freedoms guaranteed by the Bill of Rights. Education about the value of free speech, for instance, and about what could happen if we didn't have it, can help us understand our freedoms. Carl Sagan, Pulitzer Prize–winning science teacher, and Ann Druyan, secretary of the Federation of American Scientists and Sagan's wife, were quoted in the September 8, 1991, issue of *Parade Magazine* as having said the following:

> If we can't think for ourselves, if we're unwilling to question authority, then we're just putty in the hands of those in power. But if the citizens are educated and form their own opinions, then those in power work for *us*. (p. 16; emphasis in the original)

The authors of these words exercised their First Amendment freedoms of the Constitution by organizing protests against one of their concerns: continual nuclear weapons' testing. The Constitution is a courageous document because it allows for continuous change if this is the wish of the people.

1. Organize in small groups to discuss how our freedom of speech can be protected and preserved. Think especially about what *you* can do. Make a list by jotting down ideas as they are given by each student in your group.

   _____   _____

   _____   _____

   _____   _____

   _____   _____

2. Draft a paragraph about your view of freedom of speech. How do you exercise this freedom? What do you do to protect misuse of this freedom? If you feel any changes are needed in the Constitution, write about your ideas. You may want to put your suggested change(s) in the form of a new amendment.

_____

_____

_____

_____

_____

_____

_____

_____

3. Share first drafts in groups, giving and receiving feedback for improvements. Make plans for revision.

4. Rewrite your piece below, incorporating suggested changes that you feel will make your writing more meaningful. _____

_____

_____

_____

_____

_____

_____

_____

_____

_____

_____

_____

_____

_____

_____

_____

_____

_____

_____

_____

_____

_____

_____

_____

_____

_____

_____

_____

_____

_____

_____

ACTIVITY 5.4

In Charge When Home Alone

There may be times when you need to be home without a parent or other adult there. When you are home alone or with younger children, you are in charge. This is an important responsibility. It means knowing how to act and what to do. It means being prepared to deal with things that can happen. It is a challenge that can contribute to your personal growth. An unknown writer once said, "Challenges can be stepping stones or stumbling blocks. It's just a matter of how you view them."

This is a class writing activity. The finished product will be a guidebook to help you take care of yourself and handle things when you're home alone. You will work in teams. The activity will not be completed in one session; together, you and your teacher decide how much time can be devoted to this activity. Then you, along with your classmates and teacher, can decide on your specific writing schedule. The suggestions that follow will help you get started.

1. *Prewriting:* Brainstorm to generate a list of topics that could be included in your guidebook. This could be accomplished by continuing the web already started:

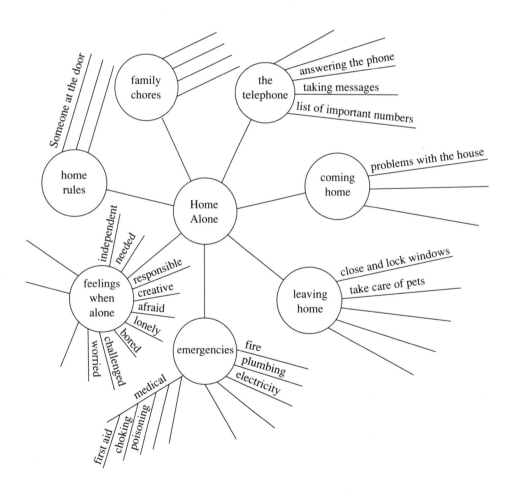

2. *First drafts:* After topics have been chosen by the class, your teacher will help divide the class into teams. For instance, if nine major topics are chosen to be included in your guidebook, and there are 27 students in your class, each team will comprise three students.

As you work in your smaller group, plan and agree on the writing task for which each member of your team will be responsible. For example, a team writing on the topic of the telephone might decide on the following subtopics: lists of important phone numbers, answering the phone, and taking phone messages. After your group has agreed on who is to be responsible for writing about each subtopic, use the space below to write a first draft.

Major topic: _____

My subtopic: _____

_____

_____

_____

_____

_____

_____

_____

_____

_____

3. *Sharing the draft:* After each team member has written a first draft, share these drafts with one another. The suggested additions and improvements will then be considered by each writer for possible revision. If necessary, rewrite your draft below:

_____

_____

_____

_____

_____

_____

_____

_____

_____

_____

_____

_____

_____

_____

4. *Sharing the final draft:* Drafts are now ready to be shared with a larger audience. The class may be divided into teams of five or six, within which each draft can be read and feedback given. Team members are encouraged to offer help with content and meaning, organization, and mechanics of writing. Each writer ends this session with plans for revision. Use the space below to rewrite your completed draft:

_____

_____

_____

_____

_____

_____

_____

_____

_____

_____

_____

_____

_____

5. *Completing the activity:* After writers have revised, edited, rewritten drafts, and proofread, writing is to be shared with the larger audience once more for final approval. The class is now ready to choose their mode of publication for this project.

_____

_____

_____

_____

_____

_____

_____

_____

_____

_____

ACTIVITY 5.5

An Historic Writing Assignment

The Bill of Rights, or the first ten admendments to the Constitution, was added to the Constitution in 1791. The source of authority for the Bill of Rights was the Declaration of Independence. In this writing activity, we will review how the Declaration of Independence came into being. We will also learn about the people who drafted this document by writing letters to the men who were the authors.

By 1776, the political relationship between Great Britain and her thirteen colonies in North America was bleak and steadily growing worse. Many members of the Continental Congress were pleading for the cause of independence. On June 7, a Virginia delegate, Richard Henry Lee, moved that the political connection between the colonies and Great Britain should be dissolved, with the colonies becoming free and independent states. The motion was seconded by John Adams of Massachusetts. Some delegates agreed with Lee, but others wanted more time to think about such a serious step. Therefore, the vote was deferred until July 1. The Congress appointed a committee of the following five men to plan and write a statement giving the reasons for the colonies' declaring their independence from Great Britain.

1. Thomas Jefferson (1743–1826) was a tall, young lawyer from Virginia. He was a fine thinker and writer; he could express his thoughts in clear, inspiring words. He was also an inventor, architect, scientist, political philosopher, and statesman. He later became the third president of the United States. He died on July 4, 1826, fifty years after the Declaration of Independence was adopted.

2. John Adams (1735–1826) was a prominent lawyer from Massachusetts who had studied at Harvard. He later was chosen the first vice-president to serve with George Washington. John Adams then became the second president of the United States. Like Thomas Jefferson, Adams died on July 4, 1826, fifty years after the adoption of the Declaration of Independence.

3. Benjamin Franklin (1706–1790) was one of a family of seventeen children and went to work when he was only ten years old in his father's candle- and soap-making shop. He studied before and after work and late at night. He became a printer, writer, inventor, philosopher, politician, scientist, wise statesman, and civic leader of Philadelphia.

4. Roger Sherman (1721–1793) was from Connecticut. Studying nights while working as a shoemaker, he was able to become a fine lawyer and judge. John Adams said he was "as firm in the cause of American independence as Mount Atlas." He later served his state—first as representative, then senator.

5. Robert R. Livingston (1746–1813) was a young statesman and lawyer from New York. He later became minister to France and was successful in arranging for the Louisiana Purchase by the United States. He also financially backed the engineer Robert Fulton in building the steamboat.

When this group of five men appointed to draft the document went to work, they chose Jefferson to prepare the draft. Adams and Franklin made a number of minor revisions before it was submitted to Congress.

On July 2, 1776, the Congress gathered to vote on the statement of independence. First, all listened carefully as the authors of the declaration read their final draft. This document stated that all men are created equal and have the right to life, liberty, and the pursuit of happiness. The audience cheered after the reading and shook hands with the members of the committee. Then the delegates went to work carefully discussing each part of the document and making a few small revisions. Late on July 4, 1776, delegates from twelve colonies voted to accept the Declaration of Independence; soon the remaining colony, New York, sent a messenger with its vote for the document. Then the Declaration of Independence was published by being engrossed on parchment and signed.

The first person to sign the Declaration was the President of the Congress, an American patriot and statesman from Massachusetts, John Hancock. He signed in large, bold handwriting so that "George the Third might read it without his spectacles." Even today, when one signs a document, the act is often referred to as putting one's "John Hancock" on the line.

Directions: Choose one of the historical figures associated with the Declaration of Independence. It can be one of the five authors or another person who was active in supporting the cause of independence. Plan a letter you will write to your chosen historical figure: _____

My historical figure is _____.

1. Brainstorm by jotting down some questions you want to ask the person to whom you are writing. You may find it helpful to read more about the person before starting your letter.

_____

_____

_____

_____

_____

2. List some things about yourself that you want to tell the person to whom you are writing.

_____

_____

_____

_____

_____

3. Write a first draft of your letter to your chosen historical figure, using the space provided.

_____

_____

_____

_____

_____

_____

_____

_____

_____

4. Gather in groups to read your letters, giving and receiving suggestions for revision.

_____

_____

_____

_____

_____

_____

_____

_____

_____

_____

5. After revising and editing your letter, write it on a piece of stationery for sending to your chosen historical figure, represented by a classmate, who will respond with an answer.

Now—exchange the letters with classmates or with other students in your school. Then, prepare an answer to the letter you receive, keeping in mind the process that you use for writing. Also, remember to proofread carefully before sending your letter; it should be free of errors.

These letters also might be used for role playing in the classroom, as historical figures from the past come alive to speak to an audience of today.

CHAPTER 6

Revising and Editing

Revision—the process of seeing what you've said to discover what you have to say—is the motivating force within most writers. They are compelled to write to see what their words tell them.

—Donald Murray, Pulitzer Prize–winning author (1982, p. 121)

Revising—the magic of writing, the joy of writing, the challenge of writing, the reward of writing—revising is often all of these. Just as the same ingredients in the kitchen can become, in qualified hands, a gourmet treat, an epicurean delight, or, in the hands of the unskilled, a chef's nightmare; so can the changes made during the revision process send an author soaring with delight over the evolving product or to the depths of despair over lack of success. Most authors have had moments at both ends of this spectrum. Many famous writers have commented that they write to learn what they have to say. James Michener (1907–), the author of *Hawaii, Iberia,* and many other highly respected works, said that instead of being a good first-draft writer, he thinks of himself as a good *reviser*—exceedingly good, if book sales and critics' reviews mean anything. Thomas Wolfe (1900–1938), another well-known North American author, reported that he'd rewritten the ending to one of his most popular novels, *Look Homeward, Angels,* thirty-nine times. It's Edison's genius formula reported in Chapter 2 of this book all over again—"one percent inspiration; ninety-nine percent perspiration." Even for the most successful writers, revision is a necessary part of the writing process. Typically, expert writers revise constantly, though not all in the same way.

Interest in improving writing gained importance in the United States throughout the 1980s, and this trend has continued to the present. Donald Murray, a professor of English at the University of New Hampshire, won a Pulitzer Prize for journalism and has published in many, many forms from poetry to nonfiction for juveniles and adults. Donald Graves, a professor of education at the University of New Hampshire and director of the Writing Process Laboratory, studied how young children become writers. With Lucy Calkins and Susan Sowers, Graves observed sixteen children of varying abilities for two years in a rural school to see how they learned the writing process. The names of these writers and researchers, among others, became synonymous with the writing process during the 1980s.

WHY TEACH REVISION?

Donald Murray (1982), author of several books about how he teaches writing, had this to say about revising:

Unfortunately most language arts and English teachers do not appreciate the importance or the excitement of revision. They teach rewriting—if they teach it at all—as punishment, the price you have to pay if you don't get it right the first time.

But few, if any writers ever get it right the first time. They write to catch a glimpse of what they may see and then revise—and revise and revise and revise—to make it come clear....

Since the writer doesn't know what the pen is going to put on the page, the first task of revision is vision. The writer must stand back from the work the way any craftsman does to see what has been done. The writer reads with wonder and with care to find out what the page may be saying. Writers often know more clearly what they don't want to say than what they do. (p. 121)

John Ashbery (Begley, Ramo, & Rosenberg, 1993), considered a genius of lyric poetry, is another writer who says he writes to find meaning. He said, "I sort of collect words that suddenly seem to have a new meaning for me, in contexts I have never thought of before. I don't plan my writing. What comes out is usually quite surprising. I write to find out what I'm thinking" (p. 50).

Teachers who are writers themselves, of course, know firsthand that revising is "a central aspect of writing" (Fitzgerald, 1988, p. 124). Since the purpose of writing is to communicate, and to do so as clearly as possible, the writer makes necessary changes in content and/or mechanics to accomplish this purpose. According to Fitzgerald (1988), "Revision means making any changes at any point in the writing process" (p.124). Cooper (1986) recommended that students examine the following two broad areas during this stage of the writing process: "(1) Content—ideas, choice of words, and so forth [and] (2) Writing mechanics—such as spelling and punctuation" (p. 324). Humes (1983), in defining revision, also included changes in organization and content as well as editing changes. Developing writers examine these two broad areas in an effort to create clarity; that is, to craft a message that is clear, or easy to understand. And as the Chinese philosopher, Confucius (c. 551–479 B.C.), espoused, "In language, clarity is everything." To achieve the worthy goal of clarity, writers must revise their content and edit for the mechanics of grammar, punctuation, and spelling; then, these steps must be repeated until writers are satisfied. For example, consider what the well-known North American writer, Mark Twain (pen name of Samuel Langhorne Clemens, 1835–1910) said about the importance of choice of words with regard to content: "The difference between the right word and the almost right word is like the difference between lightning and the lightning bug." As we continue to enjoy Twain's wit in his novels, such as *Huckleberry Finn* and *The Adventures of Tom Sawyer,* the importance of choice of words is more and more evident.

As Nold (1981) emphasized, revision is not something that occurs once after the writing is finished. Fitzgerald (1988) offered that writers may reprocess their ideas during revision, and that "revision is recursive and can occur at any point in the writing process, embedded within other subprocesses" (p. 124). Recognizing along with Graves (1984) that revision may not seem natural to students, Cooper (1986) suggested that teachers provide ample modeling and conferencing opportunities as developing writers learn to revise. These revision conferences are essential and may take place before, during, or after the writer actually makes changes; revision conferences also may take various forms, such as between teacher and student, between students with similar writing abilities, between students with different writing abilities, between student and visiting author, and so on. Through practice, students will develop the art of revision and thus will become better able to determine what changes to make as they construct and/or clarify written messages.

To help her students better understand the concept of revision, a public school teacher brainstormed with her students to develop a list of reasons a writer might choose to make changes. As you will observe, their ideas could be categorized under Cooper's two broad areas—content and writing mechanics. Some of the reasons students suggested for revision included the following:

- To discover for themselves what they want to say
- To expand their topic by adding information
- To use various styles of presentation, such as anecdotes, to create interest
- To present the material in a more interesting way, including anecdotal style
- To improve word choice
- To combine short, choppy sentences
- To clarify voice and audience
- To answer questions
- To create enticing titles and leads that capture the reader's interest
- To reorganize their material to make better sense or to make the piece flow better

Just as this teacher brainstormed with her developing writers, she also practiced the habit of writing with them. As suggested by Murray (1982, p. 127), she wrote with the students, "showing them how badly the writer writes, revealing the failures and mistakes and stupidities and awkwardness that clumsily lead the writer toward meaning, a meaning the writer did not expect, perhaps did not even want to accept." This secure teacher had the courage necessary to model revision of her own drafts. She was willing to risk being imperfect in front of her students. She shared her errors as she noted ways to improve her draft and encouraged her students to do the same. They were "sharing the challenge of their art" just as "the oboe teacher plays along with the student oboist" (Murray, 1982, p. 127). Like the mother eagle who pushes her babies out of the nest in order to teach them to use their own wings to fly, then scoops underneath them in the air after each effort, catching them and safely depositing them back in the nest to try again and again until they are ready to solo, this teacher taught revision techniques in a meaningful context. She helped her students learn *how* to move through the recursive steps associated with revision. She was preparing them to "solo" as they became more skillful writers; during this process, she always kept in mind that "there are developmental differences in the ability to revise" (Lundsteen, 1989, p. 267). As a motivational tool, as well as an example of one form of writing, she often referred students to the following stanza from Emily Dickinson's poem, "Aspiration," which they had studied together earlier in the term:

> We never know how high we are
> Till we are called to rise;
> And then, if we are true to plan,
> Our statures touch the skies.*
> —First stanza from "Aspiration"

Guidelines for Teaching Revision

Revision strategies and techniques can be nurtured, and since students "do not automatically and immediately revise" (Lundsteen, 1989, p. 268), revision in all likelihood will need to be taught. Fitzgerald (1988) offered two good reasons for nurturing the ability of revision with writers of all ages: "First, reworking thoughts and ideas can powerfully affect writers' knowledge. . . . Second, under certain circumstances, revision may improve the quality of compositions" (p. 125). With regard to the second reason, Fitzgerald stressed that "the critical aspect is not merely how many revisions are made but rather which ones" (p. 125). In a classroom where

*Source: Reprinted by permission of the publishers and the trustees of Amherst College from *The Poems of Emily Dickinson*, Thomas H. Johnson, ed., Cambridge, Mass.: The Belknap Press of Harvard University Press, Copyright © 1951, 1955, 1979, 1983 by the President and Fellows of Harvard College.

students write frequently and have ample opportunity for conferring with peers and their teacher about their work-in-progress, revision takes on the perspective of natural problem solving. Fitzgerald (1988) offered the following three guidelines for teachers interested in developing the revision ability of their students:

First, activities ought to take place in the context of a larger program of writing instruction designed to help writers develop knowledge of the content of what they want to write about and develop knowledge of characteristics of "good" text. . . . Second, activities ought to focus on the process, not the product, of revision. That is, students ought to see revision as a way of thinking, not solely as making marks on paper. . . . Third, if revision is to become a way of thinking, it should be seen as an integral aspect of many types of writing—not just creative writing, but content area report and essay writing, letter writing, and poetry writing as well. (p. 126)

How much direct instruction related to revision should be provided, given that it has received little emphasis in most public schools in the United States? As one teacher quipped, "A lot more than in the past!" In the primary grades, a more naturalistic approach can be taken, allowing for experimentation and encouraging peer conferencing. According to Fitzgerald (1988), "Direct instruction and procedural facilitation . . . have been investigated with intermediate grade children, and are likely to be most successful with students at that age level or older" (p. 126). Teacher modeling, using think-alouds, should be particularly helpful for developing writers who learn well through the vehicle of demonstrations. Of course, inherent in a direct instructional approach are guided practice opportunities in which students may work in pairs or teams, as well as other opportunities for practicing revision on their own.

As students develop their work-in-progress and seek feedback from others, including their peers and the teacher, they will begin to plan their revisions. Tompkins (1990), emphasizing the importance of the student's commitment to revision, stated the following:

At the end of the writing group, students each make a commitment to revise their writing based on the comments and suggestions of their writing group members. The final decision on what to revise always rests with the writers themselves, but with the understanding that their rough drafts are not perfect comes the realization that some revision will be necessary. When students verbalize their planned revisions, they are more likely to complete the revision stage. Some students also make notes for themselves about their revision plans. (pp. 87–88)

As students make their revisions, Tompkins (1990) suggested that both teachers and students give attention to the kinds of revisions that are being made. In that regard Tompkins (1990, p. 89) offered the revision hierarchy shown in Figure 6.1 and suggested that it could be shared "with upper-grade students so that they can know the revision options they have available."

Model Activities 6.1 through 6.6 were designed for helping student writers develop their revision abilities. Many fine teachers, from the earliest grades on up, have observed firsthand the positive results that occur when they model revision and then allow students to practice these newly introduced strategies and techniques in writing that is meaningful to them. Likewise, wise teachers also carefully choose the content for modeling; for example, the authors of this text selected interesting material that would contribute to the development of students' cultural literacy for the majority of the model activities found at the end of each chapter.

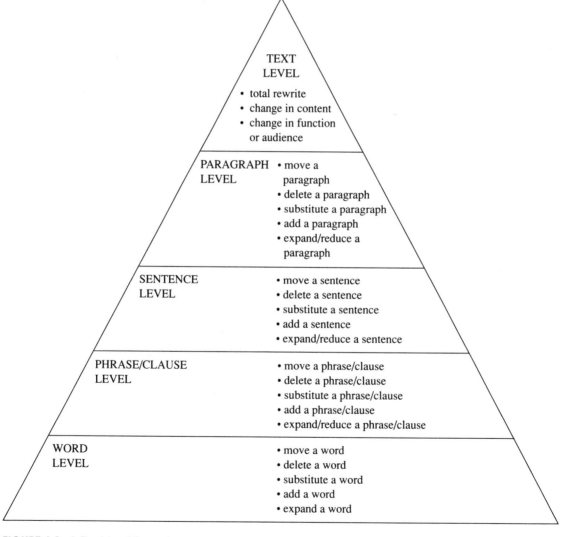

FIGURE 6.1 A Revision Hierarchy

Source: Reprinted with the permission of Merrill, an imprint of Macmillan Publishing Company, from *Teaching Writing: Balancing Process and Product* by Gail E. Tompkins. Copyright © 1990 by Merrill Publishing Company.

The Use of Reference Tools in Revision

As students learn to revise their work, reference skills also should be modeled. The best times to address reference skills and reference resources such as dictionaries and thesauri are within the meaningful context of students' work-in-progress—that is, when their use will serve the students' writing purposes. As students are revising and editing, they should have easy access to reference tools; reference books can be shared conveniently in a classroom, either at a center or on a movable cart. Goodman, Bird, and Goodman (1991) suggested that several dictionaries should be available

that vary in complexity and size. . . . The dictionary can help confirm what a pupil thinks a word means. It can confirm the standard spelling(s) of a word. It can, for what it's worth, suggest the history of a word. And, it can indicate at least one possible pronunciation, though that may vary from dialect to dialect. (p. 150)

Goodman et al. also emphasized the importance of letting students know the limitations of resources such as dictionaries. Gunning (1992), stressing the importance of the functional use of dictionaries, encouraged instruction in dictionary usage:

Many school dictionaries include generous instructions for use together with practice exercises. Use these, but concentrate on building dictionary skills through functional use. That is, show students how to use the dictionary and encourage them to incorporate it as a tool for understanding language. For instance, when they have

questions about word meaning, pronunciation, spelling, or usage, have them seek help in the dictionary. (p.152)

One of the most useful and easiest books to use for revising is the thesaurus. The following true story, told by an outstanding educator, may prove useful when introducing students to this resource tool. Her most meaningful use of the thesaurus happened many years ago when two colleagues decided to send a valentine to their principal, who was famous for his boastful comments. Proud of anything to do with their school, he would say of virtually every new idea, piece of equipment, or building part: "It has already been called the most famous . . . in . . . County." The pair of teachers wanted to send him a valentine that would keep him guessing about whether they had complimented or insulted him. They were determined to use words they thought he wouldn't know. So they created lines for the valentine that were subtly complimentary (actually, they really liked this person). Then, they looked up each adjective they had chosen in a thesaurus to find a synonym unknown to them— and (they hoped) to him also—calculating that their message would send the "show-off" to his dictionary for deciphering. They never found out whether their anonymous valentine was appreciated, but they had a wonderful time themselves during the process of writing it—and they learned new words as they used language in a context that was meaningful to them. This natural situation for using a thesaurus made them acutely aware of the need for planning activities to acquaint their students with this marvelous resource.

EDITING

At what point is the developing writer ready to move from revising and sharing drafts to editing, or as Tompkins (1990, p. 88) wrote, "putting the piece of writing into its final form"? Most writers create several drafts and share them with various others, as described earlier in this chapter, prior to polishing their writing. Of course, the number of drafts per composition varies from writer to writer and with any one writer, depending on the topic, writing form, and/or circumstances. Many published authors admit that there are days when their words seem to flow, almost as if they were prerecorded; then, there are other days when it takes much of a morning to create one acceptable paragraph. In all

likelihood, the developing writer will need to learn that this is normal; ultimately, he or she must decide when a piece is ready to move to another stage.

Whereas the focus during the revising stage was primarily on creating meaningful content, the writer at the editing stage is ready to focus on making the piece as readable as possible; this means that the writer will reread the work-in-progress, looking for all errors including mechanics. According to Tompkins (1990),

Mechanics are the commonly accepted conventions of written standard English. They include capitalization, punctuation, spelling, sentence structure, usage, and formatting considerations specific to poems, scripts, letters, and other writing forms. The use of these commonly accepted conventions is a courtesy to those who will read the composition. (p. 88)

Editing is an essential part of preparing a piece of writing for public reading or publication. "In editing, writers check spelling, capitalization, punctuation, usage, and related problems" (Hennings, 1990, p. 311). According to Hull (1987), the process of editing involves "correcting writing errors in grammar, syntax, punctuation, and spelling" and "is to be distinguished from the process of revision—reworking a text in such a way as to substantially alter its content or structure" (p. 56). Error making is viewed as part of learning language and thus as quite natural as one learns. Hull (1987) emphasized that error correcting is "a complex cognitive skill" (p. 56) and "a process that proceeds through rule induction and hypothesis testing" (p. 64). Finding errors occurs as the writer rereads what has been written thus far; errors also may be identified through requested feedback from peers and teachers. Of course, consideration must be given to the reality that students with learning disabilities may have difficulty identifying errors and proofreading. Educators working with these students report the usefulness of teaching coping strategies, such as using computer spell checkers and asking their classmates to assist them with proofreading. To the extent possible, students should be encouraged to self-edit before seeking assistance or feedback from others. In this regard, Form 6.1, A Revising and Editing Checklist, can be used as is or modified for use as a tool for developing writers.

Many students will choose (and should be encouraged) to develop their own checklists. As students reread their writings and ask others to do the same, checklists can be used as part of their decision-making and learning process. Writers may discover, for example, that they need to learn more about apostrophes in order to use them properly in the current pieces that they are fine-tuning. Addressing an authentic need will be far more meaningful to writers than having them memorize isolated rules in the non-meaning-making context of a rule book. Likewise, conferencing with students about their ideas for editing will yield better results than red-marking the errors on students' compositions. For example, it may be during these confer-

ences that students share their feelings that some things don't sound right grammatically in particular sentences of their work-in-progress, but they don't know exactly what needs to be changed. This puts teachers in an excellent position to assist instructionally without taking any responsibility away from the students. Fisher and Terry (1990) suggested that when students

are given the responsibility of editing their own writing, they engage in a meaningful learning experience. They make decisions about comma placements, spelling, sentence structure, and so on. When they check their own drafts for correctness by reading them aloud, or asking partners to read them, they discover their errors and see a need for correcting them. (p. 361)

It was during such a conference that one middle school writer said that she "suspected" that a particular word in her composition was misspelled; she had circled the word when she reread her material, reminding herself to check the spelling. The teacher, wishing to encourage the student to take responsibility for her own editing, asked her what *she* (the student) planned to do about the possible error. Smiling in a self-assured manner, the student quipped, "I could look it up in the dictionary." The teacher nodded affirmatively, leaning forward a bit to show that she was listening. It was then that the student surprised her with the following question: "Did you know that the dictionary is the only place where *success* comes before *work*?" (attributed to Arthur Brisbane). The student and teacher laughed briefly, and the student continued, "I could use a spell checker if I had access to a computer, I could ask another student who spells well, or I could ask you to tell me if it's right." And that's just what that amused, kind, and perceptive teacher did; she gave the developing writer the requested feedback immediately. She chose to do so for a couple of very good reasons. First, she wanted to continue building a better working relationship with this fledgling writer. Second, knowing that the student understood several strategies for determining the correctness of the word's spelling, the teacher chose to use their remaining time together for other things that the student still wanted to address. This flexible teacher and the developing writer continued their conference, with the writer taking the lead comfortably in a trusting relationship that had been facilitated by a teacher who responded positively to the student's risk-taking humor. This teacher observed

Name _____

Date _____

Title _____

Type _____

Intended Audience _____

Check (√) if you agree. List page number/s of possible errors.
Student   Peer   Teacher

Content
The content fits the assignment.

____   ____   ____

My writing makes sense.

____   ____   ____

Format
I used correct form.

____   ____   ____

I followed conventions.

____   ____   ____

Spelling
Errors Corrected

____   ____   ____

	Student	*Peer*	*Teacher*
Capitalization			
First words	___	___	___
Titles	___	___	___
Geographical	___	___	___
Govt. bodies	___	___	___
Languages	___	___	___
Organizations	___	___	___
Others	___	___	___
Punctuation			
Periods	___	___	___
Question marks	___	___	___
Exclamation marks	___	___	___
Commas	___	___	___
Apostrophes	___	___	___
Hyphens	___	___	___
Colons	___	___	___
Quotation marks	___	___	___
Parentheses	___	___	___
Others	___	___	___

Other Notes

Student_____

Peer _____

Teacher _____

FORM 6.1 A Revising and Editing Checklist

firsthand that this particular student, who previously had seemed hesitant to take charge of editing her own writing, was actually enjoying the new empowerment associated with assuming responsibility for decisions about her work-in-progress. A few days later, when this same student served as an editor for another writer, she modeled strategies that she had acquired earlier during her conference with the wise teacher. It was obvious to everyone that learning was taking place in this environment; furthermore, learning was viewed as an enjoyable and worthwhile endeavor.

Handwriting Legibility

A group of teachers had been discussing whether handwriting should be considered by students as they edited their compositions. With today's movement away from the idea of beautiful penmanship as an art to be taught in the classroom, and toward word processing at a computer, one teacher shared the following vignette with her colleagues:

After her students had edited their own writing with their current knowledge base of grammar, punctuation, spelling, etc., she encouraged them to work together in their next step of moving their work-in-progress toward publication. As she recalled, Lucy Calkins had recommended in one of her books that students will pass information along to one another when given the opportunity. Also, this teacher wanted to reinforce the value of cooperative learning. All seemed to be running quite smoothly in the learning environment until she heard one student sigh with exasperation and then exclaim to the other, "I can hardly read your handwriting!" It was on this day that the class decided to add handwriting legibility to their editing checklist.

The teachers concurred with the students' conclusion to consider legibility of handwriting under editing. As they discussed this concern further, they focused on how they could help students who may not have been developmentally ready for penmanship instruction during the initial stages of writing. The following suggestions were offered:

1. Observe students as they write to see how they are holding the writing tool and paper as well as how they are forming their letters and words.
2. Conference with students about their particular needs.
3. Provide modeling and practice opportunities where needed.

Spelling

The conversation about handwriting legibility flowed almost immediately into problems associated with spelling and the editing stage of the writing process. One teacher reflected, "While it's very difficult to determine what's misspelled until the handwriting is made more legible, even students composing at a computer struggle with spelling." Another teacher validated this concern and offered that her students, who were frequent users of word processors, had decided that it was okay to use invented spelling as a placeholder during the initial stages of writing; she reported that a class representative had summed up the class consensus this way: "If we stop to look up every word we're not sure is spelled correctly, or take time to ask someone, the flow of writing will be broken often." Not a single student, however, thought concern for cor-

rect spelling should be minimized during the editing stage or the final proofreading before publication.

There appears to be agreement among educators that "spelling is important in the writing process" (Allred, 1987, p. 8). As students construct meaning through the written word, spelling can be addressed within the context of their writing. Manning and Manning (1986) emphasized the importance of understanding that "spelling is for writing" (p. 10). Gentry (1987) offered that "purposeful writing is the key to learning to spell" (p. 28). Rather than being an end in itself, spelling accurately helps one become a more effective and efficient writer. As students move their work-in-progress toward a product, there is an authentic need for accurately spelled words.

As writers move to the editing stage of the writing process, the constructive developmental process of spelling is evident. It is at this point that concern is directed toward spelling accuracy; the writer rereads the composition and addresses mechanics such as the identification and correction of misspelled words. Horn (1967) stated that there was ample evidence indicating that "the mere checking of spelling errors does little good unless accompanied by an effective plan for learning the words which have been misspelled" (p. 13). Twenty years later, Allred (1987) reaffirmed the need for "a plan for correcting composition spelling errors" as well as "procedures for learning misspelled words" (p. 8); he stressed that "continued research is needed to identify the most productive means of improving spelling ability during the writing process" (p. 8). Perhaps new insights will be forthcoming, as suggested by Allred, as a result of "a shift in the nature of investigating writing and spelling from the empirical to the case study approach" (p. 8). Meanwhile, it will be prudent for educators to keep in mind the complexity of the orthography (the writing of words with letters in the proper order according to standard usage) of the English language and to reconsider the position of Hodges (1981) that learning to spell is a developmental process. In this regard, the following suggestions of Hodges (1981) should be helpful:

1. Spelling should be taught in the context of general language study. It should provide children with opportunities to explore the ways in which their knowledge of spoken language relates to writing and how to apply that knowledge to spelling.

"How can it be misspelled? I just made it up!"

© 1992; Reprinted courtesy of Bunny Hoest and Parade Magazine

2. The focus of spelling should be on presenting spelling as an integrated system.

3. A variety of instructional materials and approaches should be used to provide for individual learning styles and rates.

4. Spelling instruction should foster an exploration of English spelling, building on the natural inquisitiveness of children and providing opportunities for them to apply growing orthographic knowledge in a variety of writing situations.

5. Spelling instruction needs to provide numerous opportunities for students to assess their written words and, with teacher guidance, to use spelling errors as a springboard to new understandings about the orthography. (pp. 11–13)

As the discussion of spelling came to a close that afternoon, the teachers agreed that number 4 in the foregoing list was crucially important. If developing writers are encouraged to explore English spelling and to understand *why* the English language is hard to spell, there is a greater likelihood that they will view orthography as an interesting challenge, not a stumbling block. In that regard, the following newspaper clipping was offered:

Kids' Question

Q. Why is the English language so hard to spell?

A. There are three basic reasons. One is that the spoken language has changed over the years, but the spellings have not. For example, the word "pine" used to be pronounced "Peony." Also the "ough," in words such as "through," used to have its own special sound similar to a sound used in the German language, but it was dropped. Another reason is that we change pronunciations to fit English tradition. In the word "pneumonia," we pronounce only the "n." But in the Greek language, where the word came from, both the "p" and the "n" are pronounced. And last, different spellings emerged for words that sound alike but have different meanings, such as "to" and "too."—*Philadelphia Inquirer**

Given that students will observe the irregularities of English orthography and, as a result, make natural inquiries, teachers will need to design instruction that allows time for exploration and related discussions.

Usage

Hennings (1990), referring to usage skills, included the following: "the ability to begin and end sentences and paragraphs in writing, handle capitalization and punctuation conventions, and work with noun and verb usage patterns" (p. 356). Hennings clarified the distinction between *grammar* and *usage* by referring to the 1985 work of Robert Hillerich:

He explains that "Grammar has to do with the way words are strung together in order to make intelligible (or 'legal') sentences in the language. 'I brung the pencil' is

*Source: Tallahassee Democrat, March 31, 1992, p. 1B. Used with the permission of the Tallahassee Democrat.

grammatical; 'I the brung pencil' is not." In contrast, usage is a "matter of language habit" and social acceptability. As Hillerich further explains, "'I don't have a pencil' is socially acceptable usage in school, but 'I ain't got no pencil' is unacceptable." (p. 366)

According to Vacca, Vacca, and Gove (1991), "The key to learning oral language lies in the opportunities children have to explore and experiment with language toward purposeful ends" (p. 14). Given that grammar is learned intuitively as youngsters explore and experiment with the language spoken in their homes, many students will come to the writing table unaware that their work-in-progress deviates from standard English. Tompkins (1990) warned that "too often the correction of usage errors is a repudiation of the language spoken in children's homes rather than an explanation that written language requires a more formal language dialect or register" (p. 293). Rather than correcting errors through an oral process wherein students are asked if the corrected language sounds better, Tompkins recommended "a problem-solving approach during the editing stage of the writing process. Locating and correcting errors in students' writing is not as threatening as correcting their talk because it is not as personal" (p. 293). Tompkins offered the following guidelines for correcting students' grammar and usage errors in compositions:

1. Use a problem-solving approach to correct grammar and usage errors.
2. Correct errors in the editing stage of the writing process.
3. Consider the function, audience, and form of the composition when determining whether to correct errors or which errors to correct.
4. Let students know that correcting grammatical and usage errors is a courtesy to readers.
5. Keep explanations for the corrections brief.
6. Sometimes simply make the change and say that in writing it is written this way.
7. Don't ask students if the correction makes the writing "sound better."
8. Use sentence-building activities to rid the composition of lackluster and repetitious words and short, choppy sentences.
9. Ignore some errors, especially young children's.
10. Respect the language of children's home and community, and introduce standard written English as "book language." (p. 294)

Nancy Stanley-Burt, a professor at Florida A&M University, gives a similar message to her students. Calling standard English "broadcast grammar," she tells students: "You speak different ways for different situations. You can speak with dialects, slang words, different sentence structures, and any way you choose when you are at home or among friends and family, but it is *economically advantageous* to learn to speak and write broadcast grammar."

PROOFREADING

During conversations with teachers of primary grade children through college students, the concept of proofreading was reported to be an essential part of the writing process and an area in which students showed considerable weakness. However, there did not appear to be a consistent definition of proofreading among the surveyed teachers or in the professional literature. According to Harris (1987),

our students cannot proofread effectively because we—teachers, researchers, textbook writers—fail to use the term "proofread" in any consistent, clearly defined manner. As a result, students often make no distinction between revising and proofreading. They equate revising with copying a paper over neatly in ink and reading through it hurriedly before turning it in. In effect, they collapse the entire, complicated, highly recursive process of writing into what is essentially manuscript preparation. (p. 465)

Although proofreading does involve rereading the work-in-progress, it is unlike revising and editing in its function and purpose. According to Harris (1987), "Proofreading is limited to the final phase of the writing process and is for the explicit purpose of eliminating distracting minor errors from the manuscript" (p. 465). With this definition, proofreading would be addressed following revision and editing; it would take place after the writer had dealt with issues of substance related to content and organization. As part of manuscript preparation, good proofreaders would "attend to the text closely and deliberately—looking specifically at each word and mark of punctuation, carefully noting not only what is there but also what is not there" (Harris, 1987, p. 464). Because the task of proofreading involves competence in both reading and writing, it is complex; also, the task requires modification of the normal reading process in that the proofreader literally looks at each word and punctuation mark. Therefore, proofreading strategies will need to be modeled for many students beginning with the primary grades; others will require in-depth instruction. Heller (1991), for example, stressed teacher modeling "when teaching proofreading skills in the primary grades" (p. 93). The following strategies were among those suggested by Harris (1987) related to developing good proofreading skills:

- . . . use a pointer—a finger, pencil, whatever—in order to force ourselves to look at each word and mark of punctuation.
- . . . let time elapse between writing the paper and proofreading it.
- . . . read papers aloud. (p. 465)

Returning to the earlier example of the middle school student who suspected that she had a misspelled word in her composition, then conferred with her teacher about the word during a conference and received immediate feedback regarding the suspected misspelling, one can assume that a correction was made, if necessary, by the develop-

ing writer. Of course, if she were a student with a learning disability, the teacher could adjust expectations to meet her instructional needs. Otherwise, the following scenario could take place. After editing the work-in-progress, this writer would proofread the piece as a final check. Although she still may have spelling in mind, checking one last time to make sure that all words have been spelled accurately, she automatically will coordinate the proofreading for other types of mechanical errors, such as punctuation. In all likelihood, the writer will ask a peer or the teacher to look the piece over after she has finalized her efforts, particularly if publication is imminent. This collaborative effort at this crucial point allows the writer to achieve an optimal level of confidence regarding the evolved product. As an aside, students appreciate knowing that galley proofs must be carefully read before a book is published; they deserve to know that even famous, well-published authors have editors and proofreaders for their manuscripts. Of course, students also need to understand that it is the author who has the final say about his or her manuscript; it is the writer who, in the end, is responsible for the final product.

MODELING EDITING AND PROOFREADING

When in-depth instruction is needed, editing and proofreading should be demonstrated. One good way to accomplish this task is to use think-alouds with model paragraphs. You can avoid any possible embarrassment by using writing samples that do not come from the students for initial demonstrations. Later on, should students offer, their samples may be used for modeling purposes. An anonymous paragraph, such as the following, could be used on an overhead projector to demonstrate or model editing and proofreading; for this purpose, a list of symbols for editing, presented after the anonymous paragraph, was utilized.

The Indians of North America

by the year 1492 many different Indian tribes lived in various parts of North America. Many believe that these Indians originally came from Asia in search of food thou-

sands of years before any European discovered the continent. In reality, there were millions of Indians living in what is today the United States when the Italian explorer and navigator, Christopher Columbus (1451–1506), found the New World in 1492. Columbus is credited with calling the people he met Indians since he actually believed he had arrived in India. As one might expect, they already had names for their own tribes in their own languages.

Symbols for Editing

Purpose	Symbol
move together	⁐
spread apart	#
move	[circle with arrow]
reverse order	[reversal curve]
check spelling	(sp)
indent for paragraph	¶
omit	~~word~~
insert word(s)	∧
capitalize	≡
change to lower case	/P
insert punctuation:	
period	⊙
comma	∧,
apostrophe	∨'
quotation marks	∨". . .∨"

Naturally, educators will want to take learners' needs into account when deciding what to model first, as well as how much to model during an initial paragraph or later paragraphs. For students who have had no exposure to editing and proofreading their own writing or writings of others, much less exposure to the symbols used for editing, instruction will need to be designed to include incremental lessons with ample practice opportunities. For these students, it probably will be helpful, also, if they have a list of the symbols for reminders as they begin to edit their own work-in-progress. And there's no reason that students can't add to the list of symbols for editing as they are exposed to additional symbols or as they perceive a need for others. Keep in mind, of course, that what the teacher stresses during instruction is what students tend to remember.

Activities 6.1 through 6.6 were designed for modeling revising. Whereas Model Activities 6.7 through 6.10 focus on editing different single mechanics, the last activity, 6.11, puts editing the various mechanics all together, as in the passage, "The Indians of North America," presented earlier in this chapter. Because revising and editing skills are best taught in the context of the student's own writing, it is recommended that these activities be used for modeling during direct instruction, rather than as practice.

Finally, remember that the teacher is responsible for serving as final editor once students have readied their selections for publication. During a final conference, instructional needs may still surface; however, the writer's present skill level will be evident, and the teacher can build on this knowledge base. As these developing writers move their pieces toward publication—whether it be informal such as in a classroom display, or more formal, such as having a story published in the local paper—they will experience the good feelings that come naturally when an important piece of work has been completed and given credibility through publication. Good writers write; publication can be the impetus for writing in the future.

CONCLUSION

Revising and editing for content and mechanics are essential parts of the writing process, as well as the most recursive. For example, a first draft may undergo numerous revisions before the writer determines that it is ready to be shared with others. Then, there may be a great many peer and teacher consultations about revisions, often in the form of sharing evolving drafts. After considering everyone else's advice, the writer makes decisions about final revisions, then edits and proofreads before declaring the work finished. In the end, it is the writer who must accept the responsibility and the response from others for the finished product.

Process-based writing allows students to experience success as developing writers; thus, writing becomes an enjoyable form of communication that will enable them to achieve in every content area and will add great personal pleasure to life, both in the present and in the future. The responsibility is to teach students *how* to revise, edit, and proofread—to make these rewarding parts of the writing process.

REFERENCES

Allred, R. A. (1987). *What research says to the teacher: Spelling trends, content, and methods.* Washington, DC: National Education Association.

Barth, E. (1975). *Turkeys, pilgrims, and Indian corn—The story of the Thanksgiving symbols* (Illustrated by U. Arndt). New York: Clarion Books.

Begley, S., Ramo, J. C., & Rosenberg, D. (1993). Where do great minds come from? And why are there no Einsteins, Freuds or Picassos today? *Newsweek,* June 28, p. 50.

Cooper, J. D. (1986). *Improving reading comprehension.* Boston: Houghton Mifflin.

Dickinson, E. (1951). "Aspiration." Cambridge, MA: Belknap Press, Harvard University Press.

Fisher, C. J., Terry, C. A. (1990). *Children's language and the language arts.* Boston: Allyn and Bacon.

Fitzgerald, J. (1988). Helping young writers to revise: A brief review for teachers. *The Reading Teacher, 42,* 124–129.

Gentry, R. (1987). *Spel . . . is a four-letter word.* Portsmouth, NH: Heinemann.

Goodman, K. S., Bird, L. B., & Goodman, Y. M. (Eds.). (1991). *The whole language catalog.* Santa Rosa, CA: American School Publishers.

Graves, D. H. (1984). *A researcher learns to write.* Exeter, NH: Heinemann Educational Books.

Gunning, T. G. (1992). *Creating reading instruction for all children.* Boston: Allyn and Bacon.

Harris, J. (1987, December). Proofreading: A reading/writing skill. *College Composition and Communication, 38,* 464–466.

Heller, M. F. (1991). *Reading–writing connections: From theory to practice.* White Plains, NY: Longman.

Hennings, D. G. (1990). *Communication in action: Teaching the language arts,* 4th ed. Boston: Houghton Mifflin.

Hillerich, R. (1985). Dealing with grammar. In *Teaching children to write, K–8.* Englewood Cliffs, NJ: Prentice-Hall.

Hodges, R. E. (1981). *Learning to spell: Theory and research into practice.* Urbana, IL: National Council of Teachers of English.

Horn, E. (1967). *Teaching spelling.* Washington, DC: National Education Association.

Hull, G. (1987, September). Current views of error and editing. *Topics in Language Disorders, 7* (4), 55–65.

Humes, A. (1983). Research on the composing process. *Review of Educational Research, 53*(2), 201–216.

Juster, N. (1961). *The phantom tollbooth* (Illus. by J. Feiffer). New York: Windward Books/Random House.

Kids' question (1992). *Philadelphia Inquirer* via *Tallahassee Democrat,* March 31, p. 1B.

"Laugh Parade." (1992). *Parade Magazine.* New York: Parade Publications.

Lundsteen, S. W. (1989). *Language arts: A problem-solving approach.* New York: Harper & Row.

Manning, M. M., & Manning, G. L. (1986). *Improving spelling in the middle grades,* 2nd ed. Washington, DC: National Education Association.

Murray, D. M. (1982). *Learning by teaching: Selected articles on writing and teaching.* Montclair, NJ: Boynton/Cook.

Nold, E. W. (1981). Revising. In C. H. Frederiksen, M. F. Whiteman, & J. F. Dominic (Eds.), *Writing: The nature, development, and teaching of written communication.* Hillsdale, NJ: Erlbaum.

Reutzel, D. R., & Cooter, R. C. (1992). *Teaching children to read: From basals to books.* New York: Macmillan.

Tompkins, G. E. (1990). *Teaching writing: Balancing process and product.* Columbus, OH: Merrill.

Vacca, J. L., Vacca, R. T., & Gove, M. K. (1991). *Reading and learning to read,* 2nd ed. New York: HarperCollins.

MODEL ACTIVITIES

The activities that follow are meant to serve as models; such activities should be used as part of a total learning environment. These model activities were designed to demonstrate how the writing process can be developed while expanding the writer's knowledge base and providing opportunities for the writer to think critically.

ACTIVITY 6.1

Revising with a Dictionary or
Thesaurus to Clarify Meaning

Directions: Often we have a favorite word of the moment. It may be a slang word like *neat, cool,* or *awesome,* or a common word like *good.* The student who wrote the following paragraph overused the word *big.* Please help this student improve the paragraph by substituting different words to clarify exactly what was meant. You may use a thesaurus or dictionary to find *synonyms*—words that have the same meaning. Write the new words above the underlined words.

The big football player had his big chance in the big game last weekend. His team was the big favorite

to win. They were favored to win by 15 points, a big margin. It was a big surprise when they lost this

big game.

Next, Compare your revised paragraph with those of your classmates. Because you were all trying to say approximately the same thing, you may find that many of you used the same synonyms. When John shared his first draft of the following story, he and his teacher decided that he had overused the words that are underlined. Use a thesaurus or dictionary to find synonyms for these words to give more life to these sentences. Write the new words above the underlined words. You also may wish to do the same for other words in the paragraph.

The happiness of this day made the good man feel happy. He had always taken good care of his wife,

just as she had always taken good care of him before the accident. Her famous apple pie had made her

famous among all of their relatives and friends. Today, Thanksgiving, she was happy because she was

able to prepare the first holiday dinner in a long time.

Now, read your revised paragraph aloud to your classmates and see how many different ways there are to say the same thing. You may want to try your hand at writing a paragraph that overworks one adjective. After selecting an adjective, draft a paragraph and decide if sharing at this point would be helpful. Prepare a revised copy that clarifies the meaning, then edit for mechanics and proofread. If you're willing to share your paragraph with the whole class, let your teacher know. As you write in the future, always reread your drafts to edit for overuse of the same words.

Using Prepositional Phrases to Revise Meanings

Often you can change the meanings of sentences through the use of a prepositional phrase. A *preposition* is a word that combines with a noun, adjective, or adverb to show a relationship to another word or set of words. An easy way to determine if a word is a preposition or not, is by using the phrase *the house*. Any word, other than a verb, that can go before these two words is a preposition. Some examples follow:

over the house	*inside* the house	*by* the house
to the house	*into* the house	*beside* the house
from the house	*of* the house	*upon* the house
around the house	*under* the house	*down* the house
about the house	*through* the house	*off* the house
in the house	*with* the house	*below* the house
out of the house	*above* the house	*between* the houses

These are not the only words that are prepositions. Immediately, *during* comes to mind as an example of a word that doesn't go with *the house*. Also, prepositions are often combined, as in the sentence "He fell *off of* the house." Still, the phrase *the house* is a quick and easy way to remember many prepositions.

Directions: In the sentences that follow, use a prepositional phrase to revise the meaning.

1. Jerry spilled milk _____.

2. The soldiers drove the tanks _____.

3. The cattle grazed _____.

4. We left the campsite _____.

5. The happy children were singing _____.

Now, use the same phrases, except place them at the beginning of each sentence, and separate them with a comma from the rest of the sentence.

1. _____, Jerry spilled the milk.

2. _____, the soldiers drove the tanks.

3. _____, the cattle grazed.

4. _____, we left the campsite.

5. _____, the happy children were singing.

Sometimes, more than one prepositional phrase is used in the same sentence. Here is an example:

The soldiers drove the tanks *down the street in the parade.*

Now, write a sentence with two prepositional phrases.

_____

Georgia Mae and the Coat Hangers: Revising to Entice Your Audience

Which of the following article titles sounds most interesting to you?

Georgia Mae and the Coat Hangers

A Wonderful Woman I Once Knew

Making a Wreath

All three of those titles would be accurate for the short story I am going to share with you; but if you are anything like I am, and had not already read the last title, you would be wondering what a story involving coat hangers could possibly be about. Newspaper writers know that it takes only a few sentences for readers to decide whether or not they are going to read a feature article. For this reason, the first sentences, or *lead,* must be interesting.

Just as you read the titles, read the three proposed leads for the story of Georgia Mae and the Coat Hangers and select the one you think should start the story.

1. Georgia Mae was the housekeeper for some of my friends when I was growing up. She lived one block down Beach Court and one-half block down Georgia Avenue.
2. Georgia Mae was a special person in my life. For one thing, we shared the same birthday. For another, she always made wreaths at Christmas.
3. It was December 15th and we were as excited as we could be, for we all knew what that date meant. December 15th was the date each year that Georgia Mae, the Pied Piper of children in our neighborhood, helped us make coat-hanger, pepper-berry, gold-spray-painted wreaths.

The first two versions contained too many boring details. The comment about sharing the same birthday was straying from the topic. But the last lead stirs your interest in the first sentence, then describes Georgia Mae in such a positive way that you think the rest of the article will also be upbeat. It sets you wondering how she was capable of letting children use those items, and leads you to think that if you read on, you will find out.

Your turn:　Fill in the following blanks. Then revise the information given to change it into an enticing lead.

The most exciting day of my life was _____.

_____

_____

_____

_____

_____

_____

_____

What made it so exciting was that _____

_____

_____

_____

_____

_____

_____

_____

_____

_____

_____

The revised edition:

_____

_____

_____

_____

_____

_____

_____

_____

_____

_____

_____

_____

_____

_____

_____

_____

_____

Great job! Now, think of an interesting title to catch the interest of a reader.

_____

Early Telephones and Calling Long Distance: Revising by Combining Sentences

Directions: The paragraphs below contain interesting information, but they have been written with short, choppy sentences. Combine some of the sentences to make the thoughts flow better. You may need to add some connecting words and cross out phrases that repeat information already given.

EARLY TELEPHONES

Grandpa Larry told me a story. The story he told me was about how telephones have changed. They have changed a lot since he was a little boy. He said his grandmother had shown him a telephone that she had used. This telephone was a wooden box. It was hanging on the wall. It had a hand crank on the right side. To use it, you would lift the receiver on the left side. Then you would turn the crank on the right side once around for each number. For example, if you wanted a two, you would turn the crank twice around. You would pause between numbers. Then the operator would connect you to the right party. This was the earliest telephone Grandpa Larry ever saw.

Grandpa Larry's own first phone was not much more advanced. It also hung on the wall. There was no hand crank. You lifted the receiver off of the left side of the box. Grandpa Larry's phone number was 1–8. Grandma Marilyn lived in a much bigger town. Her phone number had three digits. It was 1-6-8. Her friend's number was 7-8-9. When you picked up the phone, an operator would answer it. The operator would say, "Number please." When Grandpa Larry was little, he couldn't remember everyone's number. He would call the operator. She was also his babysitter. He would say, "Rosie, I want to talk to Aunt Sophie." Rosie would connect him.

CALLING LONG DISTANCE

In the early 1950s, the operator did most of the work to make a long distance phone call. To call long distance, there were no phone area codes. If there were, only the operators knew them. You would pick up the receiver. When you did this the operator would say, "Number please." You would say politely, "Operator, I want to place a long distance call. I want to place a call to West Palm Beach, Florida." She would reply, "What is the number you wish to call?" Then you would give the number. Today, only person-to-person calls or collect calls are similar to calling long distance in the 1950s.

171

Miles Standish and Benjamin Franklin: Revising to Change the Style of Presentation

Directions: Read the following paragraphs about John Alden, Miles Standish, and Priscilla Mullins. Then decide which of the two was more interesting to read.

Paragraph 1 The Pilgrims left England in the early 1600s to settle in North America in what is now Massachusetts. Miles Standish was a soldier who was hired to help train the Pilgrims to defend themselves. He wanted to marry Priscilla Mullins. She married John Alden, a cooper, instead.

Paragraph 2 Miles Standish, called Captain Shrimp because he was only five feet, two inches tall, was a brave soldier, hired to help the Pilgrims learn to defend themselves. He was afraid of only one thing—proposing to Priscilla Mullins, the love of his life. Because of his shyness, he made a big mistake. He sent John Alden, a cooper who made beer barrels and kept them from leaking, to ask Priscilla to marry him. Priscilla, according to a line in the 1858 poem of Henry Wadsworth Longfellow called *The Courtship of Miles Standish,* is said to have replied, "Why don't you speak for yourself, John?" Well, John must have, because they had eleven children and lived many happy years together until John died at the age of 87. Priscilla died several years later.

Which of the two paragraphs did you find more interesting?

Check either Paragraph 1 _____ or Paragraph 2 _____. Think about why you chose Paragraph 1 or Paragraph 2. Provide your rationale (reasons) below:

_____

_____

_____

_____

_____

_____

_____

_____

_____

Your Turn: To practice changing the style of presentation, you may choose from the following four choices:

1. Rewrite the information you have just read in a new paragraph.
2. Read additional information about Miles Standish and then write your own paragraph about him.
3. Read the facts that follow and rewrite them in a more interesting form.
4. Read additional information about Benjamin Franklin and then write your own paragraph about him.

Benjamin Franklin (1706–1790) was a North American statesman, inventor, scientist, and writer. He did not want the bald eagle to be chosen as the national symbol for the United States. He liked the turkey, calling it a "true original Native of North America." He said that the eagle was of "bad moral character . . . generally poor and often very lousy."

_____

_____

_____

_____

_____

_____

Additional information for this activity can be found in books such as *Turkeys, Pilgrims, and Indian Corn— The Story of the Thanksgiving Symbols* by Edna Barth, illustrated by Ursula Arndt (New York: Clarion Books, 1975).

eagle vs. turkey

Pilgrim Clothes: Revising to Reorganize Material

Directions: Although the following information about Pilgrim dress is accurate, it needs to be revised to better organize it. After reading all of the paragraphs, give some thought to reorganization possibilities.

PILGRIM CLOTHES

Have you ever wondered how we know what kind of clothes the Pilgrims wore? Several lists of articles of clothing owned by Pilgrims were found attached to their wills. An interesting book by Edna Barth (1975) tells this and more about our Pilgrim ancestors. For instance, what colors do you think they wore? We usually see pictures of black clothes, but most Pilgrims didn't wear black—only the Elder (preacher) or formerly rich businessmen. We often think of sad colors as being black or brown, but the "sad" colors women wore back at that time meant deep, like the berries or nuts they were dyed with— mulberry and nut brown. They also wore blue, red, and green.

We see pictures of men with buckles on their shoes, but they probably didn't wear them—they aren't on the lists. Women wore blouses called "stomachers" covered by dresses often laced up the front. Over that they wore waistcoats (vests) that were usually red. Men wore stocking caps to keep their heads warm. The men wore linen shirts and wool or leather pants called breeches. Outside, women wore cloaks and hoods. When it was cold, men wore sleeveless leather jackets and sleeveless coats so they'd have their arms free.

Your Turn: The first paragraph of "Pilgrim Clothes" is fine, but the second paragraph needs to be reorganized because the descriptions of men's and women's clothing are all mixed together. One method of reorganization would be to write separate paragraphs for men's and women's clothing. Write one paragraph about women's clothing and one paragraph about men's clothing on a piece of notebook paper. Use the book by Barth or another resource of your choice if you would like more information about Pilgrim clothing. Perhaps this is a topic you'd like to research thoroughly, or you may have another topic of your own in mind.

Popular Popcorn: Editing for Capitalization and Punctuation

Directions: Read the following selection carefully. The author has written a very interesting essay about popcorn but has failed to observe the standard usage of capitalization and punctuation. As you read, mark changes needed for capitalization and for quotations, apostrophes, question marks, periods, commas, and semicolons.

POPULAR POPCORN

Anyone want popcorn. The answer to this question has been YES throughout history.

While we can't be absolutely sure about how long popcorn has been popular we do know that it's history spans at least thousands of years. In caves in North America, archeologist's found corn that was popped over 5,000 years ago. Very old popcorn also has been found in South American countries. In north America, during its early history, popcorn also was enjoyed as a soup and as a breakfast dish. It was even a gift from the indians at the first thanksgiving dinner. Today, popcorn continues its' popularity, furthermore, we know now that this popular item is very nourishing and low in calories?

Popular Popcorn: Editing for Capitalization and Punctuation—Answer Sheet

POPULAR POPCORN

Anyone want popcorn? The answer to this question has been "YES!" throughout history.

While we can't be absolutely sure about how long popcorn has been popular, we do know that its history spans at least thousands of years. In caves in North America, archeologists found corn that was popped over 5,000 years ago. Very old popcorn also has been found in South American countries. In North America, during its early history, popcorn also was enjoyed as a soup and as a breakfast dish. It was even a gift from the Indians at the first Thanksgiving dinner. Today, popcorn continues its popularity. Furthermore, we know now that this popular item is very nourishing and low in calories.

ACTIVITY 6.8

The Shy Platypus: Editing
for Sentence Construction

Directions: Read the story of "The Shy Platypus" below: The information given is accurate, but the writer needs your help in improving the sentence construction. Lightly cross through poorly written sentences, and place your version in the space above the sentences. Be sure not to omit any of the information given.

THE SHY PLATYPUS

Late in the 1700s the platypus was discovered on the continent. Of Australia by Europeans because this

shy creature appeared to be a combination. Of mammal, bird, fish, and reptile, its discovery caused

quite a stir.

Some experts in England at the time suggested that the reports a mistake were; of course, they

learned differently. The platypus is lower a form of mammal called monotremes. Like birds or reptiles.

It lays eggs and raises its babies, in a nest; it also nurses with milk its young. Its bill is duck-like. In

shape, although the bill of the platypus. Is very rubbery. Its webbed feet have claws, which might tear

the webbing. If the platypus didn't walk. On its knuckles. Being a great swimmer. The platypus

searches for in the water food where it uses its sensitive bill to tasty morsels find. Such as tadpoles and

worms. When a platypus is full grown, it covered is with soft fur. And weighs only about four pounds.

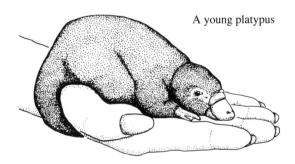

A young platypus

The Shy Platypus: Editing for Sentence Construction— Answer Sheet

(This is one possible answer sheet. Other student variations may also be acceptable.)

THE SHY PLATYPUS

Late in the 1700s, the platypus was discovered on the continent of Australia by Europeans. Because this shy creature appeared to be a combination of mammal, bird, fish, and reptile, its discovery caused quite a stir.

Some experts in England at the time suggested that the reports were a mistake; of course, they learned differently. The platypus is a lower form of mammal called monotremes. Like birds or reptiles, it lays eggs and raises its babies in a nest; it also nurses its young with milk. Its bill is duck-like in shape. Although the bill of the platypus is very rubbery, its webbed feet have claws, which might tear the webbing if the platypus didn't walk on its knuckles. Being a great swimmer, the platypus searches for food in the water where it uses its sensitive bill to find tasty morsels such as tadpoles and worms. When a platypus is full grown, it is covered with soft fur and weighs only about four pounds.

The Prairie Schooner: Editing for Spelling (History Content)

Directions: The following description of "The Prairie Schooner" is historically correct; but, alas, the writer hasn't edited for spelling. Circle the words you think are spelled incorrectly. If you are sure you know the correct spelling, write it above the circled word; if you are not sure, find the correct spelling and put it above the circled word. If you leave a word circled with no correction above it, that will signal that a word you initially thought might be misspelled was not.

THE PRAIRIE SCHOONER

As pioneers moved westward to settle the North American frontier in the mid-1800s, wagon trains made up or cuvered waigons pulled by oxon or mules were not uncommen sigtes.

The cuvered wagon, also refered to as the prarie skooner or prairie wagon, was used like modern-day moving vans to carry a family's belongings to thier destanation. Unlike the moving van of today, the cuvered wagon was very samll; the bed of the wagen was rectanguler in shape and usally mesured about four feet wide and ten to twelve feet long. Becasue of the limeted space, families offen had to leave behind things that weren't considered necessities. Given that the wagons were to carry the setlers throgh the wildernes, where the elaments were offten qwite harch, sometimes belongings had to be discartid along the way to liten the load. Taking into acount the undercarriage and covering, a loaded wagon often weighted as much as a tun.

The Prairie Schooner: Editing for Spelling (History Content)— Answer Sheet

THE PRAIRIE SCHOONER

As pioneers moved westward to settle the North American frontier in the mid-1800s, wagon trains made up of covered wagons pulled by oxen or mules were not uncommon sights.

The covered wagon, also referred to as the prairie schooner or prairie wagon, was used like modern-day moving vans to carry a family's belongings to their destination. Unlike the moving van of today, the covered wagon was very small; the bed of the wagon was rectangular in shape and usually measured about four feet wide and ten to twelve feet long. Because of the limited space, families often had to leave behind things that weren't considered necessities. Given that the wagons were to carry the settlers through the wilderness, where the elements were often quite harsh, sometimes belongings had to be discarded along the way to lighten the load. Taking into account the undercarriage and covering, a loaded wagon often weighed as much as a ton.

ACTIVITY 6.10

Measuring Angles: Editing
for Spelling (Math Content)

Directions: The author of the following paper was asked to describe how to measure angles. The paper was very well written, with one exception. The author still needs to edit for spelling. Can you help? Circle the words that you think are misspelled. Then, use a dictionary or the glossary of your math textbook to find the correct spellings, or ask others how they think the words are spelled. Write the correct spelling above the circled words.

MEASURING ANGLES

As we think mathamatically, we use numbers and cymbols; offen, words are used as well. The

meenings of terms used in math will varry from thier meenings in othur subject areas. For example,

consider the word *ray* when it is used to difine *angle:*

Angles are made when two rays meat at a point. Angels are mezured in dagrees. Take

a circle, for instence. It has 360 dagreezs or 360 equeel parts with eich part or angle

equeeling the size of one dagree. If the circel is dividied into four diferent parts, eich of

the angels equeels 90 degreezs. The 90-dagree angels are also called right angels.

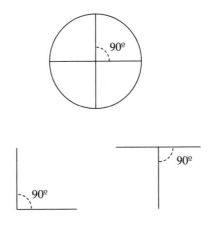

If math interests you, you might enjoy reading *The Phantom Tollbooth* by Norton Juster, illustrated by Jules Feiffer (New York: Windward Books/Random House, 1961).

181

Measuring Angles: Editing for Spelling (Math Content)— Answer Sheet

MEASURING ANGLES

As we think mathematically, we use numbers and symbols; often, words are used as well. The meanings of terms used in math will vary from their meanings in other subject areas. For example, consider the word *ray* when it is used to define *angle:*

Angles are made when two rays meet at a point. Angles are measured in degrees. Take a circle, for instance. It has 360 degrees or 360 equal parts with each part or angle equaling the size of one degree. If the circle is divided into four different parts, each of the angles equals 90 degrees. The 90-degree angles are also called right angles.

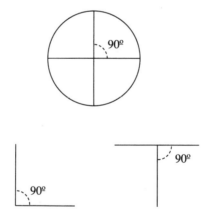

Something Old Is New: Editing for Grammar and Mechanics

Directions: The content of the essay below has been well written, but the author needs your assistance with editing. You may want to begin by checking grammar and capitalization; also, make sure correct punctuation has been used.

SOMETHING OLD IS NEW

In the 1930s grocery stores in small towns was little more than a room with shelves around the walls and tables and barrels in the middle. You carried your purchases to a counter and left them there until you was ready to pay for them. Then in the 1950s, Supremarkets arrived on the scean. These Stores had isles of shelves and you push a grocery cart around the store. When you complete selecting your purchases you pushed your cart to the front of the store where there was often several cashiers and counters at which to pay.

Small Mom and Pop Grocery Stores had a hard time competing with these new-fangled giants. So they offered a service that the big stores didn't have, You could phone in your order and *the store would assemble and deliver your groceries*—for free. This was a wonderfull advantage to the elderly, for socialites who was to busy with other things to be bothered doing her own grocery shopping, or for the cook who suddenly discovered that she needed something for dinner that was not in her familys' pantry. However, one paid for the luxury of delivery with higher prices for groceries. Then, many of these little grocery stores went out of business replace by "convenience" stores. These stores, close to home and not so busy, were convenient for many, but not for those who had enjoyed having their groceries delivered?

Today, supermarkets are offering something new You phone in your order, and *the store will assemble and deliver your groceries*—for a fee of approximately $10. The supermarket has *discovered* service. Something old is new.

ACTIVITY 6.11

Something Old Is New: Editing
for Grammar and Mechanics—
Answer Sheet

SOMETHING OLD IS NEW

In the 1930s, grocery stores in small towns were little more than a room with shelves around the walls and tables and barrels in the middle. You carried your purchases to a counter and left them there until you were ready to pay for them. Then, in the 1950s, supermarkets arrived on the scene. These stores had aisles of shelves and you pushed a grocery cart around the store. When you completed selecting your purchases, you pushed your cart to the front of the store where there were often several cashiers and counters at which to pay.

Small Mom and Pop grocery stores had a hard time competing with these new-fangled giants. So they offered a service that the big stores didn't have. You could phone in your order and *the store would assemble and deliver your groceries*—for free. This was a wonderful advantage for the elderly, for socialites who were too busy with other things to be bothered doing their own grocery shopping, or for the cook who suddenly discovered that she needed something for dinner that was not in her family's pantry. However, one paid for the luxury of delivery with higher prices for groceries. Then, many of these little grocery stores went out of business, replaced by "convenience" stores. These stores, close to home and not so busy, were convenient for many, but not for those who had enjoyed having their groceries delivered.

Today, supermarkets are offering something new. You phone in your order, and *the store will assemble and deliver your groceries*—for a fee of approximately $10. The supermarket has *discovered* service. Something old is new.

184

CHAPTER 7

Technology and Composing

The wildfire spread of the computer in recent decades has been called the single most important change in the knowledge system since the invention of movable type in the 15th century or even the invention of writing.

—Alvin Toffler, a well-known social thinker, in *Powershift,* 1985, p. 419.

One crisp evening late in the fall, Jack and Fred were exchanging comments about their school-aged children as they were riding the evening commuter train home from work. Fred, leaning just a bit in Jack's direction, inquired with real curiosity, "By the way, have you been in a classroom lately?"

"No," replied Jack, "I haven't. Peggy and I try to attend PTO regularly, but it's almost impossible to take time off during the day in my line of work. Besides, I always feel awkward and uncomfortable interrupting classes."

"Well, let me tell you, I used to feel somewhat uncomfortable myself, but not anymore. The last time we attended PTO, the president announced that recent studies have shown that parental participation helps raise student test scores. Many parents who never volunteered before are now offering, for example, one hour a week. And, I'll tell you, the teachers are welcoming the help with open arms. I went last week and couldn't believe my eyes."

"Obviously something got your attention!" offered Jack. "I'm all ears!"

And so Fred began to unfold the essence of his recent experience at his daughter's school. "Stepping into the large area, I wondered if I were in the right place. Could this be my daughter's classroom? Just for a moment I thought that perhaps this was a special club producing a video or some, kind of a presentation. Looking around, I didn't see anyone conducting a class. Finally, I saw an adult at a ma-chine that looked like a VCR, talking with a group of students. They were zipping through scenes of the Arctic tundra that they were viewing on a television set on a movable cart. Yet there was no motion between scenes as there would be on a VCR. They were using a videodisc player. The room was a veritable beehive of activity. Some students were standing with headsets on, singing into a cassette recorder in one section of the room. One person was using a camcorder on a tripod to film what looked like a skit. Several students were talking to a typist at a computer, while several others stood by a printer, eagerly scanning the words as they came rushing out" . . . and so the story continued.

What this parent was describing with great enthusiasm is today's ideal learning environment. In this classroom, a teacher/facilitator serves as a director: planning, choosing themes or topics, and teaching students how to locate information, using technology that would have been unimaginable less than two decades ago. Marshall McLuhan (1911–1980), director of the Canadian Centre of Culture and Technology at the University of Toronto, said in his 1964 book titled *Understanding Media: The Extensions of Man,* "'The medium is the message' because it is the medium that shapes and contrasts the scale and form of human association and action" (Seldes, 1985, p. 279). His saying is once again apropos as the new technological media shape today's associations and actions.

As technology has become part of the educational system in North America, teachers truly have become learners along with their students, for in most cases teachers are constantly learning to keep up with the rapid advances being made as new technology is developed. Because of the expanding knowledge base, it is impossible to learn everything; so students must become adept in accessing the many databases these powerful new educational tools offer and, then, in learning how to share the knowledge they have obtained. Through the expertise in technology that dedicated teachers have to offer, students will be taught critical thinking as they learn how to gather, disseminate, and exchange information. Thus, while working cooperatively within a curriculum that integrates the language arts across subject areas, they will evolve as creative problem solvers and become self-directed lifelong learners.

THE HISTORY OF THE COMPUTER

Heilman, Blair, and Rupley (1986) reported that, in 1946, the first electronic digital computer in the United States was built at the University of Pennsylvania. "It filled a large room and contained 18,000 vacuum tubes and 6,000 switches" (p. 516). Then, in the late 1960s, the silicon chip or microprocessor was introduced, and the size of computers was greatly reduced. Any personal computer today can more than do the work of that early room-sized computer. One can only imagine the sense of accomplishment felt in 1946 when the first computer worked. That exciting experience had to be comparable in some ways to the feelings of Orville and Wilbur Wright, reported by them in a set of books called *America: Great Changes in Our History Told by Its Makers* (1925), when, on December 17, 1903, the first man-carrying flying machine worked. Only five people witnessed that historic event, although all the people who lived nearby had been invited. But the weather was cold, and other man-carrying flying machines had not flown, so those invited had no reason to think this one would fly either. On this flight, however, for the first time in the history of the world, a man-carrying machine had lifted off the ground under its own power, had flown forward against the wind for twelve seconds, and had landed without wrecking. Three more flights that day ended safely, the final one lasting for 59 seconds. Then, while the excited pilots and spectators were discussing the flights, a gust of wind picked the plane up and rolled it over and over, ending the experiments, but not the excitement of the day.

In recent years, a vast number of new terms related to technology have become familiar to most of us; because technological advances are being made so rapidly, however, it's almost impossible for everyone to stay abreast of both the current technology and its associated language. Some examples of words new in the 1980s included *fax machines, video cameras, compact disk players,* and *laser printers.* Of course, some seemingly new things have become a part of everyday life so quickly that people forget that they have not always been around. Television is a good example; although the more senior members of any community can recall life both before and since television, today's students have a knowledge base only of life with television. In the early 1950s, it was not uncommon to see a group of family and friends gathered in front of a television store on a Friday or Saturday evening. Teenagers had television parties when something special came on to view. In rural communities, it was not uncommon to have neighbors as frequent visitors in the home of someone who had a new television set.

In 1981, *Time* magazine called the computer the "Machine of the Year" (White, 1991). People were both amused and skeptical. At first, some people predicted computers would replace millions of workers; indeed, because of the speed of the exchange of information available with computers, some workers have been replaced. Toffler (White,

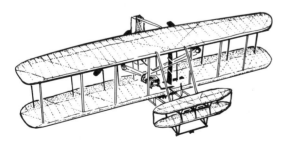

The Flyer, *the world's first successful man-carrying airplane, was built and flown by the Wright Brothers in 1903.*

1991, p. 2), told of one terminal information exchange system used, PROFS, that performed the work of 40,000 employees. However, many new jobs also have been created as the world clamors for more and better computer hardware and software and for educated people to decide how to use the information generated in computer reports. Common products using computers include microwaves, cars, video cassette recorders (VCRs), digital watches, compact disks (CDs), product and equipment bar codes, automated teller machines (ATMs), point-of-sale (POS) debit cards, credit cards, and personal computers (PCs). Scarcely a child in the decade of the 1980s grew up without playing an Atari, a Coleco, or a Nintendo computer-run video game. Whereas in 1981 it was hard to imagine life *with* computers, today it's almost impossible to imagine life *without* computers.

Because the technology of computers and software has advanced so rapidly and continues to do so, this chapter will not recommend specific programs. It was estimated in 1991 that there were more than 10,000 instructional programs on the market (O'Malley, 1991), and the number increases daily.

Zachmann (1991) predicted that "even the most sophisticated educational or game software today is little more than a primitive hint of what will be possible a few years down the road" (p. 98). He claimed that there are three keys necessary to unlock the "educational potential of modern computer technology" (p. 98):

1. Lower prices, so that everyone can afford multimedia
2. The resources to make a lot of truly educational software
3. The development, through entertainment, of a consumer market for educational software outside of our schools.

As Zachmann said, "To learn is ultimately the most entertaining thing a person can do" (p. 98). He emphasized that the challenge of the 1990s was "to make learning entertaining or, better put, to make entertainment educational . . ." (p. 98).

Two very popular educational simulation games in the late 1980s and early 1990s, which supported this hypothesis that the entertainment format works, were "The Oregon Trail" and "Where in the World Is Carmen Sandiego?" (The latter, as its name implies, is a geography program.)

Lest anyone question the need to make education more entertaining, consider this fact concerning geography reported by Allen in the February 1992 issue of *Teaching K–8* (p. 16): "A national survey conducted last year revealed that one out of five North Americans between the ages of 18 and 24 could not locate the United States on an outline map of the world."

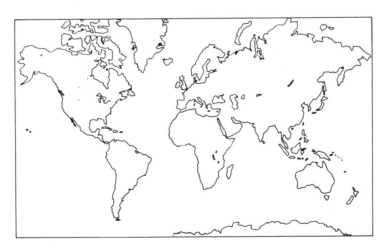

NEW SKILLS ARE NEEDED

When early computers began to be used to produce large quantities of data, people speculated that those who used computers would not need to be very skilled or knowledgeable. It was assumed that they simply would type in information requested by programs. Instead, according to Zuboff (1991):

What we are learning is that these new conditions defy the old rules of thumb about automation. Instead of *dumber* people, we are discovering that people need whole new skill-sets and the basis for competence and excellence in this new world.

People who have learned their work relying on physical cues in their environment (interaction with things or people) now require new intellectual skills that will enable them to create meaning and value from the increasingly abstract cues of electronically presented information.

These new "intellective" skills include an emphasis on abstract thinking, problem solving, and inference; an explicit theoretical understanding of the work at hand and its context; modes of reasoning that are analytic, procedural, and systemic; and finally the ability to commit one's attention to systematic mental effort for extended periods. (p. 5) (emphasis in original)

Clearly, if schools are going to produce citizens capable of using these new intellective skills in the real world, students must be expected to master more than a body of facts; they must become critical thinkers, capable of problem solving.

Early computer programs for student use included two commonly used types: tutorial and drill and practice, which taught and drilled on facts and skills. O'Malley (1991) quoted Becker, a research scientist at Johns Hopkins University: "Teachers are trained to teach kids facts and skills, which is not a good use of computers in many cases. So to change education using computers is to change what teachers conceive of as their primary purpose" (p. 14). Karen Scheingold (O'Malley, 1991), of the Bank Street College of Education, working at the national center at Bank Street on a five-year grant from the U.S. Department of Education, said, "If we continue to think of schooling as pouring information into kid's heads, then we will end up with nothing more than we have right now" (p. 13).

O'Malley, in his 1991 article "The Revolution Is Yet to Come," said that "the school environment itself may have to undergo significant restructuring before computers can be the instruments of major change" (p. 13). He quoted the opening statement of a study by the United States Congress Office of Technology Assessment (OTA) that "today's classrooms typically resemble their ancestors of fifty

years ago more closely than operating rooms or business offices resemble their [fifty-year-old] versions" (p. 13). O'Malley (p. 14) further quoted Adeline Naiman, the Director of Education at the Computer Museum in Boston, who had this to say:

When used properly, computers change the locus of control over the learning process. Instead of teachers handing down dogma, you have a situation in which both the responsibility and the pleasure of learning is in the hands of the learner. It takes a knowing adult with a certain maturity and comfort level to let go.

By the fall of 1990, Raymond Fox (1990), president of the Society for Applied Learning Technology (SALT) was acknowledging that in industry (as in education) individuals bring varying backgrounds to the learning site, and that new software programs should determine the previous background and incorporate this information into programs of instruction. One year later, Fox (1991) suggested that if we wanted to have technology-based learning systems in the schools, our teacher training should include more than a single college course in computers. He stated that limiting computer training to one course would be comparable to introducing college students to books for the first time right before graduation.

When the U.S. president and the governors in 1990 announced their educational goals for the year 2000, one of the goals was that "every school in America insure that all students learn to use their minds, in order to prepare them for responsible citizenship, further learning, and productive employment in a modern economy" (Elam, Rose, & Gallup, 1991, p. 43). Undoubtedly, being prepared for productive employment in a modern economy would include becoming computer literate. The National Education Association (NEA) committee on educational technology proposed "putting a PC and adequate software on every teacher's desk by 1991" (O'Malley, 1991, p. 14). Although this proposal was not achieved, Gary Wells of the NEA said, "If we have 2.5 million teachers using computers, you are going to see an explosion of creative uses in the classroom" (O'Malley, 1991, p. 14). Indeed, this has already happened. Although a few teachers still find themselves somewhat computer illiterate, others have made a whole new world come alive for themselves and their students.

One such teacher is Emily Sachar (1991), who, while reporting on the use of technology in the classroom, described the resource materials available to teachers at the kiosk of the St. Louis Zoo.

The kiosk, officially called the "interactive multimedia resource interface," or IMRI, is equipped with laser discs, a high-quality videocassette recorder, a laser printer, a 25-inch television set, and two speakers, all controlled by an Apple Macintosh IIci computer and some special software. . . . The laser discs are housed in a kind of jukebox that can holdup to 72 discs. (pp. 14–15)

Sachar told of a teacher planning a multimedia montage in two hours for a unit on oceans. From 500 slides, two hours of audio tape, a 799-page textbook, and four and one-half hours of video tape, she created an eighteen-minute video tape and printed out reams of teacher resource materials with a laser printer. This material was then available for background information at her convenience. She was delighted that she could pull all of the "video, audio, and written materials together in one shot. And I could get it all off the computer to take with me" (p. 14). Zoo officials said they had ordered the material to "enhance, not replace, the teacher's role as curriculum writer" (p. 15). The teacher can gather the material as a television editor would. It can be selected, reorganized, and reproduced by teachers and students alike.

Although it may seem as if this teacher had conducted most of the research for the students, in fact, she was acting in the same capacity as the classroom teacher who asks a media specialist to gather available materials for a particular unit. Students will have numerous opportunities to continue building on this knowledge base. By copying the material for students to read on a given topic and showing the prepared video, the teacher has provided students with a common background from which each can move forward. In fact, Jim Jackson and George Crossland (1992), writing in *IBM Higher Education* about "Using Multimedia to Improve Students' Cultural Literacy" told that E. D. Hirsch, Jr., author of *Cultural Literacy: What Every American Needs to Know* (1987, p. 36), said that students must be given background instruction before they can be expected to "engage in a discussion of the significance of these topics. . . . "

Individual interests will influence the direction of each student's writing and reading. For example, in the unit on oceans, one developing writer could select the Portuguese man-of-war for in-depth study, another student might choose the stingray, and so on.

Since the teacher conceptualized this as a unit, most likely the video was not planned to be viewed all at one time. One day's large group topic might be starfish; another day's topic could be whales. Classroom computers could be hooked up to large-screen televisions so the class could use information from the audio and visual encyclopedia or everyone could watch via a liquid crystal display (LCD) projection system. As all school districts move into the computer age, more and more materials will become available that will make the technology of the St. Louis Zoo available to all teachers and students. One surprising piece of information reported by media specialists is that the presence of such technology does not make students use reference materials less; in fact, they seem to use them more. Once material has been gathered through the use of technology, students will want to put their hands on "hard copy," hold the books, examine the colorful pictures closely, and read other books related to their topics.

The Buddy System Project

Indiana launched into the Information Age in 1987, when Kent Wall, president of Technology Management, Inc., and H. Dean Evans, state superintendent of public education, met for lunch one day (Hansen, 1992). They wanted to prepare their current students better and to help their students' parents, 30 percent of whom did not have high school diplomas, become better informed and skilled.

They aired their most creative visions, including all the many *who's* and *how's* involved: Who will pay? Who will train? Who will repair? How can we achieve our goals? Then they set about putting their ideas into action.

Starting with the fourth and fifth graders in five pilot schools, they purchased a computer for each student at school and a *buddy* computer to use at home. The home computer enabled students to "become proficient in keyboarding, to learn software that could be used creatively, plus offer them a tool they found to be exciting" (Hansen, 1992, p. 61).

Then, they had teachers assign computer homework. Their rationale was as follows:

First, if the parents became interested in their child's computer and its link to the school, the educational impact on the student could be significant. Second, parents might easily acquire computer skills of their own that would be valuable in the job market.

At this point in the discussion, another vista opened. If home computers were furnished with modems, communication between students, teachers and parents could take place. Moreover, a world of information could be brought directly into the home for families to access. Homes and schools could be linked to public and private information providers, and, in time, statewide networks might grow from lessons learned in a pilot project. (p. 61)

The Buddy System Project became a reality because of a true public–private partnership between phone and computer companies, funds from grants, private sectors, and the cooperation of the school system. In 1992, the legislature provided a $1.5 million annual allocation to continue the Buddy System Project and expand it to the fourth grade at seven more schools. As Hansen described it:

Annual evaluations designed by the University of Pittsburgh and conducted by Quality Performance Associates, in Chicago, Ill., show that Buddy students:
- Acquire superior computer skills;
- Produce written work of higher quality and greater length with fewer errors;
- Produce work of greater creativity and complexity;
- Complete more homework.
. . . Plus parents and siblings spend considerable amounts of time themselves using the Buddy computer. Parents report substantially increasing their computer skills and gaining knowledge they can apply in their jobs. (p. 62)

Numerous examples were given describing how the students used the computers to find out more about the Middle East when the Persian Gulf War broke out in early 1991. When a large earthquake occurred in San Francisco, California, in late 1990, the Buddy students used an earthquake database from Boulder, Colorado, to conduct research, "and then used Prodigy to contact members who lived in the San Francisco area" (p. 62).

Other examples were given of parents and of how their job-related skills were increasing. Promotions, home businesses, a high school equivalency diploma (GED), and even the inspiration to attend college were all attributed to the positive impact of the Buddy System.

Buddy leaders proposed a model with goals that were ambitious but affordable. Access to a home computer for every fourth- through sixth-grade student in their state cost the state less than $100 per student per year. Many schools may hesitate to implement this model through fear that they cannot afford it; but this school system has shown it can be done!

The Saturn School of Tomorrow

Another school using cutting-edge technology is the Saturn School of Tomorrow in St. Paul, Minnesota. When the America 2000 plan was announced in 1991 at the White House, President George Bush cited the Saturn School of Tomorrow (King, 1992) as a "break-the-mold" school. Saturn's goal was "that each and every student become a successful, lifelong learner" (p. 66). How they planned to achieve this was reflected in the school's mission statement:

Mission: The Saturn School of Tomorrow will bring together the best of what is known about effective learning research and powerful learning technologies and synthesize it into a transformed, personalized school setting that employs a Personal Growth Plan for each student, a curriculum for today and tomorrow, and the assumption of learning success for each child. (p. 66)

Begun as a districtwide magnet school in 1989, Saturn School is "high-tech, high-teach, and high-touch" (p. 67). "Author and self-taught philosopher Eric Hoffer's quote serves as a dictum at Saturn: 'Learners will inherit the earth, while the learned find themselves well equipped to deal with a world that no longer exists'" (p. 68). Peter Drucker, often called the father of management, is also quoted: "The best way to predict the future is to create it" (p. 68). In fact, Drucker (1989), in giving his opinion of "How Schools Must Change," stated that the computer has "unlimited patience and is at the command of the learner the way no teacher in a classroom can be" (p. 20).

The action plan of Saturn School addressed five principles, the fifth of which involved the use of the school's high-tech tools:

Students at Saturn use high-tech tools: video, word processing, modems. LEGO-LEGO robotics, HyperCard programming and group interaction using the ICS Discourse system (which allows the teacher, or any presenter, to see student answers or opinions typed at their desktop keyboards hooked to the teacher's computer). We call the Discourse room a place where "you can sit, but you can't hide." Because of the assumptions and passivity of textbooks, Saturn students almost never use them; learning is meant to be active "hands-on and heads-on . . . " (p. 67)

King stated that Saturn has received recognition "not for what we have done—it is for our search for a better way for all students to learn" (p. 68).

USING COMPUTERS IN THE WRITING PROCESS

"The computer offers the possibility of establishing an individualized experience in learning to write that may someday become almost as natural as learning to speak," wrote Balajthy (1986, p. 138). He later continued with this quotation from Papert (1980, p. 157):

We take for granted that there should be a gap between the spoken and written language. Children learn to speak as babies without formal instruction. But the written language comes later, if at all, and seems to require deliberate professional teaching. But why should this be so? Is writing really harder than speaking? I believe not and that the computer will close the gap.

Suid and Lincoln (1989) suggested that one of the reasons people use computers is as follows: "You can cook terrific meals on a wood-burning stove. But if you're like most people, you prefer a modern range. It's easier. It's faster. And it lets you do more" (p. 318). Life has sped up for all of us in many ways. The following examples demonstrate how modern conveniences have made many of our daily chores quicker:

Changes Change Things

Long Ago	Today
hooks and eyes	Velcro
wood-burning stoves	microwaves
washboards	automatic washers
clotheslines	dryers
handwritten	computer
abacus	calculator
operators	car phones
Pony Express	fax
horse and buggy	jet airplane

As the chart demonstrates, many of the things we use daily are much faster today than their counterparts in the past. Ken Bardach, Associate Dean of Management at Rensselaer Polytechnic Institute (RPI) in Troy, New York, offered the saying, "The only people who like change are wet babies" (Applications, 1992, p. 48). In reality, however, many people are thrilled when new products appear on the market, and they can't wait to try them.

Project SYNERGY

Project SYNERGY—Software Support for Underprepared Students—began in 1990 to gather, review, and identify software that was helpful for underprepared students and adults. The stages of implementation described by Kamala Anandam (1992), while referring to the use of the software, apply to how educators have seemed to augment all modern technology use. First, there is *awareness* when teachers are just learning about new material. Then, they *analyze* the new material; they *accommodate* the material without changing their methods of teaching; they *assimilate* the material and realize that perhaps they need to change some traditional teaching practices; finally, they *adopt* the new technology into their curriculum. Anandam reported that "the five stages of implementation require considerable time and effort" (p. 28).

When to Teach Typing on the Computer

As the word processor has been introduced and used at the elementary school level, a debate has evolved over whether teaching students to type is necessary or even worth considering. Rude (1986, p. 97) reported that, in 1983, Kaake had reviewed the literature and found that "typewriting increases children's reading, spelling, grammar, punctuation, and creative writing abilities." She also found some elementary students can type as fast as 40 words per minute. Although many typing programs are now available, Rude gives the good advice to encourage, but not pressure, young students above their developmental physical capabilities for typing. Interested and capable students, given the opportunity, will always want to excel. By middle school, however, all students should be encouraged to learn keyboarding skills. When the computer is used as a word processor, it is a tool or vehicle for translating thoughts to print form. The quality of a piece composed at a computer will reflect the writer's ability to use this tool. However, the advantages of the word processor are myriad and each stage of the writing process is enhanced through its use. Consider the following reasons word processing is helpful:

- Most people can type on a word processor much faster than they can write by hand. The mind works much faster than words can be put on paper in any way.
- It's much easier to read a typewritten draft than one written by hand.
- Changes made by moving, adding, and deleting text are much faster on a word processor. The changes are much neater—in fact, they don't even show. Type a few commands and a whole word or group of words can be changed throughout an entire manuscript.
- Spelling and grammar checkers aid in finding errors. When the words students want to spell are not in their computer dictionaries there is an opportunity to improve dictionary skills as they search for correct spellings.
- In publishing, papers are neater and more professional looking than those written by hand or typed on a typewriter. Many varied typing fonts are available, and it is simple to use boldface and italics to emphasize words.
- Programs offering clip art and various formats allow even young students to create many different types of work, including banners, newspapers, invitations, as well as illustrated reports.

Content Is Still the Main Priority

Although creating a nice-looking paper is very important, teaching students how to write adequate and clear content is still the main priority. Rifkin (1990, p. 25) reported that Dartmouth College has an Apple Macintosh in every dorm room on campus. Yet, although professors acknowledge that papers are now "clean, readable and without spelling errors, the content of papers is of no higher quality than in precomputer days." As DeGroff (1990) said, "It is teachers' beliefs about writing and writing with computers, rather than the technology it-self, that makes a difference in how instruction proceeds" (p. 570). DeGroff, citing the findings of two studies, said, "The teachers taught writing, not computing, and they taught in ways that were consistent with their established beliefs about teaching and learning to write" (p. 570). Computers were simply another tool that helped them achieve their already established goals. Dr. Linda Heller, a media specialist in a Tallahassee, Florida, elementary school, said, "To truly become a computer literate society, students must learn to think and compose on the computer—just as it is better to learn to think in a foreign language when studying that language." When students learn to revise as they compose, they are both thinking as writers and reading their material as readers. Since revision is so easy on the computer, they are more apt to take risks so that they can visualize how something looks before they lose their thoughts. They quickly learn how easily their writing can be changed. Model Activity 7.1 gives an opportunity to practice moving material to make a revised selection better. Of course, the length of this activity could be reduced or expanded to fit the needs of the learner.

Students Like Using Computers

Baer (1989), of New Mexico State University, wanted to discover if students' attitudes toward writing were changed by use of the word processor. Baer interviewed 58 seventh graders who had been given nine weeks of keyboard and word-processing practice prior to the study and then observed them during writing assignments. Students said that three things affected how much they liked to write and how much time they spent on task. They liked choosing their own topics, working in a quiet place with few distractions, and writing on the word processor. Only three students did not like using the word processor, and they had not learned enough computer skills to function well. The 55 students who liked using the word processor to write had the following things to say about using word processing: "Mistakes were easier to see and correct . . . they could concentrate better at a keyboard; [and] the keyboard also reminded some students about punctuation. Some students felt more in control of their work at the keyboard" (p. 562). Clearly, the majority of students felt that their writing experiences were better with the use of the word processor.

HOW TO BEGIN TEACHING WRITING ON A COMPUTER

In the simplest scenario in today's classroom, one might find a single computer that students use for word processing by inserting their individual disks and taking turns. Data disks can be stored in students' writing folders and used when students have computer turns so that they can continue their writing. When computers are limited in number, teachers sometimes have students write rough drafts by hand, then type their revised creations on the computer. How one school district in the southeastern United States integrated its word-processing technology with its fourth- and fifth-grade developmental writing program (DWP) was described by Moore (1989). Moore was fortunate enough to have a lab with fifteen computers. Prewriting and first drafts took place in the classroom for the first two days of the week. When the students arrived in the computer lab on the third day, they either worked on their drafts at desks or worked in pairs at the computer, with each partner alternately having two fifteen-minute turns. Partners helped each other with capitalization, punctuation, and spelling. Dictionaries and thesauri were readily available. Teachers assisted students through mini conferences. On the fourth day, students shared printed copies of their stories for editing by their peers. Three trained computer assistants helped with loading programs, checking computers before and after the class, and printing. Although Moore didn't specify whether these assistants were aides, volunteers, or peer students, any of these could be taught to serve in this capacity. Moore (1989) reported that teachers had noted that "students who had difficulty with rewriting and revising have increased their ability to edit and revise their compositions due to the ease by which editing and revising is [sic] accomplished with word processors" (p. 611). Moore continued that teachers thought that they had more time to assist in revision and that reluctant writers were completing more assignments. They felt that "students using word processors significantly improved the quality of their writing compared with students not using word processors" (p. 611).

Whereas Moore managed to help her students become computer literate with limited computer time, the stages of process-based writing can be modeled and shared with students on a computer. By use of a LCD projection system, matter on the computer screen can be projected on a full-sized movie screen or wall for viewing by a whole class, or the material can be shown on a large-screen television set.

The following was observed by one teacher when she went to visit a small technology communications center found in the media center. She eavesdropped on two girls working at a computer:

"Marsha, do you know how to spell *enormous*?"

"No, but if we get close, the spell checker will help us correct it."

"Okay, what should I put?"

"Type *e-n-o-r-m-u-s.*"

These girls were not going to let lack of skill in spelling slow down their creative writing. Another group was having a different problem.

"Okay, we're ready to print. Do you know how?"

"Well, I think I remember. We learned how in Mr. Smith's class, but you forget things like that over the summer when you don't use them. Highlight the word 'Print' on your menu bar. Click your mouse. Okay, now put your mouse on the word 'Help.' Click it again."

"Why don't we just call Judy. She's a computer assistant."

"And let her think we can't read? Look, the directions are as easy as pie."

"Hey, you're right. Even I can do this. Let's print!"

A third group was having problems of a different sort.

"C'mon, hurry up. It's my turn to type."

"I only have a little bit more to write to finish this paragraph. Please let me finish, okay? I'll let you type over your time limit a little bit, too."

"Okay, that sounds fair. Hey, back up. You wrote the word *are* two times."

These scenes and many similar ones are repeated daily as technological advances make their way into the learning environment. Today, students can use computer programs to assist them as they move through the overlapping and recursive stages of the writing process. There are programs that assist in brainstorming. Ideas are typed on the computer so that the whole class can have a printed copy, thus freeing students to think and not have to copy the brainstormed list. Several programs even "allow the teacher to create prompts to guide students at the prewriting stage" (King & Vockell, 1991, p. 145). Freewriting is another possible computer prewriting activity. Several authors (King & Vockell, 1991; Marcus & Blau, 1983) suggested turning off the monitor and having students write without seeing the screen. They believe this use of "blind typing"or "invisible writing" encourages students to concentrate on their thoughts rather than on their typing skills. Obviously, this is assuming that students can already type. Model Activity 7.2 combines both freewriting and practice in the use of a spell checker.

King and Vockell (1991) cited the following advantages of computer use compared with the use of pencil and paper:

- Students are not distracted by handwriting concerns.
- Mechanics are less likely to interfere with the flow of thoughts.
- Students tend to experiment more with phrasing and structure.
- Students create longer documents.
- Hardcopy is easy to read and encourages thorough proofreading.
- In the rewriting stage, students are more willing to edit content as well as surface errors. (p. 148)

Many programs also aid students at the revision and editing stages in checking word choice and mechanics. DeGroff (1990) cited Phenix and Hannan (1984) as noting that once students find out "how easy it is to make changes with the word processor, they are more willing to take chances with their writing. They risk invented spellings or less-than-conventional punctuation" (p. 572). They don't mind going back to make revisions in their work once they realize they won't have to recopy their whole paper. Model Activity 7.1, introduced earlier in the chapter, also gives students an opportunity to revise information in order to put it in better chronological order.

No other aspect of the computer in process-based writing is as exciting as the possibilities for audiences. Whether one student is writing on a disk to be shared and/or answered by the teacher or another student, printing a story to be shared with the class or submitted to a national or international publication, or sending letters via a modem to pen pals (nowadays, a.k.a. computer pals) around the globe, the opportunities for publication are limited only by knowledge and/or budget. The many ideas offered in Chapter 8 of this book, "Modes of Publishing," can be used readily in conjunction with the computer.

Process-based writing on the computer can be used across the curriculum. A report that is being prepared for any content area can be written on the computer using the overlapping and recursive stages of the writing process.

Simulations offer another specialized use of computers. "A computer simulation is a program that attempts to model some portion of the world that, in general, cannot be experienced due to limitations of time, circumstance, money, or physical resources" (Geisert & Futrell, 1990, p. 54). The military and commercial pilot training programs have used simulations for years. Of course, prior to computer use, the simulations must have been on films or filmstrips. Pilots report that airplane simulations make them feel as though they are really flying. Computer simulations allow students to make decisions that alter what follows. In one simulation of a deer population described by Geisert and Futrell (1990), students controlled the size of a deer herd, then saw the results of their actions on the computer screen. If they allowed too many deer to live, there was not enough space, food, or water, and the deer became weak and diseased. Students could easily use simulations as the basis for writing activities. Although each student could have used the same program, their results, based on choices they had made, would all have been different.

A media aide in a school, who also happened to be a parent, was telling the former teacher of one of her children about how excited her daughter, who was virtually aliterate (a term referring to one who is able to read, but doesn't), had been about the simulation program "Where in the World Is Carmen Sandiego?" Armed with a world atlas, the student was searching through clues given in the program, looking in the atlas for answers, and amassing a lot of good information for future writing.

PERIPHERALS AND THE VIDEODISC PLAYER

There are several attachments, known as peripherals, that can extend the use of the classroom computer. They include the compact disk read-only-memory (CD-ROM) and the telecommunications system. Videodisc players also expand the use of computer technology in the classroom.

The CD-ROM is like a musical CD and is directly descended from it. A disk player can be plugged into a computer, and the computer will read the information on the CD-ROM. King and Vockell (1991) quoted Orwig and Baumback (1989) with the following categories of information on CD-ROMs:

Reference materials such as encyclopedias, dictionaries, thesauri, and directories. Examples include BOOK-SHELF (JMH Software, ELECTRONIC ENCYCLOPE-DIA (Grolier), and MULTIMEDIA ENCYCLOPEDIA (Compton).

Indexing services such as abstracts, ERIC, and *Books in Print.* Examples include SILVERPLATTER (Silverplatter) and DIALOG ONDISC (Dialog Information Services).

Visual databases that contain clip art for desktop publishing

Software collections of public domain titles, such as PUBLIC DOMAIN FREEWARE/SHAREWARE (Alde Publishing) (p.167)

One CD-ROM can store up to 270,000 pages of text, as well as "video, graphics, numerical databases, sound, and computer programs" (King & Vockell, 1991, p. 167). Also available is a word-processing program that students can access at the same time they are using the reference materials so that they can cut and paste from references while they are writing reports. Model Activity 7.3 demonstrates how a teacher can direct students in gathering materials from various sources.

In addition to the use of the CD-ROM, one may use telecommunications to tap into information available from faraway places. Besides a computer, required equipment includes a modem, a phone line, and a subscription to an information service that will give phone numbers to access on-line databases. Telecommunications software will be provided by the service chosen. Hooked up to a standard telephone jack, a computer can be connected to other computers around the world.

Another special use of computer technology is with the videodisc player. A single videodisc can store up to 54,000 individual frames on each side. Stories can be stored just as on video tape, but a specific slide can be found, and then relocated, by using barcode numbers and scanners similar to those used for products in grocery stores. For example, one teacher used her videodisc of *Young Sherlock Holmes* (Columbus, 1985) in this way:

We've been watching the story of *Young Sherlock Holmes* today. Holmes said that Watson was from the northern part of Ireland, liked sweet tarts, was named James, was a writer, and that his father was a doctor. Examine this frame. You are seeing the same things that Holmes saw when he met Watson for the first time. Write down any clues that you see that support Holmes' statements.

After the students had been given several minutes to think and write, she used a barcode scanner to find the exact number of a prior frame that showed the clues she wanted the students to see.

Take a look at what Watson is eating on the train.

Then, by scanning other numbers, she returned to several other frames and discussed them with the students. Next, she moved to the frames in which Holmes told Watson how he'd known, or guessed in some cases, the statements he'd made, such as when Holmes told Watson that he had known he liked sweet tarts, because of both his size and the custard that he had smeared on the lapel of his jacket.

Think of how exciting a writing assignment could be if students took turns selecting three or four frames from a story and asked the class to write a story using their choices in the same or varying sequences. Videodiscs are also helpful for study and review and even for interactive instruction (INTERACTIVE, 1990, p. 6). As more practically indestructible videodiscs become available, their use will certainly aid in the development of both cultural literacy and process-based writing.

HOW COMPUTER PROGRAMS CAN HELP ADVANCED WRITERS

In the past, most word-processing programs permitted students to draft, revise, and edit for publica-

tion. If a computer were used for brainstorming, the words written became page 1 of the draft until the writers were ready to move them. But writers and teachers who valued the writing process had experienced frustration with this lack of flexibility. They wanted to be able to store ideas without having them become a part of the manuscript. Turkle (1991), a professor at Massachusetts Institute of Technology (MIT), felt this same frustration when writing computer programs. She observed that educators, industry, and academics all proposed working through programs from top to bottom. But Turkle's mind did not function that way. Turkle first experimented with one idea for a while, then began working on something else. She believed that her mistakes were "missteps" and that these were only stepping stones. As often is the case in writing, her thoughts were not linear. She said she felt that when she worked in this way, which she called "tinkering" or bricolage," she was having a conversation with a computer and not a monologue. According to Webster's dictionary, *bricolage* comes from the French and means "to putter about." *Bricoleurs* work without a precise plan, fiddling with this and that, like painters who step back from their canvases and then make changes. Turkle said that a bricoleur navigates by interaction and association. They are like writers who start without an outline and move from one idea to another by association. Bricoleurs' thought processes are seemingly different from the normal linear process used by most

processors, yet their finished products may be every bit as organized as the products of the planner.

Writing software programs of the past have given bricoleur writers little opportunity to store thoughts on one topic while working on another without completely moving from one document to another. Houlette (1991), director of the Indiana Writing Project and an associate professor of English at Ball State University, recognized the need for a program that accommodated these various activities and functions. He, too, wanted a software program that reflected how writers really write. He found that previous programs were "limited by the presumption that writers perform only one task at a time" (p. 9). So Houlette wrote a program called Write Environment, a Microsoft Windows application. For this program, he was chosen the first place winner of the 1990 Masters of Innovation II, Award for Liberal Arts and Sciences. Houlette hoped writing instructors would feel as he did, that his computer program could really improve writing content. While his software program was being field-tested by graduate students, the windows terminology included writing terms such as *file, edit, search, write,* and *revise.* Houlette said that his program was based on a model that acknowledged that writing is a nonlinear process and that different writers write in different ways. His program tried to support individual styles.

INNOVATIVE USES OF COMPUTERS IN THE LEARNING ENVIRONMENT

Two separate projects have relied heavily on computer writing. One was titled Computer Pals Across the World (formerly the Australaskan Writing Project). The other one will be referred to as The Moss Point Plan.

Computer Pals Across the World

The purposes of this ongoing whole language–based project described by Beazley (1989), its founder and director, were as follows:

- to provide students with a real context in which they can improve their written communications skills;
- to provide an opportunity for cultural exchange through reading and writing;
- to motivate the linguistically less interested student;
- to provide an opportunity for students to develop keyboard skills; and

- to familiarize students with the use of international telecommunications. (p. 599)

In this Australian-based project, students with similar interests from different countries were paired. Most schools were paired with only one country; but some schools, for example, had one class writing to France, one to England, and one to the United States.

Assignments of six activities were given. The first assignment was to write a letter to your computer pal introducing yourself. The second activity was to write a report about something familiar. The example given was "Thanksgiving." The third activity was to exchange an original poem with your computer pal. The fourth activity was to send newspaper articles, producing an on-line individual, class, or school newspaper, with the variety of articles one would find in any school newspaper. The fifth activity was an exchange on social issues in written dialogue. The students themselves debated vital world issues by writing opinion papers on their computers. The sixth and final activity was to write scripts pertaining to a myth or legend of their culture.

Throughout the project, students used the various stages of the writing process. Because of the expense of electronic transmission, students were encouraged to observe economy of expression. The focus was on English, although foreign language students also participated in the world network. The project was a very stimulating motivator to learn a foreign language. The media center became an important place as students researched information to send to their computer pals. One can only imagine the motivation and enjoyment such a project produces. Truly, reading and writing benefits could in no way be separated as students corresponded, "tele-edited," and commented on the writing of others around the globe.

The Moss Point Plan

Another story of great success involving the use of computers follows. To say the Moss Point, Mississippi, School District was disappointed with its test results would be a vast understatement. In 1986, over half of its eleventh graders failed the essay writing test, and almost one-fourth of the junior class failed the reading test. Realizing that these dismal results affected all learning, the district decided to improve in these two areas while also teaching application of computer skills. After considerable research, they chose to use a program of semantic or cognitive mapping. Cronin, Meadows, and Sinatra (1990) cited findings from the International Reading Association (1988) that this interactive organizational approach between the reader and the text helps the reader create meaning out of what is being read; it is a practical application of schema theory. The central office staff, principals, and teachers at each school worked together to plan how to implement this program. To move to a holistic curriculum, they decided to teach semantic mapping, writing, and thinking skills to every student. A highly structured computer program known as "The Thinking Networks for Reading and Writing" approach was utilized. The staffs were trained, and students were taught three types of semantic mapping: sequence, theme, and classification. Teachers modeled these maps on chalkboards and overhead projectors in each content area, but especially in science, social studies, and English classes. Teachers planned lessons incorporating the writing process. They related new vocabulary and concept ideas to previous material so that students could see the relationship between what they were learning and what they already knew. They identified main ideas of reading assignments. They asked students to map homework assignments, which were presented on the chalkboard and discussed. In writing classes, students were asked to prepare reports using the semantic maps as guides. Examples were given of semantic maps prepared by students as young as fifth grade, although the eleventh-grade scores were used for benchmark purposes. Students used computers for both the mapping and essay writing. Students became more reflective and better organized. They developed higher order thinking as they judged the relationships of parts to the whole. As they wrote essays, they combined their texts-in-the-head with new information that was presented. The results were outstanding. After two full years of implementation, not one eleventh grader failed the essay writing test (as compared to over half before the program was started); in reading, 366 eleventh graders passed the reading test and three failed, as compared to one-fourth of the students who had been failing when the program started. These results are a true tribute to a district's willingness to implement change through the use of training, computers, and the writing process.

COMPUTERS TODAY AND TOMORROW

Computers in the hands of skilled teachers who carefully select and use good software definitely can improve the education our students receive. Computers can do whatever we have programmed them to do. Computers can talk, computers can beat people in games if they have been programmed to execute the proper moves, and computers can use logic and math; but computers cannot think. Computers cannot (at this time) step inside the brain of another human being and escape with that person's thoughts. However, "virtual reality" (Associated Press, 1992) allows a person's thoughts, transferred first to their hands and then from their hands to a computer screen through the use of special sensor gloves, to be brought to life on the screen so that people can "walk through" their creations. Already appearing in video game arcades, programs using virtual reality will permit computer-equipped friends to share vacations in faraway places. Robots in satellites use virtual reality; for example, a per-

son on earth wearing sensor gloves holds a hammer, pounds it, and a robot in space does the same thing. A renowned surgeon could guide the hand of an inexperienced doctor in a distant city. Control tower pilots could steer an ill pilot's plane to safety. And master teachers could help students learn anything. While limited to one-on-one experiences today, who knows what tomorrow will bring. This is the technology of today. As for the technology of tomorrow, visualize your future—it might come true.

REFERENCES

Allen, D. (1992, February). Byte Size. *Teaching K–8, 22*(5), 14, 16.

America: Great crises in our history told by its makers. (1925). Chicago: Americanization Department, Veterans of Foreign Wars. *10,* 184–201.

Anandam, K. (1992, March). Project SYNERGY: Software support for underprepared students. *IBM Higher Education, Supplement to Technological Horizons in Education (T.H.E.) Journal,* pp. 26–28.

Applications. (1992, April). Executives in MBA program use BBS to communicate. *Technological Horizons in Education (T.H.E.) Journal, 19*(9), 48.

Associated Press. (1992, April 1). "Virtual reality" lets computer users translate body movements into changes on the screen. *Tallahassee Democrat,* p. 9D.

Baer, V. (1989, March). Revising: The fourth *r*? *Phi Delta Kappan, 70,* 561–562.

Balajthy, E. (1986). *Microcomputers in reading and language arts.* Englewood Cliffs, NJ: Prentice-Hall.

Beazley, M. R. (1989, April). Reading for a real reason: Computer pals across the world. *Journal of Reading, 32*(7), 598–605.

Columbus, C. (Writer), Spielberg, S. (Producer), & Levinson, B. (Director). (1985). *Young Sherlock Holmes* [Laser optical videodisc]. Los Angeles: Paramount Home Videos.

Cronin, H., Meadows, D., & Sinatra, R. (1990, September). Integrating computers, reading, and writing across the curriculum. *Educational Leadership, 48*(1), 57–62.

DeGroff, L. (1990, April). Is there a place for computers in whole language classrooms? *The Reading Teacher, 43*(8), 568–572.

Drucker, P. F. (1989, May). How schools must change. *Psychology Today, 23,* 18–20.

Elam, S. M., Rose, L. C., & Gallup, A. M. (1991, September). The 23rd annual Gallup poll of the public's attitudes toward the public schools. *Phi Delta Kappan, 73*(1), 43.

Fox, R. G. (1990, Fall). Letter from the president. *SALT Newsletter,* p. 1.

Fox, R. G. (1991, Fall). Letter from the president. *SALT Newsletter,* p. 1.

Geisert, P. G., & Futrell, M. K. (1990). *Teachers, computers, and curriculum / Microcomputers in the classroom.* Boston: Allyn and Bacon.

Hansen, A. G. (1992, April). A buddy computer in the home: Five-year progress report. *Technological Horizons in Education (T.H.E.) Journal, 19*(9), 61–65.

Heilman, A., Blair, T., & Rupley, W. (1986). *Principles and practices of teaching reading,* 6th ed. Columbus, OH: Merrill.

Hirsch, E. D., Jr. (1987). *Cultural literacy: What every American needs to know.* Boston: Houghton Mifflin.

Houlette, F. (1991). Write environment: A window on the writing process. *Zenith Data Systems, Supplement to Technological Horizons in Education (T.H.E.) Journal,* Special issue, pp. 9–11.

INTERACTIVE laser disc: Technology for interactive teaching and learning (1990, Spring). *Supplement to Technological Horizons in Education (T.H.E.) Journal,* p. 6.

International Reading Association. (1988). *New directions in reading instruction.* Newark, DE: International Reading Association.

Jackson, J., & Crossland, G. (1992, March). Using multimedia to improve students' cultural literacy. *IBM Higher Education, Supplement to Technological Horizons in Education (T.H.E.) Journal,* 36–37.

King, D. T. (1992, April). The Saturn School of tomorrow: A reality today. *Technological Horizons in Education (T.H.E.) Journal, 19*(9), 66–68.

King, R. E., & Vockell, E. L. (1991). *The computer in the language arts curriculum.* Watsonville, CA: Mitchell McGraw-Hill.

Marcus, S., & Blau, S. (1983, April). Not seeing is relieving: Invisible writing with computers. *Educational Technology, 23*(4), 12–15.

Moore, M. A. (1989, April). Computers can enhance transactions between readers and writers. *The Reading Teacher, 42*(8), 608–611.

O'Malley, C. (1991, Summer). The revolution is yet to come. *National Forum: The Phi Kappa Phi Journal, 71*(3), 12–14.

Orwig, G., & Baumbach, D. (1989). *What every educator needs to know about the new technologies: CD-ROM.* Orlando, FL: UCF/DOE Instruction Computing Resource Center.

Papert, S. (1980). *Mindstorms: Children, computers, and powerful ideas.* New York: Basic Books.

Phenix, J., & Hannan, E. (1984). Word processing in the grade one classroom. *Language Arts, 61*(8), 804–812.

Rifkin, G. (1990). Can technology effectively replace human teachers? *Computerworld, 24,* October 8, p. 25.

Rude, R. T. (1986). *Teaching reading using microcomputers.* Englewood Cliffs, NJ: Prentice-Hall.

Sachar, E. (1991, August). Bringing animals to class: The St. Louis Zoo creates a new multimedia center—for teachers only. *Teacher Magazine, 2*(9), 14–15.

Seldes, G. (Ed.). (1985). *The great thoughts.* New York: Ballantine, p. 279.

Suid, M., & Lincoln, W. (1989). *Recipes for writing: Motivation, skills, and activities.* Menlo Park, CA: Addison-Wesley.

Toffler, A. (1985). *Powershift: Knowledge, wealth, and violence at the edge of the 21st century.* New York: Bantam.

Turkle, S. (1991, Summer). If the computer is a tool, is it more like a hammer or more like a harpsichord? *National Forum: The Phi Kappa Phi Journal, 71*(3), 8–11.

White, S. W. (1991, Summer). The universal computer. *National Forum, 71*(3), 2.

Zachmann, W. F. (1991, August). Education: The final frontier. *PC Magazine, 10*(14), 97–98.

Zuboff, S. (1991, Summer). Informate the enterprise: An agenda for the twenty-first century. *National Forum: The Phi Kappa Phi Journal, 71*(3), 3–7.

MODEL ACTIVITIES

The activities that follow are meant to serve as models; such activities should be used as part of a total learning environment. These model activities were designed to demonstrate how the writing process can be developed while expanding the writer's knowledge base and providing opportunities for the writer to think critically.

Madame Curie: Revising on a Computer

Directions: On a word processor, type the paragraph below as written. Then, using your computer's program for moving material, rearrange the facts to put the information given in chronological (date) order.

MADAME CURIE (1867–1934)

At the age of five, Marie was a very curious little girl who was dying to learn to read. She begged her father to teach her to read and write, but instead he encouraged her to play, saying, "Marie, you'll learn to read and write soon. Remember in life there is a time to work and a time to play. Play while you can, my girl, play while you can."

Marie Sklodowska was born in Warsaw, Poland, on November 7, 1867. Although times were hard in Poland, Marie had a rather happy childhood. She was one of five children born to Professor Sklodowska, a high school teacher, and Madame Sklodowska, a former teacher.

At the age of fifteen, Marie finished high school (called the Gymnasium) with the highest honor possible, the gold medal for scholarship. At that time, only men received higher education. Her father knew she had a brilliant mind and said he would help her leave the country to complete her education.

Marie dreamed of going to the Sorbonne, the world-famous university in Paris, France. However, her family was not wealthy and her brother was already at the University of Warsaw. Marie spent several years tutoring the children of wealthy parents. Her older sister, Bronya, wanted to go the the Sorbonne to study to become a doctor. Marie said she would take a job with a wealthy family to help pay for Bronya's schooling. Bronya, 20, told Marie, 17, that she wanted her to save for her own education.

"Bronya," said Marie. "That's enough of that talk. This is the only plan that will work for me now. When you are a doctor, you can help me as I want to help you now." Marie never thought once about this sacrifice so her sister could go to the university.

Marie earned a degree in physics in 1893. One year later she earned a degree in math. She placed first among the students in physics and second in math.

The years passed, and by 1890, Marie's dreams of going to the university faded. Hope began to leave her. But Bronya wrote Marie that year and said, "Marie, I am soon to be married. I very much want you to come and live with us and go to the university." Marie spent the next year in Warsaw with her father, saving money to go live with Bronya. It was during this year that she began secretly studying science and made the decision that she wanted to be a scientist.

By the time Marie actually left to go to Paris, she was twenty-four years old. Although she had great gaps in her education, she did very well. The lectures were given in French, and often she would miss whole sentences. Also, she needed a better knowledge of mathematics and physics. Because of her educational gaps, she needed a quieter place to study. She found a place closer to the university. Her sister's place had been over an hour away. She became lost in her work and lived for weeks on buttered bread and tea. Sometimes, but not often, she would have eggs, chocolate, and some fruit. She spent all of her time studying.

Marie received her doctorate degree in June of 1903. In November of the same year she and her husband received England's highest scientific honor, the Davy Medal, and in December they received the Nobel Prize in physics.

In 1894, she met Pierre Curie (1859–1906), a brilliant thirty-five-year-old French research scientist. Marie had found a research job but needed a less-crowded laboratory in which to work. They were married in 1895. For a while, each continued with individual research, but soon Marie convinced Pierre to share her excitement about her work with the radiation of uranium. After much experimentation, they discovered two new elements, which they named *polonium,* in honor of Poland, and *radium,* because of its radiation.

Pierre had wanted to work at the Sorbonne as a professor for quite a while. Twice he was turned down, but in July 1905 he was elected to the Academy of Science.

After Pierre's death, the Sorbonne broke its tradition of having only male professors and offered Marie the professorship they had created for Pierre. As a genius, she was recognized as the only scientist who could direct the laboratory.

Disaster followed in April 1906, when Pierre was accidentally killed as he thoughtlessly walked in front of a wagon drawn by two horses. Marie was filled with sorrow and worn out by hard work. She thought about quitting her work but remembered Pierre's words: "Whatever happens, even if one of us has to go on like a body without a soul, the other must work just the same." So Marie went back to work.

Radiation treatment and X-rays are two benefits we all share today, thanks to the life work of Marie Curie. In 1934, Marie Curie died, killed by the radium that had been so much a part of her life.

From 1906 until 1910, Marie worked with another scientist, isolating and finding a better way to measure radium, a discovery that greatly aided doctors. She also continued to study polonium and its rays. In 1911, Marie Curie became the first person to receive two Nobel Prizes when she won the Nobel Prize in chemistry.

Your Turn: Although most activities allow for your own ideas, chronological order, like alphabetical order, has only one correct answer. When you are relating factual information, such as historical or biographical, keeping the events in chronological order is essential for your reader's comprehension. Type the preceding story as is. Then use the computer to rearrange paragraphs so that the dates and events in Marie Curie's life are in the order in which they occurred.

Compare the first five words of each paragraph with the order that follows to see if you revised the paragraph correctly:

Marie Sklodowska was born in
At the age of five
At the age of fifteen
Marie dreamed of going to
"Bronya," said Marie. "That's enough
The years passed, and by
By the time Marie actually
Marie earned a degree in
In 1894, she met Pierre
Marie received her doctorate degree
Pierre had wanted to work
Disaster followed in April 1906,
After Pierre's death, the Sorbonne
From 1906 until 1910, Marie
Radiation treatment and X-rays are

Now, write your reaction to the story of Marie and Pierre Curie. You might tell why you are glad you live in today's world rather than in their time, or what you think of today's scientists' work (Are any of their life stories this interesting?). Or you can give your opinion about sending a family's children to college by birth order.

You do not have to use any of the suggestions given if something else about this story appealed to you and you would like to respond to that instead. Type your response on your word processor.

Freewriting and Use of Spell Check

Directions: First, choose a topic that is very familiar to you, such as "My Family," "My Best Friend," "My Pet," or "My School." Next, set a timer for three minutes. Put your fingers on the home row of your keyboard, close your eyes, and type until the buzzer rings.

Now, open your eyes and execute the commands for a spell check. Because it might be natural to miss some words with your eyes closed, you may or may not have some words misspelled.

Note the number of errors made. Depending on your typing skill, you may find this an easy way to block out other distractions when you compose at the computer.

ACTIVITY 7.3

Directing Students' Use of Sources

Directions: You are studying ocean animals in class and you have been instructed by your teacher to choose an animal that interests you and to write about it, using at least three different sources. Find the most current information about your animal that you can by using your computer's data encyclopedia. Your media specialist or your teacher can help you with this.

The following is an example of facts you may have found:

Animal Chosen: Portuguese man-of-war

Fact 1:   The Portuguese man-of-war looks like an innocent bubble; when, in fact, it is one of the most dangerous marine animals that exists. The poison in its tentacles, which may be five to forty feet long, is as potent and toxic as that of a cobra.

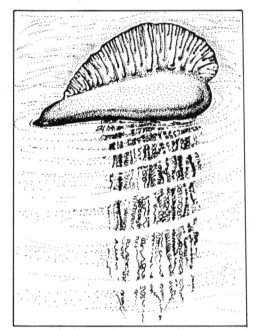

Name of Article or Topic: Interesting Sea Animals

Author: James Hunter

Year of Copyright (also give month if a magazine is used):   April 1992

Source (if not from a book):   Strange Ocean Facts Magazine

Volume (if from a set):   _____

Page/pages: p. 16

City of Publication: Not needed for a magazine article

Publisher: Not needed for a magazine article

Fact 2:   The Portuguese man-of-war can deflate its bladder and sink in the water during rough seas. Then it can blow itself up again to float on top when the sea is calm.

Name of Article or Topic: The Portuguese Man-of-War

Author: Ronald J. Bishop

Year of Copyright (also give month if a magazine is used):   1992

Source: The Book of Facts

Volume (if from a set):   _____

Page/pages: p. 231

City of Publication: New York

Publisher: Hoosier, Inc.

Fact 3:   The Portuguese man-of-war lives by feeding on fish and other marine organisms. One fish is immune to its poison and lives among its tentacles.

Title or Topic: Big Book of Strange Creatures

Author: Samuel E. Jones

Year of Copyright (also give month if a magazine is used):   1991

Source (if not from a book):   _____

Volume (if from a set):   _____

Page/pages: p. 474

City of Publication: Boston

Publisher: Sea Press

Now, combine the facts gathered to write an interesting paragraph or story as in the one below about the Portuguese man-of-war. You also may include other interesting things you know about the man-of-war. When you use each of your facts, write the author's name followed by a comma, the year followed by a comma, and the page or pages written with p. _____ or pp. _____–_____, as modeled by the fictitious references given on the next page.

THE PORTUGUESE MAN-OF-WAR

The Portuguese man-of-war looks like a giant blue bubble of bubble gum, but it is really a dangerous animal. "Its tentacles, which may be five to forty feet long, are as potent and toxic as the poison of a cobra" (Hunter, 1992, p.16). Most fish are stunned or killed by its poison, but "one fish is immune to its poison and lives among its tentacles" (Jones, 1991, p. 474).

Perhaps you may have wondered why sometimes you see "jellyfish," as they are sometimes called, floating on the water, while at other times people are stung without seeing them at all. The Portuguese man-of-war has the ability to inflate and deflate its body. The Portugese man-of-war can deflate its bladder and sink in the water during rough water. Then it can blow itself up again to float on top when the sea is calm (Bishop, 1992, p. 231). So just because you can't see them doesn't mean they aren't there. Sometimes, when there are a lot of them around, or after a storm, you'll see some of them stretched out on the beach. If stung by a Portuguese man-of-war, many people make a paste of meat tenderizer and water to counteract the poison.

Now, look at the names of your three authors. Using the last name, put them in alphabetical order. Bishop, Hunter, Jones

Using the information you found for each author, compile a list of references like the following fictitious one.

References

Bishop, R. (1992). The Portuguese man-of-war. *The book of facts.* New York: Hoosier, p. 231.
Hunter, J. (1992, April). Interesting sea animals. *Strange Ocean Facts Magazine,* p. 16.
Jones, S. E. (1991). *Big book of strange creatures.* Boston: Sea Press, p. 474.

Your turn: Choose a topic. Think of several descriptors you might use to search for your topic. For example, in searching for the Portuguese man-of-war, the words used were *Portuguese man-of-war, jellyfish,* and *fish.*

Descriptors: _____

Next, include useful information that you have found and copy the information needed from each source.

Fact/s: _____

_____

_____

_____

_____

_____

_____

_____

_____

Title or topic: _____

Author: _____

Year of copyright (also give month if a magazine is used): _____

Source (if not from a book): _____

Volume (if from a set): _____

Page/pages: _____

City of publication: _____

Publisher: _____

Continue using the same format with at least two more sources. You may wish to include other facts from other sources. Three different sources are a minimum suggested for this beginning research.

Now, on your word processor, write a draft using the interesting facts you have learned about your topic.

CHAPTER 8

Modes of Publishing

It is time to give away the secret: teaching writing is fun.

—Donald M. Murray, Pulitzer Prize–winning writer (1985, p. 1).

Written work in progress that has evolved from prewriting through a series of drafts deserves to be brought to completion; one form of completion is publication. And what better way for students to discover the importance of their own writing than by seeing it published? They recognize that their good writing also has value to others when it is published; their sense of accomplishment spurs them on to write again.

Publication offers an excellent opportunity to advance cultural literacy while improving writing. This can occur, for example, when students publish works based on knowledge gained from meaningful study of content area subject matter that has been integrated with related literature. Writing reviews, summaries, essays, research papers, or creative stories and poems about famous people and events enhances the cultural literacy of both the writer and others with whom the writing is shared. Using drama or music to publish stories, poems, and song lyrics provides an outlet for creative talents as well as an exciting vehicle for learning more about different cultures. The model activities presented in this chapter combine cultural literacy and writing; with publication as the goal, these activities strike a balance between knowledge and thinking.

Publishing, the final stage in the writing process, may range from an informal display of student writings in the classroom or having books printed and bound in a school publishing center to the sophistication of submitting a story or poem to a newspaper or magazine for formal publication. When students write and revise in groups, their drafts are read by others at various stages of development. Broadly,

this examination of student writing by other readers at any stage can be considered publication; the ongoing work of process writing affords much opportunity for this kind of publishing. Occasionally, however, the stimulation of other audiences—parents, other classes in the school, students from another school, community leaders, and others—can provide timely encouragement to the developing writer. As a result of this encouragement, writers feel more confident about making the decision to publish: in book form, letter form, or any of the many ways to publish student writing.

Published work should be representative of the best writing students can do. Students need to understand that some of their work will be published, and some will not be published, just as professional writers do not publish every draft they write. Calkins (1986) emphasized that publishing need not involve a large amount of a teacher's time to be successful. Publishing is most helpful to students if it is begun early in the year and occurs frequently and predictably throughout the rest of the year. Some teachers schedule announced times when authors will publish some of their better written work. This provides students with a deadline and a time frame for completion of their work-in-process. If students write often and keep their work in writing folders, publication can be a natural process, with no reason for panic.

A sense of authority as authors is strengthened when students are allowed to choose favorite pieces of writing for publication. Cooper and Brown (1992) discussed selecting work to include in a portfolio and recommended that students write a rationale for their choices. They reported how an eighth grader, Tanya, showed her enthusiasm for her best writing by commenting on her process as follows:

I feel it is my best piece of writing because it was exactly what I wanted to write. I just knew the poem was perfect when I finished. The first sentence of my poem says, "Starvation and misery pluck at my heart." That is the exact way I wanted those words to come out. I could scream, I think my paper is so great. (p. 43)

Cooper and Brown observed, "Selecting their best writing allows students to evaluate their own work while the rationale asks them to internalize their own standards to support that choice in writing" (p. 43).

Publishing possibilities for student writers are many and varied. Books, completed and bound, can be shared with classmates and others. Classroom literary journals can be writing outlets for many types of student writing. Classroom newspapers can be a place for students to write about school trips and visitors and to contribute feature articles, editorials, and special columns. Many local newspapers include a student section and invite school-age writers to contribute. Likewise, students can be encouraged to write letters to the editor on topics of concern to them. Editors of certain magazines encourage students to write and submit their work for publication, and student magazines regularly publish written products of developing authors. Publication can occur in the form of book reviews and research papers; and book clubs and writing workshops often engage in projects leading to publication. Dramatic and musical presentations of written work are other forms of publication.

Publicly sharing writing is a powerful motivational force to encourage students to complete pieces of writing. In the past, the only audience for student writing was often the teacher. When writing instruction revolves around writing as a process, however, the teacher is only one of the many audiences who reads the student's work-in-progress as well as the finished product when the student chooses to go "public" through one of the many modes of publication. Publishing possibilities, including some of the items found in lists offered by Fisher and Terry (1990, pp. 361–363) and Temple, Nathan, Burris, and Temple (1988, pp. 260–261), are suggested ideas that can be utilized in a responsive writing environment.

- Bulletin boards in classroom, hall or library:
  Featuring selected writing
  Featuring author of the week
  Demonstrating the writing process from first draft, through all revisions, to final product
- Mobile of chosen writings
- Displays of student work
- Instructional posters for use throughout the year: environmental concerns, health news, school rules, school achievements and awards, and so on
- Signs for class office campaigns, school bake sales, and the like
- Inspirational messages written to be read over the public address system
- Greeting cards: get well, congratulations, holiday, birthday
- Documented picture collections about class projects or class trips
- A newspaper for the classroom, another class, or the school:
  Original student writing
  Special columns: advice, fashion, social, etc.
  Editorials
  Interviews
  Sports
  Advertisements
  Comics and cartoons
- Student magazines: fashion, beauty, cars, vacation, environmental issues, careers, hobbies, etc.
- Literary journals:
  Classroom
  Grade-level
  All-school
- Yearbooks
- Instructional manuals or how-to books:
  Computer programs
  Games and game rules
  Cookbooks
- Contributions to student section of local newspaper
- Contributions to student section of student literary magazine
- Classroom mailboxes where students can exchange letters and invitations
- Letters to parents, teachers, principals, other school staff, authors, public figures, community leaders, etc.
- Letters to the editor of local newspaper
- Letters of inquiry
- Thank-you notes to school visitors and presenters
- Writing contests found in student magazines
- Books written and, if desired, illustrated by students:
  To be shared in the classroom
  To be placed in the school library
  To be placed in waiting rooms in the community
- Books written for younger children:

To be taken home for younger siblings
To be contributed to a lower grade classroom

- Chain novels produced by the class or the school
- Student anthologies of students' best writing of prose or poetry
- Classroom dictionaries
- Plays written and produced by students
- Plays written for younger children to perform
- Songs written to be performed
- Stories written for storytelling
- Program notes for class or school productions
- Puppet shows written and produced by students
- Radio shows written and produced by students and transmitted by school's public address system
- Cassette tapes of students recording selected prose or poetry they have written
- Overhead transparencies of good student papers
- Presentations by teacher of student work (with writer's permission) to other teachers and groups
- Research reports on a selected topic

The preceding list clearly shows that publication possibilities within the learning environment are endless. The teacher who takes advantage of opportunities to publish student work may be planting the seed for future writing careers. Patricia C. McKissack, a former eighth-grade English teacher and author or coauthor of more than forty books for young people, responded to the question of how she got started writing for children in an informal interview (Bishop, 1992):

I actually got started in third grade. I wrote a poem, and the teacher put it on the bulletin board and said she liked it. It was thrilling to have other people read and respond to something I had written, and I don't think that feeling ever left me. I was forever scribbling ideas and thoughts. I kept a journal; I've always kept a diary.

When I became a teacher, I was bothered by the lack of materials for African American children. I taught eighth grade, that very important age group where they're looking for self, especially in books. I wanted to give my kids Paul Laurence Dunbar. He's an American standard. My mother had recited Dunbar for me, and I grew up jumping double dutch to "Jump back, honey, jump back!" But his work wasn't in our anthologies, where my kids could get it. So I said, "OK, I'll write it myself." So I did, and that was one of my first books (*Paul Laurence Dunbar: A Poet to Remember,* Children's Press, 1984). It was the first time I had disciplined myself to write a whole manuscript—beginning, middle, and end—with purpose. Of course, it didn't get published for many years. (p. 70; emphasis in original)

Calkins (1986) explained that authorship is a process, and helping students see themselves as authors should take place as soon as possible after students start writing. If early efforts of students are published, even though less than perfect, the sense of authorship will provide motivation for future writing.

PUBLISHING BOOKS

The reading–writing connection is highlighted during the publishing stage. Students whose work is regularly published see themselves as authors; in turn, they feel confident to evaluate the writing of the authors who have written the books they read. This contributes to their reading ability as well. As Mason and Au (1990) stated,

They seem to feel that they are in a more direct *social interaction* with the author. They also seem more aware of the importance of the reader's purpose and reactions when reading a particular text. Reading, like writing, becomes an active process. (p. 64; emphasis in original)

Calkins (1986) stated, "If our children see themselves as authors, they will read with admiration, marveling at another author's efforts and learning

vicariously from another author's successes and struggles" (p. 228).

Fran Lyons Sammons (1987), realizing that her fifth-grade students were intrigued with reading plot–choice novels such as those in the *Choose Your Own Adventure* series, seized this opportunity to discover if creating their own choose-a-plot books would motivate her students to write. Prewriting included having each student read a commercially published plot-choice book, followed by group discussion and generation of a list of common qualities found in most of these books. Using a story flowchart, Sammons' students worked in pairs to create a thirteen-page book with seven different endings. Student pairs were each responsible for writing a specified part of the story after the class discussed an experimental plot, collaborating and assisting one another at every stage of the process. Teams brainstormed possible characters, settings, and action starting points as they drafted story parts; this process helped developing writers understand that creating a story is putting together parts to make a whole. These students not only enjoyed writing, they also learned skills in plot structure by thinking through a line of story action; they became aware of inventing characters by giving them physical and psychological attributes. Once the publishing phase began, students worked in groups to finalize the writing process. They designed the title, dedication, and "warning" pages. One team of Sammons' students worded a reader warning as follows: "Do not read this book straight through! This book has many choices. When you come to a choice, go to the page as shown. When you finish your adventure, start again because each choice leads to a different adventure" (Sammons, 1987, pp. 53–54). The publishing process was completed with teams organizing the pages, drawing illustrations, designing and making oaktag covers, and binding the books with heavy tape. A photocopier was used to make several copies for the school library. Sammons felt that the most valuable outcome of this project was "the surge in student writing enthusiasm and confidence. Every child is an *author*—and has a book to prove it!" (Sammons, 1987, p. 54).

Using Sammons' technique, a seventh-grade language arts teacher in New Jersey, Barbara Elaine Sargent (1991), implemented a computer writing activity for her adolescent students after she noted how popular the plot-choice stories were with these students. Objectives of this class project were to have students create, write, revise, edit, and share with a larger audience their choose-your-own-adventure stories. This writing project required at least ten forty-minute class periods and gave students opportunities for working in pairs and groups as well as conferencing regularly with the teacher. The project culminated with students printing their stories on the computer, illustrating the stories if desired, designing covers, and binding their books, using available media center equipment. Sargent (1991) shared this observation: "The students' books were placed in the school library for the rest of the student body to read. Having their stories available to a wider audience was exciting and made my students feel like real authors" (p. 159).

Publishing is a powerful motivation for writing and presents students with a real purpose for revision and editing. Students are much more willing to invest their time when they know their completed work will be shared with others. They need to understand the reason(s) for continuing to work on a particular draft before expending the energy necessary for revision and editing. Students need to become empowered enough to determine when *they* believe a piece is worth developing; although the teacher may facilitate, the student should be encouraged to be the decision maker whenever possible. Individual student-authored books should represent work that has been thoughtfully written and taken through the stages of revising and editing. When a product is published, it should be free of errors. This is important so that students can feel proud of their work and recognize the effort needed to produce good writing. Finishing touches of covers, binding, and illustrations make these books valuable additions to the classroom and school libraries. Students may also choose to use their books as gifts for family and friends.

A learning experience that gives students an opportunity to write for an audience other than their peers is to write and publish books for youngsters in the primary grades. As students make books to be enjoyed by younger students, they identify their audience and write for it. After publication of these books, the older students can visit the elementary classes as "visiting authors" to be interviewed by the younger children. This provides a positive learning experience for everyone. Model Activity 8.1 provides the opportunity for students to write and publish books for children in the primary grades.

The writing of group books allows students to collaborate by selecting a topic, then agreeing to contribute individual episodes. Other topics might be researched and published as a group project in science, social studies, or any content area. Monique Gratrix (Gratrix & Hayden, 1990) found that a sense of author community was developed in her sixth-grade classroom by writing a class memoir together. Students were encouraged to share their thoughts and discoveries in this writing project. Some days seem to be made for this kind of writing; a snowstorm, a field trip, a celebration, or a special news event all provide ideas for writing topics. A primary purpose for writing group books is to have a publication that includes writing from *every* student in the class. Model Activity 8.2 was designed as a group activity to assist students as they write and publish their class anthology.

It is important for teachers to provide a learning environment that encourages student writing of books as an ongoing process. For example, students could bring empty photo albums to school at the beginning of the year. When a final draft is completed, it could be sealed in the plastic-covered pages to be read by others during reading time. Upper-grade students might read some of these works to students in other classes. Think how important it will make a young author feel if his or her story is chosen to be read aloud to the class. A bulletin board display featuring an "Author of the Week" with a photograph and attractively presented collection of written work makes writers feel special indeed. Some teachers have found classroom publication of books to be an excellent opportunity to invite school volunteers to become involved. Printing, binding, and producing multiple copies are tasks that volunteers could undertake to enable more classroom writing to be published.

NEWSPAPER PUBLISHING

An exciting mode of publication for a school classroom is the newspaper. Opportunities abound for students to find individual areas of interest and expertise as they decide to write for a particular section of a newspaper. Writers are needed for special columns, such as literary, health, fashion, advice, foods, and social activities. Sports writers, cartoonists, and advertisement writers are necessary for the staff of a newspaper. Add to this list editors, feature writers, and reporters to conduct interviews and collect news. One can readily see that publishing a class newspaper enables students to collaborate while working on varied chosen assignments. The newspaper could be published for and circulated in a particular class, all the classes in a grade, or the entire school. The newspaper might become an ongoing publication, with the number of issues during the school year determined by the teacher and students.

One teacher, Judy Kissell (1990), found that publication of a school newspaper with four editions throughout the year was a good vehicle for publishing student writing efforts. Students began the project by studying several area newspapers to understand the types of things found in newspapers and the various layout styles. Then students brainstormed about newsworthy events and people at their school to come up with ideas for articles and interviews, want ads, comics, movie and book reviews, advice columns, and editorials. After group members agreed on writing assignments, they went to work writing rough drafts. During the next session, students read their own articles and were encouraged to revise and edit them as needed. Proofreading was accomplished by exchanging written work and reading one another's writing. In the third session, Kissell's students entered their articles on the computer, printing them in forty-character columns to achieve a newspaper style. They spent the fourth session cutting and pasting articles and deciding on a name for the paper. Finally, the completed publication was copied and distributed to everyone in the school. All students in the class had had an opportunity to publish their written efforts while serving as reporters, editors, and other newspaper staff members.

An opportune time for a classroom to publish a newspaper might be in connection with studying about Benjamin Franklin (1706–1790), one of the greatest U.S. statesmen, who started writing—and publishing—as a young teenager. Learning about how Franklin prepared for writing by reading every book he could find and how he anonymously published in the newspaper by writing articles at night and slipping them under the printshop door of his brother's newspaper publishing office can serve as both an incentive and a model for developing writers to practice process writing and increase their cultural literacy. Model Activity 8.3 will give students an opportunity to write a newspaper article while learning more about a most interesting North American figure, Benjamin Franklin.

BOOK REVIEWS

Fourth and fifth graders in a New Hampshire school surprised their school librarian, Carolyn Jenks, and their teacher, Janice Roberts, with the quality of work they produced in reviewing books. The students in this multiaged classroom practiced process writing and were accustomed to responding to reading by writing. Therefore, when Roberts received a list of the school library's new acquisitions, she saw an opportunity to provide her students with another situation to extend their reading, writing, speaking, and listening expertise beyond the classroom. "What if each child had a copy of the book list, chose and read one or more of the books, and wrote a book review so that other members of the school population could read about the new acquisition?" (Jenks & Roberts, 1990, p. 742).

The days that followed saw much collaboration among students, their teacher, and the librarian, who modeled how to write book reviews by reading sample reviews and discussing the elements of a book review. The teacher and students discussed the project further and determined that their reviews would contain the following: "Brief summary of the story; Comment about the writing; Recommendations" (p. 743). The students began writing their first drafts and decided that final ed-

ited copies, including illustrations, would be shared during the class library period the following week.

The students chose many different kinds of books, and each review reflected the student's voice as well as elements of the book reviewed. Roberts discussed with her students how they had been able to accomplish the difficult task of writing excellent book reviews. The illustrated reviews were put on display in the library, and Jenks shared with the students how other students in the school were reading the reviews and checking out the books. This writing project proved to be a valuable learning experience as these students

understood that they, as readers, had valid things to say about books and that their opinions were important when they were backed up by reasons and examples. Their history of reading and writing and the collaboration of the teacher and the librarian had led them naturally into being honest and thoughtful reviewers of books and into the kind of critical thinking which would stand them in good stead through a lifetime of reading [and writing]. (p. 745)

THE RESEARCH STORY

Engaging students in writing stories describing their search for information about particular topics provides an excellent format for students to express what they have learned in their own voices. Furthermore, writing stories about the research process itself is a powerful learning tool for students as they develop into independent thinkers and learners. Introducing students to the process of inquiry by researching topics of interest gives them the opportunity to engage in authentic uses of oral and written language. A desire to know more about themselves and their world leads students beyond their classrooms into their homes and communities in search of knowledge about their chosen topics.

McGinley and Madigan (1990) conducted a five-month project in a fifth-grade classroom in southeastern Michigan to determine how students, as independent learners, chose research topics and what kinds of instructional activities they used to think and learn. The researchers focused on the *process* by which students acquire knowledge while developing the content of their chosen topics, building on Macrorie's (1981) I-Search paper method. I-Search provides a format where details of what was learned, as well as the story of how that knowledge was acquired, are written in the students' own voices.

The findings of McGinley and Madigan's study indicated that students learned to engage in a different kind of research when both the process and the content of students' learning were addressed. The following example shows how one student carried out her search for information and meaning about the topic of banking. Kristin, a fifth grader, was identified as one who needed the additional help available from such a project. Also, she was a student willing to extend her learning beyond the limits of the classroom. Kristin's desire to learn more about banking came naturally; when she was younger, one of her favorite activities had been going with her father on his weekly trips to the local bank.

In group discussions, Kristin and her classmates reviewed what they already knew about banking and discussed where they might find more information. Kristin's notes revealed that, as a result of this collaboration, she chose the following resources for further study: what you can learn at the bank, at the library, from the telephone book, and from your parents. Group discussions also helped Kristin develop specific questions she wanted answered about her topic, along with resources for finding the answers. After several trips to the bank, Kristin still had many unanswered questions; her genuine need to know more about the topic of banking gave her the courage to set up an interview with the manager of a local bank. A peer supported Kristin by advising her how to begin: "Call them up and say hello this is Kristin and I'm doing research on banking and I have a few questions" (McGinley & Madigan, 1990, p. 478). The interview offered a new way of seeing and learning about banking with Kristin as an active participant.

Kristin's need to know more about banking led her on a search for information; this same need led her to examine her own writing to see what she had learned and still needed to learn. In communicating the story of her search to her peers, Kristin found herself referring to her notes made during interviews and discussions—as well as excerpts from books—to remember accurately everything she had learned. McGinley and Madigan (1990) documented the steps in Kristin's learning process in this way:

Through her notes she was able to examine what she had organized as useful information; and by creating her own record of the information she had encountered, Kristin came to make new knowledge in a "text" of her own—a kind of "support text" that she could revisit in order to reexamine and "see" her own learning as she sought to compose the story of her search. (p. 479)

Kristin was invited to present to the class her written story of what she had learned about banking, as well as how this knowledge had been acquired. Interestingly, in revising her draft, Kristin decided to write her research story in the third person, with herself as the main character of the story. The resulting published story became a valuable resource for readers wanting to know more about

banking or as a model for other students beginning their own research projects. McGinley and Madigan (1990) summarized the value of student publication of research stories as follows:

The research and reflection on the research enables students to explore and demystify the process by which they and others come to know, a process that involves awareness of the unique roles that reading, writing, and talking play in acquiring knowledge and an understanding of the struggle involved in making meaning. (p. 482)

Phelps (1992) recommended that research be published by writing a "three-search paper." His method includes three kinds of research—reflecting, interviewing, and reading—that are carried out as students start with their own experience, then conduct interviews and read printed sources to find out if experiences and ideas of others corroborate their own. Phelps suggested that students begin with freewriting on personal experience with the subject, followed by interviews of at least two people: peers or others with related experiences or authorities on the subject. Thus, being fairly well informed about their subjects, students are more focused and less hesitant about a visit to the library for the third area of research, reading. "Because printed sources are the last area of research, students are not likely to build papers around the quotations. Instead, printed references support, expand, explain, or otherwise elaborate their personal experience and interviews" (p. 77). As the three-search papers evolve through successive drafts along with peer and teacher critiquing, the published efforts are "interesting revelations of students integrating their experience with others" (p. 78).

AUTHORS' CONFERENCES, WRITING WORKSHOPS, AND BOOK CLUBS

Authors' conferences or writing workshops are held regularly in many schools across the country and present a highly motivating force for student writers. Individuals, classrooms, grades, and entire schools coordinate efforts over many weeks to produce drafts, revise, edit, and publish their final manuscripts. Often the end activity is a book fair or a visit from a professional author. Sometimes, work is evaluated by judges and honors given. Some authors' conferences are writing competitions among classrooms or grades; other conferences focus more on sharing than on competition. Stu-

dents in a given classroom might organize and hold their own publishing conferences, with writers selecting work from their writing folders and asking peers to read the written pieces and make suggestions about which ones to publish. Of course, the author has the final word about which piece will be published. Regardless of how the event to celebrate publication is carried out, it is important that every participant be treated as a winner. For example, an attractive certificate of participation, with a seal and ribbons, properly signed by the teacher and the principal, is appropriate for every student.

Writers' clubs are found in many schools and include activities such as publishing a literary magazine, going on field trips that provide related information and interest, sponsoring lectures by local writers, and serving as a forum for dramatic and musical works written by the students. The Institute for Research on Teaching at Michigan State University related how Deb Woodman, teacher of an upper elementary class in an urban school, used The Book Club to provide an effective literacy program for her students. Developed by McMahon and Raphael (1992), The Book Club replaced a more traditional teacher-directed reading program with a social-interactive approach encompassing four components: reading, writing, community share, and instruction. The students in Woodman's class wrote about their ideas before each session, recording those ideas in a log for use as a permanent record. "At other times students used writing to reflect on what they had learned or how their ideas had changed, or to compose original stories that extended or related to ones read previously" (McMahon & Raphael, 1992, p. 1). By writing before coming to The Book Club, students were able to engage in more mature discussions, which affected the amount and type of information included in later writing activities. One book club activity leading to publication occurred when students wrote folktales and, after a session with a local author as storyteller, became interested in becoming authors themselves.

The California Young Writers' Program of San Diego implemented a unique concept to promote, recognize, and share student writing. Students involved in this program donated finished books to children living on the state's Indian reservations (Staff, *Reading Today,* 1992).

DRAMATIC AND MUSICAL EXTENSIONS

Creative students and teachers will enjoy publishing their stories, poems, and songs through drama or music. Many students appreciate the opportunity to write stories in the form of plays or puppet shows to be produced by their class or other classes in the school. These plays might be fictional, dramatizations of some historical event, or written about a particular topic. Interested students can be offered the opportunity to participate in a drama club. Burke (1986) described how one group performed as follows: "Readers' Theatre is a group of people who perform dramatic extensions. One person presents a dynamic interpretive reading of a poem, tale, play, or song as others in the group mime the actions" (p. 61). Hoyt (1992) also wrote about using Readers' Theatre to interpret written work and stated:

While there are many published scripts which turn favorite literature selections into Readers' Theatre, the most effective scripts often are designed by the students. Students responding to literature can list the main characters and then select portions of the text to be used. (p. 582)

Students may write poems that can be adapted to choral reading, making use of voice combinations and contrasts to create meaning and mood. Voices that are high and low, loud and soft, or fast and slow can be used while a class or group of students read poetry aloud. When students experience the process of orchestrating their poems for choral reading, they will enjoy adding sound effects, exclamations, and movement. These extra features help their written words to have added meaning as well as bring delight to an audience. Practice is necessary before a work is ready for sharing; students want to do their best in front of their peers. All students can participate in choral reading; and, because there is no failure, there is little anxiety. The ready response of applause and smiles at the end of a performance delights authors and performers alike. McCauley and McCauley (1992) described their experiences with choral reading as follows:

The more choral reading you do in your class, the more the students will want to share these readings with others. Also, the children will soon be anxious to write their own poems so that they too can be performed. The students will have all sorts of ideas about who should say which line, how loud or soft the voices should be, or what gesture will help make their point more meaningful to the listener. They quickly move from readers, to performers, to authors, to directors. My fifth graders rewrote science and social studies lessons into choral readings. One eighth-grade physical education class wrote soccer rules in a choral reading format. (pp 531–532)

Some stories that students write adapt well to storytelling, another exciting forum for presenting written work to an audience. If students have been exposed to the art of storytelling by listening to a variety of tellers, they learn to discriminate and evaluate storytelling styles. A natural progression is for students to write original stories to be told. A story about an experienced event, as told to family and friends every day, can become a story for telling. Family traditions and customs provide excellent material for storytelling.

In many cultures, the tradition of storytelling has its roots in music; therefore, some storytellers bring music into the storytelling experience. Susan Flaccavento is one educator dedicated to teaching students to use their imaginations and music to construct their own stories for telling. Students attending her musical storytelling workshops write their own verses and add musical accompaniment.

As reported in *The Greeneville Sun* (Wilburn, 1991), Flaccavento's sessions at The Discovery Theatre workshop encourage students to expand their ideas for a story through the use of sound. Musical storytelling can meet the students' need to express themselves, giving them a sense of self and validating what and who they are. "Such mental stretching," Flaccavento stated, "should be a constant goal" (p. W-2).

Other opportunities for presenting written work in musical form can be offered when students are encouraged to write and perform songs and ballads. Most early adolescent students enjoy listening to music and are familiar with various musical styles. Publishing original works in a musical form can be exciting as students collaborate to write and practice their musical acts for performances before their peers and/or others.

DISPLAYING STUDENT WRITING

Much of the publication of student writing will occur as it is displayed in the classroom and throughout the school. The classroom teacher contributes greatly to the feeling of accomplishment of the student writers, and the acceptance of their work by their classmates and school, by seeing that the published work is displayed carefully and attractively. The following guidelines, offered by Temple and Gillet (1989), should be helpful as student writing is displayed around the room, in the hallways, the library, or the school office.

Change the papers frequently, every week or so.

Give the students opportunities to edit and polish their work before displaying it.

Ask permission to display any work. If a student says no, respect the refusal.

Make sure *every* child has work displayed regularly.

Use displays to demonstrate early drafts, editing, and other aspects as well as content.

Refer to displayed work; don't just post it and forget it.

Return all work to the writer when you take it down. (p. 278)

Be careful that the displaying of student work is not used primarily as a reward; instead, use displays to teach and reinforce writing fundamentals.

PUBLISHING BY THE TEACHER

Process writing programs can produce many different products worthy of publication. The student, as author, is identified as one "who writes and who is willing to work with a piece of writing and a set of ideas for more than a brief period. It takes a knowledgeable teacher to advance these outcomes" (Lipson & Wixson, 1991, p. 608).

In an environment where teachers become better

writers while writing along with their students, the stage is set for them to share their reflections on what happens in the classroom. As teachers find their writing voices, they are encouraged to participate in the process of submitting manuscripts to editors of newsletters, journals, and other forums for publication. Through their own writing, these teachers share successful teaching approaches with the general community of educators. This is a time-consuming endeavor, and teachers who expend the energy required to publish are certainly to be commended.

One special education teacher who took the risk to engage in the process of writing for professional publication, Marilyn D'Alessandro, had this to share following the publication of her article in a professional journal (D'Alessandro et al., 1992):

Besides the achievement of having my article published, my effort had a long-lasting effect on my work. In order to write the article, I had to follow my own advice to organize my notes and present my reading program in a coherent manner. As I worked with the article, I reexamined things I was doing automatically in the classroom. It is easy to tell the children to think about why they do something in a certain way. It was difficult to do it myself. Writing was an excellent self-imposed assignment—to evaluate my own work—not in terms of standardized tests or educational evaluations, but for myself and other teachers. My classroom environment was more dynamic as I experimented and formulated my classroom-based research. (p. 409)

Teachers who write discover that taking a writing draft through publication enables one to understand the process of writing firsthand. Experiencing failure and despair, success and joy, while engaged in the hard work of writing, teachers are able to understand the writing experiences of their students. Then, they are in a better position to help their students understand the process of learning to write.

CONCLUSION

The act of writing is completed through publication. Until then, work has been writing-in-process. Drafts have been written to construct meaning, shared with others, and examined carefully to see how they could be improved; then they have been revised and edited. Now the writing is in the final stage and being prepared to be shared with strangers—readers or listeners who wish to be informed, inspired, or entertained by the writing. Before releasing the work for public reading or hearing, the author and the teacher should proofread it one last time to make absolutely certain that it is ready to be published. This is a crucial point for authors, given that the quality of their publication depends primarily on them. Of course, if the process has evolved optimally, the product will be in fine shape.

When publication occurs, writers experience a new confidence along with a new identity—that of a published author. They have created something in their own voices and have been heard. In all likelihood, they will continue using process writing throughout their lives.

REFERENCES

Bishop, R. S. (1992). Profile: A conversation with Patricia McKissack. *Language Arts, 69*(1), 69–74.

Burke, E. M. (1986). *Early childhood literature: For love of child and book.* Boston: Allyn and Bacon.

Calkins, L. M. (1986). *The art of teaching writing.* Portsmouth, NH: Heinemann.

Cooper, W., & Brown, B. J. (1992). Using portfolios to empower student writers. *English Journal, 81*(2), 40–45.

D'Alessandro, M., Diakiw, J. Y., Fuhler, C. J., O'Masta, G. M., Pils, L. J., Trachtenburg, P., & Wolf, J. M. (1992). Writing for publication: Voices from the classroom. *The Reading Teacher, 45*(6), 408–414.

Fisher, C. J., & Terry, C. A. (1990). *Children's language and the language arts,* 3rd ed. Boston: Allyn and Bacon.

Gratrix, M., & Hayden, R. (1990). Short snappers for daily writing. *The Reading Teacher, 44*(3), 279–280.

Hoyt, L. (1992). Many ways of knowing: Using drama, oral interactions, and the visual arts to enhance reading comprehension. *The Reading Teacher, 45*(8), 580–584.

Jenks, C., & Roberts, J. (1990, November). Reading, writing, and reviewing: Teacher, librarian, and young readers collaborate. *Language Arts, 67,* 742–745.

Kissell, J. (1990). A school newspaper: The Crown Press. *The Reading Teacher, 44*(3), 278–279.

Lipson, M. Y., & Wixson, K. K. (1991). *Assessment and instruction of reading disability: An interactive approach.* New York: HarperCollins.

Macrorie, K. (1981). *Searching writing: The I-Search paper.* Portsmouth, NH: Heinemann.

Mason, J. M., & Au, K. H. (1990). *Reading instruction for today,* 2nd ed. Glenview, IL: Scott, Foresman/Little, Brown.

McCauley, J., & McCauley, D. (1992). Using choral reading to promote language learning for ESL students. *The Reading Teacher, 45*(7), 526–533.

McGinley, W., & Madigan, D. (1990, September). The research "story": A forum for integrating reading, writing, and learning. *Language Arts, 67,* 474–483.

McKissack, P. C. (1984). *Paul Laurence Dunbar: A poet to remember.* Chicago: Children's Press.

McMahon, S., & Raphael, T. (1992). Student book clubs. *Communication Quarterly, 14*(2), 1, 3–4.

Murray, D. M. (1985). *A writer teaches writing,* 2nd ed. Boston: Houghton Mifflin.

Phelps, T. O. (1992). Research or three-search? *English Journal, 81*(2), 76–78.

Sammons, F. L. (1987). Stories that grow on trees. *Instructor, 97*(4), 52–54.

Sargent, B. E. (1991). Writing "Choose your own adventure" stories. *The Reading Teacher, 45*(2), 158–159.

Staff. (1992). The write stuff: Helping young authors. *Reading Today, 9*(4), 10.

Temple, C., & Gillet, J. W. (1989). *Language arts: Learning processes and teaching practices,* 2nd ed. Glenview, IL: Scott, Foresman.

Temple, C., Nathan, R., Burris, N., & Temple, F. (1988). *The beginnings of writing,* 2nd ed. Boston: Allyn and Bacon.

Wilburn, B. (1991). Workshop helps kids tell musical stories. *The Greeneville Sun,* Greeneville (Tennessee), May 11, p. W-2.

MODEL ACTIVITIES

The activities that follow are meant to serve as models; such activities should be used as part of a total learning environment. These model activities were designed to demonstrate how the writing process can be developed while expanding the writer's knowledge base and providing opportunities for the writer to think critically.

ACTIVITY 8.1

Publishing Books for Children in a Primary Grade

This activity will guide you as you write and publish a book to be enjoyed by younger children. This project will require several writing and sharing sessions. Therefore, it would be helpful to keep all your work associated with this writing activity in a folder, to be worked on as time permits.

1. Before writing, interview children in the lower grades of school to find out the kinds of books they like. What did you find out? _____

_____

_____

_____

Read several books written for kindergarten through grade 3. Do you remember any favorites from when you were younger? How are these books different from the ones you read now? _____

_____

_____

_____

Brainstorm a list of things to keep in mind as you write for a younger audience:

Example: Use vocabulary that is known by younger children.

_____

_____

_____

2. Identify the setting, characters, and scenes for your story for younger children:

Setting: _____

Main characters: _____

_____

_____

Brief summary of your story: _____

_____

_____

_____

_____

A possible title for your story: _____

_____

3. On separate paper, write a first draft of your story. Share your draft with peers for feedback. List below ideas received from your peers that you think you should use in revising your draft.

_____

_____

_____

_____

_____

4. Rewrite your story, making revisions that you feel will make your story a better one to be read by younger children. For example, consider including conversation for your characters if you haven't done so already.

5. Edit your final draft for mechanics, conferring with others if you wish. Then proofread your work.

6. Plan illustrations for your book by drawing, cutting from magazines and pasting, making collages, or creating designs to fit the story you have written. Again, request feedback from peers as you share your plans for illustration. They may have suggestions for some good changes, or their positive reinforcement will let you know you are on the right track.

7. Complete your book in its final form. Design and make a cover. Be sure to include a title page, giving your name as author and the year in which your book is being published. You may wish to include a dedication page thanking people who helped you or are special to you. Examine books in your media center for examples of dedications.

8. Present completed books to the classes of students for whom they were written. You can make this a special day for everyone involved by planning a time for recognition of the student authors, when they can be interviewed by the younger children and autographs signed.

Our Class Anthology

An *anthology* is a collection of literary works, such as poems, anecdotes, short stories, or plays. The word *anthology* means "flower gathering" in the Greek language from which it comes. The goal of this project is to gather a selected piece of writing from each student in the class (and the teacher) for publication in a class anthology.

1. You will want to have an example of your very best writing included in the class anthology. Perhaps something in your writing folder or your journal would be a good choice, or you may want to write something new. Discuss with classmates and your teacher the kinds of things your class would like to include in the anthology. The following list will give you some ideas; add others that come to your mind as you think.

   poetry about students our own age _____

   personal experiences _____

   humor _____

   original fables or tall tales _____

   one-act plays _____

   stories about our school _____

   _____

   _____

   _____

   _____

   _____

   _____

2. When your draft is ready, share it with a group of your peers for critiquing. Make any necessary revisions and then edit for mechanics.

3. Prepare your final draft and proofread it for accuracy. If you choose, illustrate your contribution to the class anthology.

4. Discuss with peers and your teacher plans for compiling all the completed works into the class anthology. Plan for the title page and table of contents. Write below your choice of a title for the anthology:

   _____

   Discuss all the titles suggested and, as a group, decide which one is best.

5. As a group, decide on a cover design for the class anthology. You could choose a committee to design the cover, or you could have each student submit his or her cover design and vote on the one to be used.

ACTIVITY 8.3

Benjamin Franklin, Printer and Publisher

Benjamin Franklin (1706–1790) was born in Boston, Massachusetts, into a family of seventeen children. Benjamin attended school for only two years. Then, at the age of ten, he went to work in his father's candle and soap shop, cutting wicks and melting tallow. Although Franklin's formal schooling had ended, his education continued as he read every book he could get. "Reading was the only amusement I allowed myself. I spent no time in taverns, games, or frolicks* [sic] of any kind," said Benjamin Franklin. He also taught himself mathematics, the sciences, and several foreign languages to become one of the best educated men of his time. Life was never dull for young Ben Franklin. He had a good sense of humor; and his kindness, tact, and courtesy were evident to all he met. He was very well liked.

Franklin also worked on his writing style, using as a model a British journal called *The Spectator.* Because Benjamin did not like candle making, at the age of twelve he asked his father's permission to be an apprentice to his older brother, James, a printer. Benjamin soon became a skilled printer, but he liked to write. So he wrote newspaper articles, signed them "Mrs. Silence Dogood," and slipped them under the printshop door. The articles were very good, and James printed them until he discovered that Benjamin had written them.

Benjamin wanted to be independent; so in 1723, at the age of seventeen, he went to Philadelphia. He worked for various printers for the next several years and, at the age of twenty-four, became the owner of his own printshop. He published *The Pennsylvania Gazette* and wrote much of the material for it. Franklin liked new ideas; he was the first American editor to publish a newspaper cartoon and to illustrate a news story with a map.

Franklin received even wider acclaim for *Poor Richard's Almanac,* which he wrote and published for twenty-five years. Franklin's purpose for publishing the almanac was to communicate his wise observations on life as well as his religious and political ideas. Most popular with readers, however, were his many wise and witty sayings, called proverbs. People today still repeat many of these sayings—for example: "An ounce of prevention is worth a pound of cure"; "A penny saved is a penny earned"; "Little strokes fell great oaks." *Poor Richard's Alamanc* also included astrological predictions, jokes, and verses.

Writing, printing, and publishing were only a few examples of the many things Franklin did so well during his long and useful life. He helped draft and signed four key documents in American history: the Declaration of Independence, the Treaty of Alliance with France, the Treaty of Peace with Great Britain, and the Constitution of the United States. He was always concerned with the well-being and dignity of mankind.

In this activity, you will have an opportunity to learn more about this great American as you write a newspaper article. You'll also learn a lot about life during that particular period of history.

1. The following list names some of the many roles Benjamin Franklin played during his lifetime. Place a check mark by those topics that you would like to investigate to learn more about Benjamin Franklin. If you want to add other topics, list them.

---

*An old form of spelling for the word *frolic,* meaning fun, play, merriment, or prank.

statesman
scientist
philosopher
diplomat
writer
printer
publisher
politician
civic leader
founder of first subscription library
founder of university
founder of public hospital
organizer of fire department
leader of police reform
postmaster
president of antislavery society
researcher of electricity
military leader

inventor: for example, lightning rod,
     Franklin stove, bifocal eyeglasses
husband and father
American delegate to London
member of Continental Congress
delegate to Constitutional Convention
Minister to France
researcher of navigation and the Gulf
     Stream
candlemaker
soapmaker
gardener: cabbage grower, discov-
     ered using lime to improve acid
     soil

_____

_____

_____

2. Choose one topic from those you checked on the foregoing list that you find especially interesting. Then jot down things you already know about this chosen topic.

_____

_____

_____

3. Check sources to gather more information about your chosen topic. Your school library, the public library, and your social studies textbook can provide this information. Makes notes as you read.

4. When you are ready to write a first draft, pretend that you are a reporter of a local newspaper working in the time that Benjamin Franklin lived. Write about your topic in the style of a newspaper story reporting a current event. Write your first draft below.

_____

_____

_____

_____

_____

_____

_____

_____

_____

_____

---

5. Share your draft with a peer group for feedback. Make any necessary revisions to make the article better. Ask your group to help you brainstorm about possible headlines for your story. Taking a cue from Franklin's wit and humor, some headline examples could be:
   BEN FRANKLIN STARTS FIRE —— DEPARTMENT
   BIFOCALS HELP INVENTOR FIND NEW IDEAS
   LIGHTNING RODS SPARE THE HOUSE BUT SPOIL THE LOOKS
   ELECTRICITY IS THE KEY TO THE FUTURE

6. Now, rewrite your draft with your chosen headline, all revisions, and any illustrations that might add to the story.

(headline)

7. Edit for mechanics and then proofread your news story.

8. Complete this activity by printing *The Franklin Gazette*. The various articles written about different events in Franklin's life will provide interesting reading about this outstanding person and his many achievements.

CHAPTER 9

Journal Writing: A Heuristic Activity

If you wish to be a writer, write.

—Epictetus, first–second century Greek stoic philosopher in Rome

A heuristic activity is a hands-on, self-educating activity that improves the skillfulness of learners as they participate. Journal writing is such an activity, for writing improves as students write more frequently. The use of journals in the classroom became widespread in the late 1980s and early 1990s, but they are not new. Almost a hundred years ago, classroom use of the journal was popular; but for many years between then and now, other teaching approaches took precedence and widespread journal use was discontinued.

Outside of school, people have been keeping written records of their daily experiences for centuries. Bookkeepers call them *journals,* ships' captains call them *logs,* and children and adults alike call them *diaries;* but they all serve the same purpose—a place to record in writing things that have happened to the writers, along with their feelings about those events.

There are many kinds of journals used by adults: serious ones, like the kind of records kept on owned property so that taxes at sale time won't be higher than necessary; and ones just for fun, like the birthday book kept to remember everyone's special day. Gardening journals are loved by those who want to record what and when they've planted as well as projected dates for various maintenance needs. Birthday and holiday card lists, with all of their notes for gifts ideas, moves, and other family changes, become journals of sorts about families and friends.

We may think of artists only as producers of paintings or other works of art, but the *writing* of the nineteenth-century artist Winslow Homer is also beautiful. In a letter to his brother, he wrote, "The sun will not rise, or set, without my notice and thanks" (Victoria, 1990, p. 14). Leonardo da Vinci (1452–1519), most famous for the *Mona Lisa,* but also a famed Italian sculptor and painter of the Sistine Chapel, a scientist, and an engineer, wrote journals that contained sketches of his work and inventions, including his attempts to have man fly. Claude Monet (1840–1926), the renowned French impressionist painter, kept cooking journals (in regular school notebooks) of meals served to his family of ten in the 1880s. So inspiring were these records of family history that they were used to produce a tome now available to the public. Monet's impressionistic style as a painter contrasted with his private life, in which he was a rigid taskmaster who paid strict attention to the most minute detail of every meal; for example, he insisted that meals be served within thirty seconds from the time he sat down at the table.

From the era before radio, television, and large public libraries we have meticulous records of where people acquired their personal treasures. One gentleman from the early 1900s compiled a list describing each piece of furniture he had inherited from family members, naming the givers, their relationships to the writer, and other pertinent details such as the dates of their births and deaths. How exciting to have furniture passed down from generation to generation and know the name of the original owner as well as other personal information about the person and the antique. This gentleman listed each item he purchased, where he got it, and how much it cost. He even noted trivia like the following: "This neighbor lived down the street from us in a blue house." History becomes fascinating once we realize that it is about real people and their lives.

Had it not been for a journal, one of the most familiar American poems, the one that begins "'Twas the night before Christmas," would not be known today. Clement Moore (1779–1863), a professor of Hebrew and Greek literature at Central Theological Seminary, was a good friend of Washington Irving (1783–1859), probably most famous for his story of Ichabod Crane and the headless horseman, *The Legend of Sleepy Hollow*. Irving had written a satirical *History of New York* in which he ridiculed the Dutch people who had brought with them to this country their love of Saint Nicholas, who delivered gifts during the Christmas holidays. Irving, in his tale, portrayed Saint Nicholas bringing the gifts from a carriage in the sky down the chimneys, in the same manner as in today's familiar poem. Moore composed at least part of the poem on an 1822 errand to pick up the holiday turkey. He read the poem that same evening to his wife, his six children, and a guest, young Harriet Butler. Harriet copied the poem in her journal. She showed it to the editor of the *Troy Sentinal,* who published it as "An Account of the Visit of Saint Nicholas" on December 23, 1823. Moore didn't even know it was being published, nor did he get credit as its author until it was published in the 1837 edition of *The New York Book of Poetry*. By then the poem was very popular. Today, it is a Christmas favorite, thanks to Harriet Butler and her journal (Denker, 1991).*

Uncle Merv, a ninety-two-year-old relative of one of this book's authors, has entered into his daily journal a list of every major purchase he has ever made. At present, his new outboard motor has been used only five times, making its cost about $50 an outing. He's very interested in using it more often in order to reduce the cost per usage. Having been a fervent journal writer for most of his long life, he has bookcases of journals.

Perhaps, one might think, that was good enough for the olden days; but today's youth could not pos-

sibly be enticed into writing this much. Yes, they can! The secret has to do with the choice of topic. Personal journals deal with everyone's favorite topic—oneself. Journals can be used to record thoughts, feelings, and dreams; this kind of writing is therapeutic. When journals are read or reread, the writers are recalling their own history. Writing helps provide stability, validity, meaning, and purpose in writers' lives. Yes, they really did exist at that prior point in time. They really did have entertaining and valid opinions about things. They are worthwhile. Journals can help build self-esteem by facilitating inner happiness that isn't dependent on strokes from others. Alverman and Muth, writing in an International Reading Association (IRA) publication edited by Duffy (1990) said, "If students are to value writing as a vehicle for self-expression, they must have opportunities to write about themselves and their feelings" (p. 108). As with everything else, some students will respond more favorably to journal writing than others.

Daly, Vangelisti, and Witte (1988) found through research on writing that the frequency, amount, and type of writing assignments influenced students' attitudes toward writing. Alverman and Muth (1990) reported on a study by Fear, Anderson, Englert, and Raphael (1987) involving students in an upper elementary grade. One teacher assigned writing topics based on the social studies or science content that students were studying. The second teacher let students write on topics they had generated at the beginning of the year. A positive relationship was noted between the productivity and the self-selection of topics: "They generated significantly more ideas on three measures of productivity than did students in the first teacher's class" (p. 101). Self-selection is a motivator. Jeorski and Conry (1981) found that students' attitudes affect their satisfaction and interest in writing, as well as their feelings about writing improvement. Perhaps the most startling information comes from the National Assessment of Educational Progress (NAEP), a group of educational evaluators often known as the Nation's Report Card. Since 1969, they have been collecting information nationally and assessing what students know in reading, writing, history, geography, math, science, and other fields (Applebee, Langer, Mullis, & Jenkins, 1990). The NAEP is congressionally mandated and reports to the Commissioner of Education Statistics. In the NAEP's study of fourth, eighth, and eleventh

Source: Information from "A Gift for the Season," by Bert Denker, from *Southern Accents,* December–January 1991, pp. 46, 48, 51, is used with permission from *Southern Accents.*

graders' attitudes toward writing, only about *half* of the students assessed responded that they valued writing. For fourth, eighth, and eleventh graders, the most significant area of importance was that "writing helps me to show people that I know something" (p. 60). Students at all levels felt more strongly that "writing helps me share my ideas" than was true in a previous study in 1984, and fourth and eighth graders felt that "writing can help me get a good job." Amazingly, eleventh graders responding to that statement showed that they were not quite as optimistic as previous eleventh graders about the influence of writing on employment. Both fourth and eighth graders were more likely to feel that "people who write well are more influential"; conversely, both groups declined in the belief that "writing helps me to think more clearly." Daly and Miller (1975) indicated that students' attitudes toward writing even affect their choices of colleges.

Daly and Hailey (1984) reported that when students feel their writing is being evaluated, as in a pass/fail composition, as opposed to writing in a journal that no one will read, they become increasingly anxious. Daly and Miller (1975) found that as students' anxiety level increased, their performance level decreased. Valencia, McGinley, and Pearson (1990, p. 127), stated that "the mechanics of writing would be of little (if any) concern in journal writing. . . . " Students should have the opportunity to write material that will not be evaluated to encourage a positive attitude toward writing. When writing other than journal writing is evaluated, the teacher should try to find positive things to note to encourage the student's writing.

This chapter focuses on journals that can be used easily at school. It includes ideas about the physical journals themselves, several types of personal journals, dialogue journals, peer response or buddy journals, literature study journals or reading response journals, double-entry journals, poetry journals, process journals, academic journals, and reflective journals. Many teachers use more than one kind of journal, often beginning with just one and then adding others as they feel comfortable doing so. Some journals, such as personal journals, may be used daily; others, like reflective journals, may be used only when students want to sort through their feelings and reactions to a specific event. The current trend toward the regular use of journals in the classroom can facilitate meaningful writing practice, which is the most important factor in improving student writing. According to Vacca and Vacca (1989), journals, thought books, or learning logs, as these authors call them, are "probably one of the most versatile writing-to-learn strategies available to students and teachers in any subject area. And one of the most productive" (p. 261).

The classroom teacher has the opportunity to increase students' knowledge of cultural literary by the same technique used in this book—that is, by weaving information about artists, writers, composers of music, and geniuses in every field into daily lessons. Modeling the use of the biographical information in a dictionary might also whet students' interest in famous people and their contributions to society.

MATERIALS USED FOR JOURNAL WRITING

If students purchase their own materials, a bound notebook is preferable to a loose-leaf notebook for journal writing. This curtails the temptation for students to tear out pages they don't like, or to waste valuable time starting over as perfectionists tend to do. Bound pages will stay together forever. If the school furnishes all materials, making bound books for journal writing provides immediate ownership and gets students actively and positively involved from the outset. Another not so lasting but less time-consuming idea is to laminate a 12″ × 18″ sheet of construction paper for each student. Letting students personalize their covers prior to lami-

nation gives them a sense of ownership from the start. Directions are as follows:

1. Fold the laminated paper in half.
2. Insert thirty or forty sheets of paper.
3. Using a piece of notebook paper as a guide, punch holes in three places on the outside and fasten with paper fasteners.

The books can be stapled in three places on the outside cover instead, but books made in this way often come undone. Although wallpaper page covers bound with plastic binders are attractive, they cannot withstand daily use without tearing apart. Another option is the use of purchased folders. These are fine for journals to which you might want to add pages, such as literature study journals, but for personal journals they pose the same problems as do loose-leaf notebooks.

PERSONAL JOURNALS

Personal journals are just that: personal. Thoughts written in personal journals are not meant to be shared with other students, unless the author volunteers. If students get in the habit of beginning each period with entries in their personal journals, this becomes an excellent and routine way to start class in an orderly fashion. Also, as students choose to share their writings, they will provide much valuable information about themselves. Students should be taught always to date their logs and to leave no more than one line space between entries. Otherwise, this personal journal will become physically cumbersome. When teachers begin this process, students may not be able to think of anything to write. Modeling a journal entry on the board, and even letting students copy it as a beginning, helps them get started. A beginning entry follows:

September 1, 199–.   Today is the first day of a new school year. It was very hard to come back today, as this certainly signals the end of summer; but I was delighted to see all of my friends today. Everyone was . . .

If students need assistance on the second day, a suggestion could be shared. The one that follows models the value of family discussions:

September 2, 199–.   Last night my mom and I watched a movie on television. Two boys were trying to impress their girlfriends with fake mustaches, but the one boy's father wouldn't let them get away with that. The movie was pretty funny, and afterwards Mom started telling about something similar that had happened to her years ago. That's when it dawned on me that Mom had once been a teenager!

Sometimes, students may feel that there is nothing special to write about on a particular day. Teachers need to let students know that this happens to them, too. They might read Jack Prelutsky's poem "Today Is Very Boring" in his 1984 book of poetry, *New Kid on the Block.* Though juvenile, the poem illustrates the point that if you are feeling less than optimistic on a certain day, things that would be exciting to others can seem mundane to you.

Consider the woman who, visiting an old friend for the first time in ten years, suddenly interjected into the conversation, "Oh, by the way, I just got back from Hawaii and Australia," as if her travels were as routine as a trip to the grocery store. Her *joie de vivre*—the joy of living—seemed to be missing that day. To most people, including her old friend, such a trip would have been very exciting and noteworthy.

The student who says, "Today, there's nothing special I want to write. I didn't go anywhere or do anything last night," could be saying that she's tired, bored, or stressed out; but more than likely, she's saying that she is an inexperienced writer. Ask her what she did yesterday after school; when you hear something interesting, suggest that she write about that topic. To probe whether students are really at a loss for a topic, a teacher might ask what they had for dinner last night. Do they like that food? Who prepared dinner? Who usually prepares dinner? Who ate with them? Topic ideas will probably surface. If students think these topics are too unimportant to write about, they need to be encouraged to realize that their lives and ordinary experiences have value.

A short story such as "The Gift of the Magi" by William Sidney Porter, whose pen name was O. Henry (1862–1910), shows how an author can make a dynamic story out of seemingly mundane items. This short story about a comb and a watch chain has universal appeal because the story is really about the true meaning of love. Taking place at the turn of the twentieth century, it centered on the sacrifices a young, newlywed, New York City couple made to buy each other gifts at Christmas. Both of them sold their most prized possessions—the young wife sold her hair to a wig shop to buy her husband a gold chain for his gold pocket watch (the status symbol of the day), and he pawned his watch for the money to buy his wife a tortoise-shell comb for her beautiful waist-length hair.

Most students will find the drama in O. Henry's short stories appealing, and they should be interested in learning about the life experiences he drew on as a writer. For example, he worked as a sheep rancher and bronco buster in Texas, lived as a fugitive in Honduras, and spent three years in an Ohio prison. Although he was born in North Carolina, he moved to New York City when he was twenty and is best remembered for stories of city life. O. Henry seems to have been a cowboy! And who would have suspected that a cowboy would know so much about romance in the city! Students may be surprised to learn that most writers are not people who lock themselves in fancy offices and write. They are often ordinary people who happen to enjoy writing. Students need to realize that anyone who wants to write can and should.

A fourth-grade student who started out as a very poor reader and writer became very excited when telling of an escapade involving his sister and her boyfriend. He wanted to tell it orally, as students often want to do if someone has helped them brainstorm a topic. When this happens, the teacher knows the student is now ready to write. This particular student even wanted to know how to write conversation so he could tell the teacher what the boyfriend said to the store manager of a small market, and what the manager replied. He was so excited about this story that he did an outstanding job of including details that helped one visualize the situation:

My sister's boyfriend was standing by the potato chip rack visiting with a friend, when the manager came rushing over.

"Look what I just found on the floor," he said.

"What?" My sister's boyfriend replied.

"I just found this huge diamond ring, and if no one claims it in three weeks, I get to keep it! While that would be great for me, I guess I'd feel pretty bad if I were the one who lost it!"

This was the same student who, five minutes before, couldn't think of anything to write.

Students who finish writing their personal journal entries before others may choose to read during the remaining time. Many teachers allow ten or fifteen minutes so that every student has a chance to finish. It must be stressed to students that correct spelling is not important at this point. The teacher will note only whether or not students have written at least four sentences—or whatever minimum criterion has been established. The minimum require-

ment should start small; once students get in the habit of writing regularly, they will have a lot to say.

Students should be encouraged to keep their personal journals. As the years come and go, their entries will have special meanings to them. As an example, consider how prices have changed since the following entry was made in the 1933 personal journal of Rolland Sharp, a New Jersey engineer, advised by his doctor to take a relaxing vacation:

April 28, 1933
—Friday—
Cloudy and cool. Wind N.E. Arrived at St. Augustine at 7:00 a.m. Breakfast 50 cents and car washed for $1.00. Left at 8:15 a.m. Had a stroll around the old part of the town. Very odd narrow streets—no sidewalks. Bought some postcards. They were three for a nickel, and we paid a penny a piece for stamps, for a grand total of eight cents. Total for last night's supper, room, and today's breakfast cost $3.50. Arrived in Miami at 4:30 p.m. Total distance from New Jersey—1410 miles. Total expenses for trip, including three nights on the road plus groceries for the boat we rented, were $37.23.

This journal entry shared travel and its expenses, but what was a trip to the Florida Keys like in those days? A May entry from the same journal tells what two gentlemen on a two-week trip to the Florida Keys did to entertain themselves in a relaxing way. The first thing they did was rent a big "beautiful 54-foot boat, and buy gas, oil, food stuff, and fishing tackle." A journal entry almost two weeks later follows:

May 16, 1933
—Tuesday—
Little shower early this a.m. Not much rain. Clear and hot at 9:00 a.m. Wind S.E., moderate. Caught seven fish at the cut between Ragged Key and Little Ragged Key. Lots of fun! After dinner we went ashore on Sand Key exploring. Talk about jungle! It sure is a sight. Only thing we worried about were snakes. Walked about two miles down thru the "jungle." Killed four rabbits. Saw lots of coconuts on the trees. I shot several off and we drank the milk out of them. Certainly was an experience. We also saw where the bootleggers had made several signal fires and saw numerous blinds they had built.

Also went in the little motor boat and saw some beautiful coral and an enormous sponge bucket. Back to the boat for dinner at 5:30 p.m. Had fried rabbit for dinner. Finished the dishes and went to bed early.

Students are always amazed by these stories and try to include more details in their journals in the future. They begin to realize that their history recorded in a journal might be interesting to read to their children, and possibly their grandchildren, some day. If you use this selection with your older students, you might explain that 1933 was during Prohibition, a period of our country's history when selling drinking alcohol was illegal. *Bootleggers* were people who sold illegal alcohol. (Could they have hidden bottles in their boot legs?) *Blinds* were camouflages built to hide the stills where they produced the illegal whiskey. In another section of the same journal, Sharp tells of using a glass-bottom bucket in the clear water and finding several bottles thrown overboard by the bootleggers, desperadoes of that era, akin to today's drug dealers.

GIVING CREDIT FOR JOURNAL WRITING

A simple method for evaluating personal journal writing is simply to give each student a plus (+) or a minus (−): enough, or not enough. This can be recorded easily on a class roll on a clipboard, or in the grade book. At the bottom, write the dates, as in the following example:

Journal Writing

Mary Appleton	+	+	+	+	Ab	+	+	+
Rosa Banks	−	Ab	Ab	+	+	+	+	+
Doris Delow	+	+	+	+	−	+	+	+
Eunice Ernest	+	+	+	+	+	+	+	+
Manuel Garcia	+	+	+	+	+	+	+	+
	9/6	9/7	9/8	9/9	9/10	9/13	9/14	9/15

It is important to record student absences daily on the record sheet so that teachers can accurately excuse missing dates in student journals. It is almost impossible to get to every student each day, and journal entries are not assignments students complete as make-up work when they have been absent. Some teachers collect journals once a week, or every other week. It is simple to record five days' entries at a time on record sheets and to mark on the students' journals, also. Journals aren't being graded for content, usage, or mechanics, so a whole class set can be recorded in less than twenty minutes, including reading time. Wise teachers include some words of praise to encourage each author to keep writing.

Teachers, in discussing students' writing with them, often have a good opportunity to show one student exactly how quotation marks are used to signal conversation or, for another student, how book titles are capitalized. This is also the time for students to share information that ordinarily could not be shared orally. The student might really need help, as in this journal entry:

My dad locked me out of the house last night. I spent the night at the neighbors'. I was late coming to school today because I couldn't get in my house to get my clothes. I am afraid to go home.

This journal entry necessitated a call for protective services and helped the student obtain the phone number of an adult he could call when help was needed. Fortunately, all journal entries are not so serious. One mainstreamed student had trouble with her spelling, with almost undecipherable writing, until it was discovered that she was spelling with a lisp. When one thinks about this, it makes perfect sense. She spelled words exactly the way she heard them:

The wrote ethery day about thith girl who wath her beth thriend. The thriend had moved out oth town and thar away to Alathka.

Identification of the hearing impairment and continued work with the speech therapist helped this student improve her listening, speaking, and writing immensely. These, in turn, helped her reading improve. By the end of the year, this very motivated student showed average achievement when compared to other students in the class. Without the journal, which prompted identification of the hearing impairment that was really causing many of her learning problems, there is little reason to think she would have accomplished so much in one year.

If teachers had no other measure of accomplishment to share with a parent during a conference, the personal journal would be a wonderful way to show growth and development in writing, particularly if students have dated all entries. Fortunately, once teachers start using journals, they have many ways of showing growth, especially if more than one type of journal is used.

Many students will tell teachers that they do not enjoy writing because it has been an unsuccessful experience for them. Consequently, the most im-portant factor in improving writing, *practice,* has been lacking. Journal writing is generally free writing, not subject to editing or to being read by others, except for certain types of journals. Writing for ten to fifteen minutes at the beginning of each class period provides a good writing warm-up activity and practice.

Teachers may want to copy Model Activity 9.1 for students to glue into their personal journals as an introductory page.

ANOTHER TYPE OF PERSONAL JOURNAL

Many teachers use journals of another type, which they also call personal journals. In implementing the personal journal concept, one creative teacher had her students bring a large paper bag, maga-zines, scissors, and glue to class at the beginning of the year. Students cut out pictures that had special meaning to them and put them in the bag. Later, they cut the bag open and made a collage of their pictures. This became their identity bag; each pic-ture became a future journal topic. Then, the col-lages were used as very personal book covers. Some were even used by students to cover their journals! Students at a loss for a subject for the day had only to look at the pictures they had found meaningful earlier.

Another innovative idea is to have students make a list of thirty or more things or people that are very special to them. This activity is a good first-day icebreaker. Students have no trouble with the first ten or so items, but the fun begins when several students announce that they have included "the beach," and the others say, "Yeah!" and add "the beach" to their own lists. And so it goes. Most students really enjoy this assignment when they take it home for completion. The next day, the as-signment gets a little tougher. Students are asked to choose their ten favorite things on the list. Some-times, a student's highest priority item may not even have been thought of until #29. These favor-ites may become journal topics. Model Activity 9.2 can be used to help students think of some topics of interest to them that they can use for future journal writing.

Having students choose journal topics is not a new technique. For example, Athlene Miller, beloved mother of one of this book's authors, Marilyn Sharp, wrote the following journal entry on Octo-ber 8, 1915, in Chattanooga, Tennessee, when she was a young girl of 15.

An Afternoon Outing.   One afternoon not so very long ago, I went with some friends chestnutting. We left the automobile on the side of the road and roamed through the woods on Missionary Ridge looking for trees where the chestnuts were easy to get. The burrs were still clinging to some of the nuts and these had to be handled very carefully. We succeeded in finding a tree that was loaded and gathered all we could carry home with us.

After the chestnutting expedition, we all got in the auto and drove out to Fort Oglethorpe, where the soldiers were giving a band concert. Staying there for about half an hour, we came home.

Athlene Miller's journal, today a prized fam-ily treasure, was written in a Banner Notebook: a hardbound, cloth-covered, loose-leaf notebook. Both the rough drafts and the corrected copies of all work were included in this journal, and it appears that she had chosen her own topics for writing in 1915.

DIALOGUE JOURNALS

Dialogue journals, in which students write something to the teacher and the teacher responds in writing, are very similar to personal journals. Students love them. Students write more often and become better writers when someone responds to them! Dialogue journals are wonderful if a teacher is integrating reading and writing instruction. They give students and the teacher opportunities to engage in dialogue about books the students have read. Dialogue journals, can be personal journals, literature study journals. or other types that will be discussed later. Sometimes student responses include errors. These errors are often self-corrected if, in the teacher's response, the correct usage is modeled. An example is given in the literature study dialogue journal that follows:

Student: In the book, *The Great Gilly Hopkins* (Paterson, 1978), Gilly was hoping her mother would rescue her from Trotter. I wanted her mother to be nice, but she *weren't.* (Student error is in italics as an example of a grammatical error.)

Teacher: I thought her mother would rescue her, too. Why do you think her mother wasn't nice? (Teacher models correct form of the verb, without comment.)

Student: Her mother didn't rescue Gilly because she wasn't a very strong person. She probably wasn't mis-treated when she was little, because Nonnie *were* a very nice person. (Student has again misused *were.*)

Teacher: I agree. Nonnie was a very nice person. Do you think she was as nice as Trotter?" (Teacher again models correct usage of *was* and *were.*)

Student: Yes, she probably was as nice as Trotter. Why do you think the book ended when it did?

Notice that the student self-corrected each grammatical error when the teacher modeled the proper usage. In the last entry, the student even was ending the response with a question, in the same manner as the teacher.

Peter Johnston (1992), of the State University of New York in Albany, advocated the use of dialogue journals from first grade through college. He uses dialogue journals in his college classes as a method of self-evaluation; he has his students write analytical memos that reflect their changes in journal writing. Johnston felt that students who wrote in journals became more aware of their own knowledge, as well as what they were learning at school. He reported that if students used their journals as field notes to write their own report cards, "this would accomplish at once ownership, reflectiveness, and interest in development" (p. 143).

Nancie Atwell, in her book *In the Middle* (1987),

"Write me a sentence. Write me a paragraph. Write me a page. What are we? Her students or her pen pals?"

Source: From *Phi Delta Kappan,* June 1988, p. 717. Used with permission of Martha Campbell.

said that she had learned to stop answering as a teacher, "spitting out questions like a computer and lecturing my kids about what they're supposed to see and appreciate in the literature they read" (p. 178). Further, she said that the letters she wrote to her middle school students were personal and contextual. She'd learned to respond specifically and personally—but not too personally. She felt that the purpose of her answers was not to invite disclosures of students' personal problems or offer counsel.

Maria de la Luz Reyes, in an IRA presentation (1990) on bilingual students' journal writing, reported that dialogue journals are particularly effective in middle schools. She found that research with nonnative English speakers, also called limited English proficient (LEP) students, began to appear in the literature of the 1980s, including the writings of Graves, Gutstein et al., Flores and Garcia, Hayes and Bahruth, McGettigan, and Staton. The literature indicated increased fluency in English as a result of the informal nature of journal writing. LEP students, permitted to select their topics, became more fluent and could write longer passages that were more meaningful to them.

Luz Reyes felt as Nancie Atwell did about not getting involved too personally but learned that limiting topics can reduce a student's desire to write. She gave an example of a student whose dialogue was on a subject that Luz Reyes considered inappropriate, her fear of voodoo. The student had written many long paragraphs containing both English and Spanish. Finally, Luz Reyes wrote, "I don't think we should write about this any more. It scares me." The student replied, "O.K." Following this, the student refused to write anything for two weeks. The teacher, in effect, had said, "Your choice of topics is unacceptable." Although that is indeed what she had meant, she had turned off her student. She had first encouraged the student to write what was on her mind and then had told her it was not all right. The student, when told she could not voice her fears to her teacher, felt she had nothing more to say.

An advantage of dialogue journals is that they are nonthreatening and nongraded. The emphasis is not on language mechanics, although most teachers report that journal writing improves writing form. Students can select their topics, as well as the pace and tone of the communication. The major disadvantage of these journals is that the teacher cannot respond to every entry of each student's journal. In fact, Luz Reyes titled her 1990 speech, "How come some times you don't write back?" We have incorporated, and sometimes paraphrased, most of Luz Reyes' positive teacher responses/behaviors for English as a Second Language (ESL) students into a list of responses suitable for all students' dialogue journals:

- Share your love of learning with your students and encourage their scholarship: "Yes! That was a wonderful book. Have you read . . .?" "I think that last poem you wrote was every bit as good as . . . , don't you?"
- Encourage students to be risk takers: "Why don't you enter the computer fair? You could use something you've written in here."
- Respond personally with concern for students: "I have been worried about where you've been. I hope you and your mom are feeling better."
- Show that you value student's feelings: "I know how you feel; it always hurts my feelings when I'm left out, even though I know they can only invite a few people."
- Show enthusiasm and encouragement for students' interest: "Good luck in your game on Saturday," or "I have a friend who could help you with your butterfly collection."
- Show you value families by asking about theirs: "Tell me about your brother's wedding," or "Is your dad enjoying his guitar lessons?"
- Show respect for students' cultures and customs: "About how many people attend your family reunions? Do you have them every summer?"
- Tell students that they know more than you do about some subjects and encourage them to share: "How long does it take to learn to play a guitar? Would you play for us one day?"
- Answer compassionately without being judgmental when students ask for your advice: "If I were you, I'd consider either . . . or . . . ."
- Steer students away from poor choices: "Have you read the latest facts about that topic? There was a good article about that in yesterday's newspaper."
- Encourage good values: "That was really brave of you to . . . . I'm really proud of you."
- Encourage humor in your students: "That's really hilarious. Wasn't it funny when we got the icing all over us?"

Certainly each of these comments contains useful and important thoughts for any concerned teacher to consider in response to a student.

Barbara Bode (1989) reported on a study by Leslee Reed in 1979 in which Reed wrote dialogue journals with twenty-six students in the sixth grade. Every day students wrote in their bound journals.

Every night the teacher took the journals home and responded to the students. Reed felt this use of dialogue really empowered her students. Staton (1988, in Bode, 1989, p. 569) thought Reed's use of dialogue journals empowered both the students and the teacher. The language used by students most frequently contained their complaints but also included a myriad of other functional uses, such as predicting, giving facts, and thanking others. The second most common use of the dialogue process was in asking questions—even challenging the teacher. Several other researchers cited in Bode have noted how, in some classrooms, students quickly learn their passive roles. Dialogue journals help students become involved in their learning. Model Activity 9.3 offers students help in seeing how to begin a dialogue with the teacher. It offers the student a chance to reflect and the teacher an

opportunity to set the stage for future dialogue by giving positive feedback.

Of course, it is easy to see how time consuming dialogue journals can be, if a teacher must take twenty-six or more of them home every night. And this is only in a self-contained classroom! Teachers might try responding to five students a day (or period) or one class a day. Some type of rotation system is essential to making dialogue journals more manageable. Other teachers have suggested that students put their dialogue journals on a certain shelf or in a specific bag when they want a response; but this, too, has drawbacks—for example, some students writing and seeking responses often, and others never. Therefore, for practical reasons, many teachers choose other forms of journals for daily classroom use. One such journal is the buddy journal.

BUDDY JOURNALS

Bromley said that the use of buddy journals is "one activity that makes the connection between reading and writing natural, real, and meaningful and provides purposes for doing reading and writing together" (1989, pp. 122–123). Bode (1989) recommended that teachers clarify for students at the beginning that buddy journals are not as personal as dialogue journals; buddies may change several times during the year. Buddy journals need to be scheduled regularly to be successful. Although

Bode suggested several methods of pairing students, Atwell's (1987) method of just allowing or encouraging note-writing with whomever a student selects seems to be the best partner selection method for older students. An important point made by Bromley is that buddy journals "provide a real audience and give students reasons to write legibly and conherently" (Bromley, 1989, p. 126) (see Model Activity 9.4).

LITERATURE STUDY JOURNALS/LOGS

Of all the types of journals or logs available for educators to use, the literature study journal (also called the literature response journal) is, to many people, the most exciting. As Diane Wrobleski (1985) pointed out, "A literature log represents the interaction of the reader with the text" (p. 3). In a literature-based reading program, the journal can be the heart of the sharing time. Each student writes something about the assignment just read that he or she would like to share. Dorothy Watson, in a 1988 speech, said that the hardest thing for a teacher to do in literature-based instruction is give up control of the group. Most teachers have taught for years in a teacher-centered classroom. When the method of

teaching is changed to empower students creating a student-centered classroom, some teachers still feel insecure and want to direct the discussion of the literature. For this reason, many publishing companies that encourage the use of multiple copies of paperback books, as well as the newer literature-based basals, still provide questions to be answered for comprehension after reading stories.

Omitting direct questioning about stories read does not imply that students never need direct instruction. As they read journals, teachers can identify areas in which their students are very proficient and those in which they are less proficient; teachers can use this information when planning for instruction. In some cases, students can make the assignments of what is to be read and what is to be written in their journals after a teacher models how it is to be done for a while. As an example, one class had the names of the students in each different group highlighted on a class roll. Students in each group took turns being the leader by rotating down the list of highlighted names. The groups self-assigned the number of pages to be read and the writing assignment. They discussed what seemed to be a good writing topic for each section of the book. Often they would choose two writing topics for the day: The first topic would be a written prediction prior to reading; then, following the reading, the second topic would be their reaction to whether or not they had been correct in their prediction. This kind of reading response is not likely to happen without some modeling. A list might be given as a guide containing several choices of phrases, as in the list that follows. Students can add to this list as they become more experienced. Some teachers suggest that students glue this list onto the first page of a literature study journal for quick and easy reference until they become familiar with the suggestions provided.

Some Responses We Can Write About

1. A part I liked best was . . .
2. A friend, my mother, my dad, my brother, my sister, my aunt, my uncle, etc., reminds me of _____ _____ in this story because he or she always does the same thing. He or she . . .
3. When we were . . . , it reminded me of something that happened in this chapter. We were . . . and. . .

After students have written several times using these topics and have shared a few books mutually (especially among the ones teachers have chosen to read orally), comparisons of characters in various books can be modeled orally with students—for example: "Remember how Carlie, in *The Pinballs* (Byars, 1977), was always so grouchy? Why do you think she was so irritable? Have we read about anyone else who is irritable? Yes, Gilly, in *The Great Gilly Hopkins* (Paterson, 1978), was also a grouch. Had the two of them been treated in any similar ways that made them act so obnoxiously? Let's write about that today."

One fourth-grade student, when the group had assigned itself to compare the character in the story they were reading to a character in another story, wrote: "Bradley Chalkers (*There's a Boy in the Girls' Restroom;* Sachar, 1987) reminds me of Gilly (Paterson, 1978) because they both misbehaved when they came to a new school." Some teachers at a literature study meeting felt that this level of critical thinking was too difficult for fourth graders to achieve, but these students *chose* this topic for their journal writing. So a fourth choice of something to write about in journals is as follows:

4. Compare a character in this story to a character in another story that we have read.

After reading *The Trumpet of the Swan* (White, 1970), it is easy for the teacher to remark: "Remember how Sam Beaver always thought of a question each night as he was lying in bed before he went to sleep? Think of something this book makes you wonder about as you complete each chapter."

Diane Wrobleski (1985), in a paper she presented at the National Council of Teachers of English in Houston, Texas, said that, after reading Berthoff's 1981 book, *The Making of Meaning,* she felt that she had been doing too much thinking for her students. She felt that the reading guides she prepared for her high school students did not permit them to find their own meanings. She said that "the observations that trigger a response are internalized and students record their responses. . . . In a log, the reader is asked to think out loud on paper: to question, respond deeply, solve problems, to explore ideas" (Wrobleski, 1985, p. 3).

This type of learning log or literature response log can also be used as you study the content areas. For example, *Julie of the Wolves* (George, 1972) can be read to study the Arctic climate for geography, the habits of wolves for science, or the customs of Eskimos for anthropology. Charlotte Huck, Susan Hepler, and Janet Hickman wrote, in the fourth edition of their popular *Children's Literature in the Elementary School* (1987), that "Much of the story is based on research on wolves conducted at the Arctic Research Laboratory" and that "Survival stories have a powerful appeal to children in middle grades" (p. 491). Although their book was considered mainly for teachers of elementary school–age children, their recommendations of books are for students through age thirteen. These include the 100 books they have chosen to read aloud, although they believe—as does Jim Trelease, famed self-proclaimed cheerleader for reading—that books chosen to be read aloud should be at a higher level than students can read themselves. Thus, many of the stories named are relevant through the high school reading and interest level.

Theodore Taylor, author of *The Cay* (1969), wrote a story about the impact of World War II on a young boy living in Willemstad, Netherlands Antilles. More important, it was a book about overcoming prejudice. Taylor said that when he was young, he had loved books, but that he was eight years old before he learned a secret about books that was, to him, the best reason to read: He discovered that books contained adventure stories. Students who become devotees of reading through exciting adventure stories may also become interested in writing. Reactions and responses to the behavior of fictional characters can be written, shared, and discussed openly by students without the fear of reprisal that accompanies criticism of one's peers. Devine (1986) stated: "Thus a writer may have a message to share, and using all the linguistic and composing (or rhetorical) skills at her command, encode it in print. A reader then . . . tries to reconstruct the original text that was in the mind of the writer" (p. 10). Devine continued that this is an interactive approach because it involves the reader, the author, and the text, "as well as the interaction that takes place among them" (p. 10). As students discuss their journal writings, they often come much closer to comprehending the author's intended meaning than when one student reads alone and does not have the opportunity to share.

Many people have found that some of the most inspirational and exciting information they have learned was gained through sharing with others. Think of the best new dish you have enjoyed recently. The recipe may be contained in a cookbook you own, but it's likely that before you searched for the recipe in a book, someone had shared that food with you. You may have had the experience of seeing a movie or reading a good book, and then wanting your friends to watch that movie or read that book so that you could exchange opinions about the characters and plot. Literature response journal writing helps students put their thoughts down while they are fresh, so that when they meet to share and discuss the story, they each have something they found interesting to contribute to the group's pleasure in sharing their reading and attempting to understand the author's intended meaning. They often react critically to characters' behavior, expressing their current opinions and sometimes praising or criticizing the author for creating characters who act as they did. Discussion of their writing helps them clarify and sometimes change their values. This sharing of written information helps the students learn and appreciate the importance of the reading–writing connection.

Hancock (1992), in a pilot study for her dissertation, analyzed the literature response journal of a sixth-grade student for content and process. From her review of the literature, Hancock was convinced that "the free form of the literature response journal has provided an efficient means for tapping responses to reading by capturing the spontaneous inner language of the mind in a natural written form" (p. 37). She believed that studying possible patterns of response of students might provide information about their meaning-making processes, extend their responses beyond simple book reports, and provide a framework for figuring out the complexities of students. By studying the journal of Amy, a sixth-grade girl, she found that "readers do reflect on their own lives while encountering a text. The literature response journal provides the freedom and flexibility of revealing those personal reflections as they occur throughout the book" (Hancock, 1992, p. 40).

ORGANIZING A LITERATURE STUDY JOURNAL

For each new book students read, they will probably want to have some type of page divider. Possibilities for these include enlarging the book jacket (only with the publisher's permission), so the student can visually remember the book; having each group member draw a scene from the book read and then choosing the best one for copying for a divider; or simply writing the title on a piece of different-colored paper or a notebook divider. Then, if students later want to recall a particular book, their written responses about that book are readily accessible.

The reading level of a book is not the most important factor in literature response journals; the practice in writing and in seeing a purpose for writing is what matters most. Students will begin to learn that this is a very interesting way to record thoughts. They will be heard by an audience of their peers who, less critical than teachers about punctuation and capitalization, are probably more critical and judgmental of content. This encourages students to think carefully about having their writing make sense. Thus, without grading this written work, teachers are able to achieve one of the major goals for students' writing. Students are quick to correct one another if they have not comprehended

correctly. For example, when one student mistakenly wrote that a character in a story had jumped out of a tree, the rest of the group pointed out immediately that, in fact, the character had fallen from the tree.

Copies of the journal starters provided in List 9.1 (following Model Activity 9.9) may be made for students to put in their journals. These starters help students begin thinking critically about the literature they have read. This list combines both of the lists described in this section. Another tool that some teachers find useful both in literature and in the content areas is the double-entry notebook.

DOUBLE-ENTRY NOTEBOOKS

Double-entry notebooks offer students the opportunity to record specific parts of the text being studied and to comment on them. On one side of the page are the parts the student considers important, and on the opposite side of the notebook are comments.

Use Model Activity 9.5 to help your students begin a double-entry notebook. Here is an example from an eighth-grade student's double-entry notebook on *The Outsiders* (1969), by S. E. Hinton.

Observations	**Comments**
Page 27: "We were all four sitting there in silence [watching a movie] when suddenly a strong hand came down on Johnny's shoulder and another on mine and a deep voice said, 'Okay, greasers, you've had it.'"	I'd have been scared to death if this had happened to me or any of my friends.
Page 79: Johnny was upset because his parents didn't want him.*	I wonder how many kids have this happen to them. I'm sure lucky my parents love me.
Page 83: "I leaped out the window and heard timber crashing and the flames roaring right behind me."	This is the most exciting book I ever read. Incredible! You feel like you are right there!
Page 154: "A guy that'll really listen to you, listen and care about what you are saying, is something rare."	Johnny was a great guy. It was just so sad that he had to die.

POETRY JOURNALS

Many years ago, a wise kindergarten teacher introduced her young charges, who were four and five years old, to the great masters in art. The children memorized the names of the works of art and of the

artists as their tiny fingers glued copies of the pictures to pieces of cardboard and put these together in books that are still around to this day. Years later, the now-grown children still loved "Age of Innocence" by Sir Joshua Reynolds (1723–1792) and "Blue Boy" by Thomas Gainsborough (1727–

Note to reader: This is an observation, not a quotation.

1788), two English painters, and remembered both the names, and amazingly, the spellings. Surprisingly, it was not until almost fifty years later that two grown students, one an author of this book and the other a lifelong friend, discussed their kindergarten years and realized that most of the paintings included children, a point certainly planned by that wise teacher. For music to learn to skip by, these children danced to "Rustic Dance," an 1899 piece written by C. R. Howell (dates unknown) and came to sit down when they heard the teacher play the beginning notes of the "Fifth Symphony" by Ludwig van Beethoven (1770–1827), considered one of the greatest German composers of all time. Years later, when music lessons came along, the students could scarcely wait until the day they could play these two classical pieces. But for exposure to poetry, the children learned (as children should) and acted out nursery rhymes. In later years, there were no inspirational memories of adult poems learned in that wonderful room, as there were of adult art for the eye and adult music for the ear. In fact, with the exception of the fourth-grade memorization of "Columbus" and "My Shadow" by the Scottish author Robert Louis Stevenson (1850–1894), from *A Child's Garden of Verses,* and the tenth-grade requirement of the memorization of "Fog" by the North American author Carl Sandburg (1878–1967) and "Barter" by the North American poet Sara Teasdale (1884–1933), they learned no poetry. Although memorizing poetry individually is tedious and may be a barrier to enjoyment of poetry at the time, group memorization, as in choral readings, can provide pleasure both to the group and, later, to the individual. One has only to watch a former piano student sit down and try to recall a memorized piece to see that such a feeling of accomplishment can often bring pleasure in later years.

A college literature teacher told of classes of students who recited poetry while waiting in lines for lunch or for dismissal, or on field trips. One of her older students, an elementary teacher renewing her certification, tried this with skepticism and later reported that her students loved it! Certainly, the choice of poems would influence the pleasure. Collections should, however, include more than only humorous poems that teachers think will entice students. Remember the wise kindergarten teacher with her old masters and classical music. Although students do enjoy funny poems, the teacher can recommend a mixture of poetry with some old favorites that might be heard in other places. One fourth-grade teacher has required her students for years and years to memorize Robert Frost's "Stopping by Woods on a Snowy Evening." This well-loved poem will be a treasure to whole classes of hers forever. Young and old alike enjoy the English poet Christina Rossetti's (1830–1894) simple poem "Who Has Seen the Wind?" quoted in Model Activity 4.13.

Gunning (1992) stated that "ironically, the highest form of literary expression is the least liked by the majority of youngsters" (p. 337). Gunning, quoting the 1990 work of McClure, Harrison, and Reed, agreed that many children view poetry as the "literary equivalent of liver" (Gunning, 1992, p. 337). Possible reasons may be that poetry is neglected in the schools and that the choices teachers make are often not ones students enjoy. Gunning also reported Terry's 1974 findings that favorites were "poems that rhymed, were easy to understand, and had a pleasing rhythm. Limericks and poems with a narrative element were also favored" (Gunning, 1992, p. 337). Poems that didn't rhyme and haiku were the least liked forms of poetry. According to the 1990 writing of McClure, Harrison, and Reed, as reported in Gunning (1992), students dislike memorizing poems and "spending excessive time on analysis and interpretation" (Gunning, 1992, p. 337). Teachers should consider these findings when they make choices for students to hear and read. Because copyright laws prevent teachers from making poetry booklets for students mechanically or by photocopying, several poetry books can be passed around, and students can build their own collection of favorite poems by copying poems by hand. Classes may then use the poems chosen for choral reading or for memorization and group recitations. Model Activity 9.6 can be used to help students begin a poetry anthology of their own.

The last and possibly the most important type of poetry to include in the poetry journal is poetry written by students. As in other writing activities suggested in this section, students may wish to write several poems over a period of time, and then select one, or have a peer group choose the poem they prefer, for publication. These poems may be copied from poetry journals and then compiled as a class poetry anthology.

Although students dislike overanalyzing poetry, examining poetry's use of metaphors and other figurative language helps students learn to write their own poetry. One teacher modeled a poem she'd written in this way:

Blue is
> the sky,
> the sea,
> our planet,
> beautiful eyes,
> my mother's car,
> the baby's room,
> and
> cool lakes.

Her students continued with poems about colors, creating their own analogies before they ever heard the word *metaphor*. The poems of all who chose to participate were entered in a poetry contest. The poem of one of her students was declared a winner, and the student received a very motivating reward.

Poetry is meant to be enjoyed—when heard, when read, and when written. Poetry journals can help students achieve this goal.

ACADEMIC JOURNALS

According to Fulwiler (1987), the academic journal "stimulates classroom discussion, starts small group activity, clarifies hazy issues, reinforces learning, and stimulates imaginations" (p. 15). Brozo and Simpson (1991) suggested having students "spend five minutes responding to what they have read. They can summarize key ideas, ask questions, or merely list pages where they become lost" (p. 157). This helps students focus, react, and think about the course's objectives. Academic journals also can be used at the end of the lessons to summarize and react. As Devine (1986, p. 281) said, "The single most important way to discover what a reader has comprehended is to ask him!"

One advantage of an academic journal is that it gives students ongoing records of their summaries and thus provides them with study guides. Teachers can use academic journals to review important points to key issues or to have students reflect on the content covered. Students could share their writing with one another or with the class, or teachers might collect journals, or ask students to choose several of their best writings to rewrite and submit for grading. Some teachers give credit for each individual entry. Use Model Activity 9.7 to teach students how to record key points.

PROCESS JOURNALS

Diane Wrobleski (1985) said that in a process journal, writers describe their progress on particular pieces of writing. They describe what's happened up to now and what they plan to do next. They gain insight into their own process of writing. Students use these words: "I discovered; I realized; I thought; I reread, I changed; I decided; I tried; and I wrote" (p. 6). Students were asked to describe a place. Some samples of their process journals follow:

I reread everything that I had written so far and I kept parts of my first revision that I had liked and my group had liked including words, phrases and even a story. Then I expanded on the positive aspects to create a thrilled mood instead of stating my unhappiness from the room [*sic*]. (p. 11)

Last night while revising, I looked at the organization of my ideas. Then I decided to change the order of my sentences and complete the unfinished ones. I tried to focus my ideas on a tone and a subject. (p. 12)

One advantage of using the process journal is that it allows teachers to see the way students are organizing their thinking and writing. Thus, the process journal can supply a basis for planning instruction. Because process journals are useful in all content areas, they also provide an excellent opportunity to integrate writing across the curriculum. Model Activity 9.8 was designed to help students examine their own learning processes.

REFLECTIVE JOURNALS

John Wakefield, Associate Professor of Education at the University of North Alabama, reported in the *Educators' Forum* (1990) that in his educational psychology course he feels that what he calls "The Learning Journal" is probably the most useful writing assignment he gives. He said that students in his classes write for fifteen minutes every weekday for six weeks, describing what led to a specific learning experience and how the principles of learning were involved and applied. He found that students became more aware of themselves as learners. He cited two advantages of journal writing: First, students become more relaxed writers who don't fear writing; second, students learn the power of written communication.

Brandt (1991), executive editor of *Educational Leadership* wrote that "perhaps the most widely used process for inspiring reflection—among students, teachers, and administrators—is journal writing" (p. 3). One teacher attending a personal theory building workshop reported that, "to her, *reflection* had meant a brief mental replay of a series of events and that she did not often reflect deeply. Reflection, she now realized, was a rich source of continued personal and professional growth" (Killian & Todnem, 1991, p. 14). Students at the University of Northern Iowa (Canning, 1991), after being required to reflect, said that they had tried so hard to please professors and supervisors to make good grades that they had hidden their own opinions or "voices." After weekly assignments, students found that they were better thinkers.

Crawford (1992), who teaches senior English in Adrian, Michigan, described how she had combined the senior research paper with the study of poets. When the projects were completed, she asked students to write a reflective journal on their experiences. Pleased with the results, she was amazed when students continued to reflect on their research papers in their weekly journal entries. What had been intended as a three-week activity had effects on the students that lasted throughout a semester, and helped this teacher reevaluate her role in the classroom.

Researchers Surbeck, Han, and Moyer (1991) studied the journals of student teachers at the University of Arizona. "We knew that journal writing encourages thinking . . . " (p. 25). After reading the 1981 research of Yinger and Clark and the 1987 work of Zeichner and Liston, they thought journals would help teacher candidates integrate what they were learning about teaching with what they already knew, and would reveal their thoughts about teaching. They had students write biweekly and turn in their journals monthly, at which time each professor responded to what the students had written. Students were asked to give reactions to various feelings and concerns, elaborate by explaining and comparing, and contemplate by "thinking about personal, professional, or social/ethical problems" (p. 27). They found that a majority of students did use the "reaction-elaboration-contemplation sequence" (p. 27) at least partially, and that the students who did more contemplating seemed to integrate more information. The students also felt that this reflective journal writing was very helpful to them. Model Activity 9.9 shows students how to use this three-step model of thinking.

Alverman and Muth (1990) concluded by stating that if we are to teach our students to value writing, we must "make explicit the link between writing and self-knowledge. For example, journal writing is an excellent means of helping students learn about themselves and their feelings" (p. 108). Journal writing, along with other types of writing, helps students develop their ability as thinkers; that is, they practice analyzing, synthesizing, and evaluating as they construct meaning while writing.

CONCLUSION

Many different types of journals and the different uses teachers can make of them have been described in this chapter. Students are empowered by the use of journals in their learning process, for they are able to see their own progress. Journals, like the portfolios that will be discussed in Chapter 11, provide permanent records that can be used to demonstrate student progress clearly. One only has to compare the first pages in student journals with the ending pages to understand their heuristic nature and the two-thousand-year-old wisdom of Epic-

tetus, whose words began this chapter: "If you wish to be a writer, write."

REFERENCES

Alverman, D. E., & Muth, K. D. (1990). Affective goals in reading and writing. In G. G. Duffy (Ed.), *Reading in the middle school* (pp. 97–110). Newark, DE: International Reading Association.

Applebee, A. N., Langer, J. A., Mullis, I. V. S., & Jenkins, L. B. (1990). *The writing report card, 1984–1988: Findings from the nation's report card.* Princeton, NJ: National Assessment of Educational Progress, Educational Testing Service.

Atwell, N. (1987). *In the middle: Writing, reading, and learning with adolescents.* Portsmouth, NH: Boynton/Cook.

Bauer, M. B. (1986). *On my honor.* New York: Clarion.

Berthoff, A. E. 1981. *The making of meaning: Metaphors, models, and maxims for writing teachers.* Portsmouth, NH: Boynton/Cook.

Bode, B. A. (1989). Dialogue journal writing. *The Reading Teacher, 42*(8), 568–571.

Brandt, R. (1991). Overview: Time for reflection. *Educational Leadership, 48*(6), 3.

Bromley, K. D'A. (1989). Buddy journals make the reading–writing connection. *The Reading Teacher, 43*(2), 122–129.

Brozo, W. G., & Simpson, M. L. (1991). *Readers, teachers, learners: Expanding literacy in the secondary schools.* New York: Macmillan.

Byars, B. (1977). *The pinballs.* New York: Harper & Row.

Campbell, M. (1988). Cartoon. *Phi Delta Kappan, 69*(10), 717.

Canning, C. (1991). What teachers say about reflection. *Educational Leadership, 48*(6), 18–21.

Crawford, J. L. (1992). Redefining the research paper and the teacher's role. *English Journal, 81*(2), 79–82.

Crosby, J. (1990, September–October). Faster than a speeding bullet. *Tallahassee Magazine, 12*(5), 26–27.

Daly, J. A., & Hailey, J. L. (1984). Putting the situation into writing research: State and disposition as parameters of writing apprehension. In R. Beach & L. S. Bridwell (Eds.), *New directions in composition research.* New York: Guilford Press.

Daly, J. A., & Miller, M. D. (1975). Further studies in writing apprehension: SAT scores, success expectations, willingness to take advanced courses, and sex differences. *Research in the Teaching of English, 9,* 250–256.

Daly, J. A., Vangelisti, A., & Witte, S. P. (1988). Writing apprehension in the classroom context. In B. A. Rafoth & D. L. Rubin (Eds). *The social construction of written communication* (pp. 147–171). Norwood, NJ: Ablex.

Denker, B. (1991, December–January). A gift for the season. *Southern Accents,* pp. 46, 48, 51.

Devine, T. G. (1986). *Teaching reading comprehension: From theory to practice.* Boston: Allyn and Bacon.

Duffy, G. G. (Ed.) (1990). *Reading in the middle school.* Newark, DE: International Reading Association.

Fear, K. L., Anderson, L. M., Englert, C. S., & Raphael, T. E. (1987). The relationship between teachers' beliefs and instruction and students' conceptions about the writing process. In J. E. Readence & R. S. Baldwin (Eds.), *Research in literacy: Merging perspectives.* Thirty-sixth yearbook of the National Reading Conference. Rochester, NY: National Reading Conference.

Fulwiler, T. (1987). *Teaching with writing.* Portsmouth, NH: Boynton/Cook.

George, J. (1972). *Julie of the wolves.* Illustrated by J. Schoenherr. New York: Harper & Row.

Gunning, T. G. (1992). *Creating reading instruction for all children.* Boston: Allyn and Bacon.

Hancock, M. R. (1992). Literature response journals: Insights beyond the printed page. *Language Arts, 69*(1), 36–42.

Hinton, S. E. (1967). *The outsiders.* New York: Laurel-Leaf Library/Dell.

Huck, C. S., Hepler, S., & Hickman, J. (1987). *Children's literature in the elementary school,* 4th ed. New York: Holt, Rinehart and Winston.

Jeorski, S. F., & Conry, R. F. (1981). *Development and field application of the attitude toward writing scale.* Paper presented at the annual meeting of the American Educational Research Association, Los Angeles, California.

Johnston, P. H. (1992). *Constructive evaluation of literate activity.* New York: Longman.

Killian, J. P., & Todnem, G. R. (1991). A process for personal theory building. *Educational Leadership, 48*(6), 14–17.

Luz Reyes, M. (1990, May). *"How come some times you don't write back?": Characteristics of bilingual students' journal writing.* Paper presented at the International Reading Association Convention, Atlanta, Georgia.

Paterson, K. (1978). *The great Gilly Hopkins.* New York: Harper & Row.

Paulson, G. (1987). *Hatchet.* New York: Viking Penguin.

Prelutsky, J., & Stevenson, J. (illus.). (1984). *The new kid on the block.* New York: Greenwillow.

Rostkowski, M. I. (1986). *After the dancing days.* New York: Harper & Row.

Ruckman, I. (1984). *Night of the twisters.* New York: Harper & Row.

Sachar, L. (1987). *There's a boy in the girls' restroom.* New York: Knopf.

Surbeck, E., Han, E. P., and Moyer, J. E. (1991). Assessing reflective responses in journals. *Educational Leadership, 48*(6), 25–27.

Taylor, T. (1969). *The cay.* New York: Avon.

Vacca, J. L., & Vacca, R. T. (1989). *Content area reading,* 3rd ed. New York: Scott Foresman.

Valencia, S. W., McGinley, W., & Pearson, P. D. (1990). Assessing reading and writing. In G. G. Duffy (Ed), *Reading in the middle school* (pp. 124–153). Newark, DE: International Reading Association.

Victoria, September 1990, vol. 4, no. 9, p. 14.

Wakefield, J. F. (1990, Fall). Writing to think. *Educators' Forum, 1,* 9. Boston: Houghton Mifflin.

White, E. B. (1970). *The trumpet of the swan* (E. Frascino, Illus.). New York: Harper & Row.

Wrobleski, D. (1985, March). *Finding a meaning: Reading, writing, thinking applications: Double-entry notebooks, literature logs, process journals.* Paper presented at the National Council of Teachers of English Conference, Houston, Texas.

The activities that follow are meant to serve as models; such activities should be used as part of a total learning environment. These model activities were designed to demonstrate how the writing process can be developed while expanding the writer's knowledge base and providing opportunities for the writer to think critically.

My Personal Journal

MODEL ACTIVITIES

My personal journal is a daily writing activity. It is just what the name implies: personal. It is *for me, about me.* No one is going to read it except my teacher, if I choose. I don't need to worry about handwriting, spelling, or mistakes while I'm writing. I do not have to show this to anyone unless I choose to do so. I can write whatever is on my mind. I won't stop to correct, just write. Here are some examples:

September 12, 199__

We're having a quiz in science today on ecology. This is a lot more interesting than I thought. Ecology has to do with everybody. Terry and Susie are staying after school for a meeting. I'm staying, too. Terry is SO cute!

September 13, 199__

After school today my mom is going to drop Joey, Bill, Jane, and me off at the mall. We'll stay until 6:00 p.m. Then, Bill's dad will pick us up on his way home from work. We are going to have SO MUCH FUN! I'd really like to see a movie, but there won't be time. Maybe we can do that on the weekend.

Now I'll write my first entry in my own personal journal.

_____

_____

_____

_____

_____

_____

_____

_____

_____

_____

_____

_____

_____

_____

_____

ACTIVITY 9.2

The Thinker

The now-famous statue called "The Thinker" was created by the French sculptor Auguste Rodin (1840–1917). Sometimes, you feel as helpless as a statute when you sit down and try to think of things to write. To help you move past this impasse, or block, it's a good idea to have a list of topics on hand. Below, list some of the things you like so that, like all other authors, whenever you can't think of a thing to say, you can refer to your list.

People Important to Me

_____

_____

_____

_____

_____

_____

Things I Like to Do

_____

_____

_____

_____

_____

_____

_____

Famous People I Admire

_____

_____

_____

_____

_____

_____

_____

My Values

_____

_____

_____

_____

_____

_____

_____

Careers I Might Choose

_____

_____

_____

_____

_____

_____

Favorite Foods

_____

_____

_____

_____

_____

_____

ACTIVITY 9.3

Dialogue Journals

A dialogue is a conversation. In a dialogue journal, two people write their conversations. We are going to write about things that you are interested in, so I am going to let your write first. This practice page is only to help you get started. Later, we will write in regular journals. You can write anything you want, and I will not tell anyone, unless you write that you want me to get you some help with a problem. Let's begin!

Your Turn: I've been thinking about the first day we met.

_____

_____

_____

_____

_____

_____

My Turn: That's really interesting to me. I thought

_____

_____

_____

_____

_____

_____

Your Turn: _____

_____

_____

_____

_____

_____

My Turn: _____

_____

_____

_____

_____

_____

245

Buddy Journals

A buddy journal is written conversation you share with a friend, or buddy. During the year, you may choose or be assigned several different buddies. Your new buddy may read some of the things you and your old buddy wrote, so be careful that you don't write anything hurtful or unkind about anyone. Someone you don't care for now may be your best friend by the time we switch buddies. The first time we try this we are going to use these papers to practice on, but afterwards we will write in regular journals. Here is a sample of a buddy journal:

Buddy 1: Have you ever seen a tornado?

Buddy 2: No, I haven't. Have you? What makes you ask that?

Buddy 1: No, I haven't seen one either, but I'm reading this exciting book by Ivy Ruckman called *Night of the Twisters* (1984). It's based on a true event that happened in 1980, when seven tornadoes struck Grand Island, Nebraska, in three hours.

Buddy 2: Wow! Wouldn't that be scary? My mom saw a tornado up close one time.

Now, you and a buddy continue on with a written discussion of anything you know about tornados.

_____

_____

_____

_____

_____

_____

_____

_____

_____

_____

_____

_____

_____

_____

_____

_____

_____

_____

ACTIVITY 9.5

A Double-Entry Notebook

Directions: A double-entry notebook has two parts. The left side of the page is used for recording information or observations from a book you are reading. The book may be fiction or nonfiction, including content area texts. The right side of the page is used for your reaction to the text. On the left side below, labeled "Observations," write the page number of something you read that seems special to you in some way. Then copy the part or tell in your own words what happened. Under the section labeled "Comments" write what the part made you think about or your reaction. A sample is provided for you:

The Outsiders (1967)
by S. E. Hinton

Observations	**Comments**
Page 27: "We were all four there in silence (watching a movie) when suddenly a strong hand came down on Johnny's shoulder and a deep voice said, 'Okay, greasers, you've had it.'"	I'd have been sitting scared to death if this had happened to me or any of my friends.

Your Turn

Title _____

Author _____

Observations	**Comments**
Page __:	

_____

Beginning a Poetry Anthology

Poetry is one of the highest forms of writing. Understanding poetry is sometimes very easy and sometimes very difficult. There will be some forms of poetry that you especially enjoy and some that you may not enjoy at all. The reasons people give for liking one poem or a particular form of poetry over another are very personal. For example, one girl may enjoy poems about baseball because her dad always took her to baseball games with him; but for another girl, memories of her brother saying, "You can't play, get lost!" may give her unpleasant associations with that sport. So our reaction to the topic may be our first reason for choosing or not choosing a certain poem.

Some people always choose humorous poems—and no other kind. Some people love limericks. If you look, you can find examples of many kinds of poems you'll enjoy.

Directions: As you read poetry you like, try to decide if it fits any of the categories listed. Write the title, the name of the book where you found the poem, and the page it is on, so that you will be able to find it another day. If you need more lines, you may copy the topics on separate pieces of paper. Some titles may fit under two forms. You choose where to put them. This is not a project to be completed quickly, although when you sit down to read poetry, you may find many favorites at one time. These are only suggested categories. For some of them you may not have any favorites.

Rhymed or Unrhymed:

Humorous

Poem Title: _____

Book Title: _____

Page: _____

Poem Title: _____

Book Title: _____

Page: _____

Describe Something

Poem Title: _____

Book Title: _____

Page: _____

Poem Title: _____

Book Title: _____

Page: _____

Tell a Story

Poem Title: _____

Book Title: _____

Page: _____

Poem Title: _____

Book Title: _____

Page: _____

Others, Including Serious

Poem Title: _____

Book Title: _____

Page: _____

Poem Title: _____

Book Title: _____

Page: _____

Now, read back over your selections for each form. Copy the poems you like the best to create your own anthology. You may copy as many as you choose.

Learning about Academic Journals

Directions: Read the following article on passenger pigeons.

FASTER THAN A SPEEDING BULLET: PIGEONS RACE HOME TO TALLAHASSEE*

Throughout history, humans have capitalized on the homing instincts of certain birds. No living thing has a greater desire to return to its home than a homing pigeon, a descendant of the same family as the dove. Noah, from the Old Testament Bible story, sent a dove to see if flood waters still covered the land. Armies have used "pigeon corps" to carry urgent messages to troops in combat. Reuters news service got its start using pigeons to carry stock market prices to London, Paris, and Brussels. The remains of a pigeon called G.I. Joe are even preserved in the Smithsonian Institution in Washington, D.C., after saving many soldiers' lives carrying vital information.

Ray Munroe of Tallahassee starts familiarizing racing pigeons with their surroundings when they are twenty-five days old. He said, "Pigeons have different talent levels. It's kind of like in football. The coach is looking for the fast, smart athlete."

Variables that affect races include weather and predators. Races vary in length. Young birds race less than 300 miles. Birds are taken to a predetermined place where they are released to fly to their home loft. The owner takes the leg band off and inserts it into a man-made clock that records the time and band number. The clocks are sealed and may only be opened at the racing headquarters after the race.

Computers are used to calculate racing speed for each pigeon, since each home loft will vary in its distance from the starting point. A printout of the order of finish of all the birds is distributed to the owners. Munroe stated that the first race of the season is usually 150 miles. Later races are 200, 300, and 500 miles. Munroe's longest race was 565 air miles long; his bird made it home in twelve hours.

Pigeon racers gladly share advice with one another on all aspects of the sport. They realize that clubs won't thrive if one person always wins.

Next, look at the sample entries on the next page and add some of your own.

Source: Information from the article "Faster Than a Speeding Bullet" by Jim Crosby, *Tallahassee Magazine,* September–October 1990, vol. 12, no. 5, pp. 26–27, is used with permission of the *Tallahassee Magazine.*

Academic Journal Entry: Pigeon Racing

Statement

Comments

Throughout history, humans have capitalized on the homing instincts of certain birds.

I never thought about pigeons being that old.

No living thing has a greater desire to return to its home than a homing pigeon, a descendant of the same family as the dove.

I always thought doves and pigeons looked a lot alike.

Noah, from the Old Testament Bible story, sent a dove to see if flood waters still covered the land.

That *was* a long time ago.

Now, it's your turn.

Training starts when the pigeons are twenty-five days old.

_____

_____

_____

Variables that affect a race include weather and predators.

_____

_____

_____

Each pigeon in a race flies directly to his home loft.

_____

_____

_____

The farthest race Mr. Munroe participated in was 565 air miles.

_____

_____

_____

Mr. Munroe's bird returned in 12 hours.

_____

_____   _____

_____   _____

_____   _____

_____   _____

_____   _____

_____   _____

_____   _____

Processing My Learning

Sometimes we do things so automatically that we don't think about how we do them. When teachers do this, we say they are "going too fast." We don't realize that we, too, sometimes go too fast for others. It is only when we try to show a little child how to tie a bow, or how to put a space between words when writing, that we examine the processes we use to do things. Examining our own thought processes can help us become better at many things. Today, we are going to think about our writing.

Directions: Write a short paragraph about some aspect of school. It can be about this class, or about teachers, or about sports—anything about school. Write your paragraph below.

_____

_____

_____

_____

Now, reread what you have written. Next, consider the statements below; complete those that you think will help make your paragraph better.

I have reread what I wrote, and I found that _____

_____

I may change _____

I think that this paragraph _____

I may want to expand the part about _____

I may have tried to talk about too many things in this paragraph. Maybe I should _____

_____

I feel _____

_____

_____

I may need some help with _____

_____

_____

At first you may find it hard to put your thoughts into words when you reread your work, but practicing should prove helpful. You might say: "I always reread my writing to see if I've left out anything. If something doesn't sound right, I change it. Then I look for misspellings and punctuation and capitalization errors. If I need to copy my work over, I do."

Sometimes, figuring out *how* you processed your thinking after you've written helps you write better in the future.

251

Seeing and Knowing Yourself

Today, you are going to learn a method of thinking about things, or *reflecting,* that will help you better understand things that happen to you and others. This method will help you know yourself better and clarify what you believe. There are three steps to follow:

1. Describe an event or problem situation.
2. Describe your reaction or feelings to what happened.
3. Tell what your solution would be if you were deciding how to make the situation better.

Think about something that happened recently. It may have been something that happened to you or to a friend, or something you saw happen.

Describe what happened:

_____

_____

_____

_____

_____

Your Reaction: How did what happened make you feel? Or what did you think about what happened?

_____

_____

_____

_____

What do you think should be done? Why?

_____

_____

_____

_____

_____

Many times, while reflecting on various situations that have occurred, we think about two of these three parts of reflecting. We might know what happened and how we felt about a given event or situation. Often, however, we don't think through our own beliefs about what *we* think should be the outcome, or resolution. You can use this new reflective thinking method over and over in a variety of situations to become a better thinker and to know your own opinion or voice.

Journal Writing Starters

As you try to decide what your writing topic for the day will be, it may be helpful to consider the following starters used by other students. In parentheses are examples of how other students have completed these starters.

1. A part I liked best was . . .

2. _____ in this story reminds me of _____ (a friend, my mother, my dad, my brother, my sister, my aunt, my uncle, etc.) because he/she always does the same thing. He/she . . .

3. When . . . (Brian saw the tail of the plane sticking up out of the lake [Paulson, 1987]), it reminded me of something that happened to me. I/We were . . . and. . . .

4. Two characters in different books who remind me of one another are . . . (Gilly reminds me of Bradley Chalkers because they are both bad in school [Paterson, 1978; Sachar, 1987]).

5. I can't believe . . . (Brian burned his last $20 bill [Paulson, 1987]. He might get out of the woods and need the money).

6. I wonder why . . . (Lila's mother didn't want her to go to the veteran's hospital with her father, the doctor [Rostkowski, 1986]).

7. I noticed . . . (that in Katherine Paterson's books, the endings aren't what you think is going to happen.)

8. I think . . . (Brian shouldn't have burned the $20 bill since it was the last money he had [Paulson, 1987]).

9. I'm not sure . . . (if I like Gilly or not. Sometimes she is mean [Paterson, 1978]).

10. If I were . . . (as brave as Ponyboy, I could do anything [Hinton, 1967]).

11. I began to think . . . (that Joel was going to have to live with the secret of the drowning forever [Bauer, 1986]).

12. I realized . . . (that I'm not the only one who has ever been afraid when I read that Johnny was [Hinton, 1967]).

CHAPTER 10

Metacognitive Awareness and Self-Monitoring

In an Arabic apothegm, men were categorized as follows:

He who knows not and knows not he knows not
He who knows not and knows he knows not
He who knows and knows not he knows
He who knows and knows he knows

When this pithy saying was discussed with a group of teachers, their initial reaction addressed the emphasis on *He*. Realizing that the culture from which this saying had evolved valued education primarily for men, the group then opted to consider the content of the apothegm aside from the seemingly sexist language. However, one reflective teacher observed that this experience had made her even more aware of the similarities and differences among the many cultures represented in our classrooms today. Another teacher who was familiar with the saying's history pointed out the progression toward wisdom in the delineation of the four categories; that is, "He who knows and knows he knows" was considered wise and was to be followed by others. Model Ac-

tivity 10.1 was an outgrowth of this interesting discussion; it can be used to exemplify *cognition* (knowing) and *metacognition* (knowing about what one knows). Cognition and metacognition are important in that students need to be aware of what they know so that they can be strategic learners.

The teachers in this particular group had been participating in a seminar on how to empower developing writers. Thus, their discussion naturally turned to the importance of student awareness in the meaning-making processes of writing and reading. Specifically, these teachers addressed the need for students to learn how and when to use strategies that enhance clarity and comprehension. At this point, an astute history teacher reminded the others of the following quote by Hippocrates (c. 460–377 B.C.), the Greek physician who has become known as "the father of medicine": "The chief virtue that language can have is clearness." They agreed that self-regulation is a necessity for students to become optimally empowered as writers and readers—that is, to become capable of creating language that is clear and of understanding the written words of others.

METACOGNITION

Metacognition, which "refers to the awareness and control individuals have over their cognitive processes" (Baker, 1991, p. 2), is a concept that seems relatively new. In reality, only the term *metacognition* may be considered new; that is, the term was not related to reading comprehension until the late 1970s (Nist & Mealey, 1991, p. 44). Similar concepts were introduced after the turn of the last century by Dewey (1910) and Thorndike

(1917). "As early as 1917, the notion that comprehension is an active, constructive process was stated by Thorndike" (Tonjes, 1991, p. 203). The term *metacognition* refers to a monitoring of one's own comprehension or cognition. As Harris (1985) stated:

Cognitive processes are often automatic or unconscious and include such activities as search and storage mecha-

255

nisms, and inferential and retrieval processes. These processes shape mental representations, transforming them and constructing schemata. Personal knowledge of such cognitive processes and the ability to control them represent metacognition. (p. 376)

Metacognitive awareness, according to Brozo and Simpson (1991), "is the cognitive process that directs and orchestrates the other active learning processes" (p. 18). Reutzel & Cooter (1992, p. 460) offered that "metacognition pertains to student self-monitoring of thinking and learning processes." In the opinion of Baker (1991), "The concept of metacognition is one of the most important contributions cognitive psychologists have made to the field of reading education" (p. 2). She acknowledged the work of some of the researchers during the 1980s who produced evidence related to the important role metacognition plays in reading comprehension (Baker, 1985; Baker & Brown, 1984a, 1984b; Brown, Armbruster, & Baker, 1986; Garner, 1987). Furthermore, the more recent research of Hodge (1991) provided evidence for the importance of metacognitive awareness during reciprocal teaching with at-risk college students. Additionally, Baker (1991) pointed out that "metacognitive skills are applicable not only to reading but also to writing, speaking, listening, studying, problem solving, and any other domain requiring cognitive processes" (p. 2).

With an orientation toward whole language instruction, which involves an integration of the language processes, Goodman (1986) agreed that "it probably is true that as kids become literate they get some key insights about reading and writing which subsequently make their learning easier" (p. 53). He continued by offering the following:

- Language is always supposed to make sense. So in reading you know you've been successful if you understand what you read. In writing you keep rereading what you've written to make sure it makes sense.
- No one can understand everything. This reality can help kids maintain their self-confidence and develop some sense of when their lack of comprehension is the fault of the text, their lack of background, or other sources besides their own reading ability.
- Personal meanings may differ from the meanings of the community, in minor or major ways. Pupils need to internalize these shared meanings while maintaining and perfecting their personal meanings. (p. 53)

One creative teacher shared his experiences with a suggestion offered by Goodman (1986) that student curiosity about aspects of language can be evoked as students are encouraged to use their own ideas and insights to express themselves as writers. Model Activities 10.2 and 10.3 evolved from the classroom discussion that took place after his students heard a reading of "The Blind Men and the Elephant." This once well-known verse, created by an American author, John Godfrey Saxe (1816–1887), was based on a Hindoo (spelled Hindu today) fable. As the result of this teacher's willingness to seize the teachable moment, students became more metacognitively aware of the concept of a fable and had the opportunity to develop their thinking and writing abilities as they created their own fables. This teacher observed the benefits of combining the expansion of cultural literacy with the development of process-based writing.

LEARNING THROUGH THE READING–WRITING CONNECTION

According to Nist and Mealey (1991, p. 45), "Schema theory relates to the effect of prior knowledge on a new learning situation. Like metacognition, the concept of schema theory is not new. It emerged in the early 1930s with Bartlett's (1932) somewhat ambiguous definition of *schema*." Recent theorists, such as Anderson and Pearson (1984) and Just and Carpenter (1987), have developed a more specific definition that focuses on an abstract framework for organizing knowledge in one's memory.

In both the processes of reading and writing, meaning is constructed by the reader/writer. In reading, for example, one actively interacts with the text; comprehension will be related directly to the reader's background knowledge or schemata about the topic at hand. McNeil (1987) defined *schemata*, units of knowledge, broadly as follows:

Schemata are the reader's concepts, beliefs, expectations, processes—virtually everything from past experiences— that are used in making sense of text, the printed word evoking the reader's associated experiences, and past and potential relationships. (p. 5)

Furthermore, Devine (1986) offered that "embedded into these units of knowledge (in addition to the knowledge itself) is information on how this knowledge is to be used" (p. 39). Pearson and Johnson (1978) described the process of activating prior knowledge as bridge building between that which is known and that which is new. The extent to which comprehension is possible depends on the reader's understanding of how language works and the reader's familiarity with key concepts. A reader relies on his or her experiences and knowledge to predict meaning and to make sense of text. A reader also relies on this same knowledge base when he or she writes. This reading–writing connection is most evident as the student reads to expand his or her schemata in order to develop further a writing topic.

Model Activity 10.4 was designed to expand the reader's knowledge base for the largest land animal, the elephant. Of course, any relevant topic could be used; and students should be encouraged to select topics that reflect their interests. Also, this activity should be helpful to students as they establish the habit of making predictions as they read.

After using Model Activity 10.4 with a group of students, one observant classroom teacher was quick to point out that while going through the process of expanding the students' knowledge base for elephants, she realized that many students did not know how to take notes or even how to locate relevant information on the topic. In addition, others simply were not efficient notetakers. Furthermore, students who were poor notetakers did not seem to know that this was the case. That teacher would support strongly the position of Herrmann (1990) who, emphasizing the importance of understanding and controlling the studying process, stated that a portion of the curriculum

should focus on helping students study more effectively. Understanding the cognitive reasoning processes associated with effective studying and assuming metacognitive control of these processes are important goals. Three study strategies should be taught: notetaking, locating, and remembering. (p. 86)

Unfortunately, it appears realistic to conclude that some of the study strategies that we expect students to use, and take for granted that they know how to

use, are not even part of their knowledge base. Through teacher modeling and directed practice, students can develop their confidence and ability as notetakers. Given that this complex process of sorting and combining information from various sources so it can be remembered often requires students to locate information in the library, teachers must make certain that students know how to use the library efficiently as well. For example, the use of key words (descriptors required to access computer databases) can help develop students' metacognitive awareness during the decision-making process; specifically, in order to decide which key words are appropriate for their particular topics, students must search through their mental index of words. This should enhance their ability to identify key words for use in notetaking; thus, they become more aware that they are thinking and that their ideas can be expressed in writing. Students must learn how to identify and summarize with efficacy the important ideas of a lecture, from print material, or from any other source of worthwhile information; these are the study skills essential for success as students progress through the grades into college.

If students are to construct meaning through writing, they must have a schema for the writing process, including its many overlapping and recursive stages. Thus, as developing writers become more comfortable with their own process of writing, they are more likely to self-regulate (as opposed to being regulated by others) as they construct a meaningful message. As previously discussed, the nature and complexity of the task may influence the student's own process of writing. Also, the student's familiarity with his or her chosen topic will have an impact on the process. Naturally, when a writer has an extensive background associated with the topic, an orderly search of the writer's memory allows for easy retrieval of relevant information. For example, it is usually during the prewriting stage that relevant prior knowledge about the writer's chosen topic is activated. To be effective as writers, it would be helpful for students to understand the importance of prior knowledge and also to know how to evaluate their knowledge base in relation to their chosen topics; in all likelihood, students will need direct instruction and practice to achieve these objectives. Herrmann (1990), stressing the similarity between the reading and writing curriculum, stressed the importance of "planned learning experiences that help students understand the writing process and understand the cognitive reasoning processes associated with effective writing" (p. 89).

Reading and writing are not separate entities for, in reality, writers are constructing meaningful readings, and readers are reading writing. According to Flood and Lapp (1986), instruction in writing helps reading development. Model Activity 10.5 integrates the two complementary processes of reading and writing while directing the student's attention to the future of wild elephants. As the student's knowledge base for elephants continues to be expanded, consideration will be given to basic differences between the lives of a domesticated elephant and a wild elephant. Through an activity like this, subject areas across the curriculum will be addressed naturally—for example, science, math, history, geography, economics, and ecology. The reciprocal relationship between reading and writing is evident as students move through the complex process of learning. Also, the expansion of cultural literacy is occurring naturally as students explore a theme that has meaning for them.

When students construct meaning as readers and writers, they rely on their past experiences a great deal to make sense of the task at hand; they are both building and expressing background knowledge. Schema theory, according to Tonjes (1991), addresses "the need for interpretive frameworks"; she contended that "a text is gobbledygook unless the reader can breathe meaning into it" (p. 10). Furthermore, she emphasized the importance of learners using schemata to help with the following:

1. assimilate new information;
2. see what is important;
3. make inferences that elaborate;
4. summarize by aiding in the separation of important ideas from less important ones (e.g., with a fable schema, readers would give more weight in their summary to the moral than to the character, action, or event);
5. aid memory, as our schema influences interpretation, and it is our interpretation of the text rather than the text itself that we will recall. Our schema first influences our interpretation and, when activated, helps us recall later what was read. (pp. 10–11)

Writers who already have a working knowledge, or schemata, of conventions used for organizing their thoughts and signaling this organization to their audience have a definite advantage over those who do not. They are freed in a sense to concentrate on constructing a meaningful message; their primary energy can be directed to generating meaning, rather than to concerns for mechanics. For example, a developing writer may wish to include conversation between characters in a story, but may not yet know that quotation marks are used to signal dialogue. An observant teacher can take advantage of this opportunity to model for the student how quotation marks are used to signal conversation. As the student uses this new information, it becomes part of his or her knowledge base. In the future, this writer is freer to focus on the content of conversations, for the use of quotation marks has become automatic.

SELF-MONITORING

Educators agree that today there is more of a need than ever that learning be lifelong. To facilitate this complex process of ongoing learning, particularly in an age of rapid technological advances, teachers must encourage students to assume an ever-increasing amount of responsibility for their own learning. It would appear, of course, that this idea has had support across time; a journal as recent as 1991 (Amthor) considered the wisdom of the Scottish poet and novelist Sir Walter Scott (1771–1832), when he said that "all men who have turned out worth anything have had the chief hand in their own education." Also in recent times, Constance Weaver offered that, "Learning is seen as the result of complex cognitive processes that can be facilitated by teachers and enhanced by peer interaction" (Goodman, Bird, & Goodman, 1991, p. 382). The underlying assumption related to education is that individuals who are internally motivated and able to self-monitor their learning are more active in the process than those who rely on external motivation primarily. It also follows that internally motivated students feel better about themselves and are more likely to feel empowered enough to take positive risks in the learning process because of their confidence.

An example was given earlier of students who *did not know* how to take notes and *did not know* that they *did not know* how. Keeping in mind the need to integrate the language arts instructionally, consider the real possibility that these same students did not even know how to listen actively or critically to speakers. Unless students have had active listening modeled at home, school, or elsewhere, how can they be expected to have this receptive language process mastered?

The idea that both speakers and listeners must share responsibility for effective communication to occur is not new; a French proverb advised that "The spoken word belongs half to him who speaks and half to him who hears." Rather than advising students to be active listeners, we must model the process as well as help them emulate specific behaviors associated with this form of learning. Model Activity 10.6, or your modification of this inventory to fit your students, should prove helpful as you guide them toward becoming better listeners. After students have completed the inventory, encourage them to reflect on it, discuss their responses, and write goals for areas they would like to change. Self-evaluation checklists help students learn to be more aware of how they are functioning and to monitor themselves.

As an important aside, you also may want to share with students what the American writer Henry David Thoreau (1817–1862) had to say about listening and good manners. He said, "The greatest compliment that was ever paid me was when one asked me what I thought, and attended to my answer." Consider discussing with students the reality that good listening pays off in the real world with improved interpersonal relations. In addition, critical listening is important to them as consumers who are bombarded with advertising in print and in the media.

Model Activity 10.7 can be used with students who may not know how to deal with silence effectively, either in conversation or as a vehicle for learning. It also could be used as a springboard for figurative language interpretation in the context of studying literature. Furthermore, students could be encouraged to look at the concept of *silence* across history; for example, in the late 1700s, the North American statesman Benjamin Franklin (1706–

1790) wrote about silence in his autobiography. In addressing thirteen virtues that guide us through life, Franklin included "SILENCE—speaking only when you benefit others or yourself; for listening sometimes teaches you more." Examples like these offer natural opportunities for integrating content areas with the language arts.

Because listening also includes the mental activities of "search and storage mechanisms, and inferential and retrieval processes" quoted earlier in this chapter by Harris (1985, p. 376), it is a powerful vehicle for learning. Though not tied directly to writing when received, information added to a student's knowledge base through this receptive process is stored for use in the future and may become a part of his or her future writing. Developing writers call upon what they have heard, seen, read, felt, and so forth when they ready themselves to write. Their work-in-progress and their writing products will reflect their individual experiential base(s).

Speaking also requires self-monitoring if this expressive form of communication is to be developed optimally. Public speaking, for example, involves much more than simply presenting to an audience; it also involves thinking critically about the best content to include for the particular audience. More often than not, a formal speech begins with prewriting activities, whether on paper as an outline or a list of points to be covered, or as brainstorming in the head as one mentally selects and discards ideas. Next, a working written draft is prepared, which typically is revised, edited, and rehearsed before delivery. Sometimes, as in the 1992 State of the Union address given by the president of the United States, formal copies of a speech are distributed to the audience and members of the press (who could be seen on television flipping the pages as the speech was delivered). This formal speech became a part of recorded history, as have all written and spoken documents of the presidents of the United States for at least the last fifty years; they are preserved in each president's museum.

With less formal speaking, the kind of extemporaneous talk that people use most of the time for daily conversation, thoughts are expressed more spontaneously. For example, students may share their initial reactions to a president's address, debating major issues informally; this kind of talk can serve as a vehicle for metacognitive thinking as they process their ideas. As students practice drafting more formal, clear, persuasive speeches, they also need to perfect their delivery by developing the ability to self-regulate voice tone and nonverbal language, such as gestures. Only through self-monitoring as one practices, both verbally and nonverbally, can students learn to speak with confidence and conviction.

Finally, students need to understand that not all talk is for others; some thoughts and talk are just for themselves. This is particularly true of thinking. Strong (1991) said that "whenever we use talk or writing for learning—as opposed to communication—the main audience is ourselves, not somebody else" (p 155). Self-talk, whether in the form of thoughts or actual verbalizations, is a powerful tool for monitoring or regulating one's learning.

Because reading and writing are complementary processes, it is crucial that educators design instruction that takes their connection into account. Developing the process of reading has a positive impact on writing and vice versa. Thus, it is imperative that students learn how to self-regulate or self-monitor as both readers and writers.

Educators need to help students develop a repertoire of strategies for learning and to help them become reflective so that they will know what strategy or combination of strategies to use at any given time. For example, given that "older and better readers use a greater variety of fix-up strategies, such as rereading, looking ahead, using surrounding context, trying to make an inference to resolve the problem, and consulting an outside source" (Baker, 1991, p. 4), than younger and poorer readers, different students will require different levels of instruction to become metacognitively more aware and able to use a particular fix-up strategy or a combination of strategies appropriately. Baker (1991) said that teachers must instruct students directly in metacognitive skills, starting in the lower grades:

Good readers pick up metacognitive skills on their own, but poorer readers frequently do not. Given the apparent link between metacognition and achievement, it makes little sense to leave the acquisition of metacognitive skills to chance. Rather, teachers should give students direct instruction in using metacognitive skills from the early elementary years. (p. 6)

Process logs, which were discussed in depth in Chapter 9, are particularly useful for encouraging

students to be more reflective about their own thinking. These logs offer students the perfect opportunity to reflect on what they are learning and to think critically about how this knowledge will be useful to them in the future.

Whether students are understanding text created by others or writing their own, one fact is indisputable: They are thinking and making decisions. Swiss painter Paul Klee (1879–1940) is reported to have said that "art does not reproduce what we see—it makes us see." The same thought can be paraphrased and transferred to the writing process: Writing does not reproduce what we think—it makes us think. The writer is an active decision maker throughout the process of constructing meaning on a page; he or she is reading the writing to make sure it makes sense. As emphasized previously, for example, writers must decide when they need to learn more about their topic and when they're ready to start drafting. No teacher could possibly make, nor would a teacher choose to make, the infinite number of decisions that each student will consider as he or she moves through the overlapping and recursive stages of the writing process. However, teachers must facilitate student understanding of this process and, throughout the process, must model how to translate thoughts to print. If students do not know how to revise and edit their drafts, they will not be able to publish with pride a communicative message. Model Activities 10.8, 10.9, 10.10, and 10.11 were designed as examples of how to increase metacognitive awareness during the writing process.

Finally, the concept of self-regulation applies to content areas such as science, particularly with the theory of constructivism. Pope and Gilbert (1983) stated:

Knowledge is seen as being produced by transactions between a person and the environment. An emphasis is now placed upon the active person reaching out to make sense of events by engaging in the construction and interpretation of individual experiences. (p. 194)

As these students make the transition to self-regulation, they assume control for science learning. As they listen to instruction, read their texts, conduct experiments, and summarize their findings in written reports, they go through an active process of building a model that "requires the metacognitive skills of evaluating the plausibility of the model and revising hypotheses if necessary" (Baker, 1991, p. 7) Model Activity 10.12 demonstrates this relationship.

Students who develop their metacognitive awareness and practice self-regulation are more likely to function independently in various learning situations. Herrmann (1990), stressing the importance of focusing instruction on cognitive reasoning processes in the classroom, emphasized that many students need direct and/or indirect instruction on *how* to be more metacognitively in control. This chapter offers instructional strategies that emphasize the integration of the language arts with content from subject areas and the development of metacognitive awareness. As students evolve into more strategic thinkers over time, they will become more skilled at problem solving and self-monitoring their learning. Through the vehicles of reading and writing, for example, students will expand their schemata for what is important in their lives. Through self-regulation, they will be empowered to make decisions not only as learners but as responsible citizens in their communities. Ideally, they will begin to view learning as an enjoyable lifelong endeavor. This is in keeping with the following thoughts attributed to John Dewey (1859–1952), the North American philosopher and educator:

Education is a social process . . .
Education is growth . . .
Education is not preparation for life;
Education is life itself.

REFERENCES

Amthor, G. R. (1991, September). Interactive multimedia in education. *IBM Multimedia (Special Issue) Supplement to Technological Horizons in Education (T.H.E.) Journal*, 2–5.

Anderson, R. C., & Pearson, P. D. (1984). A schema-theoretic view of basic processes in reading. In P. D. Pearson (Ed.), *Handbook of reading research*. New York: Longman.

AWAKE! (1990). *71*(17), September 8, p. 21.

Baker, L. (1985). How do we know when we don't understand? Standards for evaluating text comprehension. In D. L. Forrest-Pressley, G. E. MacKinnon, & T. G. Waller (Eds.), *Metacognition, cognition, and human performance* (pp. 155–205). New York: Academic Press.

Baker, L. (1991). Metacognition, reading and science education. In C. M. Santa & D. E. Alvermann (Eds.), *Science learning: Processes and applications* (pp. 2–13). Newark, DE: International Reading Association.

Baker, L., & Brown, A. L. (1984a). Metacognitive skills and reading. In P. D. Pearson (Ed.), *Handbook of research in reading* (pp. 353–393). White Plains, NY: Longman.

Baker, L., & Brown, A. L. (1984b). Cognitive monitoring in reading. In. J. Flood (Ed.), *Understanding reading comprehension* (pp. 21–44). Newark, DE: International Reading Association.

Bartlett, F. C. (1932). *Remembering: A study in experimental and social psychology*. New York: Cambridge University Press.

Brown, A. L., Armbruster, B., & Baker, L. (1986). The role of metacognition in reading and studying. In J. Orasanu (Ed.), *Reading comprehension: From research to practice* (pp. 49–75). Hillsdale, NJ: Erlbaum.

Brozo, W. G., & Simpson, M. L. (1991). *Readers, teachers, learners: Expanding literacy in the secondary schools*. New York: Macmillan.

Burger, C. (1965). *All about elephants*. New York: Random House.

Chadwick, D. H. (1991, May). Elephants—Out of time, out of space. *National Geographic*, pp. 2–49.

Devine, T. G. (1986). *Teaching reading comprehension: From theory to practice*. Boston: Allyn and Bacon.

Dewey, J. (1910). *How we think*. Lexington, MA: Heath.

Flood, J., & Lapp, D. (1986). Getting the main idea of the main idea: A writing/reading process. In J. F. Baumann (Ed.), *Teaching main idea comprehension*. Newark, DE: International Reading Association.

Garner, R. (1987). *Metacognition and reading comprehension*. Norwood, NJ: Ablex.

Goodman, K. (1986). *What's whole in whole language?* Portsmouth, NH: Heinemann Educational Books.

Goodman, K. S., Bird, L. B., & Goodman Y. M. (Eds.), (1991). *The whole language catalog*. Santa Rosa, CA: American School.

Harris, K. R. (1985). Conceptual, methodological, and clinical issues in cognitive-behavioral assessment. *Journal of Abnormal Child Psychology, 13*(3), 373–390.

Herrmann, B. A. (1990). Cognitive and metacognitive goals in reading and writing. In G. G. Duffy (Ed.), *Reading in the middle school,* 2nd ed. (pp. 81–96). Newark, DE: International Reading Association.

Hodge, E. A. (1991). *An investigation of metacognitive training on the reading comprehension of at-risk college students*. Unpublished doctoral dissertation, Florida State University, Tallahassee, FL.

Just, M. A., & Carpenter, P. A. (1987). *The psychology of reading and language comprehension*. Boston: Allyn and Bacon.

Lobel, A. (1980). *Fables*. New York: Harper & Row.

McNeil, J. (1987). *Reading comprehension*. Glenview, IL: Scott Foresman.

Nist, S. L., & Mealey, D. L. (1991). Teacher-directed comprehension strategies. In R. F. Flippo & D. C. Caverly (Eds.),

Teaching reading and study strategies at the college level (pp. 42–85). Newark, DE: International Reading Association.

Pearson, P. D., & Johnson, D. D. (1978). *Teaching reading comprehension.* New York: Holt, Rinehart & Winston.

Pope, M., & Gilbert, J. (1983). Personal experience and the construction of knowledge in science. *Science Education, 67,* 193–203.

Reutzel, D. R., & Cooter, R. B., Jr., (1992). *Teaching children to read: From basals to books.* New York: Macmillan.

Strong, W. J. (1991). Writing strategies that enhance reading. In B. L. Hayes (Ed.), *Effective strategies for teaching reading* (pp. 153–172). Boston: Allyn and Bacon.

Taylor, B., Harris, L. A., & Pearson, P. D. (1988). *Reading difficulties.* New York: Random House.

Thorndike, E. L. (1917). Reading as reasoning: A study of mistakes in paragraph reading. *Journal of Educational Psychology, 8,* 323–332.

Tonjes, M. J. (1991). *Secondary reading, writing, and learning.* Boston: Allyn and Bacon.

Wexo, J. B. (1980). *Elephants.* Zoo Books. San Diego, CA: Wildlife Education Ltd.

MODEL ACTIVITIES

The activities that follow are meant to serve as models; such activities should be used as part of a total learning environment. These model activities were designed to demonstrate how the writing process can be developed while expanding the writer's knowledge base and providing opportunities for the writer to think critically. In this chapter, the majority of the model activities focus on the topic of elephants to demonstrate how a theme could be developed; of course, students should be encouraged to select theme studies that reflect their interests.

Do You Know Which Language Is Spoken Most Around the World?

Directions: Read each of the questions below and provide your answer in the accompanying space. Then, note whether your answer falls into Category 1, 2, or 3, and write that number in the box following your answer.

Category 1 = I know I don't know.
Category 2 = I think I know.
Category 3 = I know for sure that I know.

Questions:

1. Which language do you think is spoken by the largest number of people internationally?
   _____ ☐

2. Which language do you think would be second in the world league? _____ ☐
   Third? _____ ☐

Directions (Continued): Double check to make sure you have provided an answer for each of the questions above and have categorized your answers. Now, read the following passage to determine if your thinking was in keeping with the facts.

WHICH LANGUAGE IS SPOKEN MOST?*

If you were asked to name the most popular international language, you would probably answer "English." Yet, according to *The 1990 World Almanac and Book of Facts,* Mandarin Chinese, spoken by some 844 million people, is the language most used by the human family. This compares with the 437 million people, spread all over the world, who speak English. Which language do you think would be third in the world league? French or Spanish? No. It is Hindi, spoken by 338 million people, mainly in India. Hindi and Urdu, which is spoken by 90 million, mainly in Pakistan, "are essentially the same language, Hindustani," according to the same publication.

Directions (Continued): Write a few sentences telling your reaction to learning these facts. Was some of this information new to you? Were you able to build a bridge between that which was known and that which was new?

_____

_____

_____

_____

_____

_____

*Source: From AWAKE!, Vol. 71, No. 17, September 8, 1990, p. 21.

ACTIVITY 10.2

The Many Faces of Reality

Directions: A *fable* is a brief fictitious story that ends with a moral. It is intended to reinforce some useful truth about how people should behave, or to make an important point. Sometimes, animals with human qualities are the characters in the story. Some fables were written many centuries ago; for example, Aesop's fables date back to the sixth century B.C. More recently, Arnold Lobel (1980) has written original fables in the same style as Aesop. Read the following Hindoo (spelled Hindu today) fable, which was put into verse in the 1800s by John Godfrey Saxe (1816–1887), a North American author.

*The Blind Men and the Elephant: A Hindoo Fable**

It was six men of Indostan
   To learning much inclined,
Who went to see the Elephant
   (Though all of them were blind),
That each by observation
   Might satisfy his mind.

The *First* approached the Elephant,
   And happening to fall
Against his broad and sturdy side,
   At once began to bawl:
"God bless me! but the Elephant
   Is very like a wall!"

The *Second,* feeling of the tusk,
   Cried "Ho! what have we here
So very round and smooth and sharp?
   To me 'tis mighty clear
This wonder of an Elephant
   Is very like a spear!"

The *Third* approached the animal,
   And happening to take
The squirming trunk within his hands,
   Thus boldly up and spake:
"I see," quoth he, "the Elephant
   Is very like a snake!"

The *Fourth* reached out his eager hand,
   And felt about the knee.
"What most this wondrous beast is like
   Is mighty plain," quoth he:
"'Tis clear enough the Elephant
   Is very like a tree!"

*Source: "The Blind Men and the Elephant" by John Godfrey Saxe, in *The Poetic Works of John Godfrey Saxe,* pp. 111–112. Copyright © 1882 by Houghton, Mifflin and Company, Boston.

The *Fifth* who chanced to touch the ear,
    Said: "E'en the blindest man
Can tell what this resembles most;
    Deny the fact who can,
This marvel of an Elephant
    Is very like a fan!"

The *Sixth* no sooner had begun
    About the beast to grope,
Than, seizing on the swinging tail
    That fell within his scope,
"I see," quoth he, "the Elephant
    Is very like a rope!"

And so these men of Indostan
    Disputed loud and long,
Each in his own opinion
    Exceeding stiff and strong,
Though each was partly in the right,
    And all were in the wrong!

       Moral
So oft in theologic wars,
    The disputants, I ween,
Rail on in utter ignorance
    Of what each other mean,
And prate about an Elephant
    Not one of them has seen!

This story was told to make an important point—that how we *see* reality depends on our ability to *view* reality. Each of the men reporting the facts about the elephant certainly believed them to be accurate. Had you asked each one, "Do you know that you know?," each would have answered firmly "*Yes!*" As outsiders looking in, we can see readily that each man saw the elephant only from his own perspective, on the basis of his limited experience with the elephant. Do you agree with the statement that each man did *not* know that he didn't know? _____

Why or why not? Defend your answer. _____

_____

_____

_____

_____

_____

_____

_____

_____

For each of the men to know what the elephant was really like, their experiential base with the elephant would have to be broadened. Sometimes, it's difficult to understand things well when we know only a little about a subject or have had limited experiences with a topic. Can you think of a situation or topic like that in your life? _____

Please describe it. _____

_____

_____

_____

_____

_____

_____

_____

_____

_____

_____

_____

_____

_____

_____

_____

_____

_____

_____

Would you agree that you know that you need to know more about this situation or topic to be in a position to explain it to others or to write about it? _____

If you know that you need more information, you are now in a good position to control your learning; you can choose to find out more about this topic through various resources. Which resources do you think would be helpful with your topic? _____

_____

_____

_____

_____

_____

ACTIVITY 10.3

Write Your Own Fable

Directions: Before beginning to write your own fable, read several well-known fables such as "The Tortoise and the Hare," "The Ant and the Grasshopper," "The Lion and the Mouse," "The Fox and the Crow," "The Wind and the Sun," or "The Crow and the Pitcher." These works have been attributed to Aesop. What we know about Aesop (pronounced with a long *e* as the first syllable) comes from legend. Some say he was a Greek storyteller, but most people believe Aesop represents many legendary people who passed on the anonymous body of lore that we call fables.

After you have read some fables, make sure you understand clearly the lesson or moral being taught by each. Take time to share and discuss your insights with others. Then, begin to formulate your fable by giving consideration to each of the items in the following checklist:

Writing a Fable

1. The characters are (usually) animals with human qualities.
2. The story has some kind of problem or conflict.
3. The story is told to make a point (moral).
4. The moral comes at the end of the fable.
5. The animals may talk to one another in the fable.
6. The fable is usually short (one page or so) and fun to read. (Strong, 1991, p. 167)

Even though the moral of your story or fable will come at the end, it may be helpful to think about it first. What useful truth do you wish to convey? You may want to make a list and then choose one your like best.

_____

_____

_____

_____

_____

_____

_____

What kind of conflict or problem will your story have?

_____

_____

_____

_____

_____

_____

_____

Will animals with human qualities or humans serve your story better? If animals, then which animals?

_____

_____

Remember, your characters will talk; some will even become chatty. Make sure that you signal with quotation marks any conversation that you write. Begin your first draft below.

_____

_____

_____

_____

_____

_____

_____

_____

_____

_____

_____

_____

_____

_____

_____

_____

_____

_____

_____

_____

_____

_____

As your draft evolves, share it with others and revise as many times as needed. You may want to consider publishing one of your fables when you decide you are ready. Perhaps you will want to get with other writers of fables and consider publishing a collection.

ACTIVITY 10.4

As Hungry as an Elephant

Directions: Just for a moment, picture an elephant in your mind's eye. Now, think carefully to recall what you *know* about the appetite of this animal. Even if a lot of specific facts don't come to mind, you probably are able to *predict* generally that the elephant, which is the largest of all land animals, has quite a huge appetite. To explain your knowledge base about the elephant's appetite, consider the following questions and share your ideas with several classmates:

1. What do elephants eat? _____

_____

_____

2. How efficient is the elephant's digestive system? _____

_____

_____

3. How many sets of teeth does an elephant have over a lifetime? _____

4. How much water does an elephant drink in a year? _____

_____

5. How do elephants use their trunks to increase their food sources? _____

_____

_____

_____

6. What role do elephants' tusks play in their search for food? _____

_____

_____

_____

By discussing these questions and others that you may have raised with your classmates, you should have been able to expand further your knowledge base. Did you find yourselves making predictions as you chatted? In all likelihood, you realized that there was still much to be learned and that additional reading on the topic would be worthwhile. Additional reading will help you move through a learning cycle of making a prediction, then reading to evaluate the prediction, and so on. Of course, you will probably want to include some writing, in the form of notetaking, as part of this learning cycle. Perhaps you also considered viewing documentaries, such as those produced by *National Geographic,* to gain additional information. What are some of the things you would like to study further? Write down those things along with possible sources that would be helpful in this pursuit of knowledge. For example, several students who earlier studied this topic were particularly curious about the question regarding the elephant's sets of teeth. They discovered the following information by reading Zoo Books (Wexo, 1980) on *Elephants*:

Elephants have six sets of teeth during their lifetime. They need so many sets because the food they eat is very coarse. By 60 years of age, an elephant's last set of teeth is usually worn down. It can no longer chew its food, and so it dies. (p. 13)

269

ACTIVITY 10.5

Endangered Wild Elephants

Directions: Read the following passage about the wild elephant to learn more about its history and its future. Then, discuss with your classmates any thoughts or reactions that you have. Make notes as you work together, including facts you want to remember and questions that you want to research further. Perhaps you will use some of these notes should you choose this topic for a writing project. You may also want to write to individuals and groups already working to ensure the wild elephant's future.

ELEPHANTS IN THE WILD

Woolly mammoth
Mammuthus primigenius

While we can't say with certainty how long the wild elephant has been around, scientists believe that the group of mammals to which elephants belong (Proboscideans) has been around for about fifty million years. One close relative, the woolly mammoth, became extinct about ten thousand years ago. Proof of the woolly mammoth's existence consists of cave drawings and fossil remains. In Siberia, remains of entire mammoths have been found encased in ice; well-preserved fossils also have been found still frozen in the ice of Alaska. From these frozen finds, scientists learned that unlike today's elephants, the mammoths had hair to protect them from the extreme cold of the frozen north, explaining to us how the woolly mammoths got their name. What is not as easy to understand is the purpose of their strange tusks. The steppe mammoth, the imperial mammoth, and the woolly mammoth all had tusks up to thirteen feet long that curved first downward, and then upward to cross in front.

Today's wild elephants are found primarily in Africa and Asia. There are specific differences between the Asiatic (or Indian) and African elephants, such as the fact that African elephants have larger ears and weigh more, whereas Asiatic elephants live longer.

As you can see in the visual comparison on the next page, both male and female African elephants have long tusks, whereas only the male Asiatic elephants have tusks that are short. Unfortunately, they share a similar fate—on both continents the species is endangered, or threatened with extinction. Not only is their food supply constantly being reduced as land is developed, but in Africa they are dying in great numbers as greedy poachers kill them for their ivory tusks. Because ivory can be sold around the world for high prices, laws protecting the elephants continue to be broken. If these shrinking herds and habitats are not protected, the day will come when elephants will no longer exist in the wild.

Source: This illustration and those on page 271 are from *All About Elephants* by Carl Burger. Copyright © 1965 by Carl Burger. Reprinted by permission of Random House, Inc., p. 77.

AFRICAN ELEPHANT

ASIATIC ELEPHANT
(INDIAN ELEPHANT)

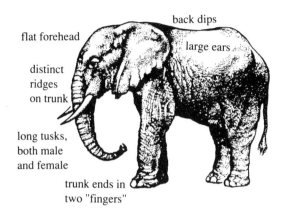

back dips

flat forehead

large ears

distinct
ridges
on trunk

long tusks,
both male
and female

trunk ends in
two "fingers"

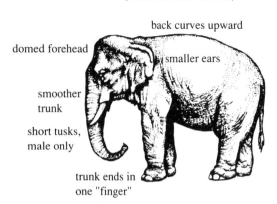

back curves upward

domed forehead

smaller ears

smoother
trunk

short tusks,
male only

trunk ends in
one "finger"

Your Notes about Elephants in the Wild

When they lived:

_____

How we know about their history:

_____

_____

Woolly mammoths:

_____

_____

Two common types of elephants today:

_____

_____

Some of their likenesses and differences:

_____

_____

Two problems elephants face today:

_____

_____

Elephants' fate if we do nothing:

_____

Other notes:

_____

ACTIVITY 10.6

Listening Self-Inventory

Directions: This activity will help you find out how well you listen to your friends. Answer the following questions by placing one check mark (✔) in the appropriate box. If you're not sure about the answer, select the last box in the row.

	Always	Often	Sometimes	Never	Don't Know
1. I am concentrating on listening when the speaker begins. I know I am ready to listen with real curiosity.	☐	☐	☐	☐	☐
2. If possible, I maintain eye contact with the speaker, which lets the speaker know I am paying attention.	☐	☐	☐	☐	☐
3. I pay attention to the speaker's voice tone, which often lets me know what the speaker considers important.	☐	☐	☐	☐	☐
4. I am aware that the speaker's nonverbal cues, such as facial expressions and hand gestures, also are used to convey meaning.	☐	☐	☐	☐	☐
5. When I don't understand something the speaker says, I ask for clarification if possible.	☐	☐	☐	☐	☐
6. To let the speaker know that I understand, I am comfortable using a physical sign such as nodding my head.	☐	☐	☐	☐	☐
7. I don't interrupt the speaker or finish the speaker's thoughts for him or her.	☐	☐	☐	☐	☐
8. I try to understand the speaker's position on issues even when I have a different opinion.	☐	☐	☐	☐	☐
9. I am able to continue listening even when there are distractions around me.	☐	☐	☐	☐	☐
10. When I take notes, such as for directions, I am able to decide what is important.	☐	☐	☐	☐	☐

Reflect on your responses. Are there areas where you'd like to change?_____

Why or why not? _____

_____

_____

You may want to discuss your responses with others. Also, you may want to set some goals to improve your listening habits. Describe those goals below:

_____

_____

_____

272

7

Copyright © 1994 by Allyn and Bacon.

ACTIVITY 10.7

Silence Is Golden

Directions: Over two thousand years ago, the following sage advice was written about the wisdom of silence:

The beginning of wisdom is silence.
The second stage is listening.

Give some thought to whether this statement still has meaning for our lives today. Discuss your ideas with others, listening carefully to their viewpoints. Then, write down what you think the word *silence* meant over two thousand years ago. Has that definition changed over time? If yes, how?

_____

_____

_____

Now, close your eyes for several minutes and sit silently. What do you hear? _____

_____

_____

Did you hear your own breathing? Perhaps you heard the sound of the air conditioner running or a door closing. Or maybe you heard sounds from the outside like thunder or an airplane overhead. How did you feel while you were sitting quietly? What thoughts went through your mind?

_____

_____

_____

You were actually listening to the sounds of silence while your eyes were closed. The phrase *sounds of silence* is a particular kind of figure of speech called an *oxymoron* (a combination of seemingly contradictory words or phrases). Some examples of oxymorons include *cruel kindness* and *cheerful pessimism.* William Shakespeare, an English poet and playwright who lived from 1564 to 1616, included several oxymorons in his famous play *Romeo and Juliet,* a story of young lovers. Among those he used are "sad joy," "sweet sorrow," and "delicious misery."

Can you think of others? List them here. _____

_____

_____

It might be fun to brainstorm with your classmates to produce a few more. List some here that you think of as you brainstorm. _____

_____

_____

Consider using oxymorons the next time you write to add interest to your meaningful message.

Think Aloud

Directions: Given the information below about the African elephant population, think aloud about your projection for the future.

1979—There were about 1,300,000 elephants in Africa.
1989—There were only about 608,000 in Africa.
1999—How many elephants do you think will be in Africa if conditions don't change?

_____

Explain to another person your reasoning for the number that you placed in the blank space above. For example, you may start your thinking process by noting the decrease by over half in the number of elephants in Africa during the ten-year span 1979–1989. You may have thought about why this has happened. You probably remembered the problems with poachers. And, of course, you may have recalled that the elephant's habitat is getting smaller and smaller as what was wilderness becomes developed land. This situation probably won't get any better, given that the number of humans in Africa will double during the next few decades.

Now, write down the steps that you went through as you reasoned your conclusion. Make sure you explain the logic you used. The Self-Monitoring Checklist provided at the bottom of this page should be helpful as you fine-tune your drafted steps. _____

_____

_____

_____

_____

_____

_____

_____

_____

_____

_____

_____

_____

Self-Monitoring Checklist:

( ) I have numbered the steps to make them clear for others.
( ) I have explained the logic of my reasoning for each step.
( ) I have capitalized the first word of each step.
( ) I have used proper spelling and have looked up words I was unsure of how to spell.
( ) I have reread my work to make sure it will be clear for others when they read it.

ACTIVITY 10.9

The Size of an Elephant's Brain

___

Directions: Read the following passage by Chadwick from the May 1991 *National Geographic* about the elephant's brain, and use the facts given to make some inferences about the elephant's intelligence.

Most mammals' brains at birth are around 90 percent of their adult weight. In a human infant the brain is only 27 percent of its adult weight. For elephants the figure is of the same order—35 percent. Their brain is highly convoluted—another measure of intelligence, which they share with humans, the great apes, and dolphins. And elephants have the largest brain of any land mammal. (p. 49)

I think elephants are very _____

because _____

_____

Now, reread the passage and identify any words that you may want to understand better. For example, the word *convoluted* may not seem clear immediately in this context. Because many words have multiple meanings, as does *convoluted*, a dictionary should be helpful as you consider the appropriate meaning in the passage. What other strategies could you use to find out more clearly the meaning of unknown words?

_____

_____

_____

If you were not sure of which strategies you *could* use, study the following lists (Taylor, Harris, & Pearson, 1988, p. 241) and practice using the information in the lists to help choose a strategy or a combination of strategies the next time you need them.

Strategies you can use when you don't understand a *word* you've read:

1. Skip over the word.
2. Sound out the word.
3. Use context clues to decode the word.
4. Use the context clues to predict what the word means.
5. Use a dictionary.
6. Ask for help.

Sometimes, you may figure out the meaning of a difficult word but still have trouble comprehending what is written. Try using the following strategies when you don't understand a *sentence, paragraph,* or *page* you have read:

1. Keep reading.
2. Reread carefully.
3. Look at the title, pictures, and headings.
4. Ask yourself important questions.
5. Put important ideas in your own words.
6. Picture the ideas in your head as you read.
7. Relate ideas to your personal experience.
8. Ask someone to clarify things.

A Memory Like an Elephant's

Have you ever heard the saying "He has a memory like an elephant's"? This saying is a *simile,* a comparison of two unlike things usually using the words *like* or *as.* A simile is called a figure of speech. In order to make an accurate prediction about the meaning of this simile, you would need a knowledge base about the memory capacity of elephants. Using your present knowledge base, make your prediction below.

My prediction of the meaning of the simile, "He has a memory like an elephant's" is this: _____

_____

_____

The book *All About Elephants* (Burger, 1965) includes the story of a German naturalist, Dr. Bernard Rensch, who decided to teach an elephant to select certain patterns from thirteen pairs of cards. Each time the elephant chose the correct patterns, he was rewarded with food. A year later, Dr. Rensch tested the elephant again. The elephant remembered the patterns with "astonishing accuracy." Dr. Rensch had to check his notes to see if the elephant was right.

Burger said that elephants also can solve problems and learn from experience. They test suspicious-looking places before they step on them; if they want to bathe in a water hole, they send a scout to see if it looks safe.

Now we want you to see if you have "the memory of an elephant." Before rereading, write everything you can remember from these reports about the intelligence of elephants.

The Memory of an Elephant

_____

_____

_____

_____

_____

_____

_____

_____

_____

_____

As you reflect about this activity, think about how your knowledge base has been expanded. Record something about what you have learned in a process journal if you wish.

ACTIVITY 10.11

What's a White Elephant?

Have you ever heard the term *white elephant?* Many adults complain that they have one. It is a thing—and it might be a house, a car, or a pet. My guess about what the term *white elephant* means is this:

_____

_____

Burger, in the book *All about Elephants* (1965, pp. 113–114), explained the term in this way. Occasionally, white elephants (called *albinos*) are born. In Thailand and other nearby countries of the Orient (the far eastern part of Asia), people used to consider white elephants sacred. Only kings were allowed to own them. The white elephants were treated as kings. They had musicians, gold coverings to keep them warm, and expensive food. People worshipped them. Even the king couldn't ride on them. They were very expensive to own. If a king didn't like another king, he might honor him with the gift of a white elephant. The rival king might not be able to afford to keep it, but to get rid of the gift would have been considered an insult. Today, a *white elephant* means something you can't afford to keep but also can't afford *not* to keep.

Think of an example of a white elephant your family owns. Often the white elephant is an ugly* gift given to the family by a favorite relative. You cannot give it away because the relative would notice its absence and be hurt. Of course you wouldn't want to offend your favorite relative, so you continue to display the gift, at the very least when your relative is present. Almost every family has at least one. Share your family's white elephant and why you keep it. _____

_____

_____

_____

_____

_____

_____

_____

How about a picture of the "white elephant"? Draw it below:

---

*Remember, "Beauty is in the eye of the beholder." For your information, this quote comes from a novel, *Molly Bawn,* written by Margaret Wolfe Hungerford in 1878.

Extremely Distant Elephant Relatives

In all writings about elephants, including the more than 350 species of Proboscideans who once lived, and the two species of Proboscideans who now live (the African and the Asiatic or Indian elephant) one would never know that there are two very distant relatives of the elephants also alive today. If we tell you about these two relatives by their family names—hyraxes and sirens—you might never be able to guess their common names. But since you are such interested scientists, make hypotheses (guesses) about these two animals.

My Hypotheses

The common name of the hyrax is the _____

The common name of the siren is the _____

Often, as we study science and other subjects, we confirm or refute our hypotheses as we read our textbooks or other reference books. Read the following information taken from Burger (1965) in *All About Elephants* and from the information found in a dictionary to confirm or refute your hypotheses.

The hyrax is a little animal similar to the guinea pig. There are more than twelve species. They are smaller than rabbits and very active. They are sometimes called hyrax shrews.

There are two kinds of sirens in the animal kingdom. A siren is a name of animals sailors used to think were mermaids, although they were nothing like the pictures we see today of mermaids. You might not recognize the siren called the dugong, but most people have heard of its endangered relative, the manatee, commonly called the sea cow. However, very few people realize that the sea cow is related to the elephant, though in a very distant way. They both had a common ancestor more than 70 million years ago. So as you can see, they are very, very distant relatives.

Did you confirm or refute your hypotheses?

_____

By reading, I learned that the two very distant relatives of the elephant are the hyrax and the siren.

The hyrax is like a _____

_____

A well-known siren is a _____

_____

Next, write the facts you know you know, and those you think you know, about the manatee. Don't hesitate for fear you are wrong. Just write quickly, and you may surprise yourself with all your knowledge about manatees. You will have the opportunity to self-correct later.

The Manatee

_____

_____

_____

_____

_____

_____

_____

_____

_____

_____

_____

_____

_____

_____

Now, check in a reference book to see if your statements are all accurate. In your text, number the statements you made that were accurate. Scratch through and correct any statements you made that were inaccurate. Were you surprised at how much you knew? _____

Take time to reflect on the process you used to confirm or refute your hypotheses. Record your thoughts below or in a process log if you wish.

_____

_____

_____

_____

_____

_____

_____

_____

_____

_____

_____

_____

CHAPTER 11

A Portfolio Approach to Assessment and Other Types of Evaluation

Good writing is within your student, and you'll hear it if you listen—and don't scrawl "awk."

—Donald Murray (1982, p. 156) English Professor and Pulitzer Prize–winning author

Have you ever been handed back papers with red marks? That's a moot question. While in college, most teachers received their share of well-intended corrections that, in retrospect, probably contributed to growth. Remember the times we've said to ourselves, "I certainly never knew that was wrong." But overall, when students have worked very hard on pieces of written work, they've been much more grateful to the teachers who have had kind words for their efforts. One first-grade teacher years ago told of putting an actual drop of honey on her young students' papers when they had tried hard. This was a lesson to some upper-grade teachers, who previously had been so overwhelmed marking stacks of papers that they barely had time to write much more than "Good Work" or "Nice Paper." As these teachers reflected on the "drop of honey" concept, they agreed that the old adage, "You can catch more flies with honey than with vinegar," also applied to teaching. They knew that building on strengths encourages growth, whereas focusing too much on weaknesses often causes students to lose motivation. As you read in Chapter 2, research findings support the importance of teachers expecting success from their students. Considering this necessary balance, evaluation seems a difficult challenge.

In addition, one might wonder, "Why is everything in education constantly changing? Are portfolios for assessment just another educational fad? Tests and red pens have worked fine for many years." But the truth is that older methods of assessment have not worked. Donald Graves (1983), a pioneer in process writing, had the following to say:

Teachers want more labor-saving devices, like easier scoring. If you have to respond to a lot of writing, there is more work involved. . . . although writing is frequently extolled, worried over, and cited as a public priority, it is seldom practiced in schools. Orders for lined paper, principally used for writing compositions, are going down. . . . Even in school systems reputed to stress writing as a major concern, there is often little writing. A survey of three such systems discovered that children from the second through the sixth grade on the average wrote only three pieces over a three-month period. Even less writing was asked for at the secondary level. Yet if writing is taken seriously, three months should produce at least seventy-five pages of drafts by students in the high school years. (p. 67)

Although educators are committed to teaching students how to learn to write, and they accept the need for accountability, they are often aware that there is not enough time to grade every piece of writing. Also, as Murray espoused in the quotation at the beginning of this chapter, it's time to stop scrawling "awk" on papers if teachers wish to encourage developing writers. Murray suggested that, as teachers start conferencing with students, the need for marking papers changes. Conferences allow the students to self-correct and make changes for improvement before they submit their papers for grading. Even as a college professor of freshman English, Murray holds as many as thirty-five conferences a day.

Times change, and we change, too—like it or not. As Harold Macmillan, British prime minister from 1957 to 1963, is reported to have said (Barwick, 1970), "It is, of course, a trite observation to say that we live 'in a period of transition.' Many people have reiterated this at many times. Adam may well have made the remark to Eve on leaving the Garden of Eden" (p. 14). Life has been changing forever! Curriculum changes, education changes, and assessment changes.

JUST WHAT IS PORTFOLIO ASSESSMENT?

What is a portfolio?
Why is it used in assessment?
How is it used in assessment?
Is it better, easier, faster?
Is portfolio assessment something worth trying?

This chapter provides an overview of portfolio assessment and offers materials that should be useful in assessing students' written work.

What is a portfolio? The following working definition grew from discussions at a conference on aggregating portfolio data, which was held in the state of Washington in August 1990 and reported in Paulson, Paulson, and Meyer (1991):

A portfolio is a purposeful collection of student work that exhibits the student's efforts, progress, and achievements in one or more areas. The collection must include student participation in selecting contents, the criteria for selection, the criteria for judging merit, and evidence of student self-reflection. (p. 60)

Paulson et al. (1991) continued, "While achievement tests offer outcomes in units that can be counted and accounted, portfolio assessment offers the opportunity to observe students in a broader context: taking risks, developing creative solutions, and learning to make judgments about their own performances" (p. 63).

The idea that writing should show the student's self-reflection has been recorded throughout recent literature (Alverman & Muth, 1990; Atwell, 1987; Calkins, 1981; Graves, 1981; Jeorski & Conry, 1981). Ownership through self-selection helps build self-esteem, a value whose importance is widely recognized. The growth shown through portfolio assessment helps those who care about student progress—teachers, parents, principals and other district administrators, and especially students—see and reflect on the gains made over time.

THE LEGACY OF GRADING

Teachers always have been accountable for grades. Even today, many school systems require teachers to grade by exact number scores and report to parents with whole number scores. The 1970s and 1980s ushered in a new era of further accountability with specific skill testing—testing little snippets of information with tests, generally of less than ten items, to determine whether students had a knowledge of certain skills. Teachers familiar with Bloom's *Taxonomy of Educational Objectives: The Classification of Educational Goals* (1964) were not satisfied with this basic level of assessment. Bloom's taxonomy proposes that there are

six levels of questioning. Categories 1 and 2 are considered questions at a low cognitive level. Levels 3 through 6 are high-order questions. Vacca, Vacca, and Gove (1987) prefer Herber's (1978) classification of levels of comprehension:

Herber has contended that a "levels" view simplifies comprehension while still dealing with the complexity of intellectual activity that is associated with more detailed and intricate classification schemes such as Bloom's or Guilford's. Although skills are assumed, levels of comprehension emphasize the interaction of comprehension skills with a broader cognitive framework. (p. 162)

Herber's first and lowest level of comprehension is the level of literal understanding: Can a reader parrot back what the text or teacher stated? The next level is the level of interpretive understanding—reading "between the lines." If the text says you are wearing your bathing suit and standing with sand between your toes and waves lapping at your ankles, where are you? The word *beach* was not given; but if you knew, then you had made an inference. This includes Bloom's comprehension level. Herber's third and highest level of comprehension involves evaluation and application—reading "beyond the lines." Can you take the information given and apply it to new situations? Here is an example: "Combine your knowledge about business letter format with your knowledge of Thomas Jefferson's Monticello to write an imaginary letter inviting Jefferson to speak to your class. Be specific about the home, describing the location, the plan, and the features you'd like for him to discuss."

National achievement tests and other standard measures such as intelligence tests often measure information in isolation. Many educators today recommend a test of application as a much more valid way to measure information learned. The problems of application testing are twofold: These tests can be much more difficult to grade, and their scoring is often very subjective.

Kenneth Goodman (Goodman, Goodman, & Hood, 1989), in the preface to *The Whole Language Evaluation Book,* stated the following about testing:

Whole language teachers have rebelled against behavioral objectives, textbooks, mastery learning, and narrow curricula. And they have rebelled against traditional evaluation, particularly standardized tests, because they find them synthetic, contrived, confining, and controlling, out of touch with modern theory and research. The tests reduce reading and writing to trivial, decontextualized, abstract skills to be tested with multiple-choice questions. (p. xi)

Goodman advocates tests that are holistic, don't fragment language, and use natural language in authentic contexts. The portfolio approach to assessment allows teachers to grade using these authentic contexts.

The whole issue of assessment gets convoluted by different factions as they debate whether or not the purpose of evaluation is criterion referenced;

that is, has a student mastered a certain number of predetermined skills. Or is the purpose of assessment to show growth of the individual student? Fortunately, portfolio assessment can show both sets of information. The teacher and school system determine what use they are going to make of the portfolio for assessment.

Baron (1989), Director of the Connecticut Assessment of Education Progress, said, "One of the things we want to know about is whether kids can produce solutions and not just recognize them." Connecticut began performance-based student assessment in the 1991–1992 school year. Richard P. Mills (1990), Vermont Commissioner of Education, rethought that state's assessment measures because state education officials were interested in "real student work, real performance, not the proxy delivered by standardized short-answer tests" (p. 53). He continued that "the objective is competence for every child and the sense of self-worth that goes with it" (p. 53).

O'Brien (1992) described teachers' acknowledgment of changes in writing assessment as follows:

Most writing teachers accept the principle of accountability. They understand the need to show what progress students are making in learning to write. However, they have learned that large-scale assessments often violate the process-centered approaches supported by research, their own classroom experiences, and workshops such as those affiliated with the National Writing Project.

Many educators have begun to feel uncomfortable with writing assessments that contradict the way writing is being taught in the classroom. This is not to say that writers never need to write impromptu memos, letters, and answers to examination questions, but large-scale writing assessments, because of the impact they can have on instruction, should reflect current composition pedagogy. . . . (p. 28)

O'Brien agreed with Wolcott (1987, p. 40) about the "need for more interplay between process and product in assessments." O'Brien also cited the work of Lederman (1986, p. 41) on the importance of product:

The best teachers do help students learn something about their own writing processes. . . . But in the end, it is a lie to tell students that "product" does not matter. . . . In the real world, product is all we can share with each other. (O'Brien, 1992, p. 29)

WHAT EXACTLY IS A PORTFOLIO?

One definition of *portfolio* in *Merriam Webster's Collegiate Dictionary,* Tenth Edition (1993) is "a hinged cover or flexible case for carrying loose papers, pictures, or pamphlets" (p. 908). Many students today have some kind of writing folder with pockets for carrying loose papers. In this folder, or portfolio, they keep everything they have written in various stages of completion—from topic idea lists, to work-in-progress, to finished products. These writings might include—but are not limited to—poetry, invitations, letters, short stories, research papers, and essays. Some teachers include audio tapes of students' reading to show progress, and some include computer disks on which their students have placed their written work. Some have even used interactive videos. In fact, although various authors and groups think portfolios should include all of a student's work, they do admit that a collection of this size could get very messy. Valencia (1990), in helping to construct a picture of a portfolio, described it in this manner. "Physically, it is larger and more elaborate than a report card. Practically, it must be smaller and more focused than a steamer trunk filled with accumulated artifacts" (p. 339).

Tierney, Carter, and Desai (1991) studied portfolio use in grades K–12 in Ohio schools over a three-year period. The first year, they studied teachers who were interested in portfolio assessment but did not use it for writing. The second year, they compared teachers who did and did not use portfolio assessment. The third year, they asked teachers to compare their own teaching: before, during, and after the use of portfolios for assessment. The most important thing that Tierney et al. felt they had learned was that portfolio assessment could be used at all grade levels (p. x).

Jongsma (1989) reported that she had asked several educators how she might use portfolio assessment as a means of evaluating reading and writing in her school. A director at Smith Research Center at Indiana State mentioned that teachers had differing opinions when deciding who should assume primary responsibility for developing the portfolio. Some believed teachers should compile this information, some felt students should select the contents, and some even thought parents should add to the portfolio as well. Several New Hampshire teachers replied that they had developed a process-oriented report card. Still, they found it necessary to add to this, so they chose a "literary folder" that seems to be a cumulative sampling of a child's work in grades K–6.

WORKING AND SHOWCASE PORTFOLIOS

According to Tierney et al. (1991), many teachers today are using at least two kinds of writing portfolios: a working portfolio and a showcase portfolio. The *working portfolio* holds lists of topics, work-in-progress, and completed work. It can be a folder in a box, in a file cabinet, or in the student's desk or locker. One creative middle school teacher described in Tierney et al. (1991) kept his students' portfolios hung by strings attached to paper clips that were hooked on a cord strung across the room. This allowed his students to have ready access to their portfolios, a feat for a teacher with over 100 students a day. Another clever feature of this idea was that students weren't all trying to squeeze into exactly the same spot to get or return their portfolios daily.

Another type of portfolio often used is a *showcase portfolio.* Students give input, and thus gain ownership, of the pieces of writing they want to enter in their showcase portfolios for each grading period. Some states require that a certain number of pieces be kept in a cumulative portfolio from grades K–6 or K–12. The number may be as low as three, and it is from the showcase portfolio that pieces can be drawn to be used for evaluation. Most people agree that if only *one* portfolio is used, it must be cleaned out at the end of the school year.

Two teachers were overheard debating whether to have one or two portfolios:

Jane: I'm all for using portfolios, but I can't see having more than one. It's confusing enough trying to store one for each student, much less *more* than one.

Bill: Well, I think of it as similar to an old loose-leaf notebook. You wouldn't want to have to wade through a student's whole notebook to find the best pieces. Besides, the portfolio should be like the ideal speech: short and sweet.

Jane: That's true. Do you think students should clear out their writing folders (working portfolios) at the end of each grading period?

Bill: No, I don't. Just because one grading period is over, there may be some papers of a student that she'd like to revise and use later. I've got some of my original poetry from when I was a child, and I wouldn't think of throwing it away.

Jane: Good point. That would be fun to keep. Then students probably need some dividers or pockets for topics, work-in-progress, and completed pieces.

Bill: I agree. Teaching students to organize their work can be very helpful to them. Also, I don't mean to say students should never throw anything away. But you know how it is: The piece you threw away yesterday is the very one you may need tomorrow.

Whether or not to use one or two portfolios is a decision that teachers will make as they mold portfolio assessment to their individual styles. What to include may be entirely up to the teacher or may be dictated by the school district or by state policy.

WE ARE WHAT WE THINK WE ARE

Mitchell and Conn (1985), in their book, *The Power of Positive Students,* told the story of Johnny Lingo, a strong, handsome man who lived long ago in a culture in which the groom bought the bride by bargaining with her father until they agreed on the number of cows they thought she was worth. An above-average bride in this culture brought two or three cows. A four- or five-cow bride was exceptional. Now the bride Johnny Lingo sought was rather plain, quiet, and much older than most other brides. The town gossips wagged their tongues about how many cows Johnny would offer, as he also was known to be a shrewd trader. To the townspeople's astonishment, Johnny offered eight cows for Sarita—the highest price ever offered for a bride. As time went by, Sarita became the most beautiful woman many people had ever seen. People asked Johnny if he had paid so much just to make Sarita happy. Johnny replied that he had wanted Sarita to be happy, but the reason he had paid so much was because he knew that the most important thing to people is **what they think of themselves.** He wanted Sarita to know that she was the most valuable woman in the town and that he loved her. But he added that he also had "wanted an eight-cow wife" (p. 129).

Our goals as educators include helping students see themselves positively as the equivalent of "eight-cow wives." Furthermore, students need to feel empowered as learners and problem solvers. If students are to grow optimally, instruction should be designed with student success in mind. Individual needs must be taken into account, for we know that all students do not learn at the same pace or in the same style. Teachers can best facilitate stu-

dents' learning by evaluating their progress and then planning the curriculum for their success.

In 1991, the mayor of the District of Columbia, Sharon Pratt-Dixon, told how, thirty years before, she had been a "C" student in high school. Teachers had told her they didn't expect her to attend college. But one history teacher had built her up and made her believe in herself. She began to make "A"s in school. In 1991, when she was sworn in as mayor, she thanked that teacher and showed her appreciation further by choosing the teacher as her civic advisor. This is another example of the power of self-fulfilling prophecies, described in Chapter 2. The importance of how we make students feel about themselves can never be overemphasized, but their pride must be for true achievement. We are fortunate to have the opportunity to help our students gain the success and pride that build self-esteem.

Evaluation should be an ongoing process. The purpose of the evaluation should not be only for reporting to parents. A good teacher evaluates constantly to assess student growth and to see if students have mastered the material being taught or if further instruction is needed. Teachers should constantly be evaluating to guide the choice of curriculum. Instruction must be designed to avoid having students repeatedly practice already mastered material. Likewise, never achieving mastery can cause a student to feel like a failure. We constantly must evaluate what we are expecting students to achieve and must guide them until they succeed in achieving it!

The National Assessment of Educational Progress (NAEP), known as the Nation's Report Card, has been collecting information nationally and assessing students since 1969. Congress, in 1988, created the National Assessment Governing Board (NAGB) to formulate policy guidelines to ensure that all aspects of evaluation were conducted fairly. In 1990, NAEP conducted a pilot portfolio study (Gentile, 1992) to develop alternative methods of assessing student writing.

From its regular, timed writing assessment, NAEP gains information about students' writing achievements on a broad range of tasks. From its special portfolio study, NAEP learns information about students: classroom experiences and school-based writing that provide a context for understanding students' overall achievements. As the various methods for collecting classroom-based writing for assessment purposes are refined, using both portfolio and traditional modes of assessment in concert may provide educators with rich, detailed portraits of students' writing abilities. (p. 74)

These findings concurred with the opinions of a multitude of educators, for across the United States in the decade of the 1990s, education has been a topic of great concern. Topics such as "The Nation's Report Card" were widely discussed and even became a foremost subject of politicians as citizens lamented the fact that the nation's schools were not meeting the needs of the students and society as a whole. In fact, "on June 8, 1989, in an unprecedented judicial decision, the Kentucky Supreme Court declared the state's public school system unconstitutional" (Foster, 1991, p. 34). Although the intention in this case was to obtain equitable funding for rural schools, specified educational objectives to be achieved by every student were identified in the reform. "Historically *all* children were not expected to master the entire curriculum. Universal education meant universal opportunity, not universal achievement" (p. 34). Kentucky's Education Reform Act of 1990 developed six new objectives, as well as more adequate methods of assessing learning. Jack D. Foster, Kentucky's Secretary of the Education and Humanities Cabinet, continued his report as follows:

As we press for more outcomes such as the ability to communicate effectively, to think critically, to reason and solve problems, and to integrate and intelligently use knowledge, we must be prepared to invest heavily in more holistic, flexible, and creative approaches to the assessment process. Much research and development is needed on how to validly and reliably document the full range of educational outcomes expected of our students.

In a world where "quality" has come to mean "zero defects," policymakers are no longer interested in how students as a group are doing "on the average." They want to know how near we are to having every student learning at the highest level of which he or she is capable. (1991, p. 36)

Foster also reported that in the newly developed method of assessment, students were required to complete various tasks. "The tasks might involve such activities as performing an experiment, assembling a portfolio of 'best works,' giving a performance, or keeping a journal that explains how to solve a particular problem" (p. 35). Authentic performances were utilized to document student achievement.

In North Carolina, a project for Rural Educational Alliance for Collaborative Humanities (REACH) (Barone, 1991), was sponsored both by private industry, many of the universities of North Carolina, and the South Carolina Humanities Council. Following the second year of the project, a final exposition was presented involving more than 100 teachers and 3,000 students. The presentation included dramatic productions, writings, and media presentations. Portfolios, including samples of students' works over time, were also on display, showing persuasively, the growth of individual students.

Manchester, New Hampshire, public schools began to explore the use of portfolios for evaluation in the fall of 1990, with the help of twelve educators from the University of New Hampshire (Hansen, 1992). The Manchester portfolios were based on the following beliefs:

Readers and writers know more about their own abilities and progress than outsiders do. Thus, they can be the prime evaluators of themselves and their work.

Choice is a hallmark of a reading-writing classroom. Thus, teachers and students will each decide what to put in their individual Literacy Portfolios.

In reading-writing workshops, teachers and students work together. Both teachers and students will create portfolios. (p. 604)

The research team, classroom teachers, and students created portfolios containing papers that explained to others who they were; these included recipes and lists of books read recently, as well as other artifacts that demonstrated literacy, and combined both the "school self and nonschool self" (p.

607). Self-reflective papers explained why each article had been chosen and, further, helped students explain both who they were and who they hoped to become. Individual literacy goals were set and students and teachers both "evaluated themselves and their work" (p. 607). Students involved in the project felt that building the portfolios and assessing themselves helped build self-esteem.

Johnston (1992) also called the portfolio "a public demonstration of one's own development as a literate person or as a learner. . . . the portfolio in this case is a demonstration of both accomplishment as a literate person and as a learner" (p. 129). He described three levels of these records: working folders, portfolios, and archival records. Johnston suggested photocopying, microfiching, or computer scanning the work saved for a permanent portfolio so that students could take home their originals. It was felt that these historical records would tie the students to the school and encourage respect and support later on. Johnston also suggested having students (and teachers) compile a portfolio two to four times a year to show development. Possible entries might include the following:

- pieces the student considers to be her best work of the semester or quarter
- a piece taken from draft through final form
- a sample taken at some earlier date and a later sample to show development
- some examples of diverse genres attempted
- a list (perhaps annotated) of books read with dates completed or abandoned
- a section from a literature log
- a copy of a letter written to an author
- a character extension
- a critical review of a book
- a parody of a book
- biographical background on an author (p. 133)

Johnston suggested having students attach a note to each piece saying why it was included. He stated that he felt the reflective act was central. He structured this reflective process with these questions:

1. What has changed most about your reading (writing)?
2. Why do you think this has changed?
3. What change would you like to see in your reading (writing)?
4. How do you plan to make that change?
5. What is the hardest part of writing (reading) for you? (p. 134)

Johnston felt that it was critical for students to select their own pieces, with some additions by teachers.

. . . If the portfolio is a principal form of communication between home and school, perhaps in place of report cards, then, the teacher might add selections with reasons too, to illustrate certain aspects that the student is not yet able to see. (p. 135)

Additionally, Johnston (1992) described double-loop learning based on the concepts of Argyris and Schon (1974). In single-loop learning, we use the current "givens" are used to solve problems. For example, narrative report cards tell more about a child's development than grades, but they are unmanageable for teachers. In double-loop learning, the problem is redefined. Why do report cards have to be sent out all at once? The use of portfolio assessment in lieu of report cards could be an example of double-loop learning. Questions to be asked in double-loop learning include the following:

- What goes on in the name of X? (Where X refers to reading instruction, individualization, writing conferences, accountability, in-service, reporting to parents, and so forth.)
- How did this come about?
- Whose interests are (and are not) being served by the way things are?
- What are the real and imagined constraints that are operating? (p. 364)

If our goal is to help all students become literate, Johnston (1992) asked us to consider these questions. What if we did not have grade levels? Imagine what could happen to the following:

- retention in grades
- transition rooms
- school readiness
- grade equivalents (p. 370)

Schools not using grade levels already exist in parts of the United States and in New Zealand. Also, Johnston said, "Although we assume that standardized testing is a necessary component of schooling and the improvement of schooling, we have ample examples of literate nations who engage in relatively little testing at all" (p. 370). It is just such double-loop thinking that has brought us to the point of having some educators use portfolio assessment as a substitute for grades in demonstrating student literacy. Double-loop thinking must also be used in finding ways to keep this assessment method manageable for teachers.

Embracing the belief that students who use the process paradigm write better than those who use a traditional approach, the Missouri Department of Elementary and Secondary Education decided to assess the writing of 54,000 eighth graders, using a process format.

Our challenge was to develop a process writing assessment that would be standardized enough to fulfill testing requirements yet allow the flexibility needed for a writing-workshop format.... In a process-oriented assessment students are invited to use process strategies and receive feedback from their peers while they are writing, but they also know that their written product will be rated by teachers who do not know them. (O'Brien, 1992, p. 29)

All eighth-grade English students in the state participated. Students were all given the same prompt and were allowed to collaborate on prewriting activities, drafting, and revising. The following questions were developed to guide them in self- and peer assessment:

1. Does my paper stay focused on the controlling ideas?
2. Does the order of my paper make sense?
3. Have I started my paper in an interesting way?
4. Does my paper have a satisfying ending?
5. Have I used description/details/examples?
6. Have I carefully edited my paper for spelling, punctuation, and grammar errors? (O'Brien, p. 30)

Teachers were trained in holistic scoring. Following this, as part of the training, they spent four to five hours scoring twenty papers. Scores were required to be within one point of the previous scorer's results 80 percent of the time. The majority scored 100 percent in agreement. Those who didn't were given additional training. Following one more practice set of papers, the raters tackled the 54,000 real papers. The majority of raters said they would participate again and enjoyed the camaraderie of a network of writing teachers. In addition to enhancing educators' awareness of the writing ability of eighth graders, the Missouri educators were pleased to support process writing and to let students know that they are accountable for their own writing development.

Cooper and Brown (1992) used student writing portfolios in teaching junior high and senior high students in California. A description of their work follows: Students were asked to write introductions to their portfolios in which they described themselves and their "characteristic writing process" (p. 40) and summarized what was in their portfolios. Contents had to include a sample of a forty-five-minute timed writing (as used in California's state assessment). Samples of writing to learn were also required, as it was felt that "one of the most valuable lessons that students can learn is that writing is a powerful tool for learning—that writing, far from simply being the product of thinking, can actually shape thinking.... " (p. 42). Other portfolio requirements included a creative writing sample, a piece the student judged to be the best with a rationale for choosing it (this piece could be one included in another category), and two pieces selected by the student and/or the teacher, allowing for individuality of portfolios. The portfolios were correlated with the California Assessment Program (CAP), administered statewide to eighth- and eleventh-grade students. The CAP test identifies ten different types of writing. For this reason, three essays, each showing a different type of writing, were included. One of the required essays must demonstrate knowledge of the writing process from start to finish. As part of showing evidence of the process approach in writing to learn, for example, notes, tapes of interviews, and interview questions could be included.

Far from constituting rigid standards, the list of required portfolio contents provides fine opportunities for flexibility. The portfolios reflect curriculum, application, and student choice. The interesting part of Cooper and Brown's work was the way the portfolios were used. At the end of the semester, they read the introductions and rationales, thumbed through the students' work (much of which they had already seen), stopped to read only the parts that appealed to them, wrote a few words of praise, and returned the portfolios to the students. This somewhat cursory glance at the finished portfolios seems unusual because most teachers still assume that, at some point in writing, final editions must be thoroughly evaluated and/or saved. Cooper and Brown view portfolios as powerful teaching tools: "the very act of compiling a portfolio can be a powerful process for many reasons, not least of which is that it helps students see themselves as writers, particularly when it involves many opportunities for self-evaluation and reflection" (p. 40).

Ballard (1992), a teacher in Terre Haute, Indiana, expressed the concerns of many when she wrote, "At the secondary level, standard portfolio use does not always seem to be practical given the constraints of producing hard evidence of achievement at given intervals" (p. 46). As an experiment, she used the students' portfolios as a final exam, giving them time to assess their own writing progress by ranking their own papers from most to least

effective, giving a rationale for good and bad points, and writing what they'd learned from that assignment. Next she had the students write what they'd learned from the course and from their own writing process. Finally, students described how they felt about writing and compared this to how they felt prior to taking the writing course. Ballard was most pleased to learn that students now saw themselves as "writers rather than as students enrolled in a composition course" (p. 48).

TEACHER AND STUDENT EXPECTATIONS

Loveless, a high school teacher, wrote that when implementing the portfolio approach, she uses student self-evaluations and student–teacher evaluation conferences. She grades "holistically on volume of writing; use of workshop time; progress toward jointly set goals; risk-taking; participation in the community of writers through sharing critiques, and so on; and use of revision strategies (as opposed to recopying only)" (Goodman, Bird, & Goodman, 1991, p. 263). *Holistically,* in this case, seems to mean "on all of the named items combined."

Atwell (1987) offered her expectations of the role of the students and the role of a teacher in a writing workshop. The roles of both seem to encourage learning and make the classroom a less threatening place for students and teacher alike. Here are some of Atwell's fifteen expectations for her grade 8 writing class:

Part I: Your Role

1. To come to class each and every day with your daily writing folder, in which you'll keep all drafts of your pieces-in-progress.
2. To take care of your folder: it's your text for this course.
3. To write every day and to finish pieces of writing.
4. To make a daily plan for your writing and to work at it during class and at home.
5. To find topics you care about.
6. To take risks as a writer, trying new techniques, topics, skills, and kinds of writing. . . .
10. To maintain your skills list and to use it as a guide in self-editing and proofreading. . . .
13. To make decisions about what's working and what needs more work in pieces of your writing; to listen

to and question other writers' pieces, giving thoughtful, helpful response. . . .
15. To discover what writing can do for you. (pp. 125–126)

Nowhere in this list of expectations did Atwell say anything like "turn in three papers a week" (or month), or anything else threatening to the student. She implied that a student should come to class prepared to work and to learn—learning for learning's sake. Included in Atwell's list of expectations for herself are the following:

Part II: My Role

1. To keep track of what you're writing, where you are in your writing, and what you need as a writer.
2. To grade your writing four times this year, based on your growth and effort as a writer.
3. To write every day and to finish pieces of writing.
4. To prepare and present mini-lessons based on what I see you need to know next. . . .
15. To help you discover what writing can do for you. (p. 126)

Atwell's list of expectations made teaching sound like a pleasure for her students and for herself—not the worrisome, harried, overworked task of most writing teachers, who face grading endless stacks of papers every night and every weekend.

Goal setting is important for students of all ages, as is willingness to master course content. Students need and deserve to know what is expected of them. When teachers, for example, take a class in college or for fun, they typically are presented with a syllabus delineating what they are going to learn in the class. Their expressed reactions to this information might include, "Oh, listen to this! We're going to learn to _____ and _____." Or, "Yuk! We *have to* _____." Often, students below the college level have no idea of what will be expected of them in a course. Giving students a writing evaluation form at the beginning of the course, and going over it with them, can help them see what the expectations will be as the writing process is taught. The form is for use with final drafts. This should be emphasized with the students. Along the way, students will be helped orally as much as possible. As mentioned before, Murray (1982) said that if we conferenced orally, there would be fewer and fewer marks on a student's page.

There is no way that one assessment form can address or adequately measure all types of writing. An example of a form that could be stapled inside a folder for writing assessment is provided for your use (Form 11.1); a marked sample is also included. Either the student or the teacher could select the genre. All items would not be marked for each genre. For instance, a student could show ability to write a business letter without consulting sources or needing to use a web. And, as Murray pointed out, all writing does not require visible prewriting; sometimes the prewriting occurs in the writer's

head. For example, Murray offered that a writer might wake up with a wonderful ending for a story already in mind. The author rushes to put it down on paper. If she is required to do prewriting first, the wonderful idea might be lost.

After a piece of writing is finished completely, the student and teacher together could mark an evaluation form, discuss the writing, and assess progress during an evaluation conference. The teacher could write additional comments beneath the items listed on the form—for example, "The rhythm in your poetry was wonderful," or "You captured the spirit of your grandmother through your use of descriptive phrases." This information is as valuable on a cumulative evaluation sheet as any marks a teacher could put in the boxes of a grade book, for it shows specific growth.

Tierney et al. (1991) cautioned against misdirecting self-evaluation by students toward what they call "low-level conventions (e.g., spelling and punctuation) rather than get at the heart or the essence of a specific selection" (p. 123). They implied this might remove the spontaneity of students' work. They also stated, "We would hate to see self-evaluation become wall charts suggesting fixed criteria by which students assess themselves" (p. 123).

PEER AND SELF-EVALUATION

Prior to the use of portfolios for assessment, emphasis was almost exclusively on the final product, with little or no value placed on work-in-progress. Although a successful finished product is still a desirable goal, it has been recognized by administrators, teachers, and students that students perform better when they have ownership of their work. One way ownership is achieved is by encouraging students to choose which pieces of their work will be assessed by the teacher. This, in itself, entails a great deal of self-assessment. Other ways of helping students take ownership of their portfolios include collaboration with other students and the teacher about their work-in-progress, in the assessment process, and in setting future goals. Tompkins (1990, p. 371) described seven different kinds of process-writing conferences; the final conference was an assessment conference in which the teacher meets with students to discuss growth and make future plans. Students are asked both to self-assess by

reflecting on competencies and to set future goals. Valencia (1990) said that "collaborative assessment strengthens the bond between student and teacher and establishes them as partners in learning" (p. 338). Portfolios become vehicles for learning. Although certain writings might have to be included in portfolios to meet state standards, students still can choose which of their works to include to meet those criteria.

Some teachers have students label their chosen works with cards that tell "Why I Chose This Piece, What I Learned, and My Future Goals" (Tierney et al., 1991, p. 83). Although fancier checklists for self-evaluation of each piece have been developed, teachers caution that these may become just another piece of work for students. The note cards described earlier can be used after many works have been completed to help students compare and evaluate their own work.

The evaluative topics just described are not very

different from the self-evaluation questions found in Faigley, Cherry, Jolliffe, and Skinner (1985) for use with college students:

Self-Evaluation

1. List the most successful things you did in writing this paper. List the things that a reader will think are successful.
2. List the things you were unable to do in this paper that would have made it more successful.
3. In the process of writing this paper, what aspects were easier than when you have written previous papers?
4. In the process of writing this paper, what aspects were more difficult than when you have written previous papers? (p. 176)

Mike Harrington, a teacher in Tallahassee, Florida, uses much more detailed forms for his high school peer evaluations. A dynamic teacher, Harrington uses the I-Search method of learning (Macrorie, 1988). An I-Search, as described by Macrorie, is what people do who have a need to know something for their own life and then write the story of what they learned and how they learned it. He used the example of his wife's search for information about several locations before deciding to move to Oaxaca, Mexico, for a year's sabbatical leave. First, she had chosen Africa, but after speaking with people who had been there, reading about Africa, and examining the costs of fares for a family of four to move there, as well as living expenses, she decided to try someplace else. So she followed the same steps before deciding on Mexico.

Macrorie thought it was important to teach students to use this process to write research papers instead of only reporting information read in reference books. Macrorie's I-Search consists of four parts:

1. What I Knew (and didn't know about my topic when I started out).
2. Why I'm Writing This Paper. (Here's where a real need should show up: the writer demonstrates that the search may make a difference in his life.)
3. The Search (story of the hunt).
4. What I Learned (or didn't learn. A search that failed can be as exciting and valuable as one that succeeded). (p. 64)

Several of Harrington's former students shared how he had helped them find their voices by conducting I-Searches for information in many areas. Class periods began by listening to and analyzing lyrics of popular music, thus further developing critical thinking. The students felt that Harrington had done an outstanding job of preparing them for the rigors of college with his use of a peer assessment form for term papers. Harrington reported that using peer evaluation for the technical aspects of a paper freed him to examine the papers for content without the endless chore of grading. Form 11.4, Harrington's most recent, was developed after students requested a chance for revision following peer editing. This cooperative learning device empowers students and helps them assume ownership of their work. Harrington's evaluation forms (Forms 11.2, 11.3, 11.4, and 11.5) are provided for your use.

INVOLVING PARENTS IN PORTFOLIO ASSESSMENT

Graves (1983) said that the questions parents commonly ask about writing address the child's improvement, the skills involved, uncorrected papers, and what they can do at home to help. From these questions, educators learn that parents share concerns similar to those of teachers when they first begin teaching the writing process.

Parents of students who have been accustomed to seeing a lot of papers coming home regularly will wonder what is going on if teachers start using portfolios or journals without explaining to them how these educational tools are used. Early in the year, a

letter can be sent home describing the use of portfolios and answering the questions Graves cited. Then, after several weeks, the portfolios are sent home and/or parents are invited to an open house. Another letter is sent home with the portfolios, encouraging the parents to give some written feedback by answering the following questions, adapted from Tierney et al. (1991, pp. 116–118), or other questions of your choosing: "Which of the pieces of writing in my portfolio did you like best?" "What did you think was a strength in my writing?" "What did you notice as an area needing growth?" Having parents date and sign the letter containing these questions is helpful.

The letter can remind parents that the student writer is growing, and growth in language mechanics will be encouraged as the year progresses. Parents have been given an opportunity to make positive remarks by being asked to pick a favorite piece and name the strengths; furthermore, they have been encouraged to offer suggestions regarding the student's next area for focus. Thus, parents participate actively in the process and assume a healthy ownership in the student writer's progress. It's easy to see why parent involvement has been recognized as a very important factor in student progress.

CONCLUSION

In this discussion of portfolio assessment, you probably have come to realize that there are as many ways to handle this type of assessment as there are teachers. Two teachers would be no more likely to handle portfolios alike than would choose to read exactly the same list of books in their entire lifetimes. The important message is that portfolios offer a valid alternative to testing, and they are an important way for students, teachers, parents, and all concerned to see the growth of the student.

Although it has not been mentioned heretofore, some serious concerns and issues have been raised concerning portfolio assessment. At the 1989 Northwest Evaluation Association (NWEA) Writing Assessment Conference (*Writing Portfolio,* 1989), many questions arose concerning management and logistics of portfolios. There were questions about how to deal with teachers who fail to maintain students' portfolios and curriculum concerns about types of assessment that might have to be given up if portfolio assessment development is supported. These are valid concerns, but the advantages of the use of portfolios, no matter how their contents are chosen, seem to outweigh the problems. Portfolios have arrived, regardless of the manner decreed by various states.

Murray (1985, p. 238) said, in answer to the question "Can Writing Be Taught?": "The answer is in the writing folders of the students." To the question, "Where is the evidence to prove they have learned to write?" he answered, "In the writing folders." The old adage, "The proof is in the pudding," holds true today in education. If you want to know if students are learning to write, check their writing. As Goodman et al. (1991) commented in *The Whole Language Catalog* (p. 428), "Vive la Difference: Long Live Diversity!" There is not one way to use portfolio assessment, just as there is not one way to teach or one writing process.

REFERENCES

Alverman, D. E., & Muth, K. D. (1990). Affective goals in reading and writing. In G. G. Duffy (Ed.), *Reading in the middle school* (pp. 97–110). Newark, DE: International Reading Association.

Argyris, C., & Schon, D. (1974). *Theory in practice: Increasing professional effectiveness.* San Francisco: Jossey-Bass.

Atwell, N. (1987). *In the middle: Writing, reading, and learning with adolescents.* Portsmouth, NH: Boynton/Cook.

Ballard, L. (1992). Portfolios and self-assessment. *English Journal, 81*(2), 46–48.

Baron, J. (1989, November–December). News: Testing a new kind of test. *Teacher Magazine, 2,* 14–15.

Barone, T. (1991, February). Assessment as theater: staging an exposition. *Educational Leadership, 48*(5), 57–59.

Barwick, D. D. (Ed.). (1970). *Great words of our time.* Kansas City, MO: Hallmark Editions.

Bloom, B. S. (1964). *Taxonomy of educational objectives: The classification of educational goals* (pp. 186–193). Handbook II. New York: Longman/Green.

Calkins, L. M. (1981). Writing taps a new energy source: The child. In R. D. Walshe (Ed.), *Donald Graves in Australia— "Children want to write . . . "* (pp. 45–54). Rosebery, NSW, Australia: Primary English Teaching Association.

Cooper, W., & Brown, B. J. (1992). Using portfolios to empower student writers. *English Journal, 81*(2). 40–45.

Duffy, G. G. (Ed.). (1990). *Reading in the middle school,* 2nd ed. Newark, DE: International Reading Association.

Faigley, L., Cherry, R. D., Jolliffe, D. A., & Skinner, A. M.

(1985). *Assessing writers' knowledge and processes of composing* (p. 176). Norwood, NJ: Ablex.

Foster, J. D. (1991). The role of accountability in Kentucky's Education Reform Act of 1990. *Educational Leadership, 48*(5), 34–36.

Gentile, C. (1992, April). *Exploring new methods for collecting students' school-based writing: NAEP's 1990 Portfolio Study.* Prepared by Educational Testing Service for the National Assessment of Educational Progress 1990 Writing Assessment, under contract with the National Center for Education Statistics, Office of Educational Research and Improvement, U.S. Department of Education. (Washington, DC: U.S. Government Printing Offices: 1–800–424–1616; Washington, DC, metropolitan area: 202–219–1651).

Goodman, K. S., Bird, L. B., & Goodman Y. M. (Eds.). (1991). *The whole language catalog.* Santa Rosa, CA: American School.

Goodman, K. S., Goodman, Y. M., & Hood, W. J. (Eds.). (1989). *The whole language evaluation book.* Portsmouth, NH: Heinemann.

Graves, D. H. (1981). Patterns of child control of the writing process. In R. D. Walshe (Ed.), *Donald Graves in Australia— "Children want to write . . . "* (pp. 17–28). Rosebery, NSW, Australia: Primary English Teaching Association.

Graves, D. H. (1983). *Writing teachers and children at work.* Portsmouth, NH: Heinemann.

Hansen, J. (1992). Literacy portfolios emerge. *The Reading Teacher, 45*(8), 604–607.

Herber, H. L. (1978). *Teaching reading in content areas,* 2nd ed. Englewood Cliffs, NJ: Prentice-Hall.

Jeorski, S. F., & Conry, R. F. (1981). *Development and field application of the attitude toward writing scale.* Paper presented at the annual meeting of the American Educational Research Association, Los Angeles, California.

Johnston, P. H. (1992). *Constructive evaluation of literate activity.* New York: Longman.

Jongsma, K. S. (1989, December). Questions and answers: Portfolio assessment. *The Reading Teacher, 43*(3), 264–265.

Lederman, M. J. (1986). Why test? In K. L. Greenberg, H. S. Weiner, & R. A. Donovan (Eds.), *Writing assessment: Issues and strategies* (pp. 35–43). New York: Longman.

Living Bible, The. (1971). Wheaton, IL: Tyndale House.

Macrorie, K. (1988). *The I-search paper:* Revised edition of *Searching writing.* Portsmouth, NH: Boynton/Cook.

Merriam-Webster's Collegiate® Dictionary (1993). Tenth Edition, p. 908. Springfield, MA: Merriam-Webster, Inc.

Mills, R. P. (1990, April). Using student portfolios to assess achievement. *The Education Digest, 55,* 51–53.

Mitchell, W., & Conn, C. P. (1985). *The power of positive students.* New York: Bantam.

Murray, D. M. (1982). *Learning by teaching: Selected articles on writing and teaching.* Portsmouth, NH: Boynton/Cook.

Murray, D. M. (1985). *A writer teaches writing.* Boston: Houghton Mifflin.

O'Brien, C. W. (1992). A large-scale assessment to support the process paradigm. *English Journal, 81*(2), 28–33.

Paulson, F. L., Paulson, P. R., & Meyer, C. A. (1991, February). What makes a portfolio a portfolio? *Educational Leadership, 48*(5), 60–63.

Tierney, R. J., Carter, M. A., & Desai, L. E. (1991). *Portfolio assessment in the reading–writing classroom.* Norwood, MA: Christopher Gordon.

Tompkins, G. E. (1990). *Teaching writing—Balancing process and product.* Columbus: Merrill.

Vacca, J. L., Vacca, R. T., & Gove, M. K. (1987). *Reading and learning to read.* Boston: Little, Brown.

Valencia, S. (1990, January). Assessment. A portfolio approach to classroom reading assessment: The whys, whats, and hows. *The Reading Teacher, 43*(3), 338–340.

Wolcott, W. (1987, February). Writing instruction and assessment: The need for interplay between process and product. *College Composition and Communication, 38,* 40, 46.

Writing portfolio assessment issues and concerns. (1989, October). NWEA Writing Assessment Conference, Draft pp. 1–3.

The activity that follows is meant to serve as a model; such activities should be used as part of a total learning environment. This model activity was designed to demonstrate how the writing process can be developed while expanding the writer's knowledge base and providing opportunities for the writer to think critically.

Judging Others

MODEL ACTIVITIES

In *The Living Bible,* there is a well-known verse called the Golden Rule:

Do for others what you want them to do for you. This is the teaching of the laws of Moses in a nutshell.

Matthew 7:12

How would this verse relate to you as you read and evaluate your classmates' writing? _____

_____

_____

_____

_____

_____

_____

_____

_____

_____

_____

_____

_____

_____

_____

_____

_____

_____

_____

_____

_____

_____

Remember, constructive criticism is intended to be helpful, and it can be offered with kindness.

FORM 11.1 Example Form—Writing Development

WRITING DEVELOPMENT FORM--An Example

Name _Jan Garlan_   Period _5_ Dates _11/9_ — _11/23/93_

Type of Work Evaluated _Historical fiction_

Prewriting   Comments

Uses several sources   _5!_   _Good research skills_
Takes notes   _✓_   _Xeroxed + highlighted_
Uses a brainstorming
  technique   _✓_   _Rough outline of plot_
Identifies audience   _✓_   _Peers_

Drafting

Puts ideas on paper   _✓_   _Fine first draft_
Shows a sense of
  audience and
  writing format   _✓_   _Followed handout well_

Sharing
                       _C.J.S._
Shares with peer(s)   _11/9_ _Good story- Move some things. 11/10 Good! C.J.S._
                       11/11 Great ending C.J.S.
Shares with teacher   _11/9_ _Content excellent 11/12 Punctuation_
                       improved

Revising and Editing

Generates more text
  if needed   _11/9_ _more needed 11/12 Must be four pages_
Revises content   _11/9 11/12 Fine Put events in chronological order_
  Literal   _11/9 Add feelings + thoughts of characters_
  Interpretive
  Application
Edits for mechanics
  Capitalization   _✓_
  Punctuation   _✓_   _Lets work on this. 11/12 Improving_
  Spelling   _11/12_ _Use computer spell checker._
  Usage   _✓_
  Sentence structure   _✓_   _Combine short sentences when possible._
  Formatting   _✓_

Published Form

Holistic Assessment   _A_   _11/23 Really moving + well written_
  Content   _A_   _Super choice of topic_
  Mechanics   _A-_   _Improving_

Comments _Jan, your completed story was better than many I've read in magazines. Check out a copy of Cobblestones from the library, and I'll help you submit it for publication._

WRITING DEVELOPMENT FORM

Name_____ Period_____ Dates_____

Type of Work Evaluated_____

Prewriting   Comments

   Uses several sources   ____   _____
   Takes notes   ____   _____
   Uses a brainstorming
     technique   ____   _____
   Identifies audience   ____   _____

Drafting

   Puts ideas on paper   ____   _____
   Shows a sense of
     audience and
     writing format   ____   _____

Sharing

   Shares with peer(s)   ____   _____

   Shares with teacher   ____   _____
                                    _____

Revising and Editing

   Generates more text
     if needed   ____   _____
   Revises content
    Literal   ____   _____
    Interpretive   ____   _____
    Application   ____   _____
   Edits for mechanics
    Capitalization   ____   _____
    Punctuation   ____   _____
    Spelling   ____   _____
    Usage   ____   _____
    Sentence structure ____   _____
    Formatting   ____   _____

Published Form

   Holistic Assessment   ____   _____
    Content   ____   _____
    Mechanics   ____   _____

Comments_____

_____

_____

_____

FORM 11.1 Example Form—Writing Development

FORM 11.2   I Search Rough Draft Check Sheet*

I Search
Rough Draft Check Sheet

1. Attention Getter:

    What kind? _____

2. Thesis Statement or Question:

    Write it here _____

    _____

3. Parenthetical Documentation? (qualifying information or explanation)

    How many? _____

4. Word Count:

    Average Words per Line   _____

    Number of Lines   × _____ (Multiply)

    Total   _____

5. Conclusion:
    Write the sentence that wraps it up.

    _____

6. Parenthetical Documentation:

    How many sources? _____

7. Interview Questions:

    How many? _____

8. Business Letters:
    How many written? _____

    Are they in business letter form? _____

*Used with permission of Mike Harrington.

FORM 11.3 I Search Final Draft Checklist

Author's Name _____ Period _____

I Search Title _____

I SEARCH
FINAL DRAFT CHECKLIST

> ENGLISH IIIH STANDARD 4.06: REVISE, PROOFREAD, AND EDIT
> ENGLISH IIIG STANDARD 4.05: REVISE, PROOFREAD, AND EDIT

Your first assignment is to read someone else's I-SEARCH paper looking for the great, interesting, fascinating parts.

☞　1.　*Place a big star* or asterisk (*) next to the parts you think are really good. You should then commu-
☞　　　nicate with the author with a little note.

The second part is to find as many mechanical errors as you can.

　　2.　*Circle and Label all mistakes.*
　　　　☞CIRCLE SPELLING ERRORS AND LABEL THEM. . . . . . *SP*
　　　　☞CIRCLE GRAMMAR ERRORS AND LABEL THEM. . . . . .*GR*
　　　　☞CIRCLE PUNCTUATION ERRORS AND LABEL THEM. . . . . .*P*
　　　　☞CIRCLE ANY OTHER ERRORS AND WRITE A SHORT NOTE OF EXPLANATION.

　　3.　When you finish, count the number of errors you found and record them on the following list. YES, YOU MAY WRITE ON MY PAPER THIS TIME.

YOU WILL BE GRADED ON EDITING. IT IS A STANDARD!

> 1ST EDIT (PEN COLOR _____)
>
> SPELLING ERRORS (SP) _____ GRAMMAR ERRORS (GR) _____ PUNCT. ERRORS (P) _____
>
> OTHER ERRORS _____ EDITOR _____
>
> COMMENTS _____
> _____

SECOND EDITOR WILL CAREFULLY EDIT THE PAPER AS WELL AS *CHECK* FIRST EDITOR'S WORK TO CERTIFY THE ERRORS FOUND WERE ACTUALLY ERRORS. **ALL ERRORS FOUND BY THE FIRST EDITOR THAT YOU AGREE WITH SHOULD BE MARKED WITH A CHECK IN YOUR PEN'S COLOR.** FIND ERRORS MISSED AND TOTAL BELOW:

> 2nd EDIT (PEN COLOR _____)
>
> SPELLING ERRORS (SP) _____ GRAMMAR ERRORS (GR) _____ PUNCT. ERRORS (P) _____
>
> OTHER ERRORS _____ EDITOR _____
>
> COMMENTS _____
> _____

*Used with permission of Mike Harrington.

FORM 11.4 I Search Final Check Sheet*

I SEARCH
FINAL CHECK SHEET

Name _____ Period _____

Partner's Name _____ Partner's Initials _____

Many of you have requested that you get a chance to check the two editors' work before I grade your papers. Here is your opportunity.

1. Get a partner.
2. Get both of your research papers out of the box.
3. Get a pen or pencil that is a different color from that used by either editor.
4. Look through *your* paper, checking the editors' work.

If you find something you think was edited incorrectly, circle it, write me a little note, and then have your partner initial that he/she agrees with you.

1. Fill out the form below, writing in the numbers you believe you deserve.
   Partial credit is acceptable. For example, if you had one of the two letters—5 pts.
2. Show your partner where you meet each of the criteria below.
   Have him/her initial each number showing he/she agrees with your assessment.
   If he/she disagrees with your assessment, he/she should write in the number he/she thinks is deserved.)
3. Total the points for Content and Formalities in the spaces provided.

_____ _____ CONTENT TOTAL

_____ _____ 10 Introductory paragraph (attention getter/topic sentence)

_____ _____ 10 Concluding paragraph

_____ _____ 10 Interview questions and answers from authority included

_____ _____ 10 Copies of two letters included

_____ _____ 20 Used a variety of sources (periodicals, books, letters, interviews, etc.)

_____ _____ 20 Body covers topic in a thorough manner

_____ _____ 20 Student's comments accompany research information.

_____ _____ FORMALITIES TOTAL

_____ _____ 10 Paper in on time (−10 for each day late)

_____ _____ 20 Clean and neat (appropriate to eleventh-grade honors standards)

_____ _____ 10 Punctuation (fewer than 3 errors per 4 typed pages)

_____ _____ 10 Grammar (fewer than 3 errors per 4 typed pages)

_____ _____ 10 Spelling (fewer than 3 errors per 4 typed pages)

_____ _____ 30 Parenthetical documentation or endnotes done correctly

_____ _____ 10 Bibliography page done correctly

↑ ↑
Numbers you think you deserve in this column.
Initials of partner or number they think more appropriate in this column.

*Used with permission of Mike Harrington.

FORM 11.5 Final Grade Check Sheet*

I SEARCH
FINAL GRADE CHECK SHEET

Name _____

Content Grade _____

——— 10 Introductory paragraph (attention getter/topic sentence)

——— 10 Concluding paragraph

——— 10 Interview questions and answers from authority included

——— 10 Copies of two letters included

——— 30 Used a variety of sources
        (periodicals, books, letters, interview, etc.)

——— 20 Body covers topic in a thorough manner

——— 10 Student's comments accompany research information.

Errors Grade _____

——— 40 Paper in on time

——— 10 Clean and neat

——— 10 Punctuation (fewer than 3 errors per 4 typed pages)

——— 10 Grammar (fewer than 3 errors per 4 typed pages)

——— 10 Spelling (fewer than 3 errors per 4 typed pages)

——— 10 Parenthetical documentation done correctly

——— 10 Bibliography page done correctly

*Used with permission of Mike Harrington.

Index

Time
  as important to writing, 10
  needed for prewriting, 59–60
Toffler, A., 186–187
Tom, D., 22
Tompkins, G. E., 155–156, 157–158, 162
Tonjes, M. J., 86, 87, 258
Topic selection
  and knowledge of subject, 257
  and student discouragement, 233
  in writing, 3, 9, 59, 86, 235
"Translating," as form of audience awareness, 91–96
Treasure Island (Stevenson), 47
Trelease, J., 236
Tremmel, R., 5–6
Trumpet of the Swan, The (White), 235
Turkle, S., 196
Twain, Mark, 154
'Twas the Night Before Christmas (Moore), 226

U

Usage, 161–162
U.S. Bureau of the Census, 25
U.S. Congress Office of Technology Assessment (OTA), 188

V

Vacca, J. L., 162, 227, 282
Vacca, R. T., 162, 227, 282
Valdivieso, R., 25
Valencia, S. W., 227, 284, 290
Vangelisti, A., 226
Vermont Commissioner of Education, 283
Videodisc player, the, in classroom, 194–195
"Virtual reality," 198
Vockell, E. L., 194–195
vos Savant, M., 4
Vygotsky, L. S., 3, 26, 85

W

Wakefield, J., 240
Walberg, H. J., 49
Wall, K., 189
Walsh, W., 84
Watson, D., 234
Weaver, C., 258

Weaver, R. L., 28
"Webbing," 50, 54
Weiss, M. J., 83
Wellington, B., 24
Wells, G., 188
West, M., 133
Wheatley, W. J., 28, 30
"Where in the World Is Carmen Sandiego?," 187, 194
White, B., 88
Whole language approach to teaching, 26–27, 88
Whole Language Catalog, The (Goodman et al.), 3, 292
Whole Language Evaluation Book, The (Goodman et al.), 283
Witte, S. P., 226
Wolcott, W., 283
Wolfe, Thomas, 153
Woodman, D., 133, 214
Word association techniques, 54
"Working portfolio," 284–285, 287
Wright, Orville, 186
Wright, Wilbur, 186
Write Environment (Microsoft), 196
Writer's Guide and Index to English (Perrin), 5
Writing
  assessment of, 226, 281–292. *See also* Portfolio Assessment
  and audience awareness, 91–96
  as beneficial to emotions, 3–4
  as beneficial to health, 4
  and classroom environment, 26
  and computers, 191–197
  and content areas, 87–91
  as enhancement to self-esteem, 4
  as a form of thinking, 5, 29, 88, 92
  forms of, 9
  and handwriting, 159–160
  history of, 4–7
  and mathematics, 89–90
  mechanics of, 154
  and metacognition, 255–256
  in the primary grades, 9–10
  and prior knowledge, 256–258
  as a process, 10
  recursive nature of, 5, 10
  as related to problem solving, 7
  and science, 90, 260
  and social studies, 90
  stages of process, 5, 7, 8
  and student self-concept, 24–25, 26, 27

Index to Model Activities